Level 2

Benchmark Series

Microsoft®
# Access®

2010

Denise Seguin

Fanshawe College
London, Ontario

Paradigm
PUBLISHING

St. Paul • Indianapolis

| | |
|---|---|
| **Managing Editor** | Sonja Brown |
| **Senior Developmental Editor** | Christine Hurney |
| **Production Editor** | Donna Mears |
| **Copy Editor** | Susan Capecchi |
| **Cover and Text Designer** | Leslie Anderson |
| **Desktop Production** | Ryan Hamner, Julie Johnston, Jack Ross |
| **Proofreader** | Laura Nelson |
| **Indexer** | Sandi Schroeder |

**Acknowledgements:** The authors, editors, and publisher thank the following instructors for their helpful suggestions during the planning and development of the books in the Benchmark Office 2010 Series: Somasheker Akkaladevi, Virginia State University, Petersburg, VA; Ed Baker, Community College of Philadelphia, Philadelphia, PA; Lynn Baldwin, Madison Area Technical College, Madison, WI; Letty Barnes, Lake Washington Technical College, Kirkland, WA; Richard Bell, Coastal Carolina Community College, Jacksonville, NC; Perry Callas, Clatsop Community College, Astoria, OR; Carol DesJardins, St. Clair County Community College, Port Huron, MI; Stacy Gee Hollins, St. Louis Community College--Florissant Valley, St. Louis, MO Sally Haywood, Prairie State College, Chicago Heights, IL; Dr. Penny Johnson, Madison Technical College, Madison, WI; Jan Kehm, Spartanburg Community College, Spartanburg, SC; Jacqueline Larsen, Asheville Buncombe Tech, Asheville, NC; Sherry Lenhart, Terra Community College, Fremont, OH; Andrea Robinson Hinsey, Ivy Tech Community College NE, Fort Wayne, IN; Bari Siddique, University of Texas at Brownsville, Brownsville, TX; Joan Splawski, Northeast Wisconsin Technical College, Green Bay, WI; Diane Stark, Phoenix College, Phoenix, AZ; Mary Van Haute, Northeast Wisconsin Technical College, Green Bay, WI; Rosalie Westerberg, Clover Park Technical College, Lakewood, WA.

The publishing team also thanks the following individuals for their contributions to this project: checking the accuracy of the instruction and exercises—Robertt (Rob) W. Neilly, Traci Post, and Lindsay Ryan; developing lesson plans, supplemental assessments, and supplemental case studies—Jan Davidson, Lambton College, Sarina, Ontario; writing rubrics to support end-of-chapter and end-of-unit activities—Robertt (Rob) W. Neilly, Seneca College, Toronto, Ontario; writing test item banks—Jeff Johnson; writing online quiz item banks—Trudy Muller; and developing PowerPoint presentations—Janet Blum, Fanshawe College, London, Ontario.

**Trademarks:** Access, Excel, Internet Explorer, Microsoft, PowerPoint, and Windows are trademarks or registered trademarks of Microsoft Corporation in the United States and/or other countries. Some of the product names and company names included in this book have been used for identification purposes only and may be trademarks or registered trade names of their respective manufacturers and sellers. The authors, editors, and publisher disclaim any affiliation, association, or connection with, or sponsorship or endorsement by, such owners.

We have made every effort to trace the ownership of all copyrighted material and to secure permission from copyright holders. In the event of any question arising as to the use of any material, we will be pleased to make the necessary corrections in future printings. Thanks are due to the aforementioned authors, publishers, and agents for permission to use the materials indicated.

ISBN 978-0-76384-304-5 (Text)
ISBN 978-0-76384-307-6 (Text + CD)

© 2011 by Paradigm Publishing, Inc.
875 Montreal Way
St. Paul, MN 55102
Email: educate@emcp.com
Website: www.emcp.com

Printed in the United States of America

19 18 17 16 15 14 13 12 11 10   1 2 3 4 5 6 7 8 9 10

# Contents

Preface         vii

## Microsoft Access 2010 Level 2

### Unit 1 Advanced Tables, Relationships, Queries, and Forms   1

**Chapter 1 Designing the Structure of Tables**     3

| | |
|---|---|
| *Model Answers* | 4 |
| Designing Tables and Fields for a New Database | 5 |
|    Diagramming a Database | 7 |
|    Assigning Data Types | 7 |
|    Using the Field Size Property to Restrict Field Length | 8 |
| Restricting Data Entry and Data Display Using Field Properties | 10 |
|    Adding Captions | 10 |
|    Requiring Data in a Field | 10 |
|    Disallowing Zero-Length Strings in a Field | 10 |
|    Creating a Custom Format for a Text Field | 13 |
|    Creating a Custom Format for a Numeric Field | 15 |
|    Creating a Custom Format for a Date/Time Field | 17 |
|    Restricting Data Entry Using Input Masks | 18 |
| Working with Memo Fields | 22 |
| Creating an Attachment Field and Attaching Files to Records | 24 |
|    Editing an Attached File | 26 |
|    Saving an Attached File to Another Location | 27 |
|    Removing an Attached File | 27 |
| *Chapter Summary, Commands Review, Concepts Check,* | |
| *Skills Check, Visual Benchmark, Case Study* | 27 |

**Chapter 2 Building Relationships and Lookup Fields**     35

| | |
|---|---|
| *Model Answers* | 36 |
| Building Relationships | 37 |
|    Establishing a One-to-Many Relationship | 37 |
|    Editing Relationship Options | 40 |
|    Establishing a One-to-One Relationship | 42 |
|    Establishing a Many-to-Many Relationship | 44 |
| Defining a Multiple-Field Primary Key | 45 |
| Creating a Field to Look Up Values in Another Table | 46 |
| Creating a Field That Allows Multiple Values | 50 |
| Creating Indexes | 53 |
| Normalizing the Database | 56 |
|    First Normal Form | 56 |
|    Second Normal Form | 56 |
|    Third Normal Form | 56 |
| *Chapter Summary, Commands Review, Concepts Check,* | |
| *Skills Check, Visual Benchmark, Case Study* | 57 |

| **Chapter 3 Advanced Query Techniques** | **67** |
|---|---|
| *Model Answers* | 68 |
| Extracting Records Using Select Queries | 70 |
|    Saving a Filter as a Query | 70 |
|    Prompting for Criteria Using a Parameter Query | 72 |
| Modifying Join Properties in a Query | 75 |
|    Specifying the Join Type | 75 |
|    Adding Tables to and Removing Tables from a Query | 78 |
|    Creating a Self-Join Query | 80 |
|    Creating an Alias for a Table | 81 |
|    Running a Query with No Established Relationship | 82 |
| Creating and Using Subqueries | 83 |
| Selecting Records Using a Multiple-Value Field | 86 |
| Performing Operations Using Action Queries | 88 |
|    Creating A New Table Using a Query | 89 |
|    Deleting a Group of Records Using a Query | 91 |
|    Adding Records to a Table Using a Query | 91 |
|    Modifying Records Using an Update Query | 93 |
| *Chapter Summary, Commands Review, Concepts Check,* | |
| *Skills Check, Visual Benchmark, Case Study* | 94 |
| **Chapter 4 Creating and Using Custom Forms** | **103** |
| *Model Answers* | 104 |
| Creating Custom Forms Using Design View | 105 |
|    Bound, Unbound, and Calculated Control Objects | 106 |
|    Creating Titles and Label Objects | 106 |
|    Adding Fields to a Form | 108 |
|    Moving and Resizing Control Objects | 111 |
|    Formatting Controls | 112 |
|    Changing the Tab Order of Fields | 115 |
|    Adding a Tab Control to a Form | 116 |
|    Creating a Subform | 118 |
| Adding Calculations to a Form in Design View | 124 |
| Adjusting Objects for Consistency in Appearance | 126 |
|    Aligning Multiple Controls at the Same Position | 126 |
|    Adjusting the Sizing and Spacing between Controls | 127 |
| Adding Graphics to a Form in Design View | 129 |
| Anchoring Controls to a Form | 133 |
| Creating a Datasheet Form and Restricting Actions | 134 |
| Creating a Form Using the Blank Form Tool | 137 |
|    Adding a List Box to a Form | 137 |
|    Adding a Combo Box to a Form | 137 |
| Sorting and Finding Records in Forms | 141 |
| *Chapter Summary, Commands Review, Concepts Check,* | |
| *Skills Check, Visual Benchmark, Case Study* | 145 |
| **Unit 1 Performance Assessment** | **157** |

## Unit 2 Advanced Reports, Access Tools, and Customizing Access    167

### Chapter 5 Creating and Using Custom Reports    169

*Model Answers*    170
Creating Custom Reports Using Design View    172
   Connecting a Table or Query to the Report and Adding Fields    174
   Moving Control Objects to Another Section    176
   Applying a Theme    177
   Inserting a Subreport    178
Adding Page Numbering and Date and Time Controls    182
Adding Graphics to a Report    186
Grouping Records and Adding Functions in a Report    188
Modifying Section Properties    195
Keeping a Group Together on the Same Page    196
Inserting, Editing, and Formatting a Chart into a Report    198
Creating a Report Using the Blank Report Tool    204
   Adding a Tab Control to a Report    204
   Adding a List Box or a Combo Box to a Report    204
   Adding Hyperlinks to a Report    205
   Changing the Shape of a Control Object    205
   Changing the Tab Order of Fields    205
*Chapter Summary, Commands Review, Concepts Check,*
*Skills Check, Visual Benchmark, Case Study*    209

### Chapter 6 Using Access Tools and Managing Objectives    219

*Model Answers*    220
Creating a New Database Using a Template    221
Creating Objects Using an Application Part Template    226
Setting Form Control Defaults and Creating a User-Defined
Form Template    232
Copying Table Structure to Create a New Table    234
Modifying a Table Using the Table Analyzer Wizard    236
Optimizing Performance Using the Performance Analyzer    240
Splitting a Database    243
Documenting a Database    246
Renaming and Deleting Objects    248
*Chapter Summary, Commands Review, Concepts Check,*
*Skills Check, Visual Benchmark, Case Study*    250

### Chapter 7 Automating, Customizing, and Securing Access    251

*Model Answers*    258
Creating a Macro    258
Editing and Deleting a Macro    264
Creating a Command Button to Run a Macro    266
Creating a Navigation Form    273
Customizing the Access Environment    277
   Limiting Ribbon Tabs and Menus in a Database    279
   Customizing the Navigation Pane    279
   Configuring Error Checking Options    282
Customizing the Ribbon    283
   Creating a New Tab    284
   Renaming a Tab or Group    285

Adding Buttons to a Tab Group 285
Resetting the Ribbon 288
Creating an ACCDE Database File 289
Viewing Trust Center Settings for Access 290
*Chapter Summary, Commands Review, Concepts Check,*
*Skills Check, Visual Benchmark, Case Study* 292

**Chapter 8 Integrating Access Data** **301**

*Model Answers* 302
Importing Data from Another Access Database 303
Linking to a Table in Another Access Database 307
Deciding between Importing versus Linking to Source Data 309
Resetting a Link Using Linked Table Manager 310
Importing Data to Access from a Text File 311
Saving and Repeating Import Specifications 312
Exporting Access Data to a Text File 317
Saving and Repeating Export Specifications 319
Publishing and Viewing Database Objects as XPS Documents 321
Summarizing Data in a PivotTable and PivotChart 324
Summarizing Data in a PivotTable 324
Summarizing Data in a PivotTable Form 329
Summarizing Data Using PivotChart View 331
*Chapter Summary, Commands Review, Concepts Check,*
*Skills Check, Visual Benchmark, Case Study* 334

**Unit 2 Performance Assessment** **343**
**Access Level 2 Index** **351**

*Benchmark Microsoft Access 2010* is designed for students who want to learn how to use this feature-rich data management tool to track, report, and share information. No prior knowledge of database management systems is required. After successfully completing a course using this textbook, students will be able to

- Create database tables to organize business or personal records
- Modify and manage tables to ensure that data is accurate and up to date
- Perform queries to assist with decision making
- Plan, research, create, revise, and publish database information to meet specific communication needs
- Given a workplace scenario requiring the reporting and analysis of data, assess the information requirements and then prepare the materials that achieve the goal efficiently and effectively

Upon completing the text, students can expect to be proficient in using Access to organize, analyze, and present information.

## Achieving Proficiency in Access 2010

Since its inception several Office versions ago, the Benchmark Series has served as a standard of excellence in software instruction. Elements of the book function individually and collectively to create an inviting, comprehensive learning environment that produces successful computer users. The following visual tour highlights the text's features.

**UNIT OPENERS** display the unit's four chapter titles. Each level has two units, which conclude with a comprehensive unit performance assessment.

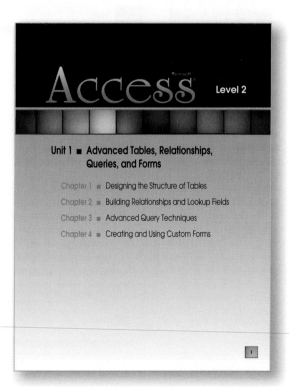

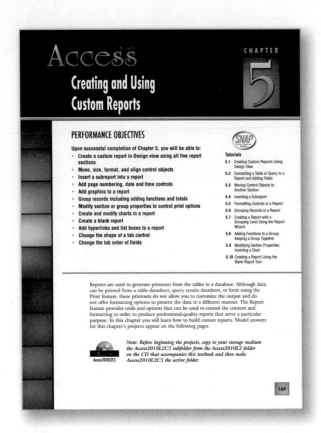

**CHAPTER OPENERS** present the performance objectives and an overview of the skills taught.

**SNAP** interactive tutorials are available to support chapter-specific skills at www.snap2010.emcp.com.

**DATA FILES** are provided for each chapter. A prominent note reminds students to copy the appropriate chapter data folder and make it active.

# PROJECT APPROACH: Builds Skill Mastery within Realistic Context

**MODEL ANSWERS** provide a preview of the finished chapter projects and allow students to confirm they have created the materials accurately.

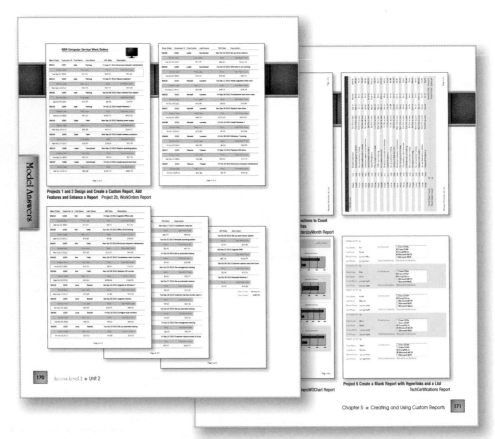

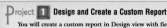

MULTIPART PROJECTS provide a framework for the instruction and practice on software features. A project overview identifies tasks to accomplish and key features to use in completing the work.

Between project parts, the text presents instruction on the features and skills necessary to accomplish the next section of the project.

STEP-BY-STEP INSTRUCTIONS guide students to the desired outcome for each project part. Screen captures illustrate what the student's screen should look like at key points.

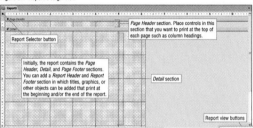

### Prompting for Criteria Using a Parameter Query

**♦ Quick Steps**

**Create Parameter Query**
1. Start new query in Design view.
2. Add desired table(s).
3. Close Show Table dialog box.
4. Add desired fields to query design grid.
5. Click in Criteria row in field to be prompted.
6. Type message text encased in square brackets.
7. Repeat Steps 5–6 for each additional criteria field.
8. Save query.
9. Close query.

**HINT**

If you are creating a parameter query that will be used by other people, consider adding an example of an acceptable entry in the message. For example, the message *Type the service date in the format mmm-dd-yyyy (example Oct-31-2012)* is more informative than *Type the service date.*

In a **parameter query**, specific criteria for a field are not stored with the query design. Instead, the field(s) used to select records have a prompt message that displays when the query is run. The prompt message instructs the user to type the criteria by which to select records. Figure 3.1 illustrates an Enter Parameter Value dialog box that is displayed when a parameter query is run to select by a technician's name. The message that is shown in the dialog box is created in the field for which the criterion will be applied. When the query is run, the user types the criterion at the Enter Parameter Value dialog box and Access selects the records based on the entry. If more than one field contains a parameter, Access prompts the user one field at a time.

A parameter query is useful if you run a query several times on the same field but use different criteria each time. For example, if you require a list of work orders by individual technician, you would have to create a separate query for each technician. This would create several query objects in the Navigation pane. Creating a parameter query that prompts you to enter the technician's name means you only have to create one query.

To create a parameter query, start a new query in Design view and add the desired tables and fields to the query design grid. Type a message encased in square brackets to prompt the user for the required criterion in the *Criteria* row of the field to be used to select records. The text inside the square brackets is displayed in the Enter Parameter Value dialog box when the query is run. Figure 3.2 displays the entry in the *Criteria* row of the *FName* field that generated the Enter Parameter Value message shown in Figure 3.1.

**Figure 3.1** Enter Parameter Value Dialog Box

**Figure 3.2** Criterion to Prompt for the Name in the *FName* Field

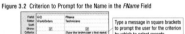

Type a message in square brackets to prompt the user for the criterion by which to select records.

---

**Project 1b**  Creating a Query to Prompt for Technician Names  Part 2 of 3

1. With the **AL2-C3-RSRCompServ.accdb** database open, create a query in Design view to select records from the Technicians table and the WorkOrders table by completing the following steps:
   a. Click the Create tab and then click the Query Design button in the Queries group.
   b. At the Show Table dialog box, add the Technicians table and the WorkOrders table to the query.

---

   c. Close the Show Table dialog box.
   d. Drag the bottom border of each table's field list box at the top of the query until all field names are visible in the box.
   e. Add the following fields in order to the query design grid: *WO, FName, LName, ServDate, Hours, Rate.*

Step 1e

2. Click the Run button to run the query.
3. Add parameters to select records by a technician's first and last names by completing the following steps:
   a. Switch to Design view.
   b. Click in the *Criteria* row in the *FName* column in the query design grid, type [Type the technician's first name], and then press Enter.
   c. Position the pointer on the vertical line between *FName* and *LName* in the gray field selector bar above the field names until the pointer changes to a vertical line with a left- and right-pointing arrow and then double-click to expand the width of the *FName* column so that you can see the entire criteria entry.

Step 3c

Step 3b

   d. With the insertion point positioned in the *Criteria* row in the *LName* column, type [Type the technician's last name] and then press Enter.
   e. Expand the width of the *LName* column so that you can see the entire criteria entry.
4. Click the Save button on the Quick Access toolbar, type PromptedTechnicianLabor in the *Query Name* text box at the Save As dialog box, and then press Enter or click OK.
5. Close the query.
6. Run the prompted query and extract a list of work orders for the technician named Pat Hynes by completing the following steps:
   a. Double-click the query named *PromptedTechnicianLabor* in the Navigation pane.

Step 6a

Step 6b

   b. Type pat at the Enter Parameter Value dialog box that displays the message *Type the technician's first name* and then press Enter or click OK. Note that Access is not case-sensitive when typing text strings.
   c. Type hynes at the second Enter Parameter Value dialog box that displays the message *Type the technician's last name* and then press Enter or click OK.

Step 6c

7. Review the records in the query results datasheet.
8. Print the query results datasheet.
9. Close the query.

# CHAPTER REVIEW ACTIVITIES: A Hierarchy of Learning Assessments

## Chapter Summary

- When building relationships consider the frequency of matching data in the common field in both tables to determine if the relationship is one-to-many, one-to-one, or many-to-many.
- One-to-many relationships are the most common type of relationship that involves joining the tables by dragging the primary key from the "one" table to the foreign key in the "many" table.
- In a one-to-many relationship, only one record for a matching field value exists in the primary table while many records for the same value can exist in the related table.
- A relationship diagram depicts the tables joined in the relationship as well as the type of relationship between the two tables.
- At the Edit Relationships dialog box you can turn on referential integrity and the two cascade options.
- Referential integrity places restrictions on new data entered into the related table. A record is not allowed in the related table if a matching record does not already exist in the primary table.
- *Cascade Update Related Fields* automatically u[...] data in the foreign key field when a change [...]
- *Cascade Delete Related Records* automatically c[...] is deleted from the primary table.
- In a one-to-one relationship only one record [...] joined field in both tables.
- In a many-to-many relationship many record[...] the joined field in both tables.
- To create a many-to-many relationship, a ju[...] minimum of two fields which are the prima[...] many-to-many relationship.
- Two one-to-many relationships using the jur[...] relationship.
- In some tables, two or more fields are used t[...] field is not guaranteed to hold unique data.
- A primary key that is made up of two or mo[...]
- A lookup field displays a drop-down list in a[...] clicks to enter the field value. The list can be[...] table, or by typing in a value list.
- Once the lookup field is created, use the Loo[...] in Table Design view to modify individual p[...]
- The Limit To List property allows you to res[...] within the lookup list.
- A field that allows multiple entries to be sele[...] created by clicking *Allow Multiple Values* at th[...]

**CHAPTER SUMMARY** captures the purpose and execution of key features.

## Commands Review

| FEATURE | RIBBON TAB, GROUP | BUTTON | KEYBOARD SHORTCUT |
|---|---|---|---|
| Add existing fields | Form Design Tools Design, Tools | | |
| Adjust size of multiple controls | Form Design Tools Arrange, Sizing & Ordering | | |
| Align multiple controls at same position | Form Design Tools Arrange, Sizing & Ordering | | |
| Anchor controls to form | Form Design Tools Arrange, Position | | |
| Blank Form | Create, Forms | | |
| Change tab order of fields | Form Design Tools Design, Tools | | |
| Combo Box control object | Form Layout Tools Design, Controls | | |
| Create datasheet form | Create, Forms | | |
| Design view | Home, Views | | |
| Equal spacing between controls | Form Design Tools Arrange, Sizing & Ordering | | |
| Find | Home, Find | | Ctrl + F |
| Form view | Form Design Tools Design, Views | | |
| Insert Image | Form Design Tools Design, Controls | | |
| Label control object | Form Design Tools Design, Controls | Aa | |
| List Box control object | Form Layout Tools Design, Controls | | |
| Line | Form Design Tools Design, Controls | | |
| Property Sheet | Form Design Tools Design, Too[...] | | |
| Sort ascending order | Home, Sort & Filter | | |
| Sort descending order | Home, Sort & Filter | | |
| Subform | Form Design Tools Design, Cor[...] | | |
| Tab control object | Form Design Tools Design, Cor[...] | | |
| Text box control object | Form Design Tools Design, Cor[...] | | |
| Title | Form Design Tools Design, Hea[...] | | |

**COMMANDS REVIEW** summarizes visually the major features and command options.

## Concepts Check  Test Your Knowledge

**Completion:** In the space provided at the right, indicate the correct term, command, or number.

1. A new form in Design view initially displays only this section in the form.

2. These are the three types of control objects found in a form.

3. Use this button from the Controls group to create an object in the *Form Footer* section in which to display a form's version number.

4. Before you can add fields to the table you must first connect a table to the form in this property box in the form's Property Sheet.

5. The large dark gray handle at the top left of a selected control is referred to by this name.

6. Hold down this key while clicking controls to select multiple control objects to be formatted.

7. Open this dialog box to change the order in which fields are selected when the Tab key is pressed in Form view.

8. Add this object to the bottom of a form to display subforms in individual pages.

9. Make sure this feature is active in the Controls group before clicking the Subform/Subreport button so that the Subform Wizard is available.

10. Click this button in the Controls group to add a calculation to a form.

11. The *Equal Vertical* option is located on this button's drop-down list in the Form Design Tools Arrange tab.

12. Change this property for a control object containing a clip art image to *Zoom* to proportionately adjust the image to the resized object's height and width.

13. The *Datasheet* form is available from this button's drop-down list in the Forms group in the Create tab.

14. Click this tab in a form's Property Sheet to locate the *Allow Deletions* property box.

15. This form tool opens as a blank white page in Layout view.

16. These two controls are used to add list boxes to a form.

**CONCEPTS CHECK** questions assess knowledge recall.

 Access Level 2 ▪ Unit 1

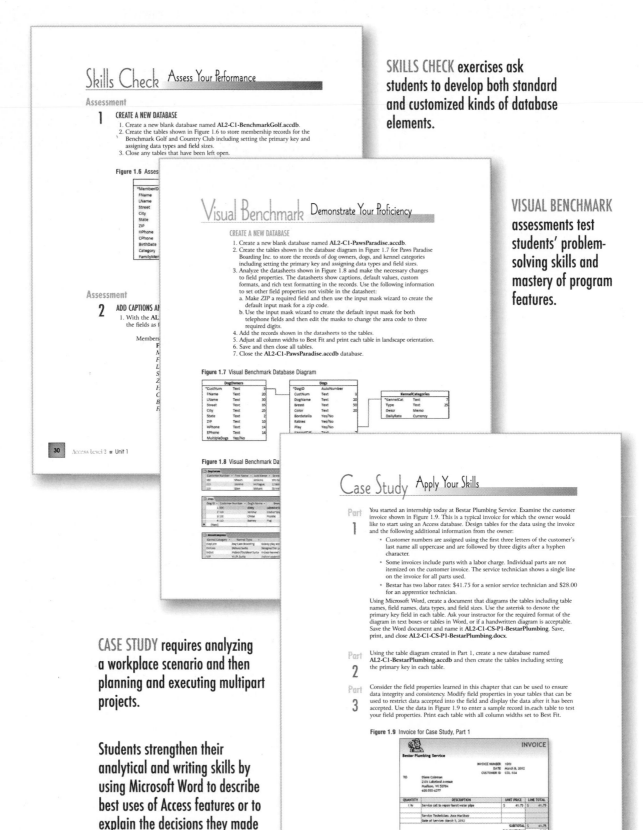

**SKILLS CHECK exercises ask students to develop both standard and customized kinds of database elements.**

## Skills Check  Assess Your Performance

**Assessment**

**1  CREATE A NEW DATABASE**

1. Create a new blank database named **AL2-C1-BenchmarkGolf.accdb**.
2. Create the tables shown in Figure 1.6 to store membership records for the Benchmark Golf and Country Club including setting the primary key and assigning data types and field sizes.
3. Close any tables that have been left open.

**Figure 1.6 Asses**

\*MemberID
FName
LName
Street
City
State
ZIP
HPhone
CPhone
BirthDate
Category
FamilyMem

**Assessment**

**2  ADD CAPTIONS A**

1. With the AL
the fields as

Members
F
M
F
L
S
Z
H
C
B
F

30  Access Level 2 ■ Unit 1

---

**VISUAL BENCHMARK assessments test students' problem-solving skills and mastery of program features.**

## Visual Benchmark  Demonstrate Your Proficiency

**CREATE A NEW DATABASE**

1. Create a new blank database named **AL2-C1-PawsParadise.accdb**.
2. Create the tables shown in the database diagram in Figure 1.7 for Paws Paradise Boarding Inc. to store the records of dog owners, dogs, and kennel categories including setting the primary key and assigning data types and field sizes.
3. Analyze the datasheets shown in Figure 1.8 and make the necessary changes to field properties. The datasheets show captions, default values, custom formats, and rich text formatting in the records. Use the following information to set other field properties not visible in the datasheet:
   a. Make *ZIP* a required field and then use the input mask wizard to create the default input mask for a zip code.
   b. Use the input mask wizard to create the default input mask for both telephone fields and then edit the masks to change the area code to three required digits.
4. Add the records shown in the datasheets to the tables.
5. Adjust all column widths to Best Fit and print each table in landscape orientation.
6. Save and then close all tables.
7. Close the **AL2-C1-PawsParadise.accdb** database.

**Figure 1.7 Visual Benchmark Database Diagram**

**Figure 1.8 Visual Benchmark Da**

---

**CASE STUDY requires analyzing a workplace scenario and then planning and executing multipart projects.**

**Students strengthen their analytical and writing skills by using Microsoft Word to describe best uses of Access features or to explain the decisions they made in completing the Case Study.**

## Case Study  Apply Your Skills

**Part 1**

You started an internship today at Bestar Plumbing Service. Examine the customer invoice shown in Figure 1.9. This is a typical invoice for which the owner would like to start using an Access database. Design tables for the data using the invoice and the following additional information from the owner:

• Customer numbers are assigned using the first three letters of the customer's last name all uppercase and are followed by three digits after a hyphen character.
• Some invoices include parts with a labor charge. Individual parts are not itemized on the customer invoice. The service technician shows a single line on the invoice for all parts used.
• Bestar has two labor rates: $41.75 for a senior service technician and $28.00 for an apprentice technician.

Using Microsoft Word, create a document that diagrams the tables including table names, field names, data types, and field sizes. Use the asterisk to denote the primary key field in each table. Ask your instructor for the required format of the diagram in text boxes or tables in Word, or if a handwritten diagram is acceptable. Save the Word document and name it **AL2-C1-CS-P1-BestarPlumbing**. Save, print, and close **AL2-C1-CS-P1-BestarPlumbing.docx**.

**Part 2**

Using the table diagram created in Part 1, create a new database named **AL2-C1-BestarPlumbing.accdb** and then create the tables including setting the primary key in each table.

**Part 3**

Consider the field properties learned in this chapter that can be used to ensure data integrity and consistency. Modify field properties in your tables that can be used to restrict data accepted into the field and display the data after it has been accepted. Use the data in Figure 1.9 to enter a sample record in each table to test your field properties. Print each table with all column widths set to Best Fit.

**Figure 1.9 Invoice for Case Study, Part 1**

34  Access Level 2 ■ Unit 1

---

# UNIT PERFORMANCE ASSESSMENT: Cross-Disciplinary, Comprehensive Evaluation

## Access Microsoft

### Performance Assessment

UNIT 2

Access2010L2U2

*Note: Before beginning unit assessments, copy to your storage medium the Access2010L2U2 subfolder from the Access2010L2 folder on the CD that accompanies this textbook and then make Access2010L2U2 the active folder.*

## Assessing Proficiency

In this unit you have learned to design and create reports with grouping, sorting, totals, and subreports; to use Access tools to analyze tables and improve database efficiency; to automate a database using macros and a Navigation form; to configure startup options and customize the database and Navigation pane; to integrate Access data with other programs; and to summarize data using PivotTables and PivotCharts.

**Assessment 1  Import Data from Text Files and Create Reports for a Property Management Database**

1. Open **AL2-U2-BenchmarkPropMgt.accdb** from the Access2010L2U2 folder on your storage medium and enable content. In this unit you will continue working with the residential property management database started in Unit 1. The database design and objects have been modified since Unit 1 based on feedback from the property manager and the office staff.
2. Import data into tables from two text files as follows. Save each set of import specifications for future use. You determine an appropriate description for each set of import steps.
   a. Append the data in the text file named *TenantsU2.csv* to the Tenants table.
   b. Append the data in the text file named *LeasesU2.csv* to the Leases table.
3. Design and create reports as follows:
   a. A report based on the LeasesByBldg query with all fields included except the building code field. Group the records by the building name and sort by Unit No within each group. Name the report *BuildingsAndLeases*. Include the current date and page numbering in the page footer. Add your name as the report designer in the report footer. Insert an appropriate clip art image in the report header. You determine the remaining layout and formatting elements including a descriptive report title.

**ASSESSING PROFICIENCY** checks mastery of features.

**WRITING ACTIVITIES** involve applying program skills in a communication context.

## Writing Activities

The following activities give you the opportunity to practice your writing skills along with demonstrating an understanding of some of the important Access features you have mastered in this unit. Use correct grammar, appropriate word choices, and clear sentence constructions when required.

**Activity 1  Create a New Database for Renovation Contracts by Importing Data**

You work for a sole proprietor home renovation contractor. The contractor has an old computer in his basement that he has been using to keep invoice records for renovation contracts. The computer is from the Windows XP operating system era and the software program the contractor used is no longer being sold or updated. The contractor was able to copy data from the old system in a tab-delimited text file named **DavisRenos.txt**. Create a new Access database named **AL2-U2-DavisRenos.accdb** and import the data from the old system into a new table. Modify the table design after importing to change the *Amount* field to Currency. Design and create a form based on the table to be used for entering new records. Design and create a report to print the records including a total of the invoice amount column. The proprietor is not familiar with Access and would like you to create a user-friendly menu that can be used to add new records using the form you designed and view the report. Create the menu using a Navigation form and configure startup options so that the menu is the only object displayed in the work area when the database is opened. Test your menu to make sure each tab functions correctly. Using Microsoft Word, compose a quick

**INTERNET RESEARCH** project reinforces research and word processing skills.

## Internet Research

**Buying a Home**

Within the next few years you plan on buying a home. While you save money for this investment, you decide to maintain a database of the homes offered for sale within the area where you are interested in buying. Design and create tables and relationships in a new database named **AL2-U2-Homes4Sale.accdb**. Include fields to store data that would be of interest to you such as: the address, asking price, style of home (condominium, ranch, two stories, semi-detached, etc.), number of bedrooms, number of bathrooms, type of heating/cooling system, property taxes, basement, and garage. Design and create a form to be used to enter the information into the tables. Research on the Internet at least five listings within the area that you wish to live and use the form to enter records for each listing. Design and create a report that groups the records by style of home. Calculate the average list price at the end of each group and at the end of the report. Include five hyperlink control objects that will link to the web page from which you retrieved the information for each listing. Include appropriate titles and other report elements. Add your name in the footer as the report designer. Publish and print the report as an XPS document named **AL2-U2-AvgHousePrices.xps**.

## Job Study

**JOB STUDY** at the end of Unit 2 presents a capstone assessment requiring critical thinking and problem solving.

**Meals on Wheels Database**

You are a volunteer working in the office of your local Meals on Wheels community organization. Meals on Wheels delivers nutritious, affordable meals to citizens in need of the service such as seniors, convalescents, or people with disabilities. The organization requires volunteers using their own vehicle to drive to the meal depot, pick up meals, and deliver them to clients' homes. The volunteer coordinator has expressed an interest in using an Access database to better organize and plan volunteer delivery routes. Create a new database named **AL2-U2-MealsOnWheels.accdb**. Design and create tables and relationships to store the following information. Remember to apply best practices in database design to minimize data redundancy and validate data whenever possible to ensure accuracy.

- Client name, address, telephone, gender, age, reason for requiring meals (senior, convalescent, or disability), meals required (breakfast, lunch, dinner), date service started, and estimated length of service required.
- Volunteer name, address, telephone, gender, age, date started, availability by day and by meal (breakfast, lunch, dinner), and receipt of police check clearance.
- Incorporate in your design an assignment for both the client and the volunteer to the quadrant of the city or town in which he or she is located. The volunteer coordinator divides the city or town by north, south, east, and west and tries to match drivers with clients in the same quadrant.
- Any other information you think would be important to the volunteer coordinator for this service.

# Student Courseware

**Student Resources CD** Each Benchmark Series textbook is packaged with a Student Resources CD containing the data files required for completing the projects and assessments. A CD icon and folder name displayed on the opening page of chapters reminds students to copy a folder of files from the CD to the desired storage medium before beginning the project exercises. Directions for copying folders are printed on the inside back cover.

**Internet Resource Center** Additional learning tools and reference materials are available at the book-specific website at www.emcp.net/BenchmarkAccess10. Students can access the same files that are on the Student Resources CD along with study aids, web links, and tips for using computers effectively in academic and workplace settings.

**SNAP Training and Assessment** SNAP is a web-based program offering an interactive venue for learning Microsoft Office 2010, Windows 7, and Internet Explorer 8.0. Along with a web-based learning management system, SNAP provides multimedia tutorials, performance skill items, document-based assessments, a concepts test bank, an online grade book, and a set of course planning tools. A CD of tutorials teaching the basics of Office, Windows, and Internet Explorer is also available if instructors wish to assign additional SNAP tutorial work without using the web-based SNAP program.

**eBook** For students who prefer studying with an eBook, the texts in the Benchmark Series are available in an electronic form. The web-based, password-protected eBooks feature dynamic navigation tools, including bookmarking, a linked table of contents, and the ability to jump to a specific page. The eBook format also supports helpful study tools, such as highlighting and note taking.

# Instructor Resources

**Instructor's Guide and Disc** Instructor support for the Benchmark Series includes an *Instructor's Guide and Instructor Resources Disc* package. This resource includes planning information, such as Lesson Blueprints, teaching hints, and sample course syllabi; presentation resources, such as PowerPoint slide shows with lecture notes and audio support; and assessment resources, including an overview of available assessment venues, live model answers for chapter activities, and live and PDF model answers for end-of-chapter exercises. Contents of the *Instructor's Guide and Instructor Resources Disc* package are also available on the password-protected section of the Internet Resource Center for this title at www.emcp.net/BenchmarkAccess10.

**Computerized Test Generator** Instructors can use the EXAMVIEW® Assessment Suite and test banks of multiple-choice items to create customized web-based or print tests.

**Blackboard Cartridge** This set of files allows instructors to create a personalized Blackboard website for their course and provides course content, tests, and the mechanisms for establishing communication via e-discussions and online group conferences. Available content includes a syllabus, test banks, PowerPoint presentations with audio support, and supplementary course materials. Upon request, the files can be available within 24–48 hours. Hosting the site is the responsibility of the educational institution.

## System Requirements

This text is designed for the student to complete projects and assessments on a computer running a standard installation of Microsoft Office 2010, Professional Edition, and the Microsoft Windows 7 operating system. To effectively run this suite and operating system, your computer should be outfitted with the following:

- 1 gigahertz (GHz) processor or higher; 1 gigabyte (GB) of RAM
- DVD drive
- 15 GB of available hard-disk space
- Computer mouse or compatible pointing device

Office 2010 will also operate on computers running the Windows XP Service Pack 3 or the Windows Vista operating system.

Screen captures in this book were created using a screen resolution display setting of 1280 × 800. Choose the resolution that best matches your computer; however, be aware that using a resolution other than 1280 × 800 means that your screens may not match the illustrations in this book.


## About the Author

**Denise Seguin** has been teaching at Fanshawe College in London, Ontario, since 1986. She has taught a variety of software applications to learners in postsecondary Information Technology diploma programs and in Continuing Education courses. In addition to co-authoring books in the *Benchmark Office 2010* series, she has authored *Microsoft Outlook 2010, 2007, 2003, 2002,* and *2000*. She has also co-authored *Our Digital World*; *Marquee Series: Microsoft Office 2010, 2007,* and *2003*; *Office 2003*; *Office XP*; and *Using Computers in the Medical Office 2007* and *2003* for Paradigm Publishing, Inc.

# Microsoft® Access®

## Level 2

# Unit 1 ■ Advanced Tables, Relationships, Queries, and Forms

Chapter 1 ■ Designing the Structure of Tables

Chapter 2 ■ Building Relationships and Lookup Fields

Chapter 3 ■ Advanced Query Techniques

Chapter 4 ■ Creating and Using Custom Forms

# Access
Microsoft®

# Designing the Structure of Tables

## PERFORMANCE OBJECTIVES

**Upon successful completion of Chapter 1, you will be able to:**

- **Design the structure of tables to optimize efficiency and accuracy of data**
- **Select the appropriate field data type based on analysis of source data**
- **Disallow blank field values**
- **Allow or disallow zero-length strings in a field**
- **Create a custom format for text, number, and date fields**
- **Create a custom input mask**
- **Define rich text formatting for a memo field**
- **Store history of changes to a memo field**
- **Define and use an attachment field with multiple attachments**

**Tutorials**

**1.1** Diagramming a Database
**1.2** Creating Tables in Design View
**1.3** Restricting Data Entry and Data
**1.4** Creating a Custom Format for a Text Field, a Numeric Field, and a Date/Time Field
**1.5** Restricting Data Entry Using Input Masks
**1.6** Working with Memo Fields
**1.7** Creating an Attachment Field
**1.8** Attaching Files to Records

Designing tables in Access is the most important task when creating a database since tables are the objects upon which all other objects are based. A query, form, or report relies on a table for the data source. Designing a new database involves planning the number of tables needed, the fields that will be included in each table, and the methods with which Access can be used to check and/or validate new data as the data is being entered. In this chapter you will learn the basic steps to plan a new database by analyzing existing data. In addition to organizing the data structure, you will also learn to select appropriate data types and use field properties to control, restrict, or otherwise validate data.

In this chapter, prior knowledge of the steps to create a new table, including changing the data type and field size and assigning the primary key, as well as the meaning of the terms *field*, *record*, *table*, and *database* is assumed.

Model answers for this chapter's projects appear on the following page.

Access
Access2010L2C1

*Note: Before beginning the projects, copy to your storage medium the Access2010L2C1 subfolder from the Access2010L2 folder on the CD that accompanies this textbook. Steps on how to copy a folder are presented on the inside of the back cover of this textbook. Do this every time you start a chapter's projects.*

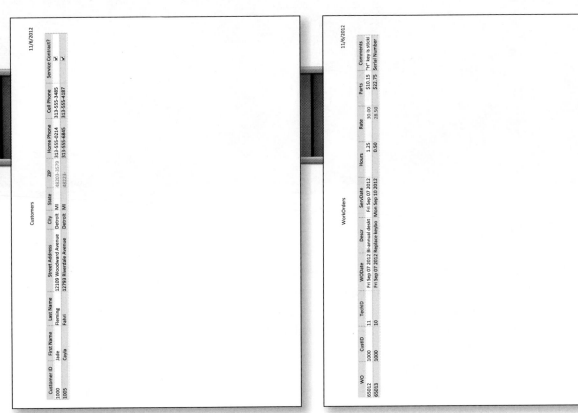

**Project 1 Create Tables by Analyzing Sample Data and Applying Database Design Techniques** Project 1c, Customers Table

Project 1f, WorkOrders Table

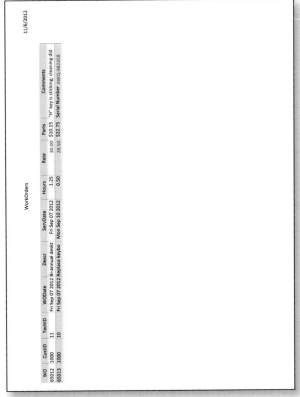

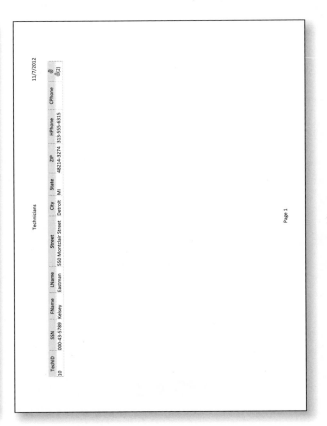

**Project 2 Work with Memo and Attachment Fields**
Project 2a, WorkOrders Table

Project 2b, Technicians Table

**Create Tables by Analyzing Sample Data and Applying Database Design Techniques**                    **6 Parts**

You will use sample data to decide how to structure a new database to track computer service work orders using best practices for table design and then create the tables.

# Designing Tables and Fields for a New Database ∎∎∎∎∎∎∎

Most of the databases you will work with in the workplace will have already been created by database designers. An introduction to the process involved in creating a new database will be of benefit to you so that you will better understand the reasons why objects are organized and related. Creating a new database from scratch involves careful advance planning. Database designers spend considerable time analyzing existing data and asking questions of users and managers. Designers will want to know how data will be used to help identify the required forms, queries, and reports to be generated from the data. Often, designers begin by modeling a report required from the database to see data that is required to populate the report. A *data dictionary* (a list of fields and attributes of each field) is then compiled from which the designer can next map out the number of required tables.

In Project 1, you will be analyzing a sample work order for RSR Computer Services. RSR started out as a small computer service company. The owners used Excel worksheets to enter information from service records and then produced revenue reports. The company's success has led to a need to move to a relational database to track customer information. The owners want to be able to generate queries and reports from the service records to assist with decision making. Examine the data in a typical work order shown in Figure 1.1. The work order form that the technicians have been filling out at the customer site will be used as the input source document for the database.

**Figure 1.1** Sample Work Order for RSR Computer Services

Designers analyze all input documents and output requirements to capture the entire set of data elements that need to be created. Once all data has been identified, the designer maps out the number of tables required to hold the data. During the process in which the designer is mapping the tables and fields to be associated with each table, the designer incorporates the following techniques:

- Each table is considered an *entity* and should describe a single person, place, object, event, or other subject. Each table should store facts that are related to the entity's subject only.

- Data should be segmented until it is in its smallest unit that you will want to manipulate. For example, in the work order shown in Figure 1.1, the customer's name and address would be split into separate fields for first name, last name, street address, city, state, and ZIP code. This approach provides maximum flexibility for generating other objects and allows the designer to sort or filter by any individual data element.

- Fields that can be calculated by using data in other fields are not included. For example, the total labor and total due amounts in the work order can be calculated using other numeric data elements.

- Identify fields that can be used to answer questions from the data. Queries and reports can be designed to extract information based on the results of a conditional expression (sometimes referred to as Boolean logic). For example, the technician enters on the work order whether the customer has a service contract or not. A field that stores a Yes or No (true or false) condition for the service contract data element allows the business to generate reports of customers that have subscribed to a service contract (true condition) and those that have not subscribed (false condition).

- Identify a field in each table that will hold data that uniquely identifies each record. This field becomes the primary key. If the source documents used for design do not reveal a unique identifier, Access provides an ID field automatically in new tables with the AutoNumber data type that can be used as a primary key.

- Determine each table that will relate to another table and the field you will use to join the two when you create relationships. Identifying relationships at this stage helps you determine if you need to add a field to a related table to allow you to join the table.

- Relational databases are built upon the concept that data redundancy should be avoided except for fields that will be used to join tables in a relationship. *Data redundancy* means data in one table is repeated in another table. Repeating fields in multiple tables wastes storage space, promotes inefficiency, inconsistency, and increases the likelihood that errors will be made when adding, updating, and deleting field values.

The design process may seem time-consuming; however, the time expended to produce a well-designed database saves time later. A database that is poorly designed will likely have logic errors or structure errors that require redefining of data or objects after live data has been entered.

# Diagramming a Database

Recall from Level 1, Chapter 1 that designers often create a visual representation of the database's structure in a diagram similar to the one shown in Figure 1.2. Each table is represented in a box with the table name at the top of the box. Within each box, the fields that will be stored in the table are listed with the field names that will be used when the tables are created. The primary key field is denoted with an asterisk. Tables that will be joined have lines drawn connecting them together at the common field that exists in both tables. You will begin to build this database in the remainder of this chapter and create the relationships in Chapter 2.

Notice that many of the field names in the diagram are abbreviated. Although a field name can contain up to 64 characters, field names that are short enough to be understood are easier to manage and type into expressions. For abbreviated field names, the Caption property is used to display descriptive headings that contain spaces and/or longer words when viewing the data in a datasheet, form, or report. Also notice that none of the field names contain spaces. Spaces are allowed in field names; however, most database designers avoid using spaces and separate compound words by changing the case, by using an underscore character (_) or by using a hyphen (-) as a separator.

Words such as *Name* and *Date* are reserved words in Access and cannot be used as a field name. Access prompts you if the field name you used is a reserved word when you try to save the table.

# Assigning Data Types

Each field is assigned a data type by the designer based on the type of entries that the designer wants to allow into the field and the operations that will need to be used to manipulate the data. Selecting the appropriate data type is important since restrictions will be placed on a field based upon the field's data type. For example, in a field designated with the Number data type, only numbers, a period to represent a decimal point, and a plus or minus sign can be entered into the field in a datasheet or form. Table 1.1 reviews the available data types.

**Figure 1.2**  Diagram of Table Structure for RSR Computer Services Database

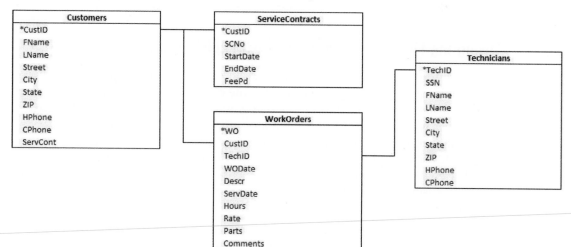

**Table 1.1** Data Types

| Data Type | Description |
| --- | --- |
| Text | Alphanumeric data up to 255 characters such as a name or address. Text fields can also store values such as a customer number, telephone number, or social security number that is used as an identifier and not for calculating. |
| Memo | Alphanumeric data longer than 255 characters with up to 65,535 characters displayed in the field. Use a Memo field to store longer passages of text in a record. You can add rich text formatting in a Memo field such as bold, italics, or font color. |
| Number | Positive or negative values that can be used in calculations. Do not use for monetary values (see *Currency*). |
| Date/Time | Accepts only valid dates and times into the field. Use to ensure dates and times are entered and sorted properly. |
| Currency | Holds monetary values. Access does not round off during calculations. |
| AutoNumber | Field value is automatically assigned by Access by sequentially incrementing the field value by 1 when a new record is added. |
| Yes/No | Entry in the field is restricted to conditional logic of Yes or No, True or False, On or Off. |
| OLE Object | Stores an embedded or linked object created in other Microsoft Office applications. |
| Hyperlink | Links to a URL. |
| Attachment | Attach a file to the record such as a picture, Word document, or Excel worksheet. |
| Calculated | The field's value is calculated using a mathematical expression that uses data from other fields within the same table. |

## Using the Field Size Property to Restrict Field Length

By default, text fields are set to a width of 255 in the Field Size property. Access uses only the amount of space needed for the data that is entered even when the field size allows for more characters, so you may wonder why one would change the property to a smaller value. One reason to consider is that changing the Field Size property becomes a means to restrict the length of data allowed into the field. For example, if RSR Computer Services has developed a 4-character numbering system for customer numbers, setting the field size for the *CustID* field to *4* will ensure that no one enters a customer number longer than 4 characters by accident since Access will disallow all characters typed after the fourth character.

Figure 1.3 shows the table structure diagram for the RSR Computer Services database expanded to include each field's data type and field size property. You will use this diagram in Project 1a to create the tables.

**Figure 1.3** Expanded Table Structure Diagram with Data Types and Field Sizes for Project 1a

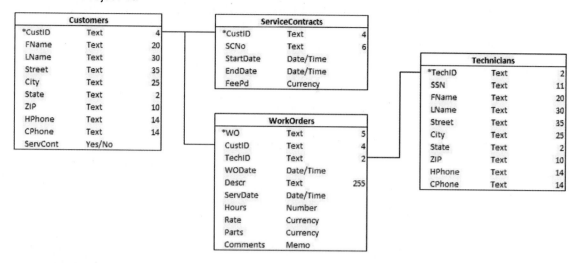

| Customers | | |
|---|---|---|
| *CustID | Text | 4 |
| FName | Text | 20 |
| LName | Text | 30 |
| Street | Text | 35 |
| City | Text | 25 |
| State | Text | 2 |
| ZIP | Text | 10 |
| HPhone | Text | 14 |
| CPhone | Text | 14 |
| ServCont | Yes/No | |

| ServiceContracts | | |
|---|---|---|
| *CustID | Text | 4 |
| SCNo | Text | 6 |
| StartDate | Date/Time | |
| EndDate | Date/Time | |
| FeePd | Currency | |

| Technicians | | |
|---|---|---|
| *TechID | Text | 2 |
| SSN | Text | 11 |
| FName | Text | 20 |
| LName | Text | 30 |
| Street | Text | 35 |
| City | Text | 25 |
| State | Text | 2 |
| ZIP | Text | 10 |
| HPhone | Text | 14 |
| CPhone | Text | 14 |

| WorkOrders | | |
|---|---|---|
| *WO | Text | 5 |
| CustID | Text | 4 |
| TechID | Text | 2 |
| WODate | Date/Time | |
| Descr | Text | 255 |
| ServDate | Date/Time | |
| Hours | Number | |
| Rate | Currency | |
| Parts | Currency | |
| Comments | Memo | |

## Project 1a   Creating Tables in Design View

Part 1 of 6

1. Start Access.
2. At the New tab Backstage view, complete the following steps to create a new database to store the work orders for RSR Computer Services:
   a. Click the Browse button located at the right of the *File Name* text box (currently displays *Database1.accdb*) in the *Blank database* section.
   b. At the File New Database dialog box, navigate to the Access2010L2C1 folder on your storage medium, select the current text in the *File Name* text box, type **AL2-C1-RSRCompServ**, and then click OK.
   c. Click the Create button located below the *File Name* text box.

3. Close the Table1 blank table datasheet that displays. You will work with tables in Design view to access all of the field properties available for fields.
4. Click the Create tab and then click the Table Design button in the Tables group. Create the fields shown in the Customers table in Figure 1.3 including the data type and field size setting.
5. Assign the primary key to the *CustID* field.
6. Save the table and name it *Customers*.

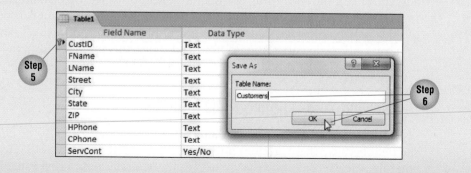

7. Close the table.
8. Create the ServiceContracts, WorkOrders, and Technicians tables shown in Figure 1.3 by completing steps similar to those in Steps 4–7. Assign the primary key in each table using the field denoted with an asterisk in Figure 1.3.
9. Make sure all tables are closed.

# Restricting Data Entry and Data Display Using Field Properties ■■■■■■■■■■■■■■■■■■■■■■■■

The properties that are available for a field depend on the field's data type. For example, a Yes/No field has 7 properties while a Text field has 14 and a Number field has 12. Use the options available in the *Field Properties* section in Design view to place restrictions on data accepted into the field and to ensure data is entered and displayed consistently. Field properties should be defined for the fields before other objects, such as forms or reports are created. The properties carry over to the other objects and taking the time to define the properties when the table is created reduces the number of times you have to make changes if you decide to modify properties later on.

You have already used the Field Size property in Project 1a to restrict the length of entries allowed in fields. In this section you will learn to apply other field properties to fields to further control data entry and display.

## Adding Captions

In Level 1 you learned about the Caption property in the Name & Caption dialog box when creating a new table using a Table datasheet. The same property appears in Design view in the *Field Properties* section. Recall that the Caption property allows you to enter a more descriptive title for the field if the field name has been truncated or abbreviated. You can also use a caption to display spaces between words in a field name rather than underscore or hyphen characters. In the absence of an entry in the Caption property, Access displays the field name in datasheets, queries, forms, and reports.

## Requiring Data in a Field

A field that you want to make sure is never left empty when a new record is added can be controlled using the Required field property. By default, the Required property is set to No. Change this value to Yes to make sure data is typed into the field when a new record is added. For example, you can force all new records to have a ZIP code entry. You do not need to set this property for a field that is defined as a primary key, since a primary key field cannot be left empty.

## Disallowing Zero-Length Strings in a Field

A zero-length field can be used to indicate a value is not going to be entered into the field because the field does not apply to the current record. When you are entering a new record and leave a field blank, Access records a null value in the field. For example, if you are adding a new record for a customer and you do not know the customer's cell phone number, you can leave the field empty with the intention

**▼ Quick Steps**

**Add a Caption to Existing Field**
1. Open table in Design view.
2. Activate desired field.
3. Click in *Caption* property box.
4. Type descriptive text.
5. Save table.

**Require Data in Field**
1. Open table in Design view.
2. Activate desired field.
3. Click in *Required* property box.
4. Click down-pointing arrow.
5. Click Yes.
6. Save table.

**Disallow Zero-Length String in Field**
1. Open table in Design view.
2. Activate desired field.
3. Click in *Allow Zero Length* property box.
4. Click down-pointing arrow.
5. Click No.
6. Save table.

of updating the field at a later time. This is an example of leaving the field blank with a null value. Alternatively, if you know the customer does not own a cell phone, you can enter a zero-length string in the field to indicate no field value applies to this record.

To enter a zero-length string, type two double quotation symbols with no space between (""). When viewing the field in a datasheet, query, form, or report, you cannot distinguish between a field with a null value and a field with a zero-length string because both display as blanks; however, you can create a control in a form or report that returns a user-defined message in the blank fields that distinguishes one from the other. For example, you could display the word *Unknown* in a field with a null value and *Not applicable* in a field with a zero-length string. In some cases, you will want to see in a form or report which records will not have a value in the field as opposed to those records that are incomplete.

By default, Text, Memo, and Hyperlink data fields can have zero-length strings entered into the field. Change the Allow Zero Length property to *No* to disallow zero-length strings.

You can also press the spacebar to insert a zero-length string.

Set the *Required* field to *Yes* and *Allow Zero Length* to *No* to make sure a field value (and not a space) has to be entered at the time the record is added.

---

**Project 1b**  **Modifying Field Properties to Add Captions and Disallow Blank Values in a Field**

Part 2 of 6

1. With the **AL2-C1-RSRCompServ.accdb** database open, add captions to the fields in the Customers table by completing the following steps:
    a. Right-click *Customers* in the Tables group of the Navigation pane and then click *Design View* at the shortcut menu.
    b. With *CustID* the active field, click in the *Caption* property box in the *Field Properties* section and then type Customer ID.
    c. Click in the *FName* field row to activate the field, click in the *Caption* property box in the *Field Properties* section, and then type First Name.
    d. Add captions to the following fields by completing a step similar to Step 1c.

    | | |
    |---|---|
    | *LName* | Last Name |
    | *Street* | Street Address |
    | *HPhone* | Home Phone |
    | *CPhone* | Cell Phone |
    | *ServCont* | Service Contract? |

    e. Click the Save button on the Quick Access toolbar.
    f. Click the View button (do not click the down-pointing arrow on the button) to switch to Datasheet view and then select all columns in the datasheet. If necessary, click the Shutter Bar Open/Close button (two left-pointing chevrons located at the top of the Navigation pane) to minimize the Navigation pane.
    g. Click the More button in the Records group in the Home tab, click *Field Width* at the drop-down list, and then click the Best Fit button at the Column Width dialog box to adjust the widths to the length of the longest entry.
    h. Click in the *Customer ID* field in the first row of the datasheet to deselect the columns.

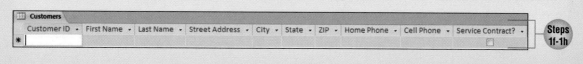

2. Switch to Design View and click the Shutter Bar Open/Close button (two right-pointing chevrons) to redisplay the Navigation pane if you minimized the pane in Step 1f.
3. You want to ensure that no record is entered without an entry in the *ZIP* field and you also want to disallow blank values in the field, including zero-length strings.
   a. Click in the *ZIP* field row to activate the field.
   b. Click in the *Required* property box in the *Field Properties* section (currently displays *No*), click the down-pointing arrow that appears, and then click *Yes* at the drop-down list.

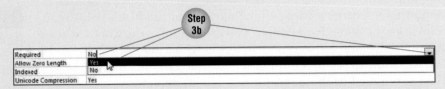

Step 3b

| Required | No |
| Allow Zero Length | Yes |
| Indexed | No |
| Unicode Compression | Yes |

   c. Click in the *Allow Zero Length* property box (currently displays *Yes*), click the down-pointing arrow that appears, and then click *No* at the drop-down list.

Step 3c

| Required | Yes |
| Allow Zero Length | Yes |
| Indexed | Yes |
| Unicode Compression | No |
| IME Mode | No Control |

   d. Save the changes to the table design.
4. Test the restrictions on the *ZIP* field using a new record by completing the following steps:
   a. Switch to Datasheet view.
   b. Add the following data in the fields indicated.

   | | |
   |---|---|
   | *Customer ID* | 1000 |
   | *First Name* | Jade |
   | *Last Name* | Fleming |
   | *Street Address* | 12109 Woodward Avenue |
   | *City* | Detroit |
   | *State* | MI |

   c. At the *ZIP* field, press Enter or Tab to move past the field, leaving the field blank.
   d. Type 313-555-0214 in the *Home Phone* field.
   e. Type 313-555-3485 in the *Cell Phone* field.
   f. Press the spacebar in the *Service Contract?* field to insert a check mark in the check box.
   g. Press Enter. Access displays an error message since the record cannot be saved without an entry in the *ZIP* field.
   h. Click OK at the Microsoft Access message box.
   i. Click in the *ZIP* field, type 48203-3579, and then press Enter four times to move to the *Customer ID* field in the second row of the datasheet.

Microsoft Access

⚠ You must enter a value in the 'Customers.ZIP' field.

OK    Help

Step 4h

5. Double-click the right column boundary of the *Street Address* and *ZIP* columns to adjust the widths so that you can read the entire field value in the columns.

Step 5

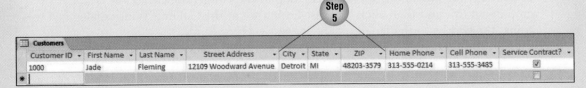

| Customer ID ▾ | First Name ▾ | Last Name ▾ | Street Address ▾ | City ▾ | State ▾ | ZIP ▾ | Home Phone ▾ | Cell Phone ▾ | Service Contract? ▾ |
|---|---|---|---|---|---|---|---|---|---|
| 1000 | Jade | Fleming | 12109 Woodward Avenue | Detroit | MI | 48203-3579 | 313-555-0214 | 313-555-3485 | ☑ |
| * | | | | | | | | | ☐ |

6. Close the Customers table. Click Yes when prompted to save changes to the layout of the table.

# Creating a Custom Format for a Text Field

The Format property controls how data is displayed in the field in the datasheet, query, form, or report. The available formats that you can use are dependent on the field's data type. Some data types have predefined formats available which can be selected from a drop-down list in the *Format* property box. No predefined formats exist for Text or Memo fields. If no predefined format exists or if the predefined format options do not meet your needs, you can create your own custom format. Table 1.2 displays commonly used format codes for text or memo fields. The Format property does not control how data is entered into the field. Formatting a field controls the display of accepted field values. Refer to the section on input masks (starting on page 18) to learn how to control new data as the data is being entered.

Refer to the section on input masks (starting on page 18)

**Table 1.2** Format Codes for Text or Memo Fields

| Code | Description | Format Property Example |
|------|-------------|-------------------------|
| @ | Use as a placeholder, one symbol for each character position. Unused positions in a field value are replaced with blank spaces to the left of the text entered into the field. | @@@@<br>Field value is 123.<br>Access displays one blank space follwed by 123, left-aligned in the field. |
| ! | Access fills the placeholder positions with characters from left to right instead of the default right to left sequence. | !@@@@<br>Field value entered is 123.<br>Access displays 123 left-aligned in the field with one blank space after 3. |
| > | All text is converted to uppercase. | ><br>Field value is mi.<br>Access displays MI in the field. |
| < | All text is converted to lowercase. | <<br>Field value is Jones@EMCP.NET.<br>Access displays jones@emcp.net in the field. |
| [color] | Text is displayed in the font color specified. Available colors are: black, blue, cyan, green, magenta, red, yellow, and white. | [red]@@@@@-@@@@<br>Field value entered is 482033579.<br>Access displays 48203-3579. |

1. With the **AL2-C1-RSRCompServ.accdb** database open, format the *State* field to ensure all text is displayed uppercase by completing the following steps:
   a. Right-click *Customers* in the Tables group of the Navigation pane and then click *Design View* at the shortcut menu.
   b. Click in the *State* field row to activate the field.
   c. Click in the *Format* property box and then type >.
   d. Save the table.

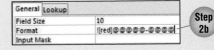

2. Format the *ZIP* field to fill the field with characters from left to right, display the text in red, and provide for the five-plus-four–character U.S. ZIP code separated by a hyphen by completing the following steps:
   a. Click in the *ZIP* field row to activate the field.
   b. Click in the *Format* property box and then type ![red]@@@@@-@@@@.
   c. Save the table.
3. Test the custom formats in the *State* and *ZIP* fields using a new record by completing the following steps:
   a. Switch to Datasheet view.
   b. Add the following data in a new record. Type the text for the *State* field as indicated in lowercase text. Notice when you move to the next field, Access automatically converts the lowercase text to uppercase. As you type the ZIP text, notice the text is displayed in red. Since no field values are entered for the last four characters of the ZIP field, Access displays blank spaces in these positions.

   | | |
   |---|---|
   | *Customer ID* | 1005 |
   | *First Name* | Cayla |
   | *Last Name* | Fahri |
   | *Street Address* | 12793 Riverdale Avenue |
   | *City* | Detroit |
   | *State* | mi |
   | *ZIP* | 48223 |
   | *Home Phone* | 313-555-6845 |
   | *Cell Phone* | 313-555-4187 |
   | *Service Contract?* | Press spacebar for *Yes* |

4. Look at the data in the *ZIP* field for the first record. This data was entered before you formatted the *ZIP* field. Since a hyphen was typed when the data was entered and the field is now formatted to automatically add the hyphen, two hyphen characters appear in the existing record. Edit the field value for record 1 in the *ZIP* field to remove the extra hyphen.

| Customer ID ▾ | First Name ▾ | Last Name ▾ | Street Address ▾ | City ▾ | State ▾ | ZIP ▾ |
|---|---|---|---|---|---|---|
| 1000 | Jade | Fleming | 12109 Woodward Avenue | Detroit | MI | 48203-3579 |
| 1005 | Cayla | Fahri | 12793 Riverdale Avenue | Detroit | MI | 48223- |

Step 4

5. Display the datasheet in Print Preview. Change the orientation to landscape. Set the margins to a top margin of 1-inch and the bottom, left, and right margins of 0.25 inch. Print the datasheet and then close Print Preview.
6. Close the Customers table.

# Creating a Custom Format for a Numeric Field

Access provides predefined formats for Number, AutoNumber, and Currency fields that include options for fixed decimal places, commas in the thousands, the currency symbol, percentages and exponential notation. Table 1.3 displays commonly used format codes that you can use to create a custom format. Use the placeholders shown in Table 1.3 in combination with other characters such as a dollar symbol, comma, and period to create the desired custom numeric format.

You can specify up to four different formats for a numeric field to include different options for displaying positive values, negative values, zero values, and null values. Examine the following custom format code:

#,###.00;-#,###.00[Red];0.00;"Unknown"

Each of the four sections is separated with a semicolon (;). The first section *#,###.00* defines the format for positive values that includes the comma in thousands and two decimal places with zeros used if no decimal value is entered. The second section *-#,###.00[Red]* defines negative values with the same placeholders as positive but starts the field with a minus symbol and displays the numbers in red. The third section *0.00* instructs Access to show 0.00 in the field if a zero is entered. Finally, a field value that is left blank would display the text *Unknown* [italics for emphasis only] in the field. Note that the example shown indicates the text that you want shown in the field includes a quotation symbol at the beginning and end of the desired text.

▼ **Quick Steps**

**Format Number Field**
1. Open table in Design view.
2. Activate desired field.
3. Click in *Format* property box.
4. Type desired format codes or select from predefined list.
5. Save table.

**Table 1.3** Format Codes for Numeric Fields

| Code | Description | Format Property Example |
|------|-------------|-------------------------|
| # | Used as a placeholder to display a number. | #.## <br> Field value entered is 123.45. Access displays 123.45 in the field. <br> Note that the number of placeholder positions does not restrict the data entered into the field. |
| 0 | Used as a placeholder to display a number. Access displays a zero in place of a position for which no value is entered. | 000.00 <br> Field value entered is 55.4. Access displays 055.40 in the field. |
| % | Multiplies the value times 100 and adds a percent symbol. | #.0% <br> Field value entered is .1242. Access displays 12.4% in the field. <br> Notice that only one decimal position causes rounding up or down to occur. |

1. With the **AL2-C1-RSRCompServ.accdb** database open, format the *Rate* field in the WorkOrders table with a custom format by completing the following steps:
    a. Open the WorkOrders table in Design view.
    b. Make the *Rate* field active.
    c. Click in the *Format* property box, delete the current entry, and then type #.00[blue];;;"Not Available". Notice that three semicolons are typed after the first custom format option *#.00[blue]*. When you do not need a custom format for negative or zero values in the property you include the semicolon to indicate no format setting for each option not specified. Since an hourly rate would never be a negative value or a zero value, you do not need to include custom formats for those situations since they would never occur.

    | Hours | Number |
    |-------|--------|
    | Rate | Currency |
    | Parts | Currency |
    | Comments | Memo |

    **Step 1b**

    | General | Lookup |
    |---------|--------|
    | Format | #.00[blue];;;"Not Available" |
    | Decimal Places | Auto |

    **Step 1c**

    d. Save the table.
2. Format the *Hours* field using a predefined format and change the field size by completing the following steps:
    a. Make the *Hours* field active.
    b. Click in the *Field Size* property box, click the down-pointing arrow that appears, and then click *Double*. The default setting for a Number field is *Long Integer*, which stores whole numbers only, meaning a decimal value entered into the field is rounded. Changing the field size property to *Double* allows you to store decimal values.
    c. Click in the *Format* property box, click the down-pointing arrow that appears, and then click *Standard* at the drop-down list.
    d. Click in the *Decimal Places* property box, click the down-pointing arrow that appears and then click *2* at the pop-up list.
    e. Save the table.

    | Hours | Number |
    |-------|--------|
    | Rate | Currency |
    | Parts | Currency |
    | Comments | Memo |

    **Step 2a**

    **Step 2b**

    **Step 2c**

    | General | Lookup |
    |---------|--------|
    | Field Size | Double |
    | Format | Standard |
    | Decimal Places | 2 |
    | Input Mask | |

    **Step 2d**

3. Switch to Datasheet view.
4. Add the following data in a new record to test the custom format and the predefined format. Notice when you move past the Rate field, the value is displayed in blue.

    | | |
    |-------|-------|
    | *WO* | 65012 |
    | *CustID* | 1000 |
    | *TechID* | 11 |
    | *WODate* | 09-07-2012 |
    | *Descr* | Bi-annual desktop computer cleaning and maintenance |
    | *ServDate* | 09-07-2012 |
    | *Hours* | 1.25 |
    | *Rate* | 30 |
    | *Parts* | 10.15 |
    | *Comments* | "H" key is sticking; cleaning did not resolve. Customer is considering buying a new keyboard. |

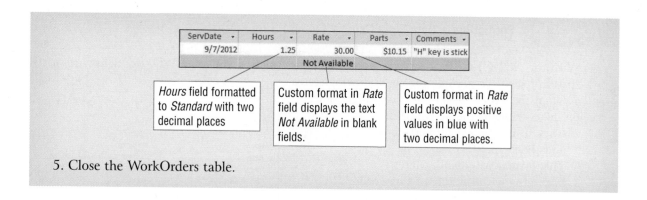

Hours field formatted to Standard with two decimal places

Custom format in Rate field displays the text Not Available in blank fields.

Custom format in Rate field displays positive values in blue with two decimal places.

5. Close the WorkOrders table.

## Creating a Custom Format for a Date/Time Field

Access provides predefined formats for fields with a data type of Date/Time that provide for a variety of combinations of month, day, and year display options for dates, and hours and minutes display options for time. If the predefined formats do not meet your needs, you can create your own custom format using a combination of the codes described in Table 1.4 along with the desired symbols such as hyphens or slashes between parts of the date. If you do not specify a format option for a Date/Time field, Access displays the date in the format m/d/yyyy. For example, in Project 1d, the date entered into the *WODate* field displayed as 9/7/2012.

A custom format for a Date/Time field can contain two sections separated by a semicolon. The first section specifies the format for displaying dates. To add a format for displaying times, type a semicolon and then add the format codes to specify the time.

▼ **Quick Steps**

**Format Date Field/ Time Field**
1. Open table in Design view.
2. Activate desired field.
3. Click in *Format* property box.
4. Type desired format codes or select from predefined list.
5. Save table.

**Table 1.4** Format Codes for Date/Time Fields

| Code | Description |
|------|-------------|
| d or dd | Displays the day of the month as one digit (d) or two digits (dd). |
| ddd or dddd | Spells out the day of the week abbreviated (ddd) or in full (dddd). |
| m or mm | Displays the month as one digit (m) or two digits (mm). |
| mmm or mmmm | Spells out the month abbreviated (mmm) or in full (mmmm). |
| yy or yyyy | Displays the year as the last two digits (yy) or all four digits (yyyy). |
| h or hh | Displays the hour as one digit (h) or two digits (hh). |
| n or nn | Displays the minutes as one digit (n) or two digits (nn). |
| s or ss | Displays the seconds as one digit (s) or two digits (ss). |
| AM/PM | Displays 12-hour clock values followed by AM or PM. |

1. With the **AL2-C1-RSRCompServ.accdb** database open, format the *WODate* field with a custom format by completing the following steps:

    a. Open the WorkOrders table in Design view.

    b. Make *WODate* the active field.

    c. Click in the *Format* property box and then type ddd mmm dd yyyy. This format will display dates beginning with the day of the week in abbreviated form, followed by the month in abbreviated form, the day of the month as two digits, and then the year as four digits. A space separates each section of the date.

    d. Save the table.

    | TechID | Text |
    | WODate | Date/Time |
    | Descr | Text |
    | ServDate | Date/Time |
    | Hours | Number |
    | Rate | Currency |
    | Parts | Currency |
    | Comments | Memo |

    General | Lookup
    Format | ddd mmm dd yyyy

    Step 1b
    Step 1c

2. Switch to Datasheet view.

3. If necessary, adjust the column width of the *WODate* field to read the entire entry.

    WorkOrders

    | WO | CustID | TechID | WODate | Descr |
    | 65012 | 1000 | 11 | Fri Sep 07 2012 | Bi-annual desk |

    Step 3

    Custom format for *WODate* field created at Step 1c.

4. Switch to Design view.

5. Format the *ServDate* field using the same custom format as the one entered for *WODate* by completing steps similar to those in Steps 1b through 1c.

6. Save the table and then switch to Datasheet view.

7. Double-click the right column boundary of the *ServDate* field and view the custom date format.

    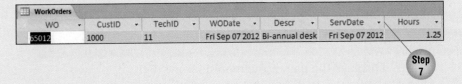

    WorkOrders

    | WO | CustID | TechID | WODate | Descr | ServDate | Hours |
    | 65012 | 1000 | 11 | Fri Sep 07 2012 | Bi-annual desk | Fri Sep 07 2012 | 1.25 |

    Step 7

8. Close the WorkOrders table. Click Yes when prompted to save changes to the table layout.

## Restricting Data Entry Using Input Masks

▼ **Quick Steps**

**Create Custom Input Mask**
1. Open table in Design view.
2. Activate desired field.
3. Click in *Input Mask* property box.
4. Type input mask codes.
5. Save table.

An *input mask* is used when you want to control the type of data and the pattern in which the data is entered into a field. Using input masks ensures data is entered consistently in all records. For example, to force all telephone numbers to have the area code entered, you can create an input mask that requires ten numbers. As you learned in Level 1, Chapter 4, Access includes the Input Mask Wizard that can be used to create an input mask for a text or date field. Commonly used masks are predefined within the wizard for telephone numbers, social security numbers, ZIP codes, dates, and times. To create your own input mask without the wizard, use the codes described in Table 1.5.

**Table 1.5** Commonly Used Input Mask Codes

| Code | Description |
|------|-------------|
| 0 | Required digit. |
| 9 | Optional digit. |
| # | Digit, space, plus or minus symbol. If no data is typed at this position, Access leaves a blank space. |
| L | Required letter. |
| ? | Optional letter. |
| A | Required letter or digit. |
| a | Optional letter or digit. |
| & | Required character or space. |
| C | Optional character or space. |
| ! | The field is filled from left to right instead of right to left. |
| \ | Access displays the character that immediately follows in the field. |

An input mask can contain up to three sections separated by semicolons. The first section contains the input mask codes for the data entry in the field. The second section instructs Access to store the display characters used in the field (such as hyphens or brackets) or not store the characters. A zero indicates that Access should store the characters. Leaving the second section blank means the display characters will not be stored. The third section specifies the placeholder character to display in the field when the field becomes active for data entry.

An example of an input mask to store a four-digit customer identification number with a pound symbol (#) as the placeholder would be: 0000;;#. The first section *0000* is the four required digits for the customer identification. Since the mask contains no display characters (such as a hyphen), the second section is blank. The pound symbol after the second semicolon is the placeholder character.

In addition to the symbols in Table 1.5, you can include the format code > to force characters to be uppercase or < to force characters to be lowercase, as well as decimal points, hyphens, slashes, or other punctuation symbols between parts of the mask.

**HINT**

If you create a custom input mask for a date field that also contains a custom format, make sure the two properties do not conflict to avoid confusion. For example, a format code that displays dates with the year first followed by the month and then the day would be confusing if the input mask required the date to be entered as month first followed by day and then year.

1. With the **AL2-C1-RSRCompServ.accdb** database open, create a custom input mask for the work order numbers by completing the following steps:
   a. Open the WorkOrders table in Design view.
   b. With *WO* the active field, click in the *Input Mask* property box and then type 00000;;_.
   This mask will require that a five-digit work order number is entered. The underscore character is used as the placeholder character that displays when the field becomes active.

   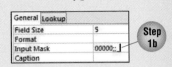

   c. Save the table.
2. Create an input mask to require the two date fields to be entered as three characters for the month with the first letter uppercase followed by two digits for the day and four digits for the year by completing the following steps:
   a. Make *WODate* the active field.
   b. Click in the *Input Mask* property box and then type >L<LL\-00\-0000;0;_. This mask requires three

   letters for the month with the first letter converted to uppercase and the remaining two letters converted to lowercase. The \- symbols instruct Access to display the hyphen character after the month as data is entered. Two digits are required for the day followed by another hyphen character and then four digits required for the year. The zero after the first semicolon instructs Access to store the display characters. Ending the mask, the underscore character is again used as the placeholder character.
   c. Make *ServDate* the active field, click in the *Input Mask* property box, and then type >L<LL\-00\-0000;0;_.
   d. Save the table.
3. Switch to Datasheet view.
4. Test the input masks using a new record by completing the following steps:
   a. Click the New button in the Records group of the Home tab.
   b. Type 6501. Notice that as soon as you type the first character, the placeholders appear in the field.
   c. Press Tab or Enter to move to the next field in the datasheet. Since the mask contained five zeros indicating five required digits, Access displays a message box informing you the value entered is not appropriate for the input mask.
   d. Click OK at the Microsoft Access message box.

   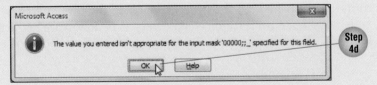

   e. Type 3 in the last position in the *WO* field and then press Tab or Enter to move to the next field.
   f. Type 1000 in the *CustID* field and then press Tab or Enter.
   g. Type 10 in the *TechID* field and then press Tab or Enter.
   h. Type sep072012 in the *WODate* field and then press Tab or Enter. Notice that the placeholder characters and the hyphens appear as soon as you type the first letter. Notice also that the first character is converted to uppercase and you do not need to type the hyphen characters since Access moves automatically to the next position after the month and the day are typed.
   i. Type **Replace keyboard** in the *Descr* field and then press Tab or Enter.

j. Type **sep102012** in the *ServDate* field and then press Tab or Enter.

k. Complete the remainder of the record as follows.

| | |
|---|---|
| *Hours* | .5 |
| *Rate* | 28.50 |
| *Parts* | 22.75 |
| *Comments* | Serial Number AWQ-982358 |

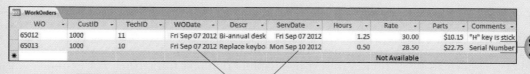

| WO | CustID | TechID | WODate | Descr | ServDate | Hours | Rate | Parts | Comments |
|---|---|---|---|---|---|---|---|---|---|
| 65012 | 1000 | 11 | Fri Sep 07 2012 | Bi-annual desk | Fri Sep 07 2012 | 1.25 | 30.00 | $10.15 | "H" key is stick |
| 65013 | 1000 | 10 | Fri Sep 07 2012 | Replace keybo | Mon Sep 10 2012 | 0.50 | 28.50 | $22.75 | Serial Number |
| * | | | | | | | Not Available | | |

Steps 4e-4k

Notice that once the date is accepted into the field, the custom Format property controls how the date is presented in the datasheet with the abbreviated day of the week at the beginning of the field and spaces between month, day, and year instead of hyphens.

5. Display the datasheet in Print Preview. Change the orientation to landscape. Set the margins to a top margin of 1-inch and the bottom, left, and right margins of 0.25 inch. Print the datasheet and then close Print Preview.

6. Close the WorkOrders table.

Other field properties that should be considered for data accuracy when designing database tables include the Default Value, Validation Rule, and Validation Text properties. Use the Default Value property to populate the field in new records with a field value that is used most often. For example, in a table where most employees have an address within the same city and state, you could use a default value to ensure consistent spelling and capitalization. The text appears automatically in the fields when new records are added to the table. The user can choose to either accept the default value by pressing Tab or Enter to move past the field, or type new data in the field. In Level 1 you learned how to create a default value using the Default Value button in the Properties group of the Table Tools Fields tab. In Design view, the Default Value property is located below the Caption property.

Use the Validation Rule and Validation Text properties to enter conditional statements that are checked against new data entered into the field. Invalid entries that do not meet the conditional statement test are rejected. For example, a validation rule on a field used to store labor rates could check that a minimum labor rate value is entered in all records. In Level 1 you learned to add a validation rule using the Validation button in the Field Validation group of the Table Tools Fields tab. In Design view, the Validation Rule and Validation Text properties are located just above the Required property.

Project **2** **Work with Memo and Attachment Fields** **2 Parts**

You will edit properties for a Memo field, apply rich text formatting to text, and attach files to records using an Attachment field.

▼ **Quick Steps**

**Enable Rich Text Formatting in Memo Field**
1. Open table in Design view.
2. Select desired field defined as Memo.
3. Click in *Text Format* property box.
4. Click down-pointing arrow that appears.
5. Click *Rich Text*.
6. Click Yes.
7. Save table.

**Track Changes in a Memo Field**
1. Open table in Design view.
2. Select desired field defined as Memo.
3. If necessary, scroll down General tab.
4. Click in *Append Only* property box.
5. Click down-pointing arrow that appears.
6. Click Yes.
7. Save table.

# Working with Memo Fields ▪■▪■▪■▪■▪■▪■▪■▪■

By default, Access formats a Memo field as plain text; however, you can apply formatting attributes to text by enabling rich text formatting. For example, you can change the font, apply bold or italic formatting, or add font color to text in a Memo field. To add rich text formatting capability, change the Text Format property to *Rich Text*.

The Append Only property for a Memo field is set to *No* by default. Change the property to *Yes* to track changes made to the field value in the datasheet. You may need to scroll down the General tab in the *Field Properties* section to locate the Append Only property. When this property is set to *Yes*, Access maintains a history of additions to the field which can be viewed in the datasheet. Changing the Append Only property to *No* causes Access to delete any existing history.

Project 2a **Enabling Rich Text Formatting and Maintaining a History of Changes in a Memo Field** Part 1 of 2

1. With the **AL2-C1-RSRCompServ.accdb** database open, enable rich text formatting and turn on tracking of history in a field defined as a Memo field by completing the following steps:
   a. Open the WorkOrders table in Design view.
   b. Make *Comments* the active field.
   c. Click in the *Text Format* property box (currently reads *Plain Text*), click the down-pointing arrow that appears, and then click *Rich Text* at the drop-down list.

Step 1c

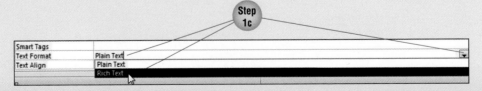

d. At the Microsoft Access message box indicating that the field will be converted to Rich Text, click Yes.

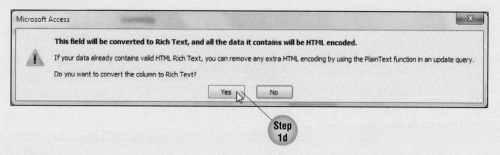

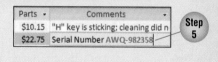

Step
1d

e. If necessary, scroll down the General tab in the *Field Properties* section until you can see the *Append Only* property box.
f. Click in the *Append Only* property box, click the down-pointing arrow that appears, and then click *Yes* at the drop-down list.

Step
1f

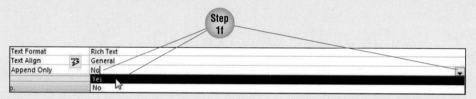

g. Save the table.
2. Switch to Datasheet view.
3. Minimize the Navigation pane and then adjust all column widths *except* the *Descr* and *Comments* fields to Best Fit.
4. Change the column width of the *Comments* field to 25.
5. Select the serial number text (AWQ-982358) in the second record in the *Comments* field and then apply bold and red font color using the buttons in the Text Formatting group of the Home tab. Click at the end of the serial number to deselect the text.

Step
5

6. Click in the *Comments* field in the first record. Press the End key to move the insertion point to the end of the existing text. Press the spacebar once, type **Microsoft wireless keyboard was recommended.**, and then press Enter to save the changes and move to the next row.
7. Right-click the *Comments* field in the first record and then click *Show column history* at the shortcut menu.
8. Click OK after reading the text in the History for Comments dialog box.
9. Click in the *Comments* field in the first record. Press the End key to move the insertion point to the end of the current text. Press the spacebar once, type **See work order 65013 for replacement keyboard request.**, and then press Enter.

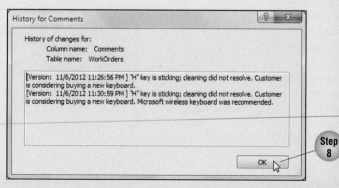

Step
8

10. Right-click the *Comments* field in the first record and then click *Show column history* at the shortcut menu.
11. Click OK after reading the text in the History for Comments dialog box.
12. Display the datasheet in Print Preview. Change the orientation to landscape. Set the margins to a top margin of 1-inch and bottom, left, and right margins of 0.25-inch. Print the datasheet and then close Print Preview.
13. Close the WorkOrders table. Click Yes when prompted to save changes to the layout of the table and then redisplay the Navigation pane.

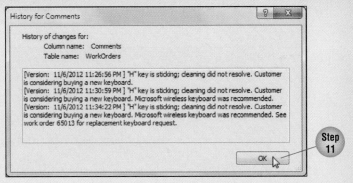

Step 11

▼ **Quick Steps**

**Create Attachment Field**
1. Open table in Design view.
2. Click in first blank field row.
3. Type desired field name.
4. Click in *Data Type* column.
5. Click down-pointing arrow.
6. Click *Attachment*.
7. Save table.

**Attach Files to Record**
1. Open table in Datasheet view.
2. Double-click paper clip in desired record.
3. Click Add button.
4. Navigate to drive and/or folder location.
5. Double-click file name.
6. Click OK.

**View Attached File**
1. Open table in Datasheet view.
2. Double-click paper clip in desired record.
3. Double-click file name.
4. View file contents.
5. Exit source program.
6. Click OK.

# Creating an Attachment Field and Attaching Files to Records

Using an Attachment field you can store several files in a single field attached to a record. The attachments can be opened within Access and are viewed and edited in the program from which the document originated. For example, you can attach a Word document to a field in a record. Opening the attached file in the Access table causes Microsoft Word to start with the document opened for editing. A file that is attached to a record cannot be larger than 256 megabytes.

An Attachment field displays with a paper clip in Datasheet view. Double-click the paper clip to open the Attachments dialog box shown in Figure 1.4 in which you manage attached files. A field that is created with a data type set to Attachment cannot be changed. You can attach multiple files to a record provided the total size of all files attached does not exceed two gigabytes.

Any file created within the Microsoft Office suite can be attached to a record as well as image files (.bmp, .jpg, .gif, .png), log files (.log), text files (.txt), and compressed files (.zip). Some files, such as files ending with .com and .exe are considered potential security risks and are blocked by Access.

**Figure 1.4** Attachments Dialog Box

1. With the **AL2-C1-RSRCompServ.accdb** database open, create a new field in which you will store file attachments by completing the following steps:

   a. Open the Technicians table in Design view.

   b. Click in the blank row below *CPhone*, type Attachments, and then press Tab or Enter.

   c. Click the down-pointing arrow in the *Data Type* column and then click *Attachment* at the drop-down list.

   d. Save the table.

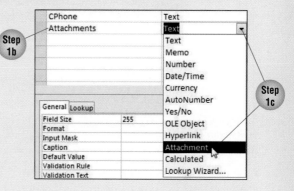

Step 1b

Step 1c

2. Switch to Datasheet view.

3. Add the following data in the first row of the datasheet.

   | | |
   |---|---|
   | *TechID* | 10 |
   | *SSN* | 000-43-5789 |
   | *Fname* | Kelsey |
   | *Lname* | Eastman |
   | *StreetAdd* | 550 Montclair Street |
   | *City* | Detroit |
   | *State* | MI |
   | *ZIP* | 48214-3274 |
   | *HPhone* | 313-555-6315 |
   | *CPhone* | "" (Recall that double quotation marks indicate a zero-length field.) |

4. Attach two files to the record for Kelsey Eastman by completing the following steps:

   a. Double-click the paper clip in the first row of the datasheet. Attachment fields display a paper clip in each record in a column with a paper clip in the field name row. The number in brackets next to the paper clip indicates the number of files attached to the record.

   b. At the Attachments dialog box, click the Add button.

   c. At the Choose File dialog box, navigate to the Access2010L2C1 folder on your storage medium.

   d. Click the file named ***EastmanResume.docx***.

   e. Hold down the Ctrl key and click the file named ***KelseyEastman.jpg***.

   f. Click the Open button.

   g. Click OK. Access closes the Attachments dialog box and displays *(2)* next to the paper clip in the first record.

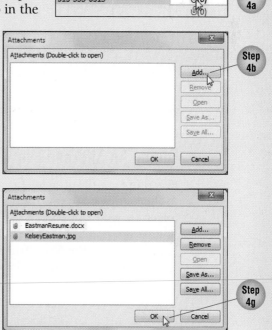

Step 4a

Step 4b

Step 4g

5. Open the attached files by completing the following steps:

   a. Double-click the paper clip in the first row of the datasheet to open the Attachments dialog box.

   b. Double-click ***EastmanResume.docx*** in the *Attachments* list box to open the Word document.

c. Read the resume in Microsoft Word and then exit Word.

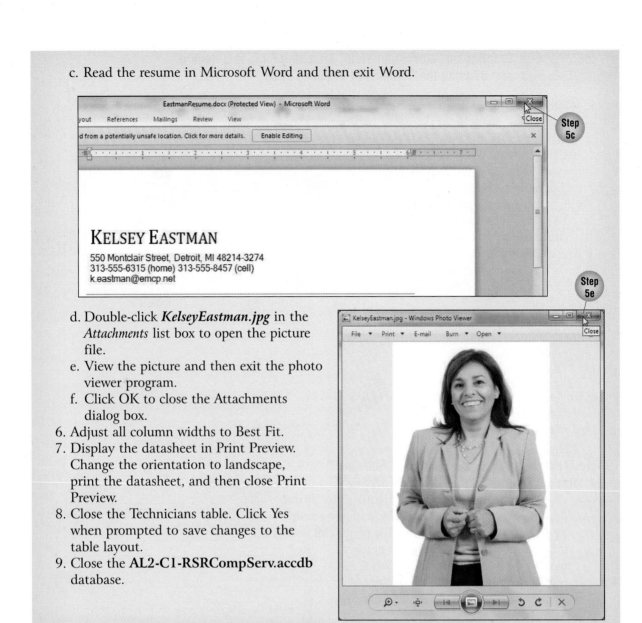

d. Double-click *KelseyEastman.jpg* in the *Attachments* list box to open the picture file.

e. View the picture and then exit the photo viewer program.

f. Click OK to close the Attachments dialog box.

6. Adjust all column widths to Best Fit.

7. Display the datasheet in Print Preview. Change the orientation to landscape, print the datasheet, and then close Print Preview.

8. Close the Technicians table. Click Yes when prompted to save changes to the table layout.

9. Close the **AL2-C1-RSRCompServ.accdb** database.

## Editing an Attached File

If you open a file attachment and make changes to the file, click the Save button in the source program to save changes. The changes are saved to a temporary folder on your computer's hard drive. To save the changes permanently, exit the Source program and then click OK at the Attachments dialog box in Access. Access displays the Save Attachment dialog box shown in Figure 1.5. Click Yes to update the changes in the database.

**Figure 1.5** Save Attachment Dialog Box

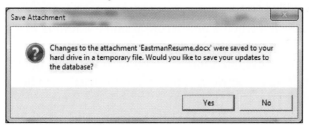

## Saving an Attached File to Another Location

You can export a file that is attached to a record to make a copy of the document in another storage location by selecting the file and then clicking the Save As button in the Attachments dialog box. At the Save Attachment dialog box, navigate to the drive and/or folder in which you want to save the duplicate copy of the file, click the Save button, and then click OK to close the Attachments dialog box.

## Removing an Attached File

If you no longer need to store a file attached to a record in the database, open the Attachments dialog box in the record containing the file attachment, click the file name for the file you want to delete, click the Remove button, and then click OK to close the Attachments dialog box.

# Chapter Summary

- Database designers plan the tables needed for a new database by analyzing sample data, input documents, and output requirements to generate the entire set of data elements needed.
- Once all data has been identified, the designer maps out the number of tables required.
- Each table holds data for a single topic only with data split out into the smallest unit that will be manipulated.
- Designers also consider relationships that will be needed in case a field needs to be added to a table in order to join the tables.
- Data redundancy should be avoided, which means a field should not be repeated in another table except for those fields needed to join tables in a relationship.
- A diagram of a database portrays the database tables with field names, data types, field sizes, and notation of the primary key.
- Fields are assigned a data type by selecting a data type appropriate for the kind of data that will be accepted into the field.
- Changing the field size property can be used to restrict entries in the field to a maximum length as one way to prevent longer entries that might be added to the field by accident.

- Change the Required property to *Yes* to force an entry into the field when a new record is added to the table.
- Leaving a field blank when a new record is entered results in a null value stored in the field.
- A zero-length field is entered into a record by typing two double quotation symbols with no space between. This method is used to indicate a field value does not apply to the current record.
- You can disallow zero-length strings by changing the Allow Zero Length property to *No*.
- The Format property controls the display of data accepted into a field. A custom format can be created by typing the appropriate format codes in the *Format* property box.
- A custom numeric format can contain four sections; one section for positive values, one section for negative values, one section for zero values, and the last section for null values.
- Use an input mask to control the type and pattern of data entered into the field.
- Create a custom input mask for a Text or Date/Time field by typing the appropriate input mask codes in the *Input Mask* property box.
- A Memo field can be formatted using rich text formatting options in the Text Formatting group of the Home tab by changing the Text Format property to Rich Text.
- Change the Append Only property of a Memo field to *Yes* to track changes made to field values.
- A field with the data type set to *Attachment* can be used to store files associated with a record.
- Double-click the paper clip in the Attachment field for a record to add, view, save, or remove a file attachment.

# Commands Review

| FEATURE | RIBBON TAB, GROUP | BUTTON | KEYBOARD SHORTCUT |
|---|---|---|---|
| Create table in Design view | Create, Tables | | |
| Minimize Navigation pane | | ≪ | F11 |
| Redisplay Navigation pane | | ≫ | F11 |
| Switch to Datasheet view from Design view | Table Tools Design, Views | | |
| Switch to Design view from Datasheet view | Home, Views | | |

# Concepts Check Test Your Knowledge

**Completion:** In the space provided at the right, indicate the correct term, command, or number.

1. Use this data type for a field that will hold numeric data that is not a monetary value. _____

2. Use this data type to store alphanumeric text longer than 255 characters. _____

3. This data type is restricted to a field value used to test conditional logic that can be one of only two conditions. _____

4. The available properties that display for a field in the *Field Properties* section in Design view are dependent on this option. _____

5. This property is used to display a more descriptive title for the field in the datasheet. _____

6. To ensure a field is never left empty, set this property to *Yes*. _____

7. Typing two double quotation symbols with no space between assigns this field value. _____

8. This is the format code to convert all text in the field to uppercase. _____

9. This placeholder in a custom numeric format instructs Access to display a zero if the position is not used. _____

10. Type this entry in the *Format* property box of a Date/Time field to display dates beginning with the day of the week abbreviated, followed by the month as two digits, the day of the month as two digits, and the year as two digits with all sections separated with a hyphen character. _____

11. Type this entry in the *Input Mask* property box to require a three-digit identification number to be entered with the pound symbol (#) used as the placeholder. _____

12. Rich text formatting is enabled for a Memo field by changing this property option to *Rich Text*. _____

13. For a Memo field with the Append Only property active, right-click in a record and click this option at the shortcut menu to display a dialog box with the history of the text changes made to the field. _____

14. Create a field with this data type to store a file with the record. _____

15. Add a file to the record by double-clicking this object in the record in Datasheet view. _____

# Skills Check  Assess Your Performance

## Assessment

### 1  CREATE A NEW DATABASE

1. Create a new blank database named **AL2-C1-BenchmarkGolf.accdb**.
2. Create the tables shown in Figure 1.6 to store membership records for the Benchmark Golf and Country Club including setting the primary key and assigning data types and field sizes.
3. Close any tables that have been left open.

**Figure 1.6** Assessment 1

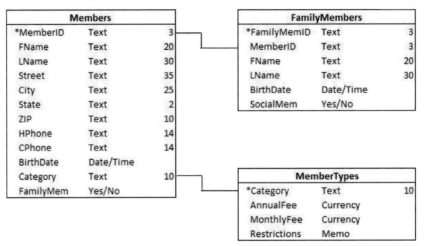

## Assessment

### 2  ADD CAPTIONS AND DISALLOW BLANK VALUES

1. With the **AL2-C1-BenchmarkGolf.accdb** database open, create captions for the fields as follows:

Members Table

| Field Name | Caption |
|---|---|
| *MemberID* | ID Number |
| *FName* | First Name |
| *LName* | Last Name |
| *Street* | Street Address |
| *ZIP* | ZIP Code |
| *HPhone* | Home Phone |
| *CPhone* | Cell Phone |
| *BirthDate* | Birth Date |
| *FamilyMem* | Family Member? |

FamilyMembers Table

| **Field Name** | **Caption** |
| --- | --- |
| *FamilyMemID* | Family ID Number |
| *MemberID* | Member ID Number |
| *FName* | First Name |
| *LName* | Last Name |
| *BirthDate* | Birth Date |
| *SocialMem* | Social Member? |

MemberTypes Table

| **Field Name** | **Caption** |
| --- | --- |
| *AnnualFee* | Annual Fee |
| *MonthlyFee* | Monthly Fee |

2. Make the *ZIP* field a required field and disallow zero-length strings.
3. Save and then close all tables.

## Assessment

### 3 CREATE CUSTOM FORMATS AND INPUT MASKS

1. With the **AL2-C1-BenchmarkGolf.accdb** database open, create the following custom formats:
   a. Display the state text in uppercase characters.
   b. Display all birth dates with the month spelled out in abbreviated form followed by the day of the month as two digits and the year as four digits with one space separating each section.
   c. Display the monthly fee in blue with two decimal values that will show zeros if no value is entered.
2. Create the following custom input masks:
   a. In the *MemberID* field in the Members table and the *FamilyMemID* field in the FamilyMembers table, require all three digits and display the underscore character as the placeholder.
   b. Require the *ZIP* field in the Members table to be entered in the pattern five required digits followed by a hyphen and then four required digits. Display the pound symbol (#) as the placeholder.
   c. Use the input mask wizard to create the standard input mask for the two telephone fields in the Members table. When the mask is finished, edit the codes in the property to make the three characters in the area code required digits as opposed to the optional digits that the wizard created.
   d. Create an input mask for both birth date fields that will match the custom format pattern created in Step 1b except include hyphens between each section. Store the display characters in the field and display the underscore character as the placeholder. For example, the custom format should display the date as *May 03 1964* in the datasheet. ***Hints: You do not need to worry about the first letter of the month being uppercase since the Format property will automatically use proper capitalization. Once you have the input mask created correctly, you can copy and paste the entry to the other birth date field***.
3. Save and then close all tables.

## 4  ADD RECORDS

1. With the **AL2-C1-BenchmarkGolf.accdb** database open, add the following records. Type the text in the *State* field as shown to test your format code. Type ZIP codes, telephone numbers, and dates, being careful to watch the placeholders and enter in the required pattern.

Members Table

| Field | Record 1 | Record 2 |
|---|---|---|
| *ID Number* | 100 | 110 |
| *First Name* | Hilary | Jesse |
| *Last Name* | Sampson | Reynolds |
| *Street Address* | 300 South Saguaro Drive | 7229 E University Drive |
| *City* | Apache Junction | Mesa |
| *State* | Az | Az |
| *ZIP Code* | 85220 4956 | 85207 6501 |
| *Home Phone* | 602 555 1587 | 480 555 1385 |
| *Cell Phone* | 602 555 3496 | 480 555 1699 |
| *Birth Date* | May 03 1964 | Oct 15 1977 |
| *Category* | Gold | Silver |
| *Family Member?* | Yes | No |

FamilyMembers Table

| Field | Record 1 | Record 2 |
|---|---|---|
| *Family ID Number* | 610 | 611 |
| *Member ID Number* | 100 | 100 |
| *First Name* | Kayla | Roy |
| *Last Name* | Sampson | Sampson |
| *Birth Date* | Jul 18 1992 | Mar 16 1994 |
| *Social Member?* | No | No |

MemberTypes Table

| Field | Record 1 | Record 2 | Record 3 |
|---|---|---|---|
| *Category* | Gold | Silver | Bronze |
| *Annual Fee* | 2500 | 1775 | 1550 |
| *Monthly Fee* | 60 | 52 | 35 |
| *Restrictions* | Unlimited weekdays and weekends; weekend ballot first | Unlimited weekdays; weekend ballot second | Unlimited weekdays; weekends after 3 P.M. |

2. Adjust all column widths to Best Fit and print each table in landscape orientation.
3. Close any tables that have been left open saving layout changes.
4. Close the **AL2-C1-BenchmarkGolf.accdb** database.

# Visual Benchmark    Demonstrate Your Proficiency

## CREATE A NEW DATABASE

1. Create a new blank database named **AL2-C1-PawsParadise.accdb**.
2. Create the tables shown in the database diagram in Figure 1.7 for Paws Paradise Boarding Inc. to store the records of dog owners, dogs, and kennel categories including setting the primary key and assigning data types and field sizes.
3. Analyze the datasheets shown in Figure 1.8 and make the necessary changes to field properties. The datasheets show captions, default values, custom formats, and rich text formatting in the records. Use the following information to set other field properties not visible in the datasheet:
   a. Make *ZIP* a required field and then use the input mask wizard to create the default input mask for a zip code.
   b. Use the input mask wizard to create the default input mask for both telephone fields and then edit the masks to change the area code to three required digits.
4. Add the records shown in the datasheets to the tables.
5. Adjust all column widths to Best Fit and print each table in landscape orientation.
6. Save and then close all tables.
7. Close the **AL2-C1-PawsParadise.accdb** database.

## Figure 1.7  Visual Benchmark Database Diagram

**DogOwners**

| *CustNum | Text | 3 |
| FName | Text | 20 |
| LName | Text | 30 |
| Street | Text | 35 |
| City | Text | 25 |
| State | Text | 2 |
| ZIP | Text | 10 |
| HPhone | Text | 14 |
| EPhone | Text | 14 |
| MultipleDogs | Yes/No | |

**Dogs**

| *DogID | AutoNumber | |
| CustNum | Text | 3 |
| DogName | Text | 20 |
| Breed | Text | 50 |
| Color | Text | 20 |
| Bordetella | Yes/No | |
| Rabies | Yes/No | |
| Play | Yes/No | |
| KennelCat | Text | 7 |

**KennelCategories**

| *KennelCat | Text | 7 |
| Type | Text | 25 |
| Descr | Memo | |
| DailyRate | Currency | |

## Figure 1.8  Visual Benchmark Datasheets

**DogOwners**

| Customer Number | First Name | Last Name | Street Address | City | State | ZIP Code | Home Telephone | Emergency Telephone | Multiple Dogs? |
|---|---|---|---|---|---|---|---|---|---|
| 100 | Shawn | Jenkins | 101 Davis Street | Bradford | PA | 16701- | (814) 555-8446 | (814) 555-7469 | ☑ |
| 110 | Valerie | McTague | 12 Bishop Street | Bradford | PA | 16701- | (814) 555-3456 | (814) 555-1495 | ☐ |
| 115 | Glen | Waters | 35 Vista Avenue | Bradford | PA | 16701-2760 | (814) 555-7496 | (814) 555-6124 | ☐ |

**Dogs**

| Dog ID | Customer Number | Dog's Name | Breed | Color | Bordetella Vaccine Checked? | Rabies Vaccine Checked? | Play with other dogs? | Kennel Category |
|---|---|---|---|---|---|---|---|---|
| 1 | 100 | Abby | Labrador Retriever | Black | ☑ | ☑ | ☑ | VIP |
| 2 | 100 | Winnie | Cocker Spaniel | Buff | ☑ | ☑ | ☑ | VIP |
| 3 | 110 | Chloe | Poodle | White | ☑ | ☑ | ☐ | Deluxe |
| 4 | 115 | Barney | Pug | Black | ☐ | ☐ | ☐ | InOut |
| * | (New) | | | | ☑ | ☑ | ☑ | |

**KennelCategories**

| Kennel Category | Kennel Type | Description | Daily Rate |
|---|---|---|---|
| DayCare | Day Care Boarding | Grassy play area where dogs can play with staff and other dogs throughout the day. | $16.50 |
| Deluxe | Deluxe Suite | Designed for *geriatric or special needs dogs*. Raised beds and quiet location. | $29.50 |
| InOut | Indoor/Outdoor Suite | Indoor kennel attached to covered outdoor patio. | $25.50 |
| VIP | V.I.P. Suite | *Indoor upgraded kennel* attached to covered outdoor patio and grass play area. | $38.50 |

# Case Study  Apply Your Skills

**Part 1**

You started an internship today at Bestar Plumbing Service. Examine the customer invoice shown in Figure 1.9. This is a typical invoice for which the owner would like to start using an Access database. Design tables for the data using the invoice and the following additional information from the owner:

- Customer numbers are assigned using the first three letters of the customer's last name all uppercase and are followed by three digits after a hyphen character.
- Some invoices include parts with a labor charge. Individual parts are not itemized on the customer invoice. The service technician shows a single line on the invoice for all parts used.
- Bestar has two labor rates: $41.75 for a senior service technician and $28.00 for an apprentice technician.

Using Microsoft Word, create a document that diagrams the tables including table names, field names, data types, and field sizes. Use the asterisk to denote the primary key field in each table. Ask your instructor for the required format of the diagram in text boxes or tables in Word, or if a handwritten diagram is acceptable. Save the Word document and name it **AL2-C1-CS-P1-BestarPlumbing**. Save, print, and close **AL2-C1-CS-P1-BestarPlumbing.docx**.

**Part 2**

Using the table diagram created in Part 1, create a new database named **AL2-C1-BestarPlumbing.accdb** and then create the tables including setting the primary key in each table.

**Part 3**

Consider the field properties learned in this chapter that can be used to ensure data integrity and consistency. Modify field properties in your tables that can be used to restrict data accepted into the field and display the data after it has been accepted. Use the data in Figure 1.9 to enter a sample record in each table to test your field properties. Print each table with all column widths set to Best Fit.

**Figure 1.9** Invoice for Case Study, Part 1

**INVOICE**

**Bestar Plumbing Service**

| | | |
|---|---|---|
| INVOICE NUMBER | 1001 | |
| DATE | March 8, 2012 | |
| CUSTOMER ID | COL-104 | |

TO    Diane Coleman
2101 Lakeland Avenue
Madison, WI 53704
608-555-6377

| QUANTITY | DESCRIPTION | UNIT PRICE | LINE TOTAL |
|---|---|---|---|
| 1 hr | Service call to repair burst water pipe | $ 41.75 | $ 41.75 |
| | | | |
| | Service Technician: Jose Martinez | | |
| | Date of Service: March 5, 2012 | | |
| | | SUBTOTAL | $ 41.75 |
| | | 5 % SALES TAX | 2.09 |
| | | TOTAL | $ 43.84 |

# Microsoft® Access®

# CHAPTER 2

# Building Relationships and Lookup Fields

## PERFORMANCE OBJECTIVES

**Upon successful completion of Chapter 2, you will be able to:**

- Create and edit relationships between tables including one-to-many, one-to-one, and many-to-many relationships
- Define a table with a multiple-field primary key
- Create and modify a lookup field to populate records with data from another table
- Create a lookup field that allows multiple values in records
- Create single-field and multiple-field indexes
- Define what is meant by normalization
- Determine if a table is in first, second, and third normal form

**Tutorials**

2.1 Creating a One-to-Many Relationship

2.2 Creating a Second One-to-Many Relationship

2.3 Editing Relationship Options

2.4 Establishing a Many-to-Many Relationship

2.5 Defining a Multiple-Field Primary Key

2.6 Creating a Field to Look Up Values in Another Table

2.7 Creating a Field that Allows Multiple Values

2.8 Creating Indexes

2.9 Normalizing a Database

Once table design is completed, establishing relationships and relationship options between tables involves analyzing the type of relationship that exists between two tables. Some database designers will draw a relationship diagram to depict the primary table and the related table's matching record frequency. You will create and edit relationships and lookup fields, multiple-field primary keys, multiple-value fields, and indexes in this chapter. The concept of database normalization and three forms of normalization are introduced to complete the examination of database design fundamentals. Model answers for this chapter's projects appear on the following page.

Access2010L2C2

*Note: Before beginning the projects, copy to your storage medium the Access2010L2C2 subfolder from the Access2010L2 folder on the CD that accompanies this textbook and then make Access2010L2C2 the active folder.*

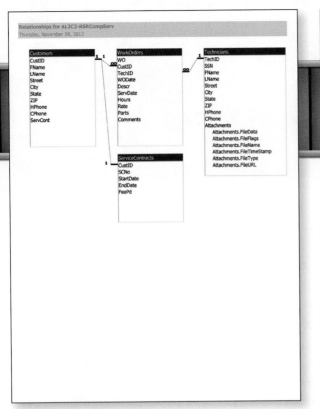

**Project 1 Create and Edit Relationships**

Project 1d, Relationships Report

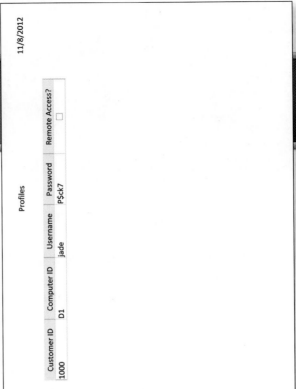

**Project 2 Create a Table with a Multiple-Field Primary Key and Lookup Fields**

Project 2c, Profiles Datasheet

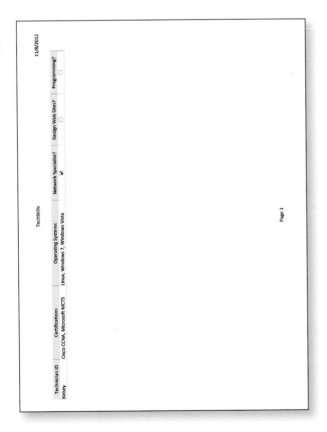

Project 2e, TechSkills Table

**Project** **1** **Create and Edit Relationships** **4 Parts**

You will create relationships and edit relationship options for the tables designed to track work orders for RSR Computer Services.

# Building Relationships ▪▪▪▪▪▪▪▪▪▪▪▪▪▪▪▪▪▪▪▪▪▪▪▪▪

Continuing the process of designing tables discussed in Chapter 1, which included determining which tables would be related to each other, the next step is to examine the types of relationships that exist. A relationship is based upon an association between two tables. For example, in the computer service database created in Chapter 1 for RSR Computer Services there is an association between the Customers table and the WorkOrders table. A customer is associated with all of his or her work orders involving computer maintenance requests, and a work order is associated with the individual customer for which the service was requested.

When building relationships, consider associations between tables and how the associations affect data that will be entered into the tables. In the database diagram presented in Chapter 1, relationships were shown by lines connecting the common field name between tables. In this chapter, you consider the type of relationship that should exist between the tables and the relationship options that you want to use to place restrictions on data entry. Access provides for three types of relationships: one-to-many, one-to-one, and many-to-many. In Access Level 1, Chapter 2, you learned about one-to-many and one-to-one relationships. You will begin by reviewing these two relationship types before you learn how to establish a many-to-many relationship.

## Establishing a One-to-Many Relationship

In the computer service database in Chapter 1, the Customers table is related to the WorkOrders table. This relationship exists because a work order involves computer maintenance for a specific customer. The customer is identified by the customer's number stored in the Customers table. In the Customers table only one record exists per customer. In the WorkOrders table, the same customer number can be associated with several work orders. This means the relationship between the Customers table and the WorkOrders table is a one-to-many relationship.

One-to-many relationships are the most common type of relationship created in Access. A common field is needed to join the Customers table and the WorkOrders table, so the *CustID* field was included in both tables. In the Customers table, *CustID* is the primary key field because each customer has only one record with a unique identification number. In the WorkOrders table, *CustID* cannot be the primary key because the same customer could be associated with several computer service work orders. In the WorkOrders table, *CustID* is the *foreign key*. A foreign key is a field included in a table for the purpose of creating a relationship to a field that is a primary key in the other table. The Customers-to-WorkOrders one-to-many relationship can be illustrated using a diagram similar to the one shown in Figure 2.1.

**HINT**

Not sure if two tables should be related? Consider if you would ever need to extract data from both tables in the same query, form, or report. If yes, then the tables should be joined in a relationship.

Relationships

▼ **Quick Steps**

**Create One-to-Many Relationship**
1. Click Database Tools tab.
2. Click Relationships button.
3. Add tables from Show Table dialog box.
4. Close Show Table dialog box.
5. Drag primary key field name from primary table to foreign key field name in related table.
6. Click Create button.

**Figure 2.1** One-to-Many Relationship between Customers Table and
WorkOrders Table

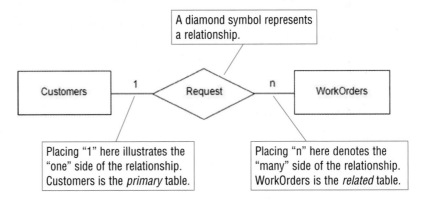

More than one method can be used to diagram a relationship if a database designer chooses to show relationships in a separate diagram from the database diagram shown in Chapter 1. In the version shown in Figure 2.1, table names are displayed in rectangles with lines drawn to a diamond symbol that represents a relationship. Inside the diamond, a word (usually a verb) describes the action that relates the two tables. For example, in the relationship shown in Figure 2.1, the word *Request* is used to show that "Customers *Request* WorkOrders." On the join line, a *1* is placed next to the table that represents the primary table, or the "one" side in the relationship, and *n* is placed next to the related table, or the "many" side of the relationship.

| Project 1a | Creating a One-to-Many Relationship | Part 1 of 4 |

1. Open **AL2-C2-RSRCompServ.accdb**. This database has the same structure as the database created in Chapter 1; however, additional field properties have been defined and several records have been added to each table to provide data with which to test relationships and lookup lists.
2. If the Security Warning message bar appears with the message indicating that some active content has been disabled, click the Enable Content button.
3. Create a one-to-many relationship between the Customers table and the WorkOrders table by completing the following steps:
   a. Click the Database Tools tab.
   b. Click the Relationships button in the Relationships group.
   c. At the Show Table dialog box with the Tables tab active and with *Customers* selected in the Tables list box, hold down the Ctrl key, click *WorkOrders*, and then click the Add button.
   d. Click the Close button to close the Show Table dialog box.
   e. Drag the bottom border of each table's field list box to resize the box until all field names are shown.

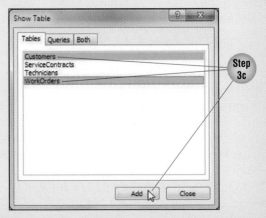

f. Drag the *CustID* field from the Customers table field list box to the *CustID* field in the WorkOrders table field list box. Be careful to drag the common field name starting from the primary table (Customers) in a relationship.

g. At the Edit Relationships dialog box, notice *One-To-Many* appears in the *Relationship Type* section. Access detected the correct type of relationship because the field used to join the tables is a primary key in only one of the tables. Always check that the correct table and field names are shown below the *Table/Query* and *Related Table/Query* list boxes. If the table name and/or the common field name is not shown correctly in the *Table/Query* list boxes and/or the *Related Table/Query* list boxes, click the Cancel button. This error occurs when you drag the mouse starting or ending at the wrong table or field. Return to Step 3f and try again.

h. Click the Create button.

4. Click the Close button in the Relationships group of the Relationship Tools Design tab.

5. Click Yes at the Microsoft Access message box asking if you want to save changes to the layout of the 'Relationships' window.

Another one-to-many association exists between the Technicians table and the WorkOrders table. A technician is associated with all of the work orders that he or she has been assigned and a work order is associated with the technician that carried out the service request. The Technicians to WorkOrders relationship diagram is shown in Figure 2.2.

**Figure 2.2** One-to-Many Relationship between Technicians Table and WorkOrders Table

1. With the **AL2-C2-RSRCompServ.accdb** database open, display the Relationships window by clicking the Database Tools tab and then clicking the Relationships button in the Relationships group.
2. Click the Show Table button in the Relationships group in the Relationships Tools Design tab.
3. Click *Technicians* in the Tables list at the Show Table dialog box, click the Add button, and then click the Close button.
4. Drag the bottom border and the right border of the Technicians table field list box until all field names are fully visible.
5. Drag the *TechID* field from the Technicians table field list box to the *TechID* field in the WorkOrders table field list box.
6. Check that the correct table and field names appear in the *Table/Query* and *Related Table/Query* list boxes. If necessary, click Cancel, and try Step 5 again.
7. Click the Create button at the Edit Relationships dialog box.

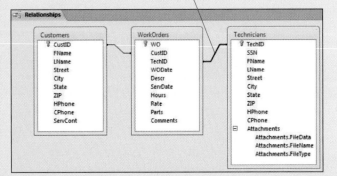

one-to-many relationship created between Technicians and WorkOrders at Steps 1 through 7

8. Click the Close button in the Relationships group of the Relationship Tools Design tab.
9. Click Yes at the Microsoft Access message box asking if you want to save changes to the layout of the 'Relationships' window.

**▼ Quick Steps**

**Edit Relationship**
1. Click Database Tools tab.
2. Click Relationships button.
3. Click black join line between tables.
4. Click Edit Relationships button.
5. Select desired options.
6. Click OK.

## Editing Relationship Options

At the Edit Relationships dialog box shown in Figure 2.3 you can elect to turn on relationship options and/or specify the type of join to create. The *Cascade Update Related Fields* and *Cascade Delete Related Records* options do not become active unless referential integrity is turned on.

**Figure 2.3** Edit Relationships Dialog Box

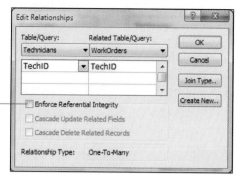

*Enforce Referential Integrity* places restrictions on data entry. A record will not be allowed in the related table (WorkOrders) with a value in the foreign key field (*TechID*) for which no matching record is already in existence in the primary table (Technicians).

In other words, you cannot assign a technician to a work order if the technician does not exist in the Technicians table.

Edit
Relationships

Turning on referential integrity in a one-to-many relationship is a good idea to ensure that orphan records do not occur. An **orphan record** is a record in a related table for which no "parent" record exists in the primary table. Assigning a technician to a work order in the WorkOrders table with no matching technician record in the Technicians table creates an orphan record in the WorkOrders table. Once referential integrity is turned on, Access checks for the existence of a matching record in the primary table as a new record is added to the related table. If no match is found, Access does not allow the record to be saved.

With referential integrity active, Access can automatically update all occurrences of the same data in the foreign key field in the related table when a change is made to the primary key field in the primary table (Cascade Update Related Fields). If a record is deleted from the primary table for which related records exist in the related table, Access can automatically delete the related records (Cascade Delete Related Records).

You will learn about join types and situations in which changing the join type is warranted in Chapter 3.

**HINT**

To enable referential integrity, the primary key and foreign key fields must be the same data type.
If you receive an error message when attempting to activate referential integrity, open each table in Design view and compare the data type for each field used to join the tables.

## Project 1c — Editing Relationships

Part 3 of 4

1. With the **AL2-C2-RSRCompServ.accdb** database open, edit the one-to-many relationship between the Customers table and the WorkOrders table by completing the following steps:
   a. Open the Relationships window.
   b. Click to select the black join line between the Customers table and the WorkOrders table.
   c. Click the Edit Relationships button in the Tools group in the Relationship Tools Design tab.
   d. At the Edit Relationships dialog box, click the *Enforce Referential Integrity* check box, the *Cascade Update Related Fields* check box, and the *Cascade Delete Related Records* check box.
   e. Click OK at the Edit Relationships dialog box. The *1* at the primary table (one side) of the join line and the infinity symbol (∞) at the related table (many side) of the join line indicate referential integrity has been turned on.

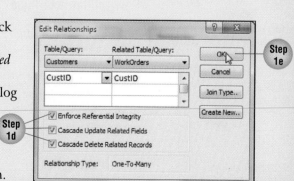

2. Edit the one-to-many relationship between the Technicians table and the WorkOrders table by completing the following steps:

  a. Double-click the black join line between the Technicians table and the WorkOrders table in the Relationships window. (You can also right-click the join line and click *Edit Relationship* at the shortcut menu.)

  b. At the Edit Relationships dialog box, turn on referential integrity and the two cascade options.

  c. Click OK.

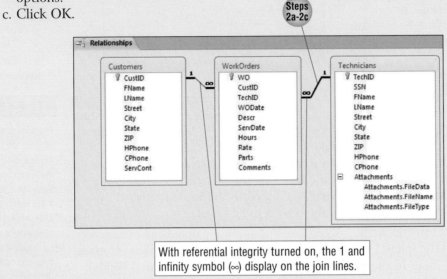

With referential integrity turned on, the 1 and infinity symbol (∞) display on the join lines.

3. Close the Relationships window.

# Establishing a One-to-One Relationship

In the database for RSR Computer Services, a table is used to store service contract information for each customer. This table, named ServiceContracts, is associated with the Customers table. Only one record exists for a customer in the Customers table and each customer subscribes to only one service contract in the ServiceContracts table. This means the two tables are related in a one-to-one relationship as shown in Figure 2.4.

**Figure 2.4** One-to-One Relationship between Customers Table and ServiceContracts Table

1. With the **AL2-C2-RSRCompServ.accdb** database open, create a one-to-one relationship between the Customers table and the ServiceContracts table by completing the following steps:
   a. Open the Relationships window.
   b. Click the Show Table button in the Relationships group.
   c. Double-click *ServiceContracts* in the Tables list box and then click the Close button.
   d. Drag the *CustID* field from the Customers table field list box to the *CustID* field in the ServiceContracts table field list box.
   e. At the Edit Relationships dialog box, check that the correct table and field names appear in the *Table/Query* and *Related Table/Query* list boxes. If necessary, click Cancel, and try Step 1d again.
   f. Notice *One-To-One* appears in the *Relationship Type* section. Access detected the correct type of relationship because the field used to join the tables is a primary key in both tables.
   g. Click the *Enforce Referential Integrity* check box, the *Cascade Update Related Fields* check box, and the *Cascade Delete Related Records* check box.
   h. Click the Create button.
2. Drag the title bar of the ServiceContracts table field list box to the approximate location shown in the Relationships window. By moving the table field list box you are better able to view the join line and the *1* at each end of the line between Customers and ServiceContracts.

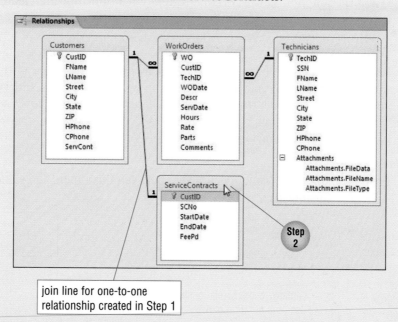

join line for one-to-one
relationship created in Step 1

3. Create a relationships report by clicking the Relationship Report button in the Tools group of the Relationship Tools Design tab.
4. Access displays the report in Print Preview. Click the Print button in the Print group of the Print Preview tab and then click OK at the Print dialog box.

5. Close the Relationships for AL2-C2-RSRCompServ report. Click Yes to save the report and click OK to accept the default name at the Save As dialog box.
6. Close the Relationships window. Click Yes to save changes to the layout.

## Establishing a Many-to-Many Relationship

Consider the association between the Customers table and the Technicians table in the RSR Computer Services database. Over time, any individual customer can have computer service work done by many different technicians and any individual technician can perform computer service work at any number of different customer locations. In other words, a record in the Customers table can be matched to many records in the Technicians table and a record in the Technicians table can be matched to many records in the Customers table. This is an example of a many-to-many relationship.

The diagram to show the many-to-many relationship between Customers and Technicians is depicted in Figure 2.5.

A many-to-many relationship is problematic because the nature of the relationship creates duplicate records. If the same customer number is associated with many technicians, and vice versa, many duplicates occur in the two tables and Access may experience data conflicts when trying to identify a unique record. To resolve the duplication and create unique entries, a third table is used to associate or link the many-to-many tables. The third table is called a junction table. A *junction table* is a table that contains at least two foreign keys—the primary key field from each table in the many-to-many relationship. Using the junction table, two one-to-many relationships are created. Examine the Relationships window shown in Figure 2.6.

In Figure 2.6, the WorkOrders table is the junction table. Notice the WorkOrders table contains two foreign keys—*CustID*, which is the primary key in the Customers table, and *TechID*, which is the primary key in the Technicians table. A one-to-many relationship exists between Customers and WorkOrders and a one-to-many relationship also exists between Technicians and WorkOrders. These two one-to-many relationships create a many-to-many relationship between Customers and Technicians.

**Figure 2.5** Many-to-Many Relationship between Customers Table and Technicians Table

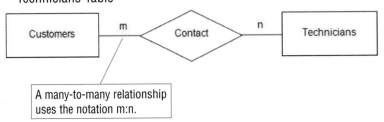

**Figure 2.6** Relationships Window Showing Many-to-Many Relationship between Customers Table and Technicians Table

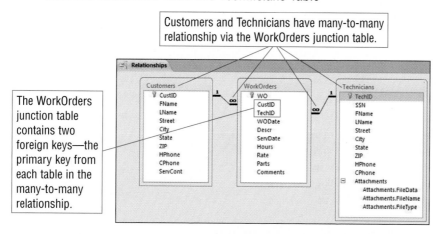

Customers and Technicians have many-to-many relationship via the WorkOrders junction table.

The WorkOrders junction table contains two foreign keys—the primary key from each table in the many-to-many relationship.

---

**Project 2** **Create a Table with a Multiple-Field Primary Key and Lookup Fields**   **5 Parts**

You will create a new table that requires two fields to uniquely identify each record. To restrict data entry in the table, you will create fields that display a list from which the user selects the field value(s).

---

# Defining a Multiple-Field Primary Key

In most tables one field is designated as the primary key. However, in some situations, a single field may not always be guaranteed to hold unique data. Look at the fields in the table shown in Figure 2.7. This is a new table you will create in the RSR Computer Services database to store computer profiles for RSR customers. The company stores the profiles as a service to RSR clients in case the client forgets his or her logon credentials. Technicians can also access the credentials data when troubleshooting at the customer's site.

Some customers may have more than one computer in their home or office and each computer can have a different profile for each username. The *CustID* field will not serve as the primary key field if the customer has more than one record in the Profiles table. However, a combination of the three fields *CustID*, *CompID*, and *Username* will uniquely identify each record. In this table, you will define all three fields as a primary key. A primary key that is made up of two or more fields is called a **composite key**.

**Figure 2.7** Project 2a Profiles Table

| Profiles | | |
|---|---|---|
| *CustID | Text | 4 |
| *CompID | Text | 2 |
| *Username | Text | 15 |
| Password | Text | 15 |
| Remote | Yes/No | |

▼ **Quick Steps**

**Create Multiple-Field Primary Key**
1. Open table in Design view.
2. Select first field.
3. Hold down Shift key (adjacent row) or Ctrl key (nonadjacent row) and select second field.
4. Click Primary Key button.
5. Save table.

**HINT**

Delete a primary key by opening the table in Design view, activating the primary key field, and then clicking the Primary Key button to remove the key.

Primary Key

1. With the **AL2-C2-RSRCompServ.accdb** database open, create a new table to store customer profiles by completing the following steps:
    a. Click the Create tab and then click the Table Design button in the Tables group.
    b. Type the field names, assign the data types, and change the field sizes as per the data structure shown in Figure 2.7.
2. Point in the field selector bar (blank column at left of field names) next to *CustID* until the pointer changes to a right-pointing black arrow and then click to select the field.
3. Hold down the Shift key and click in the field selector bar next to *Username*. The three adjacent fields *CustID*, *CompID*, and *Username* are now selected.
4. Click the Primary Key button in the Tools group in the Table Tools Design tab. Access displays the key icon next to each field.
5. Click in any field to deselect the first three rows.
6. Save the table and name it *Profiles*.
7. Close the table.

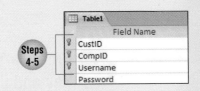

| Steps 2-3 | | |
|---|---|---|

**Table1**

| Field Name | Data Type |
|---|---|
| CustID | Text |
| CompID | Text |
| Username | Text |
| Password | Text |
| Remote | Yes/No |

| Steps 4-5 | |
|---|---|

**Table1**

| Field Name |
|---|
| CustID |
| CompID |
| Username |
| Password |

▼ **Quick Steps**

**Create Lookup Field to Another Table**
1. Open table in Design view.
2. Click in *Data Type* column of lookup field.
3. Click down-pointing arrow.
4. Click *Lookup Wizard*.
5. Click Next.
6. Choose table and click Next.
7. Choose fields to display in column.
8. Click Next.
9. Choose field by which to sort.
10. Click Next.
11. If necessary, expand column widths.
12. Clear *Hide key column* if desired.
13. Click Next.
14. Choose field value to store in table.
15. Click Next.
16. Click Finish.
17. Click Yes.

# Creating a Field to Look Up Values in Another Table

In Level 1, Chapter 4, you learned how to create a lookup list in which you typed the values that you wanted to appear in the list as you worked through the steps of the Lookup Wizard. A lookup field can also be created in which you display in the drop-down list the values found in records from another table. The user enters data by pointing and clicking rather than typing the field's entry. A lookup field that draws its data from a field in another table has many advantages. Data can be restricted to items within the list, which avoids orphan records, data entry errors, or inconsistencies in spelling. The lookup list can display more than one clue to the user so that the correct data is selected. For example, assume a lookup field requires the user to select a customer's identification number. Looking at a drop-down list of identification numbers is not very helpful; however, if the lookup field displayed the identification number as well as the customer's name, the correct entry is easily identifiable. By choosing the field entry based on the name, the correct identification number is automatically entered by Access. To assist with creating lookup fields, Access provides the Lookup Wizard. Create lookup list fields before you create relationships. If a relationship already exists between the table for the lookup field and the source data table, Access prompts you to delete the relationship before the Lookup Wizard can run.

1. With the **AL2-C2-RSRCompServ.accdb** database open, open the Profiles table in Design view.
2. Create a lookup field to enter a customer's identification number by selecting from a list of customers in the Customers table by completing the following steps:
   a. With *CustID* the active field, click in the *Data Type* column, click the down-pointing arrow that appears, and then click *Lookup Wizard* at the drop-down list.
   b. At the first Lookup Wizard dialog box with *I want the lookup field to get the values from another table or query* selected, click Next.

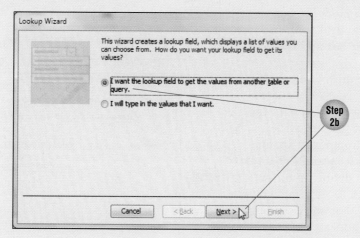

   c. At the second Lookup Wizard dialog box with *Table: Customers* already selected in the *Which table or query should provide the values for your lookup field?* list box, click Next.

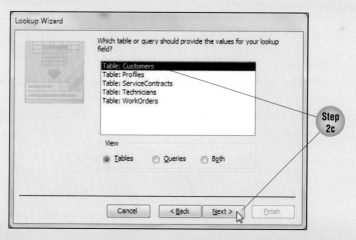

d. At the third Lookup Wizard dialog box you choose the fields you want to display in the drop-down list when the user clicks in the field. Double-click *FName* in the *Available Fields* list box to move the field to the *Selected Fields* list box.

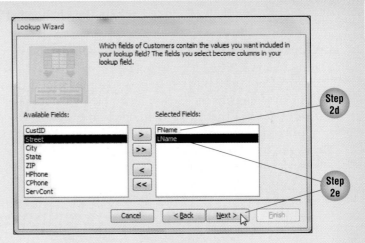

e. Double-click *LName* in the *Available Fields* list box to move the field to the *Selected Fields* list box and then click Next.

f. At the fourth Lookup Wizard dialog box, click the down-pointing arrow next to the first sort list box, click *LName* at the drop-down list, and then click Next. Notice that you can define up to four sort keys to sort the lookup list and that an Ascending button appears next to each *Sort* list box. You can change the sort order from Ascending to Descending by clicking the Ascending button.

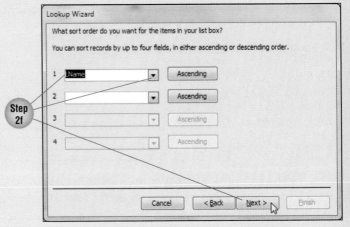

g. At the fifth Lookup Wizard dialog box you can expand column widths if necessary to display all data. Scroll down the list of entries in the dialog box. Notice the column widths are sufficient to show all of the text.

h. In order to view the customer identification numbers with the names while the list is opened in a record, click the *Hide key column (recommended)* check box to clear the check mark. Clearing the check mark displays the *CustID* field values as the first column in the lookup list.

i. Click Next.

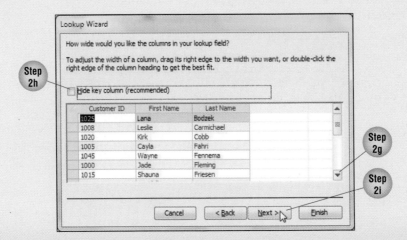

j. At the sixth Lookup Wizard dialog box with *CustID* already selected in the *Available Fields* list box, click Next. At this dialog box you choose the field value that you want to store in the table when an entry is selected in the drop-down list.

k. Click Finish at the last Lookup Wizard dialog box to accept the existing field name for the lookup field of *CustID*.

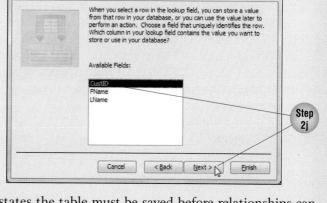

l. Click Yes to save the table at the Lookup Wizard message box that states the table must be saved before relationships can be created. Access automatically creates a relationship between the Customers table and the Profiles table based on the *CustID* field used to create the lookup field.

3. Close the Profiles table.

---

**Project 2c** **Modifying Lookup List Properties and Using a Lookup List Field in a Record**

Part 3 of 5

1. With the **AL2-C2-RSRCompServ.accdb** database open, open the Profiles table in Design view.

2. Add the following text to the Caption property of the fields noted.

| | |
|---|---|
| *CustID* | Customer ID |
| *CompID* | Computer ID |
| *Remote* | Remote Access? |

3. Modify the lookup list properties to restrict entries in new records to an item within the list by completing the following steps:

a. Make *CustID* the active field.

b. Click the Lookup tab in the *Field Properties* section.

c. Look at the entries in each of the Lookup tab's property boxes. These entries were created by the Lookup Wizard.

d. Click in the *Limit To List* property box, click the down-pointing arrow that appears, and then click *Yes* at the drop-down list. Changing *Limit To List* to *Yes* means that the field will accept data from existing customer records only. A user will not be able to type in an entry that is not in the list.

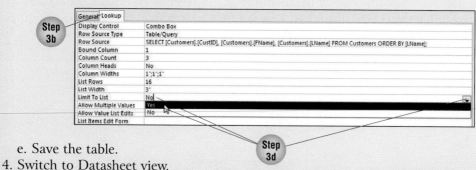

e. Save the table.

4. Switch to Datasheet view.

5. With *Customer ID* in the first row of the datasheet the active field, click the down-pointing arrow in the field and then click *Jade Fleming* at the drop-down list. Notice Access inserts *1000* as the field value in the first column. You were able to select the correct entry for *Customer ID* by clicking a customer's name and then Access filled in the customer number associated with the name for you.

6. Type the remaining fields as indicated.
   Computer ID   D1
   Username      jade
   Password      P$ck7
   Remote Access? No (leave blank)

7. Adjust all column widths to Best Fit.

8. Print and then close the Profiles datasheet. Click Yes when prompted to save changes to the table layout.

# Creating a Field That Allows Multiple Values ■■■■■■■■■

**Quick Steps**

**Create Multiple-Value Lookup List**
1. Open table in Design view.
2. Start Lookup Wizard for desired field.
3. Create list by typing values or binding data to field in another table.
4. At last Lookup Wizard dialog box, click *Allow Multiple Values*.
5. Click Finish.
6. Click Yes.

**HINT**

Multiple-value fields are suited to those occasions where you want to store more than one choice from a small list without having to create an advanced database design.

Assume you want to keep track of the industry certifications a technician has achieved. You could organize this data by creating a separate field for each certification. However, this approach might cause the table to require numerous fields in which only one or two technicians might have an entry. As an alternative, you can create a single field that displays a list of certifications with check boxes. Look at the fields in the table structure shown in Figure 2.8. In this table, for each technician, you would open a list in the *Certifications* field and click the check box next to the applicable certification title. In the field named *OperatingSys*, another list could be used to keep track of the operating systems for which the technician is considered an expert.

Create a field to store multiple values using the Lookup Wizard. You can choose to look up the values in a field in another table or create your own value list. At the last Lookup Wizard dialog box, click the *Allow Multiple Values* check box. Do not create a multiple-value field if the possibility exists the Access database could be moved to Microsoft SQL Server in the future. An Access multiple-value field upsizes to a memo field in a SQL database, causing additional conversion work to be required.

**Figure 2.8** Project 2d TechSkills Table

| TechSkills | | |
|---|---|---|
| *TechID | Text | 2 |
| Certifications | Text | 20 |
| OperatingSys | Text | 20 |
| NetworkSpc | Yes/No | |
| WebDesign | Yes/No | |
| Progamming | Yes/No | |

1. With the **AL2-C2-RSRCompServ.accdb** database open, create a new table to store technician competencies by completing the following steps:
   a. Create a new table using Design view.
   b. Type the field names, assign the data types, and change the field sizes as per the data structure shown in Figure 2.8.
   c. Assign the primary key to the field denoted with the asterisk.
   d. Save the table and name it *TechSkills*.
2. Create a lookup field to select the technician from a list of technician names in the Technicians table by completing the following steps:
   a. Click in the *Data Type* column for the *TechID* field, click the down-pointing arrow that appears, and then click *Lookup Wizard*.
   b. Click Next at the first dialog box to look up the values in a table or query.
   c. Click *Table: Technicians* and then click Next.
   d. Double-click *FName* in the *Available Fields* list box to move the field to the *Selected Fields* list box.
   e. Double-click *LName* in the *Available Fields* list box and then click Next.
   f. Sort by *LName* and then click Next.
   g. With the *Hide key column* check box selected, click Next to accept the current column widths. In this lookup example, you are electing not to show the technician's ID field value. Although you will view and select by the names, Access stores the primary key value in the table. *TechID* is considered the bound field, while *FName* and *LName* are considered display fields.

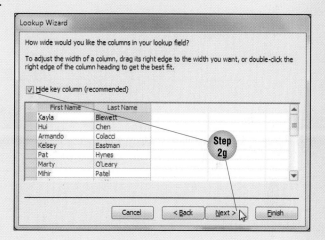

   h. Click Finish and then click Yes to save the table.
3. Create a lookup field that allows multiple values for certification information by completing the following steps:
   a. Click in the *Data Type* column for the *Certifications* field, click the down-pointing arrow that appears, and then click *Lookup Wizard*.
   b. Click *I will type in the values that I want* and then click Next.
   c. At the second Lookup Wizard dialog box, type the entries in *Col1* as shown at the right.
   d. Click Next.

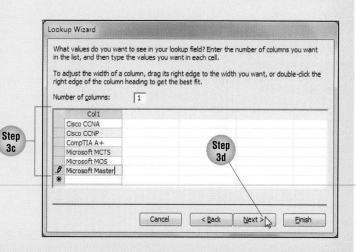

e. At the last Lookup Wizard dialog box, click the *Allow Multiple Values* check box and then click Finish.

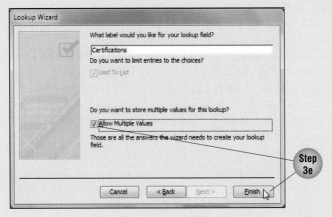

Step 3e

f. At the message box indicating that once the field is set to store multiple values, the action cannot be undone, click Yes to change the *Certifications* field to multiple values.

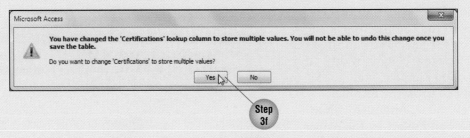

Step 3f

4. Create a lookup list to store multiple values in the *OperatingSys* field using the value list shown below by completing steps similar to those in Steps 3a through 3f.

      Windows 7
      Windows Vista
      Windows XP
      Linux
      Unix
      Mac OS X

5. Save and close the TechSkills table.

## Project 2e   Assigning Multiple Values in a Lookup List       Part 5 of 5

1. With the **AL2-C2-RSRCompServ.accdb** database open, open the TechSkills table in Design view.
2. Add the following text to the Caption property of the fields noted.

| | |
|---|---|
| *TechID* | Technician ID |
| *OperatingSys* | Operating Systems |
| *NetworkSpc* | Network Specialist? |
| *WebDesign* | Design Web Sites? |
| *Programming* | Programming? |

3. Save the table and then switch to Datasheet view.

4. Add a new record to the table by completing the following
   steps:
   a. With the insertion point positioned in the *Technician ID*
      column, click the down-pointing arrow and then click
      *Kelsey Eastman* at the drop-down list. Notice Access
      displays the technician's first name in the column. *FName*
      is considered a display field for this column; however, the
      identification number associated with Kelsey Eastman is
      stored in the table.
   b. Press Tab and then click the down-pointing arrow in the
      *Certifications* column.
   c. Since *Certifications* is a multiple-value field, the drop-
      down list displays with check boxes next to each item
      in the list. Click the *Cisco CCNA* check box and the
      *Microsoft MCTS* check box and then click OK.
   d. Press Tab and then click the down-pointing
      arrow in the *Operating System* column.
   e. Click the *Windows 7, Windows Vista*, and *Linux*
      check boxes and then click OK.
   f. Press Tab and then press the spacebar to insert a
      check mark in the *Network Specialist?* check box.
   g. Press Tab three times to finish the record, leaving the
      check boxes blank in the *Design Web Sites?* and
      *Programming?* columns.
5. Adjust the width of all columns to Best Fit.
6. Print the TechSkills table in landscape orientation
   with a left and right margin of 0.25-inch.
7. Close the TechSkills table. Click Yes when prompted to
   save changes to the layout.

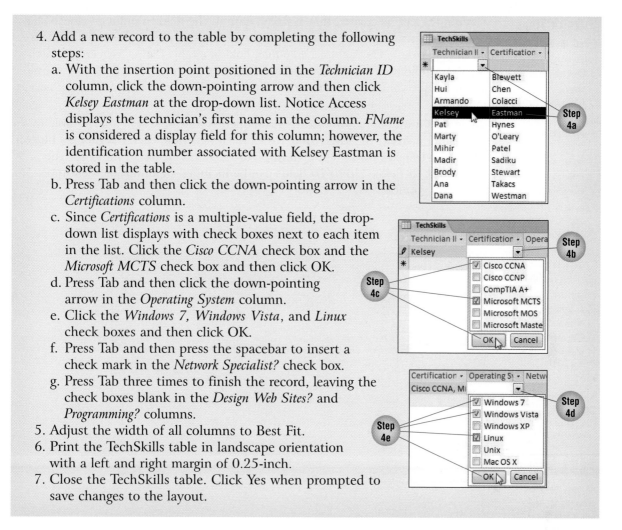

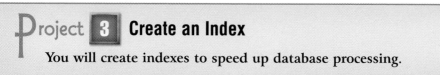

Project **3** **Create an Index**                                           **1 Part**

You will create indexes to speed up database processing.

# Creating Indexes ■■■■■■■■■■■■■■■■■■■■■■

An *index* is a list created by Access containing pointers that direct Access to the
location of a record in a table. A database index is very similar to an index you would
find printed at the back of a textbook. You search an index for a keyword that is
associated with the topic you want to find and are directed to the page number(s) in
the book. You use a book's index because you want to find the information quickly
and more directly. Access table indexes operate the same way. Access uses the index
to locate a record in a table more quickly. A field that is specified as the primary key
has an index generated by Access automatically. You can add additional indexed fields
to the database to speed up sorting and searching. For example, in the Customers
table in the RSR Computer Services database, creating an index for the *LName* field
is a good idea since the table data will be frequently sorted by last names.

▼ **Quick Steps**
**Create Single-Field
Index**
1. Open table in Design
   view.
2. Make desired field
   active.
3. Click in *Indexed*
   property box.
4. Click down-pointing
   arrow.
5. Click *Yes (Duplicates
   OK)* or *Yes (No
   Duplicates)*.
6. Save table.

## Quick Steps

**Create Multiple-Field Index**

1. Open table in Design view.
2. Click Indexes button.
3. Click in first blank row in *Index Name* column.
4. Type name for index.
5. Press Tab.
6. Click down-pointing arrow in *Field Name* column.
7. Click desired field.
8. If necessary, change sort order.
9. Click in *Field Name* column in next row.
10. Click down-pointing arrow.
11. Click desired field.
12. If necessary, change sort order.
13. Continue Steps 9–12 until finished.
14. Close Indexes window.

An index can be created that restricts data in the field to unique values. This creates a field similar to a primary key in that Access will not allow two fields to hold the same data. For example, an e-mail field in a table that is frequently searched is a good candidate for an index. To avoid data entry errors in a field that should contain unique values (and is not the primary key), set up the index to not accept duplicates.

Create a multiple-field index if you frequently sort or search a large table by two or more fields at the same time. In Table Design view, click the Indexes button to open the Indexes window shown in Figure 2.9 and create an index for the combination of fields. Up to 10 fields can be included in a multiple-field index in the Indexes window.

**Figure 2.9** Indexes Window

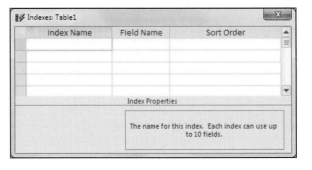

**HINT**

An index cannot be generated for fields with a data type of OLE Object or Attachment.

Indexes

---

**Project 3**  **Creating Indexes**                                     Part 1 of 1

1. With the **AL2-C2-RSRCompServ.accdb** database open, open the Customers table in Design view.
2. Create a single-field index for the *ZIP* field by completing the following steps:
   a. Make *ZIP* the active field.
   b. Click in the *Indexed* property box, click the down-pointing arrow that appears, and then click *Yes (Duplicates OK)* at the drop-down list.

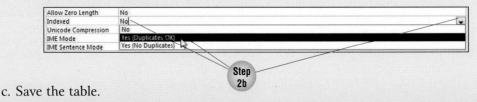

   c. Save the table.

3. Create a multiple-field index for the *LName* and *FName* fields by completing the following steps:
   a. Click the Indexes button in the Show/Hide group in the Table Tools Design tab.
   b. At the Indexes: Customers window, click in the first blank row in the *Index Name* column (below *ZIP*) and then type Names.
   c. Press Tab, click the down-pointing arrow that appears in the *Field Name* column, and then click *LName* at the drop-down list. The sort order for *LName* defaults to *Ascending*.

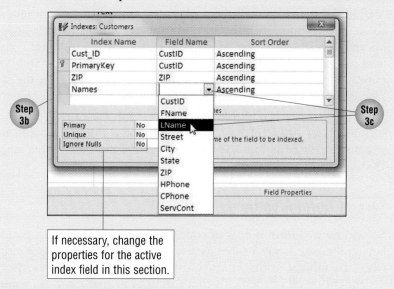

If necessary, change the properties for the active index field in this section.

   d. Click in the row in the *Field Name* column below *LName*, click the down-pointing arrow that appears, and then click *FName*.
   e. Close the Indexes: Customers window.

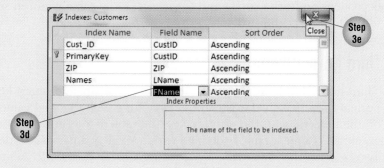

   f. Save the table.
4. Close the Customers table.
5. Close the **AL2-C2-RSRCompServ.accdb** database.

You cannot view an index. Access uses the index behind the scenes to work more efficiently. In a database with a large number of records, consider fields other than the primary key that are sorted or searched and create indexes for these fields.

# Normalizing the Database ▪■▪▪■▪▪■▪▪■▪▪■▪▪■▪▪■▪▪■■■

Normalizing a database involves reviewing the database structure and ensuring the tables are set up to eliminate redundancy. Three normalization states are tested: first normal form, second normal form, and third normal form.

## First Normal Form

A table meets first normal form when the table does not contain any fields that could be broken down into smaller units and when the table does not have similar information stored in several fields. For example, a table that contains a single field called *TechnicianName* that stores the technician's first and last names in the same column is in violation of first normal form. To correct the structure, split *TechnicianName* into two fields such as *TechLastName* and *TechFirstName*.

A table that has multiple fields set up with each field containing similar data, such as *Week1*, *Week2*, *Week3*, and *Week4* violates first normal form. To correct this structure, delete the four week fields and replace them with a single field named *WeekNumber*.

## Second Normal Form

Second normal form is only of concern for a table that has a multiple-field primary key (composite key). A table with a composite key meets second normal form when the table is in first normal form and when all of the fields in the table are dependent on all of the fields that form the primary key. For example, assume a table is defined with two fields that form the primary key: *CustID* and *ComputerID*. A field in the same table is titled *EmailAdd*. The contents of the *EmailAdd* field are dependent on the customer only (not the computer). Since *EmailAdd* is not dependent on **both** *CustID* **and** *ComputerID*, the table is not in second normal form. To correct the structure, delete the *EmailAdd* field.

## Third Normal Form

Third normal form applies to a table that has a single primary key and is in first normal form. If a field exists in the table for which the field value is not dependent on the field value of the primary key, the table is not in third normal form. For example, assume a table is defined with a single primary key titled *TechnicianID*. Two fields in the same table are titled *PayCode* and *PayRate*. Assume also that a technician's pay rate is dependent on the pay code assigned to the technician. Since a pay rate is dependent on the field value in the pay code field and not on the technician's identification number, the table is not in third normal form. To convert the table to third normal form, delete the *PayRate* field from the table. (The *PayRate* field would belong in another table in the database.)

Normalizing a database often involves splitting fields into smaller units, and/or breaking larger tables down into smaller tables and creating relationships to remove repeating groups of data.

# Chapter Summary

- When building relationships consider the frequency of matching data in the common field in both tables to determine if the relationship is one-to-many, one-to-one, or many-to-many.

- One-to-many relationships are the most common type of relationship that involves joining the tables by dragging the primary key from the "one" table to the foreign key in the "many" table.

- In a one-to-many relationship, only one record for a matching field value exists in the primary table while many records for the same value can exist in the related table.

- A relationship diagram depicts the tables joined in the relationship as well as the type of relationship between the two tables.

- At the Edit Relationships dialog box you can turn on referential integrity and the two cascade options.

- Referential integrity places restrictions on new data entered into the related table. A record is not allowed in the related table if a matching record does not already exist in the primary table.

- *Cascade Update Related Fields* automatically updates all occurrences of the same data in the foreign key field when a change is made to the primary key data.

- *Cascade Delete Related Records* automatically deletes related records when a record is deleted from the primary table.

- In a one-to-one relationship only one record exists with a matching value in the joined field in both tables.

- In a many-to-many relationship many records can exist with a matching value in the joined field in both tables.

- To create a many-to-many relationship, a junction table is used that contains a minimum of two fields which are the primary key fields from each table in the many-to-many relationship.

- Two one-to-many relationships using the junction table form a many-to-many relationship.

- In some tables, two or more fields are used to create the primary key if a single field is not guaranteed to hold unique data.

- A primary key that is made up of two or more fields is called a composite key.

- A lookup field displays a drop-down list in a field in which the user points and clicks to enter the field value. The list can be generated from records in a related table, or by typing in a value list.

- Once the lookup field is created, use the Lookup tab in the *Field Properties* section in Table Design view to modify individual properties.

- The Limit To List property allows you to restrict entries in the field to items within the lookup list.

- A field that allows multiple entries to be selected from a drop-down list can be created by clicking *Allow Multiple Values* at the last Lookup Wizard dialog box.

- A field that is defined as a multiple-value field cannot be changed back to a single-value field.
- Access displays check boxes next to items in the drop-down list if the field has been set to allow multiple values.
- An index is a list generated by Access that includes pointers that direct Access to the location of records in a table.
- Access creates an index for a primary key field automatically.
- Create a single-field table index by changing the Indexed property to *Yes (Duplicates OK)* or *Yes (No Duplicates)*.
- A multiple-field index is created using the Indexes window.
- Normalizing a database involves reviewing the database structure to eliminate redundancy. Three normalization states are checked: first normal form, second normal form, and third normal form.

# Commands Review

| FEATURE | RIBBON TAB, GROUP | BUTTON |
|---------|-------------------|--------|
| Edit relationships | Relationship Tools Design, Tools | |
| Indexes | Table Tools Design, Show/Hide | |
| Primary key | Table Tools Design, Tools | |
| Print relationships report | Relationship Tools Design, Tools | Relationship Report |
| Relationships window | Database Tools, Show/Hide | |
| Show table | Relationship  Tools Design, Relationships | |

# Concepts Check Test Your Knowledge

**Completion:** In the space provided at the right, indicate the correct term, command, or number.

1. This is the term for a field added to a related table for the purpose of creating a relationship that is the primary key in the other table.

   _____

2. The Relationships button is found in this tab in the ribbon.

   _____

3. Add a table to the Relationships window using this dialog box.

   _____

4. At the Edit Relationships dialog box, the two cascade options do not become active until this option is turned on.

   _____

5. This symbol appears on the join line next to the many side of a relationship when referential integrity is on.

   _____

6. Open the Edit Relationships dialog box for an existing relationship by doing this action with the mouse while pointing at the black join line in the Relationships window.

   _____

7. This type of relationship exists if only one matching record will be found in both tables in the relationship.

   _____

8. A many-to-many relationship is created by establishing two one-to-many relationships using a third table referred to by this term.

   _____

9. A primary key that is made up of two or more fields is referred to by this term.

   _____

10. A lookup field can be restricted to items within the list by setting this property to *Yes*.

    _____

11. Specify a field as a multiple-value field by clicking this check box at the last Lookup Wizard dialog box.

    _____

12. Set the *Indexed* property to this option for an index field that is likely to contain more than one record with the same field value, such as a zip code.

    _____

13. Open this window to create an index that uses two or more fields.

    _____

14. These are the three normalization states that are tested.

    _____

15. If a field exists in a table for which the field value is not dependent on the primary key, the table is not in this normalization state.

    _____

# Skills Check  Assess Your Performance

## Assessment

### 1  CREATE A LOOKUP LIST

1. Open the database named **AL2-C2-VantageVideos** and enable content.
2. Open each table in Datasheet view and review the table's fields and records to familiarize yourself with the database. Close all tables when finished.
3. Open the Relationships window and close the Show Table dialog box. Notice that no relationships have been created in the database. Close the Relationships window.
4. The *CustID* field in the WebOrders table can be made easier to use if the field is changed to a lookup list that presents customer names and numbers from the WebCustomers table. Open the WebOrders table in Design view, make *CustID* the active field, and create a lookup list to display values from another table using the following information.
   a. Display the *CustID*, *FirstName*, and *LastName* fields from the WebCustomers table.
   b. Sort the list in ascending order by the *LastName* field.
   c. Clear the *Hide key column* check box.
   d. Store the *CustID* value.
   e. Accept the default label for the column of *CustID*.
5. Modify the Lookup property for the *CustID* field that will ensure only items within the list are allowed to be entered into the field.
6. Save the table, switch to Datasheet view, and then enter the following record to test the lookup list.

   | | |
   |---|---|
   | *Web Order ID* | 10007 |
   | *Customer ID* | Select *106 Gary Gallagher* in the lookup list. |
   | *Date Ordered* | Feb 26 2012 |

7. Print the datasheet.
8. Close the WebOrders table.

## Assessment

### 2  CREATE A TABLE WITH A MULTIPLE-FIELD PRIMARY KEY AND LOOKUP LISTS

1. With the **AL2-C2-VantageVideos** database open, create a new table using Design view to track the videos ordered by a customer using the following information.

   | Field Name | Data Type | Field Size | Caption |
   |---|---|---|---|
   | WebOrdID | Text | 5 | Web Order ID |
   | WebProdID | Text | 7 | Product ID |
   | Qty | Number | | Quantity |

2. A customer can choose to buy more than one video on the same order. When this occurs, the same order number can be associated with more than one record in the table; therefore, the primary key cannot be based on the *WebOrdID* field alone. Assign a multiple-field primary key using both the *WebOrdID* and *WebProdID* fields. The combination of the order identification number and product identification number will uniquely describe each record in the table.
3. Save the table and name it *WebOrderDetails*.

4. Create a lookup list for the *WebOrdID* field that connects to the *WebOrdID* field in the WebOrders table. Add all three fields in the WebOrders table to the lookup list, do not specify a sort field, clear the *Hide key column*, store *WebOrdID* in the field, and accept the default field name. Modify the Lookup property to ensure only items within the list are allowed to be entered into the field.

5. Create a lookup list for the *WebProdID* field that connects to the *WebProdID* field in the WebProducts table. Display the *Product* field sorted in ascending order, make sure the column width is wide enough to display the entire video title in the list, hide the key column, and accept the default field name. Modify the Lookup property to ensure only items within the list are allowed to be entered into the field.

6. Save the table and switch to Datasheet view. Add the following records to the WebOrderDetails datasheet to test the lookup lists.

| Web Order ID | Product ID | Quantity |
|---|---|---|
| 10001 | To Kill a Mockingbird | 1 |
| 10001 | Blue Hawaii | 1 |
| 10002 | The Great Escape | 2 |
| 10003 | Cool Hand Luke | 1 |
| 10003 | Doctor Zhivago | 1 |
| 10003 | The Longest Day | 2 |
| 10004 | Dial M for Murder | 1 |

7. Adjust all column widths to Best Fit and print the datasheet.

8. Close the WebOrderDetails table. Click Yes when prompted to save changes to the layout.

## Assessment

### 3 EDIT RELATIONSHIPS

1. With the **AL2-C2-VantageVideos** database open, open the Relationships window to view the relationships created by Access when the lookup lists were created.

2. Resize and move the table field list boxes to the approximate size and location shown in Figure 2.10.

3. Edit the relationships as follows:
   a. Edit the one-to-many relationship between WebCustomers and WebOrders to turn on referential integrity and the two cascade options.
   b. Edit the one-to-many relationship between WebOrders and WebOrderDetails to turn on referential integrity and the two cascade options.
   c. Edit the one-to-many relationship between WebProducts and WebOrderDetails to turn on referential integrity and the two cascade options.

**Figure 2.10** Assessment 3

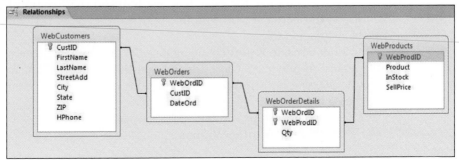

4. Create and print a relationship report.
5. On your relationship report printout write the type of relationship that exists between WebOrders and WebProducts.
6. Close the Relationships for **AL2-C2-VantageVideos** report. Click Yes to save the report and accept the default name in the Save As dialog box.
7. Close the Relationships window.

## Assessment

**4** CREATE A TABLE WITH A ONE-TO-ONE RELATIONSHIP

1. With the **AL2-C2-VantageVideos** database open, create a new table using Design view to store a customer's credit card information using the following information.

| Field Name | Data Type | Field Size | Caption |
|---|---|---|---|
| CustID | Text | 3 | Customer ID |
| CCType | Text | 20 | Credit Card Type |
| CCNumber | Text | 16 | Credit Card Number |
| CCExpMonth | Number | | Expiry Month |
| CCExpYear | Number | | Expiry Year |
| EmailAdd | Text | 30 | Email Address |

2. Assign the primary key to the *CustID* field.
3. Save the table and name it *WebCustPymnt*.
4. Create a lookup list for the *CustID* field that connects to the *CustID* field in the WebCustomers table by following steps similar to those in Assessment 1, Step 4. Modify the Lookup property to ensure only items within the list are allowed to be entered into the field.
5. Save the table, switch to Datasheet view, and enter the following record.

| | |
|---|---|
| Customer ID | Select *106 Gary Gallagher* in the lookup list |
| Credit Card Type | Visa |
| Credit Card Number | 0009100876453152 |
| Expiry Month | 7 |
| Expiry Year | 2014 |
| Email Address | garyg@emcp.net |

6. Adjust all column widths to Best Fit and print the datasheet in landscape orientation.
7. Close the WebCustPymnt table. Click Yes when prompted to save changes to the layout.
8. Open the Relationships window and open the Show Table dialog box.
9. Add the WebCustPymnt table to the window. Edit the one-to-one relationship between WebCustomers and WebCustPymnt to turn on referential integrity and the two cascade options.
10. If necessary, rearrange the table field list boxes in the Relationships window until you can better see the join line between the WebCustPymnt and WebCustomers tables.
11. Print a relationship report changing page layout options as necessary to fit the report on one page. Close the Relationships report. Click Yes to save the report and type **Relationships-Assessment4** as the report name in the Save As dialog box.
12. Close the Relationships window.
13. Close the **AL2-C2-VantageVideos** database.

# Visual Benchmark Demonstrate Your Proficiency

## CREATE LOOKUP LISTS AND EDIT RELATIONSHIPS

1. Open **AL2-C2-PawsParadise.accdb**.
2. This database is similar to the Visual Benchmark database created in Chapter 1; however, an additional table has been created and several records added to the database. Spend a few moments familiarizing yourself with the tables and records.
3. Create the following lookup lists, making sure the field value saved is always the primary key field:
   a. In the Dogs table, look up the Kennel Category in the KennelCategories table. Hide the key column in this list.
   b. In the Dogs table, look up the Customer Number in the DogOwners table. Clear the *Hide key column* in this list.
   c. In the Reservations table, look up the Customer Number in the DogOwners table. Clear the *Hide key column* in this list.
4. Open the Relationships window and edit relationships to enforce referential integrity and turn on both cascade options for each relationship.
5. Rearrange and move table field list boxes as necessary so that your Relationships window appears similar to the one shown in Figure 2.11.
6. Create and print a relationships report.
7. Save the relationships report using the default name and then close the report and the Relationships window.
8. Close the **AL2-C2-PawsParadise.accdb** database.

**Figure 2.11** Visual Benchmark Relationships Window

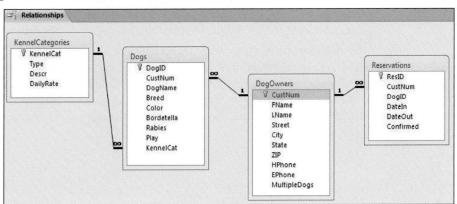

# Case Study Apply Your Skills

**Part 1**

You are working as an intern at Hillsdale Realty. The intern that worked at the company before you started work on a database to be used for managing sales agents, listings, sales, and commission quotas. The previous intern did not have time to finish the database. Open **AL2-C2-HillsdaleRealty.accdb** and enable content. Open each table and review the fields and records to familiarize yourself with the database. The Agents table is not in first normal form. The field named *AgentName* contains both the first and last names of each sales agent. To improve the table design, modify the table so that two separate fields are used for representative names. Add captions to the name fields. Correct the data in the datasheet so that the names are correctly split into the two columns. Print the revised Agents table datasheet with all column widths adjusted to Best Fit. Close the table.

**Part 2**

You decide to improve the efficiency of data entry by creating lookup lists as follows:

- In the Listings table you want to be able to select the correct Agent ID by viewing the agent names in a sorted drop-down list. Display the *AgentID* as the value in the field.
- In the Agents table you want to be able to select the quota code by viewing all of the quota codes and amounts in a drop-down list. Display the Commission Quota in the datasheet but store *QuotaID* as the field value. Edit the caption for the field to read *Quota* (instead of *Quota Code*).
- In the SalesAndComm table you want to be able to select the correct Listing Number by viewing the listing numbers and addresses from the Listings table. Make sure the column width is wide enough to display all of the street address information. Display the *ListingNo* as the value in the field.

Open the Relationships window. If necessary, add all of the tables to the window. Resize and arrange boxes so that the join lines between tables are easy to follow and understand. Edit each relationship to turn on referential integrity and the two cascade options. Create, print, and save a relationships report. Close the relationships report and close the relationships window.

You have decided to add another table named *Preferences* to the database. Create the table using the information below. You determine appropriate data types and other field properties.

| Field Name | Lookup Lists |
|---|---|
| *ClientID* | |
| *ListingNo* | Create a lookup list to the Listings table. |
| *AgentID* | Create a lookup list to the Agents table. |
| *Preferences* | Create a multiple-value list with the following items: |
| | Exclusive listing |
| | MLS listing |
| | Pre-sale inspection |
| | Staging service |

A client could have more than one listing at Hillsdale Realtors so you do not want to use *ClientID* as the primary key. Assign the primary key as a combination of two fields: *ClientID* and *ListingNo*. Add a sample record to the table to test your lookup lists and multiple-value field. Adjust all column widths to Best Fit, print the datasheet, and close the table saving the layout. Open the relationships window, add the new table, and arrange the layout so that join lines are not overlapping. Edit the relationships between Preferences and Listings and Agents to turn on referential integrity and the two cascade options. Create, print, and save a new relationships report named *Relationships-Part3*.

# Advanced Query Techniques

## PERFORMANCE OBJECTIVES

**Upon successful completion of Chapter 3, you will be able to:**

- Save a filter as a query
- Create and run a parameter query to prompt for criteria
- Add tables to and remove tables from a query
- Create an inner join, left join, and right join to modify query results
- Create a self-join to match two fields in the same table
- Create a query that includes a subquery
- Assign an alias to a table and a field name
- Select records using a multiple-value field in a query
- Create a new table using a make-table query
- Remove records from a table using a delete query
- Add records to the end of an existing table using an append query
- Modify records using an update query

**Tutorials**

3.1  Saving a Filter as a Query
3.2  Prompting for Criteria Using a Parameter Query
3.3  Creating a Query with Right Outer Join
3.4  Creating a Self-Join Query
3.5  Creating and Using Subqueries
3.6  Assigning Aliases and Using a Multivalued Field in a Query
3.7  Performing Operations Using Action Queries
3.8  Creating a New Table Using a Query
3.9  Adding and Deleting Records to a Table Using a Query
3.10 Modifying Records Using an Update Query

In this chapter you create, save, and run queries that incorporate advanced query features such as saving a filter as a query, prompting for criteria on single and multiple fields, modifying join properties to view alternative query results, and using action queries to perform operations on groups of records. In addition to these topics, you will also create an alias for a table and a field and incorporate subqueries to manage multiple calculations. Model answers for this chapter's projects appear on the following pages.

Access2010L2C3

*Note: Before beginning the projects, copy to your storage medium the Access2010L2C3 subfolder from the Access2010L2 folder on the CD that accompanies this textbook and then make Access2010L2C3 the active folder.*

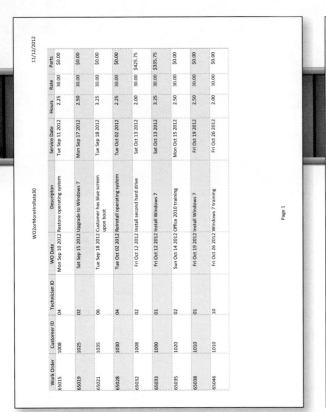

**Project 1 Select Records Using Filtered Criteria and Prompted Criteria**    Project 1a, WO2orMoreHrsRate30 Query

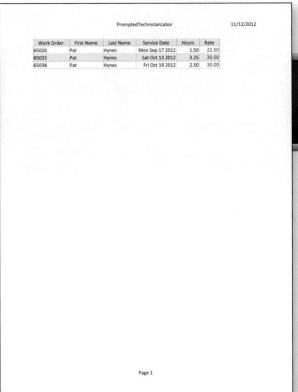

Project 1b, PromptedTechnicianLabor Query

**Project 2 Modify Query Results by Changing the Join Property**
Project 2c, UnassignedWorkOrders Query

Project 1c, PromptedServiceDate Query

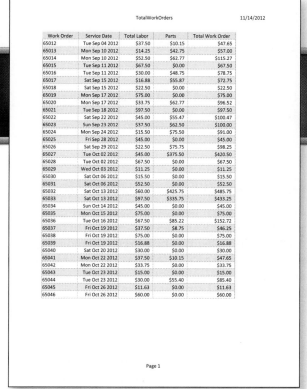

TotalWorkOrders     11/14/2012

| Work Order | Service Date | Total Labor | Parts | Total Work Order |
|---|---|---|---|---|
| 65012 | Tue Sep 04 2012 | $37.50 | $10.15 | $47.65 |
| 65013 | Mon Sep 10 2012 | $14.25 | $42.75 | $57.00 |
| 65014 | Mon Sep 10 2012 | $52.50 | $62.77 | $115.27 |
| 65015 | Tue Sep 11 2012 | $67.50 | $0.00 | $67.50 |
| 65016 | Tue Sep 11 2012 | $30.00 | $48.75 | $78.75 |
| 65017 | Sat Sep 15 2012 | $16.88 | $55.87 | $72.75 |
| 65018 | Sat Sep 15 2012 | $22.50 | $0.00 | $22.50 |
| 65019 | Mon Sep 17 2012 | $75.00 | $0.00 | $75.00 |
| 65020 | Mon Sep 17 2012 | $33.75 | $62.77 | $96.52 |
| 65021 | Tue Sep 18 2012 | $97.50 | $0.00 | $97.50 |
| 65022 | Sat Sep 22 2012 | $45.00 | $55.47 | $100.47 |
| 65023 | Sun Sep 23 2012 | $37.50 | $62.50 | $100.00 |
| 65024 | Mon Sep 24 2012 | $15.50 | $75.50 | $91.00 |
| 65025 | Fri Sep 28 2012 | $45.00 | $0.00 | $45.00 |
| 65026 | Sat Sep 29 2012 | $22.50 | $75.75 | $98.25 |
| 65027 | Tue Oct 02 2012 | $45.00 | $375.50 | $420.50 |
| 65028 | Tue Oct 02 2012 | $67.50 | $0.00 | $67.50 |
| 65029 | Wed Oct 03 2012 | $11.25 | $0.00 | $11.25 |
| 65030 | Sat Oct 06 2012 | $15.50 | $0.00 | $15.50 |
| 65031 | Sat Oct 06 2012 | $52.50 | $0.00 | $52.50 |
| 65032 | Sat Oct 13 2012 | $60.00 | $425.75 | $485.75 |
| 65033 | Sat Oct 13 2012 | $97.50 | $335.75 | $433.25 |
| 65034 | Sun Oct 14 2012 | $45.00 | $0.00 | $45.00 |
| 65035 | Mon Oct 15 2012 | $75.00 | $0.00 | $75.00 |
| 65036 | Tue Oct 16 2012 | $67.50 | $85.22 | $152.72 |
| 65037 | Fri Oct 19 2012 | $37.50 | $8.75 | $46.25 |
| 65038 | Fri Oct 19 2012 | $75.00 | $0.00 | $75.00 |
| 65039 | Fri Oct 19 2012 | $16.88 | $0.00 | $16.88 |
| 65040 | Sat Oct 20 2012 | $30.00 | $0.00 | $30.00 |
| 65041 | Mon Oct 22 2012 | $37.50 | $10.15 | $47.65 |
| 65042 | Mon Oct 22 2012 | $33.75 | $0.00 | $33.75 |
| 65043 | Tue Oct 23 2012 | $15.00 | $0.00 | $15.00 |
| 65044 | Tue Oct 23 2012 | $30.00 | $55.40 | $85.40 |
| 65045 | Fri Oct 26 2012 | $11.63 | $0.00 | $11.63 |
| 65046 | Fri Oct 26 2012 | $60.00 | $0.00 | $60.00 |

Page 1

**Project 3 Calculate Work Order Totals**

Project 3b, TotalWorkOrders Query

TechniciansOperatingSys     11/14/2012

| First Name | Last Name | Operating System |
|---|---|---|
| Pat | Hynes | Windows 7 |
| Hui | Chen | Windows 7 |
| Madir | Sadiku | Windows 7 |
| Armando | Colacci | Windows 7 |
| Kelsey | Eastman | Windows 7 |

Page 1

**Project 4 Query a Multiple-Value Field**

TechnicianOperatingSys Query

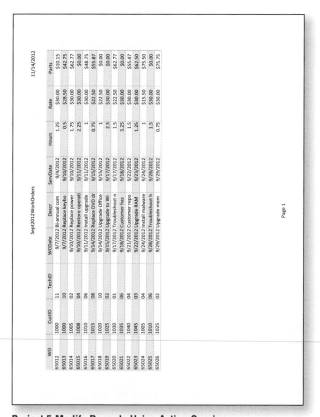

Sept2012WorkOrders     11/14/2012

| WO | CustID | TechID | WODate | Descr | ServDate | Hours | Rate | Parts |
|---|---|---|---|---|---|---|---|---|
| 65012 | 1000 | 11 | 9/7/2012 | Bi-annual com | 9/4/2012 | 1.25 | $30.00 | $10.15 |
| 65013 | 1000 | 10 | 9/7/2012 | Replace keybo | 9/10/2012 | 0.5 | $28.50 | $42.75 |
| 65014 | 1005 | 02 | 9/10/2012 | Replace power | 9/10/2012 | 1.75 | $30.00 | $62.77 |
| 65015 | 1008 | 04 | 9/10/2012 | Restore operati | 9/11/2012 | 2.25 | $30.00 | $0.00 |
| 65016 | 1010 | 06 | 9/11/2012 | Install upgrade | 9/11/2012 | 1 | $30.00 | $48.75 |
| 65017 | 1015 | 08 | 9/14/2012 | Replace DVD dr | 9/15/2012 | 0.75 | $22.50 | $55.87 |
| 65018 | 1020 | 10 | 9/14/2012 | Upgrade Office | 9/15/2012 | 1 | $22.50 | $0.00 |
| 65019 | 1025 | 01 | 9/15/2012 | Upgrade to Wi | 9/17/2012 | 2.5 | $30.00 | $0.00 |
| 65020 | 1030 | 06 | 9/17/2012 | Troubleshoot n | 9/17/2012 | 1.5 | $22.50 | $62.77 |
| 65021 | 1040 | 04 | 9/18/2012 | Customer has | 9/18/2012 | 3.25 | $30.00 | $0.00 |
| 65022 | 1045 | 03 | 9/21/2012 | Customer repo | 9/22/2012 | 1.5 | $30.00 | $55.47 |
| 65023 | 1005 | 04 | 9/22/2012 | Upgrade RAM | 9/23/2012 | 1.25 | $30.00 | $62.50 |
| 65024 | 1010 | 06 | 9/24/2012 | Install malware | 9/24/2012 | 1 | $15.50 | $75.50 |
| 65025 | 1010 | ? | 9/28/2012 | Troubleshoot h | 9/28/2012 | 1.5 | $30.00 | $0.00 |
| 65026 | 1025 | 02 | 9/29/2012 | Upgrade mem | 9/29/2012 | 0.75 | $30.00 | $75.75 |

Page 1

**Project 5 Modify Records Using Action Queries**

Project 5c, Sept2012WorkOrders Table

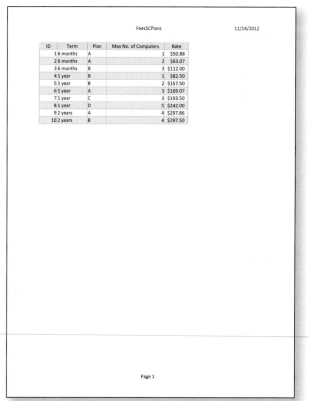

FeesSCPlans     11/14/2012

| ID | Term | Plan | Max No. of Computers | Rate |
|---|---|---|---|---|
| 1 | 6 months | A | 1 | $50.88 |
| 2 | 6 months | A | 2 | $63.07 |
| 3 | 6 months | B | 3 | $112.00 |
| 4 | 1 year | B | 1 | $82.50 |
| 5 | 1 year | B | 2 | $157.50 |
| 6 | 1 year | A | 3 | $169.07 |
| 7 | 1 year | C | 3 | $193.50 |
| 8 | 1 year | D | 5 | $242.00 |
| 9 | 2 years | A | 4 | $297.86 |
| 10 | 2 years | B | 4 | $297.50 |

Page 1

Project 5d, FeesSCPlans Table

You will create queries to select records by saving a filter's criteria and by creating a query that prompts the user for the criteria when the query is run.

**▼ Quick Steps**

**Save Filter as Query**
1. Open table.
2. Filter table as desired.
3. Click Advanced Filter Options button.
4. Click *Filter By Form*.
5. Click Advanced Filter Options button.
6. Click *Save As Query*.
7. Type desired query name.
8. Click OK.
9. Close Filter By Form datasheet.
10. Close table.

**H I N T**

Consider filtering a datasheet and saving the filter as a query if you are more comfortable using filters to select records than typing criteria expressions in Query Design view.

Advanced Filter Options

# Extracting Records Using Select Queries ▪▪▪▪▪▪▪▪▪▪

A *select query* is the query type that is most often used in Access. Select queries extract records from a single table or from multiple tables that meet criteria that you specify. The subset of records that is displayed can be edited, viewed, and/ or printed. In Query Design view, the criteria used to select records are entered by typing expressions in the *Criteria* row for the required field(s). Access provides other methods for which criteria can be specified for a query.

## Saving a Filter as a Query

A *filter* is used in a datasheet or form to temporarily hide records that do not meet specified criteria. For example, you can filter a WorkOrders datasheet to display only those work orders completed on a specified date. The subset of records can be edited, viewed, or printed. Use the Filter by Form feature to filter a datasheet by multiple criteria using a blank datasheet. A filter is active until the filter is removed or the datasheet or form is closed. When the object is reopened, all records are redisplayed.

If you filter a datasheet and then decide that you may want to reuse the criteria, save the filter as a query. To do this, display the criteria in the Filter by Form datasheet, click the Advanced Filter Options button in the Sort & Filter group in the Home tab, and then click *Save as Query* at the drop-down list. Type a query name at the Save as Query dialog box and press Enter or click OK.

Saving a filter as a query means all columns in the table display in the query results datasheet. Use the Hide Fields feature to remove field(s) in the results.

**Project 1a** **Saving a Filter as a Query** Part 1 of 3

1. Open the **AL2-C3-RSRCompServ.accdb** database and enable content.
2. Display only those service calls that required two or more hours of labor by technicians billed at $30.00 per hour using the Filter by Form feature by completing the following steps:
   a. Open the WorkOrders table in Datasheet view.
   b. Minimize the Navigation pane.
   c. Hide the *Comments* field by right-clicking the *Comments* column heading in the datasheet and then clicking *Hide Fields* at the shortcut menu.

d. Click the Advanced Filter Options button in the Sort & Filter group in the Home tab and then click *Filter By Form* at the drop-down list.

e. Click in the empty record in the *Hours* column. Use the down-pointing arrow if you want to filter the table by a specific value within the field. Type >=2 and then press Tab.

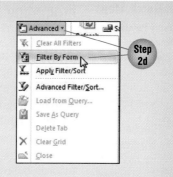

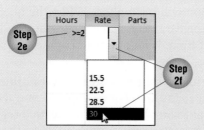

f. With the insertion point positioned in the *Rate* column, click the down-pointing arrow that appears and then click *30* at the drop-down list.

g. Click the Toggle Filter button (displays the ScreenTip *Apply Filter*) in the Sort & Filter group in the Home tab to apply the filter's criteria and display records that meet the filter conditions.

3. Review the nine filtered records in the datasheet.

4. Click the Toggle Filter button (displays the ScreenTip *Remove Filter*) to redisplay all records.

5. Click the Advanced Filter Options button and then click *Filter By Form* at the drop-down list. Notice the filter criteria in the *Hours* and *Rate* columns are intact.

6. Save the filter as a query so that you can reuse the criteria by completing the following steps:

a. Click the Advanced Filter Options button and then click *Save As Query* at the drop-down list.

b. At the Save As Query dialog box, type **WO2orMoreHrsRate30** in the *Query Name* text box and then press Enter or click OK.

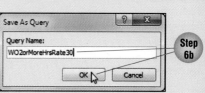

c. Click the Advanced Filter Options button and then click *Close* at the drop-down list to close the Filter By Form datasheet.

d. Close the WorkOrders table. Click No when prompted to save changes to the table design.

7. Expand the Navigation pane.

8. Double-click the query object named *WO2orMoreHrsRate30* to open the query and review the query results.

9. Hide the *Comments* column in the query results datasheet.

10. Print the datasheet in landscape orientation with the left and right margins set to 0.5 inch.

11. Switch to Design view. Notice a query created from a filter creates columns in the query design grid for only those columns upon which a criterion has been defined.

12. Close the query. Click Yes when prompted to save changes to the query layout.

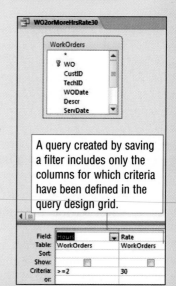

A query created by saving a filter includes only the columns for which criteria have been defined in the query design grid.

## Quick Steps

**Create Parameter Query**
1. Start new query in Design view.
2. Add desired table(s).
3. Close Show Table dialog box.
4. Add desired fields to query design grid.
5. Click in *Criteria* row in field to be prompted.
6. Type message text encased in square brackets.
7. Repeat Steps 5–6 for each additional criteria field.
8. Save query.
9. Close query.

If you are creating a parameter query that will be used by other people, consider adding an example of an acceptable entry in the message. For example, the message *Type the service date in the format mmm-dd-yyyy (example Oct-31-2012)* is more informative than *Type the service date.*

# Prompting for Criteria Using a Parameter Query

In a **parameter query**, specific criteria for a field are not stored with the query design. Instead, the field(s) used to select records have a prompt message that displays when the query is run. The prompt message instructs the user to type the criteria by which to select records. Figure 3.1 illustrates an Enter Parameter Value dialog box that is displayed when a parameter query is run to select by a technician's name. The message that is shown in the dialog box is created in the field for which the criterion will be applied. When the query is run, the user types the criterion at the Enter Parameter Value dialog box and Access selects the records based on the entry. If more than one field contains a parameter, Access prompts the user one field at a time.

A parameter query is useful if you run a query several times on the same field but use different criteria each time. For example, if you require a list of work orders by individual technician, you would have to create a separate query for each technician. This would create several query objects in the Navigation pane. Creating a parameter query that prompts you to enter the technician's name means you only have to create one query.

To create a parameter query, start a new query in Design view and add the desired tables and fields to the query design grid. Type a message encased in square brackets to prompt the user for the required criterion in the *Criteria* row of the field to be used to select records. The text inside the square brackets is displayed in the Enter Parameter Value dialog box when the query is run. Figure 3.2 displays the entry in the *Criteria* row of the *FName* field that generated the Enter Parameter Value message shown in Figure 3.1.

**Figure 3.1** Enter Parameter Value Dialog Box

**Figure 3.2** Criterion to Prompt for the Name in the *FName* Field

| Field: | WO | FName |
|---|---|---|
| Table: | WorkOrders | Technicians |
| Sort: | | |
| Show: | ☑ | ☑ |
| Criteria: | | [Type the technician's first name] |
| or: | | |

Type a message in square brackets to prompt the user for the criterion by which to select records.

---

**Project 1b**  **Creating a Query to Prompt for Technician Names**  Part 2 of 3

1. With the **AL2-C3-RSRCompServ.accdb** database open, create a query in Design view to select records from the Technicians table and the WorkOrders table by completing the following steps:
   a. Click the Create tab and then click the Query Design button in the Queries group.
   b. At the Show Table dialog box, add the Technicians table and the WorkOrders table to the query.

c. Close the Show Table dialog box.

d. Drag the bottom border of each table's field list box at the top of the query until all field names are visible in the box.

e. Add the following fields in order to the query design grid: *WO, FName, LName, ServDate, Hours, Rate*.

**Step 1e**

| Field: | WO | FName | LName | ServDate | Hours | Rate |
|---|---|---|---|---|---|---|
| Table: | WorkOrders | Technicians | Technicians | WorkOrders | WorkOrders | WorkOrders |
| Sort: | | | | | | |
| Show: | ✓ | ✓ | ✓ | ✓ | ✓ | ✓ |

2. Click the Run button to run the query.

3. Add parameters to select records by a technician's first and last names by completing the following steps:

a. Switch to Design view.

b. Click in the *Criteria* row in the *FName* column in the query design grid, type [Type the technician's first name], and then press Enter.

**Step 3c**

c. Position the pointer on the vertical line between *FName* and *LName* in the gray field selector bar above the field names until the pointer changes to a vertical line with a left- and right-pointing arrow and then double-click to expand the width of the *FName* column so that you can see the entire criteria entry.

**Step 3b**

| FName | LName |
|---|---|
| Technicians | Technicians |
| ✓ | ✓ |
| [Type the technician's first name] | |

d. With the insertion point positioned in the *Criteria* row in the *LName* column, type [Type the technician's last name] and then press Enter.

e. Expand the width of the *LName* column so that you can see the entire criteria entry.

4. Click the Save button on the Quick Access toolbar, type PromptedTechnicianLabor in the *Query Name* text box at the Save As dialog box, and then press Enter or click OK.

5. Close the query.

6. Run the prompted query and extract a list of work orders for the technician named Pat Hynes by completing the following steps:

a. Double-click the query named *PromptedTechnicianLabor* in the Navigation pane.

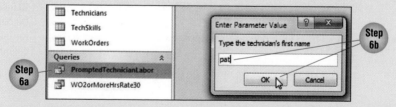

b. Type pat at the Enter Parameter Value dialog box that displays the message *Type the technician's first name* and then press Enter or click OK. Note that Access is not case-sensitive when typing text strings.

c. Type hynes at the second Enter Parameter Value dialog box that displays the message *Type the technician's last name* and then press Enter or click OK.

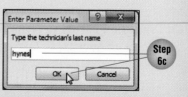

7. Review the records in the query results datasheet.

8. Print the query results datasheet.

9. Close the query.

1. With the **AL2-C3-RSRCompServ.accdb** database open, create a query in Design view to prompt the user for a starting and ending date by which to select records using the WorkOrders table by completing the following steps:
   a. Click the Create tab and then click the Query Design button in the Queries group.
   b. At the Show Table dialog box, add the WorkOrders table to the query and then close the Show Table dialog box.
   c. Drag the bottom border of the table's field list box until all field names are visible.
   d. Add the following fields in order to the query design grid: *WO, CustID, Descr, ServDate, Hours, Rate, Parts*.
   e. Click in the *Criteria* row in the ServDate column, type the entry Between [Type starting date] And [Type ending date], and then press Enter.

Step 1e

   f. Expand the *ServDate* column width until the entire criteria entry is visible.
2. Save the query, type PromptedServiceDate at the Save As dialog box, and then press Enter or click OK.
3. Close the query.
4. Double-click *PromptedServiceDate* in the Navigation pane. At the first Enter Parameter Value dialog box with *Type starting date* displayed, type October 1, 2012 and press Enter or click OK. At the second Enter Parameter Value dialog box with *Type ending date* displayed, type October 15, 2012 and press Enter or click OK.

**PromptedServiceDate**

| Work Order ▾ | Customer ID ▾ | Descripton ▾ | Service Date ▾ | Hours ▾ | Rate ▾ | Parts ▾ |
|---|---|---|---|---|---|---|
| 65027 | 1010 | Replace hard drive | Tue Oct 02 2012 | 1.50 | 30.00 | $375.50 |
| 65028 | 1030 | Reinstall operating system | Tue Oct 02 2012 | 2.25 | 30.00 | $0.00 |
| 65029 | 1035 | Set up automatic backup | Wed Oct 03 2012 | 0.50 | 22.50 | $0.00 |
| 65030 | 1000 | Clean malware from system | Sat Oct 06 2012 | 1.00 | 15.50 | $0.00 |
| 65031 | 1045 | Customer reports noisy hard drive | Sat Oct 06 2012 | 1.75 | 30.00 | $0.00 |
| 65032 | 1008 | Install second hard drive | Sat Oct 13 2012 | 2.00 | 30.00 | $425.75 |
| 65033 | 1000 | Install Windows 7 | Sat Oct 13 2012 | 3.25 | 30.00 | $335.75 |
| 65034 | 1035 | File management training | Sun Oct 14 2012 | 1.50 | 30.00 | $0.00 |
| 65035 | 1020 | Office 2010 training | Mon Oct 15 2012 | 2.50 | 30.00 | $0.00 |

records selected within the date range October 1, 2012 to October 15, 2012 for the *Service Date* column at Step 4

5. Print the query results datasheet in landscape orientation.
6. Close the query.

You will create and modify queries that obtain various results based on changing the join properties for related tables.

# Modifying Join Properties in a Query ■■■■■■■■■■■■■

*Join properties* refers to the manner with which Access matches the field values in the common field between the two tables in a relationship. The method used determines how many records are selected for inclusion in the query results datasheet. Access provides for three join types in a relationship: an inner join, a left outer join, and a right outer join. By default, Access uses an inner join between the tables, which means that records are selected for display in a query only when a match on the joined field value exists in both tables. If a record exists in either table with no matching record in the other table, the record is not displayed in the query results datasheet. This means that in some cases you may not be viewing all records from both tables when you run a query.

## Specifying the Join Type

Double-click the black join line between tables in a query to open the Join Properties dialog box shown in Figure 3.3. By default, option 1 is selected, which is referred to as an ***inner join***. In an inner join, only those records where the primary key field value in the primary table matches a foreign key field value in the related table are displayed.

Options 2 and 3 are referred to as ***outer joins***. Option 2 is a ***left outer join***. In this type of join, the primary table (referred to as the left table) displays all rows whereas the related table (referred to as the right table) shows only rows with a matching value in the foreign key field. For example, examine the query results datasheet shown in Figure 3.4. This query was created with the Technicians and TechSkills tables. All technician records are shown in the datasheet; however, notice that some technician records display with empty field values for the columns from the TechSkills table. These are the technicians who have not yet had a record created in the TechSkills table with their information. In a left outer join, all records from the primary table in the relationship are shown in the query results datasheet.

**HINT**

You can edit a relationship if you always want the join type to be a left or right outer join. To do this, click the Join Type button in the Edit Relationships dialog box to open the Join Properties dialog box. Select the desired join type and click OK.

**HINT**

Changing the join type at a query window does not alter the join type for other objects based on the relationship—the revised join property applies to the query only.

**Figure 3.3** Join Properties Dialog Box

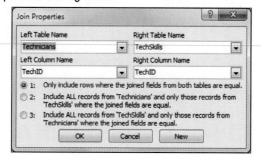

**Figure 3.4** Left Outer Join Example

| First Name | Last Name | Certifications | Operating Systems | Network Specialist? | Design Websites? | Programming? |
|---|---|---|---|---|---|---|
| Pat | Hynes | Cisco CCNP, CompTIA A+, Microsoft MCTS | Linux, Unix, Windows 7, Windows XP | ☑ | ☐ | ☑ |
| Hui | Chen | Cisco CCNP, CompTIA A+ | Linux, Unix, Windows 7 | ☑ | ☑ | ☐ |
| Kayla | Blewett | | | ☐ | ☐ | ☐ |
| Mihir | Patel | CompTIA A+, Microsoft MCTS | Unix, Windows Vista, Windows XP | ☐ | ☐ | ☑ |
| Madir | Sadiku | CompTIA A+, Microsoft MCTS | Mac OS X, Windows 7, Windows Vista | ☐ | ☐ | ☐ |
| Brody | Stewart | | | ☐ | ☐ | ☐ |
| Ana | Takacs | Cisco CCNA | Mac OS X, Windows XP | ☑ | ☐ | ☑ |
| Marty | O'Leary | Cisco CCNP | Linux, Unix | ☑ | ☑ | ☐ |
| Armando | Colacci | Microsoft Master | Windows 7, Windows Vista, Windows XP | ☐ | ☐ | ☑ |
| Kelsey | Eastman | Cisco CCNA, Microsoft MCTS | Linux, Windows 7, Windows Vista | ☑ | ☑ | ☐ |
| Dana | Westman | | | ☐ | ☐ | ☐ |
| * | | | | ☐ | ☐ | ☐ |

Left outer join query results show related TechSkills fields blank for those technicians who do not yet have a record in the TechSkills table.

Option 3 is a ***right outer join.*** In this type of join, the related table (or right table) shows all rows whereas the primary table (or left table) shows only rows with a matching value in the common field. For example, examine the partial query results datasheet shown in Figure 3.5. This datasheet illustrates 15 of the 39 records in the query results datasheet from the Technicians and WorkOrders tables. Notice the first four records have no technician first or last name. These are the work orders that have not yet been assigned to a technician. In a right outer join, all records from the related table in the relationship are shown in the query results datasheet. In a left or right outer join, Access displays an arrow at the end of the join line pointing to the table that shows only matching rows.

To illustrate the difference in query results when no change is made to the join type, examine the query results datasheet shown in Figure 3.6. This is the datasheet you will create in Project 2a. In this project, you will create a list with the technician names and qualifications. Compare the number of records shown in Figure 3.6 with those shown in Figure 3.4. Notice that fewer records display in the datasheet. Since an inner join displays only those records where a matching entry exists in both tables, records from either table that do not have a matching

**Figure 3.5** Right Outer Join Example

Right outer join query results show related technician fields blank for those work orders that have yet to be assigned to a technician.

| First Name | Last Name | Work Order | Customer ID | WO Date | Descripton |
|---|---|---|---|---|---|
| | | 65047 | 1030 | Sat Oct 27 2012 | Set up automatic backup |
| | | 65048 | 1020 | Mon Oct 29 2012 | Replace LCD monitor |
| | | 65049 | 1040 | Tue Oct 30 2012 | Set up dual monitor system |
| | | 65050 | 1045 | Tue Oct 30 2012 | Reinstall Windows 7 |
| Pat | Hynes | 65020 | 1030 | Mon Sep 17 2012 | Troubleshoot noisy fan |
| Pat | Hynes | 65033 | 1000 | Fri Oct 12 2012 | Install Windows 7 |
| Pat | Hynes | 65038 | 1010 | Fri Oct 19 2012 | Install Windows 7 |
| Hui | Chen | 65014 | 1005 | Mon Sep 10 2012 | Replace power supply |
| Hui | Chen | 65019 | 1025 | Sat Sep 15 2012 | Upgrade to Windows 7 |
| Hui | Chen | 65026 | 1025 | Sat Sep 29 2012 | Upgrade memory |
| Hui | Chen | 65032 | 1008 | Fri Oct 12 2012 | Install second hard drive |
| Hui | Chen | 65035 | 1020 | Sun Oct 14 2012 | Office 2010 training |
| Kayla | Blewett | 65023 | 1045 | Sat Sep 22 2012 | Upgrade RAM |
| Kayla | Blewett | 65036 | 1008 | Mon Oct 15 2012 | Set up home network |
| Kayla | Blewett | 65041 | 1020 | Mon Oct 22 2012 | Bi-annual computer maintenance |

record in the other table are not displayed. Understanding that an inner join (the default join type) may not display all records that exist in the tables when you run a query is important.

**Figure 3.6** Inner Join Example

| First Name | Last Name | Certifications | Operating Systems | Network Specialist? | Design Websites? | Programming? |
|---|---|---|---|---|---|---|
| Cat | Hynes | Cisco CCNP, CompTIA A+, Microsoft MCTS | Linux, Unix, Windows 7, Windows XP | ☑ | ☐ | ☑ |
| Hui | Chen | Cisco CCNP, CompTIA A+ | Linux, Unix, Windows 7 | ☑ | ☑ | ☐ |
| Mihir | Patel | CompTIA A+, Microsoft MCTS | Unix, Windows Vista, Windows XP | ☐ | ☐ | ☑ |
| Madir | Sadiku | CompTIA A+, Microsoft MCTS | Mac OS X, Windows 7, Windows Vista | ☐ | ☐ | ☐ |
| Ana | Takacs | Cisco CCNA | Mac OS X, Windows XP | ☑ | ☐ | ☑ |
| Marty | O'Leary | Cisco CCNP | Linux, Unix | ☑ | ☑ | ☐ |
| Armando | Colacci | Microsoft Master | Windows 7, Windows Vista, Windows XP | ☐ | ☐ | ☑ |
| Kelsey | Eastman | Cisco CCNA, Microsoft MCTS | Linux, Windows 7, Windows Vista | ☑ | ☑ | ☐ |
| * | | | | ☐ | ☐ | ☐ |

An inner join displays a record only when a matching value in the joined field exists in both tables—no blank records appear in the query results. However, notice that you are not viewing all records in the technicians table.

## Project 2a    Selecting Records in a Query Using an Inner Join            Part 1 of 4

1. With the **AL2-C3-RSRCompServ.accdb** database open, create a query in Design view to display a list of technicians with each technician's skill specialties by completing the following steps:
   a. Create a new query in Design view. At the Show Table dialog box, add the Technicians and the TechSkills tables. Close the Show Table dialog box and then drag the bottom border of each table's field list box until all field names are visible in the box.
   b. Double-click the black join line between the two tables to open the Join Properties dialog box.
   c. At the Join Properties dialog box, notice that *1* is selected by default. Option 1 selects records only when the joined fields from both tables are equal. This represents an inner join. Click OK.
   d. Add the following fields in order to the query design grid: *FName, LName, Certifications, OperatingSys, NetworkSpc, WebDesign,* and *Programming*.
   e. Run the query.

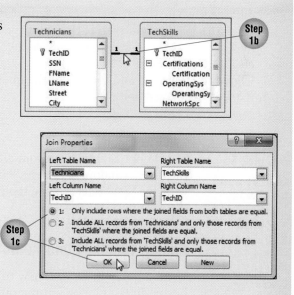

2. Minimize the Navigation pane and then compare your results with the query results datasheet displayed in Figure 3.6.
3. Save the query and name it TechnicianSpecialties.
4. Close the query.
5. Expand the Navigation pane.

1. With the **AL2-C3-RSRCompServ.accdb** database open, modify the TechnicianSpecialties query to a left outer join to check if any technicians do not have a matching record in the TechSkills table by completing the following steps:

   a. Right-click the TechnicianSpecialties query and then click *Design view* at the shortcut menu.

   b. Right-click the black join line between the two tables and then click *Join Properties* at the shortcut menu.

   c. At the Join Properties dialog box, click *2* and then click OK. Option 2 includes all records from the Technicians table and only those records from TechSkills where the joined fields are equal. The left table (Technicians) is the table that will show all records. If a technician does not have a matching record in the other table, the columns display empty fields next to the technician's name.

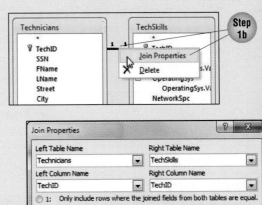

   d. Notice the join line between the two tables now displays with an arrow pointing to the joined field in the TechSkills table.

   e. Run the query.

2. Minimize the Navigation pane and then compare your results with the query results datasheet displayed in Figure 3.4 on page 76. Notice that 11 records display in this datasheet whereas only eight records displayed in the query results from Project 2a.

3. Click the File tab and then click Save Object As. At the Save As dialog box, type AllTechnicianSkills in the *Save 'TechnicianSpecialties' to* text box and then press Enter or click OK.

4. Click the Home tab and then close the query.

5. Expand the Navigation pane.

---

### ▼ Quick Steps

**Create Query with Left Outer Join**

1. Create new query in Design view.
2. Add tables to query window.
3. Double-click join line between tables.
4. Select option *2*.
5. Click OK.
6. Add desired fields to query design grid.
7. Save and run query.

Do not assume a left join always occurs with the table that is the left table in the query window. Although Technicians was the left table in the Project 2b query window, "left" refers to the table that represents the one side (primary table) in the relationship.

## Adding Tables to and Removing Tables from a Query

Open a query in Design view to add a table to a query. Click the Show Table button in the Query Setup group in the Query Tools Design tab and then add the desired table using the Show Table dialog box. Close the Show Table dialog box when finished.

To remove a table from a query, click any field within the table field list box to activate the table in the query window and then press the Delete key. The table is removed from the window and all fields associated with the table that were added to the query design grid are automatically removed. You can also right-click the table in the query window and click *Remove Table* at the shortcut menu.

Show Table

Part 3 of 4

**Project 2c**   **Selecting Records in a Query Using a Right Outer Join**

1. With the **AL2-C3-RSRCompServ.accdb** database open, create a new query to check for work orders that have not been assigned to a technician by modifying an existing query by completing the following steps:
   a. Open the TechnicianSpecialties query in Design view.
   b. Right-click the TechSkills table in the query window and then click *Remove Table* at the shortcut menu. Notice that the last five columns are removed from the query design grid along with the table.

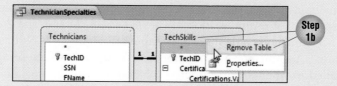

   c. Click the Show Table button in the Query Setup group in the Query Tools Design tab.
   d. At the Show Table dialog box, double-click *WorkOrders* in the Tables list, click the Close button, and then drag the bottom border of the WorkOrders table field list box until all fields are visible in the box.
   e. Double-click the black join line between the two tables.
   f. At the Join Properties dialog box, click *3* and then click OK. Option 3 includes all records from the WorkOrders table and only those records from the Technicians table where the joined fields are equal. The right table (WorkOrders) is the table that will show all records. If a work order does not have a matching record in the other table, the columns display empty fields for the technician names.

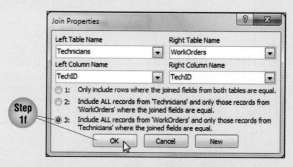

   g. Notice the join line between the two tables now displays with an arrow pointing to the joined field in the Technicians table.
   h. Add the following fields in order from the WorkOrders table to the query design grid: *WO*, *WODate*, and *Descr*.
2. Click the File tab and then click Save Object As. At the Save As dialog box, type UnassignedWorkOrders in the *Save 'TechnicianSpecialties' to* text box and then press Enter or click OK.
3. Click the Query Tools Design tab and then run the query.

4. Compare your results with the partial query results datasheet shown in Figure 3.5 on page 76. Notice the first four records in the query results datasheet have empty fields in the *First Name* and *Last Name* columns.
5. Double-click the right column boundary of the *Description* column to adjust the column width and then print the query results datasheet with the right margin set to 0.5-inch.
6. Close the query. Click Yes to save changes.

▼ **Quick Steps**

**Create Query with Right Outer Join**
1. Create new query in Design view.
2. Add tables to query window.
3. Double-click join line between tables.
4. Select option 3.
5. Click OK.
6. Add desired fields to query design grid.
7. Save and run query.

In a self-join query, the two fields joined together must have the same data type.

Do not assume a right join always occurs with the table that is the right table in the query window. Although WorkOrders was the right table in the Project 2c query window, "right" refers to the table that represents the *many* side (related table) in the relationship.

## Creating a Self-Join Query

Assume you have a table in which two fields in the same table contain similar field values. For example, look at the *Technician ID* and *Tier 2 Supervisor* columns in the Technicians table datasheet shown in Figure 3.7. Notice that each column contains a technician's ID number. Tier 2 supervisors are senior technicians who are called in when a work order is too complex for the regular technician to solve. The ID number in the *Tier 2 Supervisor* column is the senior technician's ID who is assigned to the technician.

You may find it more informative to view the list of technicians with the Tier 2 supervisor's last name instead of ID number. If you have a table that has matching values in two separate fields, you can create a *self-join query*, which creates a relationship between fields in the same table. To create a self-join query, two copies of the same table are added to the query window. The second occurrence of the table is named using the original table name with *_1* added to the end. You can assign an alias to the second table to provide the table with a more descriptive name in the query. Next, join the two tables by dragging the field with matching values from one table field list to the other. Add the required fields to the query design grid and then run the query.

**Figure 3.7** Technician's Table Datasheet with Fields Used in Self-Join Query

| | Technician ID | SSN | First Name | Last Name | Street Address | City | State | ZIP Code | Home Phone | Cell Phone | 🔗 | Tier 2 Supervisor |
|---|---|---|---|---|---|---|---|---|---|---|---|---|
| ⊞ | 01 | 000-45-5368 | Pat | Hynes | 206-31 Woodland Street | Detroit | MI | 48202-1138 | 313-555-6874 | 313-555-6412 | 🔗(1) | 03 |
| ⊞ | 02 | 000-47-3258 | Hui | Chen | 12905 Hickory Street | Detroit | MI | 48205-3462 | 313-555-7468 | 313-555-5234 | 🔗(0) | 06 |
| ⊞ | 03 | 000-62-7468 | Kayla | Blewett | 1310 Jarvis Street | Detroit | MI | 48220-2011 | 313-555-3265 | 313-555-6486 | 🔗(0) | |
| ⊞ | 04 | 000-33-1485 | Mihir | Patel | 8213 Elgin Street | Detroit | MI | 48234-4092 | 313-555-7458 | 313-555-6385 | 🔗(1) | 11 |
| ⊞ | 05 | 000-48-7850 | Madir | Sadiku | 8190 Kenwood Street | Detroit | MI | 48220-1132 | 313-555-6327 | 313-555-8569 | 🔗(0) | 03 |
| ⊞ | 06 | 000-75-8412 | Brody | Stewart | 3522 Moore Place | Detroit | MI | 48208-1032 | 313-555-7499 | 313-555-3625 | 🔗(0) | |
| ⊞ | 07 | 000-55-1248 | Ana | Takacs | 14902 Hampton Court | Detroit | MI | 48215-3616 | 313-555-6142 | 313-555-4586 | 🔗(0) | 11 |
| ⊞ | 08 | 000-63-1247 | Marty | O'Leary | 14000 Vernon Drive | Detroit | MI | 48237-1320 | 313-555-9856 | 313-555-4125 | 🔗(0) | 11 |
| ⊞ | 09 | 000-84-1254 | Armando | Colacci | 17302 Windsor Avenue | Detroit | MI | 48224-2257 | 313-555-9641 | 313-555-8796 | 🔗(0) | 06 |
| ⊞ | 10 | 000-43-5789 | Kelsey | Eastman | 550 Montclair Street | Detroit | MI | 48214-3274 | 313-555-6315 | 313-555-7411 | 🔗(2) | 06 |
| ⊞ | 11 | 000-65-4185 | Dana | Westman | 18101 Keeler Streeet | Detroit | MI | 48223-1322 | 313-555-5488 | 313-555-4158 | 🔗(0) | |
| ＊ | | | | | | | | | | | 🔗(0) | |

These two fields contain technician identification numbers. Tier 2 supervisors are senior-level technicians and are assigned to handle complex cases for other technicians.

# Creating an Alias for a Table

An **alias** is another name that you want to use to reference a table in a query. The alias is temporary and applies to the query only. Generally, you create an alias if you want to assign a shorter name to a table or a more descriptive name in the case of a self-join query. For example, one of the tables that you will use in the query in Project 2d is named Technicians_1. You can assign the table a more descriptive name such as Supervisors to more accurately describe the second table's role in the query.

To assign an alias to a table, right-click the table name in the query window and click *Properties* at the shortcut menu to open the Property Sheet task pane. Click in the *Alias* property box, delete the existing table name, and type the name by which you want the table referenced. Access replaces all occurrences of the table name with the alias in the query design grid.

▼ **Quick Steps**

**Create Self-Join Query**
1. Create query in Design view.
2. Add two copies of the table to the query.
3. Right-click second table name.
4. Click *Properties.*
5. Click in *Alias* property box and delete existing table name.
6. Type alias table name.
7. Close the Property Sheet.
8. Drag field name from left table to field name with matching values in right table.
9. Add fields as required to query design grid.
10. Run query.
11. Save query.

**Project 2d**  **Creating a Self-Join Query**  Part 4 of 4

1. With the **AL2-C3-RSRCompServ.accdb** database open, create a self-join query to display the last name of the Tier 2 supervisor instead of the identification number by completing the following steps:
   a. Create a new query in Design view.
   b. At the Show Table dialog box, double-click *Technicians* in the *Tables* list box twice to add two copies of the Technicians table to the query and then close the Show Table dialog box. Notice the second copy of the table is named *Technicians_1*.
   c. Drag the bottom border of both table field list boxes down until all field names are visible.
   d. Create an alias for the second table by completing the following steps:
      1) Right-click the *Technicians_1* table name.
      2) Click *Properties* at the shortcut menu.
      3) Select and delete the current name in the *Alias* property box in the Property Sheet task pane.

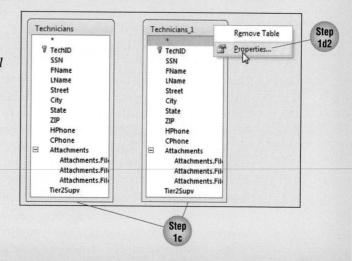

4) Type Supervisors and then close the Property Sheet task pane.

e. Drag the field named *Tier2Supv* from the Technicians table field list box at the left to the field named *TechID* in the Supervisors table field list box at the right. This creates a join line between the two tables.

f. Add the *FName* and *LName* fields from the Technicians table to the query design grid.

g. Add the *LName* field from the Supervisors table to the query design grid.

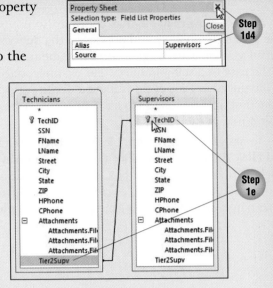

Step 1d4

Step 1e

Steps 1f–1g

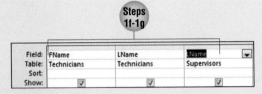

2. Run the query. The last names displayed in the second *Last Name* column represent the *Tier2Supv* name.

3. Switch to Design view.

4. Right-click the second *LName* column (from the Supervisors table) and click *Properties* at the shortcut menu. Click in the *Caption* property box in the Property Sheet task pane, type Tier 2 Supervisor, and then close the Property Sheet task pane.

5. Save the query. Type Tier2Supervisors at the Save As dialog box and then press Enter or click OK.

6. Run the query.

7. Double-click the right column boundary of the *Tier 2 Supervisor* column to adjust the width and then compare your results to the datasheet shown at the right.

8. Close the query. Click Yes to save changes.

Step 7

## Running a Query with No Established Relationship

If a query is created from two tables for which no join is established, Access will not know how to relate records in each table. For example, if one table contains 20 records and the other table contains 10 records and no join is established between the tables, Access produces a query results datasheet containing 200 records (20 × 10). Absent a relationship, Access produces a datasheet representing every combination of records between the two tables. This type of query is called a **cross product** or **Cartesian product** query. The results of such a query in most cases would provide data that serves no purpose.

If you add two tables to a query and no join line appears, create a join by dragging a field from one table to a compatible field in the other table. The two fields should contain the same data type and be logically related in some way.

## Project 3 — Calculate Work Order Totals

**2 Parts**

You will use a subquery nested within another query to calculate the total amount earned from each work order.

# Creating and Using Subqueries ▪▪▪▪▪▪▪▪▪▪▪▪▪▪▪▪

When performing multiple calculations based on numeric fields you may decide to create a separate query for each individual calculation and then use subqueries to generate the final total. A *subquery* is a query nested inside another query. Using subqueries to break the calculations into individual objects allows you to reuse a calculated field in multiple queries. For example, assume that you want to calculate the total amount for each work order. The WorkOrders table contains fields with the number of hours for each service call, the labor rate, and the total amount of the parts used. To find the total for each work order, you need to calculate the total labor by multiplying the hours times the rate and then add the parts value to the total labor value. However, you may want the total labor value to be in a separate query so that you can perform other calculations such as finding the average, maximum, or minimum labor on work orders. To be able to reuse the total labor value, you will need to create the calculated field in its own query.

Once the query is created to calculate the total labor, you can nest the query inside another query to add the labor to the parts to calculate the total for all work orders. Creating subqueries provides you with the flexibility to reuse calculations, thus avoiding duplication of effort and reducing the potential for calculation errors.

In Level 1, Chapter 3 you learned how to insert a calculated field in a query. Recall the format for an equation in a query is to type in a blank *Field* row the desired field name followed by a colon and then the equation with field names in square brackets. For example, Total:[Sales]+[SalesTax].

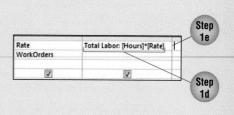

**▼ Quick Steps**

**Nest Query within a Query**
1. Start new query in Design view.
2. At Show Table dialog box, click Queries tab.
3. Double-click query to be used as subquery.
4. Add other queries or tables as required.
5. Close Show Table dialog box.
6. Add fields as required.
7. Save and run query.

**H I N T**

Subqueries are not restricted to nested calculations—use a subquery for any combination of fields that you want to be able to reuse in multiple queries.

## Project 3a — Creating a Query to Calculate Total Labor

**Part 1 of 2**

1. With the **AL2-C3-RSRCompServ.accdb** database open, create a query to calculate the total labor for each work order by completing the following steps:
   a. Create a new query in Design view. At the Show Table dialog box, add the WorkOrders table to the query window and then close the Show Table dialog box.
   b. Drag the bottom border of the WorkOrders table field list box down until all fields are visible.
   c. Add the following fields in order to the query design grid: *WO*, *ServDate*, *Hours*, and *Rate*.
   d. Click in the blank *Field* row next to *Rate* in the query design grid, type Total Labor: [Hours]*[Rate], and then press Enter.
   e. Expand the width of the calculated column until you can see all of the formula in the *Field* row.

2. Run the query and view the query results. Notice the *Total Labor* column does not display a consistent number of decimal values.
3. Switch to Design view.
4. Format the *Total Labor* column by completing the following steps:
   a. Click the insertion point anywhere within the *Total Labor* field row to activate the field.
   b. Click the Property Sheet button in the Show/Hide group in the Query Tools Design tab.
   c. Click in the *Format* property box in the Property Sheet task pane, click the down-pointing arrow that appears, and then click *Standard* at the drop-down list.
   d. Close the Property Sheet task pane.

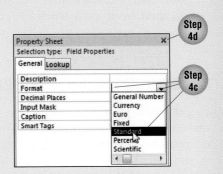

5. Save the query. Type **TotalLabor** at the Save As dialog box and then press Enter or click OK.
6. Run the query. Notice the last four rows contain no values since the service calls have not yet been completed.
7. Switch to Design view. Click in the *Criteria* row in the *Hours* column, type **>0**, and then press Enter.
8. Save the revised query and then run the query.
9. Close the query.

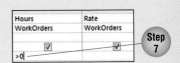

---

**Project 3b** | **Nesting a Query within a Query** | Part 2 of 2

1. With the **AL2-C3-RSRCompServ.accdb** database open, create a new query to calculate the total value of all work orders using the TotalLabor query as a subquery by completing the following steps:
   a. Create a new query in Design view.
   b. At the Show Table dialog box, click the Queries tab.
   c. Double-click *TotalLabor* in the Queries list.
   d. Click the Tables tab.
   e. Double-click *WorkOrders* in the Tables list and then close the Show Table dialog box. Notice that Access has automatically joined the two objects on the *WO* field.
2. Add fields from the TotalLabor subquery and from the WorkOrders table by completing the following steps:
   a. Double-click the asterisk (*) at the top of the TotalLabor field list box. Access adds the entry *TotalLabor.** to the first column in the query design grid. This entry adds all of the fields from the query. Individual columns do not display in the grid; however, when you run the query, the datasheet will show all fields.

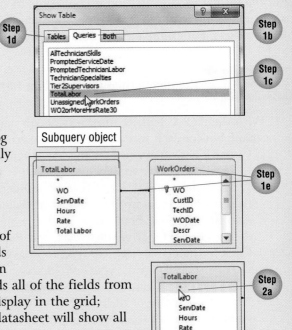

b. Run the query. Notice the query results datasheet shows all five columns from the TotalLabor query.

c. Switch to Design view. You decide to format the *Total Labor* column to *Currency* for this new query. In order to do this, you need to add the column to the query design grid.

d. Right-click in the field selector bar (gray bar above the *Field* row) for the *TotalLabor.*\* column and then click *Cut* at the shortcut menu to remove the column from the design grid.

e. Add the following fields from the TotalLabor query field list box in order to the query design grid: *WO*, *ServDate*, and *Total Labor*.

f. Format the *Total Labor* column to *Currency*.

g. Drag the bottom border of the WorkOrders table field list box down until all fields are visible and then double-click *Parts* to add the field to the query design grid.

3. Create the calculated field to add the total labor and parts by completing the following steps:

a. Click in the blank *Field* row next to *Parts* in the query design grid, type Total Work Order: [Total Labor]+[Parts], and then press Enter.

b. Expand the width of the *Total Work Order* column until the entire formula is visible.

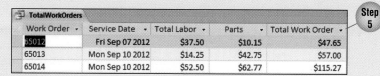

c. Format the *Total Work Order* column to *Currency*.

4. Save the query. Type TotalWorkOrders at the Save As dialog box and then press Enter or click OK. Run the query.

5. Double-click the column boundary for the *Total Work Order* column to adjust the column width and then print the query results datasheet.

6. Close the query. Click Yes to save changes.

Smaller queries are easier to build and troubleshoot. Another reason to use subqueries is when you need to create a complex query. Create subqueries to build and test each section individually and then combine the subqueries into the final query.

---

P roject **4** **Query a Multiple-Value Field** **1 Part**

You will select records using a multiple-value field in a query.

---

## Selecting Records Using a Multiple-Value Field ■ ■ ■ ■ ■ ■ ■

**Show Multiple-Value Field in Separate Rows in Query**
1. Open query in Design view.
2. Click in *Field* box of multiple-value field in design grid.
3. Move insertion point to end of field name.
4. Type period (.).
5. Press Enter to accept *.Value*.
6. Save query.

You learned to create and use multiple-value fields in Chapter 2. In a query, a multiple-value field can display as it does in a table datasheet with the multiple field values in the same column separated by commas, or you can elect to show each field value in a separate row. To show each value in a separate row, add the multiple-value field name with *.Value* at the end in the *Field* box in the query design grid. Figure 3.8 displays the query design grid for the query you will use in Project 4 that displays each entry in the *OperatingSys* field in a separate row in the datasheet.

To select records using criteria in a multiple-value field, type the criteria using the same procedures you would for a single-value field. For example, in the TechnicianSpecialties query, typing *Windows 7* in the *Criteria* row in the *OperatingSys* column causes Access to return the records of any technician with Windows 7 as one of the multiple field values.

**Figure 3.8** Project 4 Query Design Grid

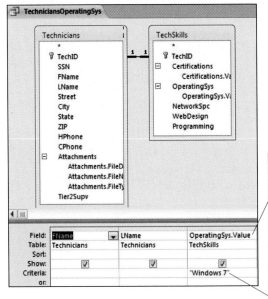

Adding *.Value* to the end of the multiple-value field *OperatingSys* causes Access to display each value in a separate row in the datasheet.

Only those records with *Windows 7* as one of the multiple-value field entries will be selected in the query results.

**Project 4** **Using a Multiple-Value Field in a Query** Part 1 of 1

1. With the **AL2-C3-RSRCompServ.accdb** database open, open the TechnicianSpecialties query in Design view.
2. Right-click in the field selector bar above the *Certifications* field and click *Cut* at the shortcut menu to remove the field from the query design grid.
3. Delete the *NetworkSpc*, *WebDesign*, and *Programming* columns from the query design grid by completing a step similar to Step 2.

Step 2

4. Run the query. Notice each record in the *Operating Systems* column displays the multiple values separated by commas.
5. Switch to Design view.
6. Click in the *OperatingSys* field box in the query design grid, move the insertion point to the end of the field name and then type a period (.). Access displays *.Value* in the *Field* box. Press Enter to accept the .Value property in the field name. *Note: When creating a query from scratch, drag the multiple-value field name with the .Value property already attached from the table's field list box to the query design grid.*

Step 6

7. Click the File tab, click Save Object As, type TechniciansOperatingSys at the Save As dialog box, and then press Enter or click OK.
8. Click the Query Tools Design Tab and then run the query. Notice that each entry in the multiple-value field is now displayed in a separate row.
9. Switch to Design view.
10. Click in the *Criteria* row in the *OperatingSys.Value* column in the query design grid, type Windows 7, and then press Enter.

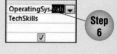
Step 10

11. Run the query. Notice the column title for the multiple-value field in the query results datasheet is now *TechSkills. OperatingSys.Value*. Change the column heading for the field by completing the following steps:
    a. Switch to Design view.
    b. Click the insertion point anywhere within the *OperatingSys.Value* Field box in the query design grid.
    c. Click the Property Sheet button in the Show/Hide group of the Query Tools Design tab.
    d. Click in the *Caption* property box, type Operating System, and then press Enter.
    e. Close the Property Sheet task pane.

Step 11e

Step 11d

12. Run the query.

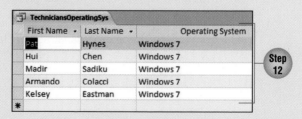
Step 12

13. Print the query results datasheet and then close the query. Click Yes to save changes.

---

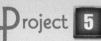roject **5** **Modify Records Using Action Queries**          **4 Parts**

You will create a new table, add and delete records, and update field values using action queries.

Create Make-Table
Query
1. Create query in
Design view.
2. Add desired table(s)
to query.
3. Add desired fields to
query design grid.
4. If necessary, enter
criteria to select
records.
5. Run query.
6. Switch to Design
view.
7. Click Make Table
button.
8. Type table name.
9. If necessary, select
destination database.
10. Click OK.
11. Run the query.
12. Click Yes.
13. Save query.

# Performing Operations Using Action Queries ■■■■■■■■

*Action queries* are used to perform an operation on a group of records. Building an action query is similar to building a select query with the extra step of specifying the action to perform on the group of selected records. Four types of action queries are available and are described in Table 3.1.

To create an action query, first build a select query by adding tables, fields, and criteria to the query design grid. Run the select query to make sure the desired group of records is being targeted for action. Once you are satisfied the correct records will be modified, change the query type using the Make Table, Append, Update, or Delete buttons in the Query Type group in the Query Tools Design tab shown in Figure 3.9.

Clicking the Run button once the query type has been changed to an action query causes Access to perform the make-table, append, update, or delete operation. Once an action query has been run, the results cannot be reversed.

**Table 3.1** Action Query Types

| Query Type | Description |
| --- | --- |
| Make Table | A new table is created from selected records in an existing table. For example, you could create a new table that combines fields from two other tables in the database. |
| Append | Selected records are added to the end of an existing table. This action is similar to performing a copy and paste. |
| Update | A global change is made to the selected group of records based on an update expression. For example, you could increase the labor rate by 10 percent in one step. |
| Delete | The selected group of records is deleted from a table. |

**Figure 3.9** Query Type Group in Query Tools Design Tab

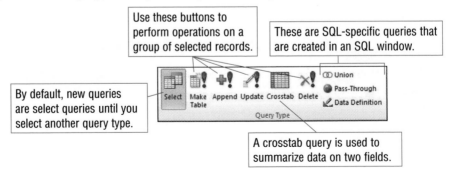

Use these buttons to perform operations on a group of selected records.

These are SQL-specific queries that are created in an SQL window.

By default, new queries are select queries until you select another query type.

A crosstab query is used to summarize data on two fields.

# Creating a New Table Using a Query

A *make-table query* creates a new table from selected records placed in the same database or in another database. This type of query is useful to create a history table prior to purging old records that are no longer required. The history table can be placed in the same database or in another database used as an archive copy. Once you have created a select query that will extract the records you want to copy to a new table, click the Make Table button in the Query Type group in the Query Tools Design tab to open the Make Table dialog box shown in Figure 3.10. Enter a table name, choose the destination database, and click OK.

**Once you have run a make-table query, do not double-click the query name in the Navigation pane since doing so instructs Access to run the query again. Open the query in Design view to make changes to the criteria and/or query type if you need to use the query again.**

Make Table

**Figure 3.10** Make Table Dialog Box

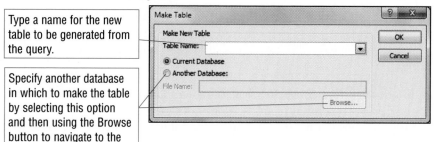

Type a name for the new table to be generated from the query.

Specify another database in which to make the table by selecting this option and then using the Browse button to navigate to the other database file name.

---

## Project 5a   Creating a New Table Using a Query

Part 1 of 4

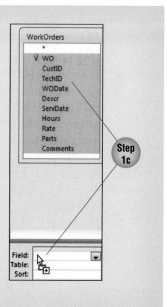

1. With the **AL2-C3-RSRCompServ.accdb** database open, create a select query to select work order records for September 1, 2012 to September 15, 2012 inclusive by completing the following steps:

   a. Create a new query in Design view. Add the WorkOrders table to the query window and then close the Show Table dialog box. Drag the bottom border of the table field list box until you can see all of the field names.

   b. Double-click the WorkOrders table field list box title bar. This selects all records within the table.

   c. Position the arrow pointer anywhere within the selected field names in the field list box and drag the pointer to the first column in the query design grid. All fields in the table are added to the query design grid.

   d. Click in the *Criteria* row in the *ServDate* column, type Between September 1, 2012 and September 15, 2012, and then press Enter.

e. Run the query. The query results datasheet displays seven records.

| Work Order | Customer ID | Technician ID | WO Date | Descripton |
|---|---|---|---|---|
| 65012 | 1000 | 11 | Fri Sep 07 2012 | Bi-annual computer maintenance |
| 65013 | 1000 | 10 | Fri Sep 07 2012 | Replace keyboard |
| 65014 | 1005 | 02 | Mon Sep 10 2012 | Replace power supply |
| 65015 | 1008 | 04 | Mon Sep 10 2012 | Restore operating system |
| 65016 | 1010 | 06 | Tue Sep 11 2012 | Install upgraded video card |
| 65017 | 1015 | 08 | Fri Sep 14 2012 | Replace DVD drive |
| 65018 | 1020 | 10 | Fri Sep 14 2012 | Upgrade Office suite |

records selected for make-table query at Step 1e

f. You decide you do not need to archive the *Comments* field data. Switch to Design view and then delete the *Comments* column from the query design grid.

2. Make a new table from the selected records and store the table in a history database used for archive purposes by completing the following steps:

a. If necessary, switch to Design view.

b. Click the Make Table button in the Query Type group in the Query Tools Design tab.

c. With the insertion point positioned in the *Table Name* text box, type Sept2012WorkOrders.

d. Click *Another Database* and then click the Browse button.

e. At the Make Table dialog box, navigate to the Access2010L2C3 folder on your storage medium and then double-click the file named *AL2-C3-RSRCompServHistory.accdb*.

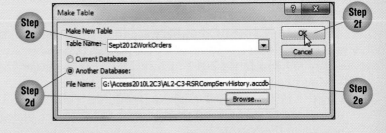

Step 2c

Step 2f

Step 2d

Step 2e

f. Click OK.

g. Click the Run button.

h. Click Yes at the Microsoft Access message box indicating you are about to paste seven rows to a new table.

3. Save the query. Type Sept2012MakeTable at the Save As dialog box and then press Enter or click OK.

4. Close the query.

5. Close the **AL2-C3-RSRCompServ.accdb** database.

6. Open the **AL2-C3-RSRCompServHistory.accdb** database and enable content. Click OK to continue if a message appears stating that Access has to update object dependencies.

7. Open the Sept2012WorkOrders table.

8. Review the records that were copied to the new table from the make-table query.

9. Close the table.

10. Close the **AL2-C3-RSRCompServHistory.accdb** database.

## Deleting a Group of Records Using a Query

A *delete query* is used to delete a group of records that meet specified criteria in one step. You can use this action query in any instance where the records to be deleted can be selected using a criteria statement. Using a query to remove the records is more efficient and reduces the chances of removing a record in error if deleting is done manually in the table.

The make-table query used in Project 5a created a duplicate copy of the records in the new table. The original records still exist in the WorkOrders table. The make-table query used to archive the records can be modified by changing the query type to a delete query and then using it to remove the records from the original table.

Action query names display with a black exclamation mark in the Navigation pane next to an icon that indicates the type of action that will be performed if the query is run.

### ▼ Quick Steps
**Create Delete Query**
1. Create query in Design view.
2. Add desired table to query.
3. Add desired fields to query design grid.
4. Enter criteria to select records.
5. Run query.
6. Switch to Design view.
7. Click Delete button.
8. Run the query.
9. Click Yes.
10. Save query.

Delete

---

**Project 5b** **Deleting Records Using a Query**                                          Part 2 of 4

1. Open the **AL2-C3-RSRCompServ.accdb** database and enable content.
2. Right-click the Sept2012MakeTable query and then click *Design View* at the shortcut menu.
3. Click the Delete button in the Query Type group in the Query Tools Design tab.
4. Click the File tab, click Save Object As, type Sept2012Delete at the Save As dialog box, and then press Enter or click OK.
5. Click the Query Tools Design tab and then run the query.
6. At the Microsoft Access message box indicating you are about to delete seven rows from the table and informing you the action cannot be reversed, click Yes to delete the selected records.
7. Close the query.
8. Open the WorkOrders table. Notice that no records exist with a *Service Date* before September 15, 2012.
9. Close the table.

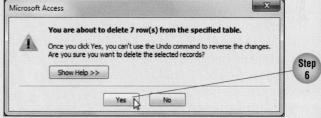

---

## Adding Records to a Table Using a Query

The *append query* is used to copy a group of records from one or more tables to the end of an existing table. Consider using an append query in any situation where you want to make a duplicate copy of records. For example, in Project 5a, the make table query was used to create a new table to store archive records. Once the table exists, you can use append queries to copy subsequent archive records to the end of the existing history table.

Append

**Create Append Query**
1. Create query in Design view.
2. Add desired table to query.
3. Add desired fields to query design grid.
4. Enter criteria to select records.
5. Run query.
6. Switch to Design view.
7. Click Append button.
8. Type table name.
9. Select destination database.
10. Click OK.
11. Run the query.
12. Click Yes.
13. Save query.

Clicking the Append button in the Query Type group in the Query Tools Design tab causes the Append dialog box to open with the same options as the Make Table dialog box, as shown in Figure 3.11.

The receiving table should have the same structure as the query from which the records are selected.

**Figure 3.11** Append Dialog Box

---

**Project 5c**    **Adding Records to a Table Using a Query**      Part 3 of 4

1. With the **AL2-C3-RSRCompServ.accdb** database open, open the Sept2012MakeTable query in Design view.
2. Modify the criteria to select work order records for the last half of September 2012 by completing the following steps:
   a. Expand the width of the *ServDate* column until you can see the entire criteria statement.
   b. Click the insertion point in the *Criteria* row in the *ServDate* column, insert and delete text as necessary to modify the criteria statement to read Between #9/16/2012# And #9/30/2012#, and then press Enter.

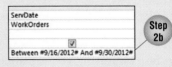

3. Click the Append button in the Query Type group in the Query Tools Design tab.
4. Since the query is being changed from a make-table query, Access inserts the same table name and database that was used to create the table in Project 5a. Click OK to accept the table name *Sept2012WorkOrders* and the *AL2-C3-RSRCompServHistory.accdb* database located in the Access2010L2C3 folder on your storage medium.

If you are appending to a table in the existing database, you can select the table name from the drop-down list.

5. Click the File tab, click Save Object As, type Sept2012Append at the Save As dialog box, and then press Enter or click OK.
6. Click the Query Tools Design tab and then run the query.
7. Click Yes at the Microsoft Access message box indicating you are about to append eight rows and the action cannot be undone.

8. Close the query.
9. Close the **AL2-C3-RSRCompServ.accdb** database.
10. Open the **AL2-C3-RSRCompServHistory.accdb** database.
11. Open the Sept2012WorkOrders table and print the datasheet in landscape orientation.
12. Close the table.
13. Close the **AL2-C3-RSRCompServHistory.accdb** database.

## Modifying Records Using an Update Query

When you need to make a change to a group of records that can be selected in a query and the change to be incorporated is the same for all records, you can instruct Access to modify the data using an update query. Making a global change using an update query is efficient and reduces the potential for errors that could occur from manual editing of multiple records.

Clicking the Update button in the Query Type group in the Query Tools Design tab causes an *Update To* row to appear in the query design grid. Click in the *Update To* box in the column to be modified and type the expression that will change the field values as needed. Run the query to make the global change.

Update

▼ **Quick Steps**

**Create Update Query**
1. Create query in Design view.
2. Add desired table to query.
3. Add desired fields to query design grid.
4. Enter criteria to select records.
5. Run query.
6. Switch to Design view.
7. Click Update button.
8. Click in *Update To* box in field to be changed.
9. Type update expression.
10. Run the query.
11. Click Yes.
12. Save query.

**Project 5d**  **Changing Service Plan Rates Using an Update Query**  Part 4 of 4

1. Open the **AL2-C3-RSRCompServ.accdb** database and enable content.
2. Open the table named FeesSCPlans and review the current values in the *Rate* column. For example, take note that the current rate for Plan A's six month term for one computer is $48.00. Close the table when you are finished reviewing the current rates.
3. Create an update query to increase Plan A service contract rates by 6% by completing the following steps:
   a. Create a new query in Design view.
   b. Add the table named FeesSCPlans to the query and then close the Show Table dialog box.
   c. Add the *Plan* and *Rate* fields to the query design grid.
   d. Click in the *Criteria* row in the *Plan* column, type **A**, and then click in the Criteria row in the next column in the query design grid. *Note: The AutoComplete feature will show a list of functions as soon as you type A. You can ignore the AutoComplete drop-down list since you are not entering a mathematical expression for the criteria; however, pressing Enter causes Access to add Abs to the Criteria row. Clicking in another box in the query design grid will remove the AutoComplete drop-down list.*

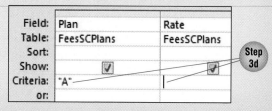

e. Run the query. Review the four records shown in the query results datasheet.
f. Switch to Design view.
g. Click the Update button in the Query Type group in the Query Tools Design tab. Access adds a row labeled *Update To* in the query design grid between the *Table* and *Criteria* rows.
h. Click in the *Update To* row in the *Rate* column, type [Rate]*1.06, and then press Enter.

4. Save the query. Type **RateUpdate** at the Save As dialog box and then press Enter or click OK.

5. Run the query. Click Yes at the Microsoft Access message that says you are about to update four rows.

6. Close the query.

7. Open the FeesSCPlans table. Notice the *Rate* values for Plan A records have increased. For example, the value in the Rate column for Plan A's six month term for one computer is now $50.88. Print the datasheet.

8. Close the table and then close the **AL2-C3-RSRCompServ.accdb** database.

| Query1 | |
|---|---|
| Plan | Rate |
| A | $48.00 |
| A | $59.50 |
| A | $159.50 |
| A | $281.00 |

Step 3e

| Field: | Plan | Rate |
|---|---|---|
| Table: | FeesSCPlans | FeesSCPlans |
| Update To: | | [Rate]*1.06 |
| Criteria: | "A" | |

Step 3h

Create a backup copy of the database before running an action query.

Exercise caution when running any action query since the queries perform changes in database tables. For example, in Project 5d, if you ran the update query a second time, the rates for the Plan A service plans would increase another six percent. Once changed, the rates cannot be undone. To reverse the update, you would need to create a mathematical expression in a new update query to remove six percent from the prices if you ran the query twice by mistake.

# Chapter Summary

- A filter can be saved as a query by displaying the filter criteria in a Filter By Form window, clicking the Advanced Filter Options button, and then clicking *Save as Query* at the drop-down list.

- Parameter queries prompt the user for the criteria by which to select records when the query is run.

- To create a parameter query, type a prompt message encased in square brackets in the *Criteria* row in the field you want to use to select records.

- Changing the join property can alter the number of records that are displayed in the query results datasheet.

- An inner join selects records only if a matching value is found in the joined field in both tables.

- A left outer join selects all records from the left table and matching records from the related table; empty fields display if no matching records exist in the related table.

- Click the Show Table button in the Query Setup group in the Query Tools Design tab to add a table or query to the query window.

- Remove a table from the query by clicking a field within the table's field list box and pressing the Delete key, or by right-clicking the table and clicking *Remove Table* at the shortcut menu.

- A right outer join selects all records from the right table and matching records from the primary table; empty fields display if no matching records exist in the primary table.

- A self-join query is created by adding two copies of the same table to the query window and joining the tables on a field containing matching field values.

- An alias is another name that you want to use to reference a table in a query.

- Right-click a table name in the query window, click *Properties* at the shortcut menu, and then enter the alias for the table in the *Alias* property box at the Property Sheet task pane.

- A query that contains two tables that are not joined creates a cross product or Cartesian product query, which means Access creates records for every possible combination from both tables, the results of which are generally not meaningful.

- A subquery is a query nested inside another query. Use subqueries to break down a complex query into manageable units. For example, a query with multiple calculations could be created by combining subqueries in which each calculation is built individually.

- Another reason for using subqueries is to have the ability to reuse a smaller query in many other queries, meaning you do not have to keep recreating the same structure.

- Create select queries on multiple-value fields using the same methods you would use for single-field criteria.

- Adding *.Value* to the end of a multiple-value field name in the *Field* box in the query design grid causes Access to place each field value in a separate row in the query results datasheet.

- A make-table query creates a new table in the active database or in another database with the structure defined in the query design grid and containing records selected by a criteria statement.

- Delete a group of records in one step by creating and running a delete query.

- Add a group of records to the bottom of an existing table in the active database or in another database using an append query.

- An update query allows you to make a global change to records by entering an expression such as a mathematical formula in the query design grid.

# Commands Review

| FEATURE | RIBBON TAB, GROUP | BUTTON |
|---|---|---|
| Advanced Filter Options | Home, Sort & Filter | |
| Append query | Query Tools Design, Query Type | |
| Create query in Design view | Create, Queries | |
| Delete query | Query Tools Design, Query Type | |
| Make table query | Query Tools Design, Query Type | |
| Run query | Query Tools Design, Results | |
| Show Table | Query Tools Design, Query Setup | |
| Update query | Query Tools Design, Query Type | |

# Concepts Check  Test Your Knowledge

**Completion:** In the space provided at the right, indicate the correct term, command, or number.

1. Click this button at a Filter By Form datasheet to save the filter's criteria as a query.

2. This is the name for a query which prompts the user to type the criteria in a dialog box when the query is run.

3. Double-clicking the black join line between tables in a query window opens this dialog box.

4. This join type displays all records from the related table and empty fields if no matching record exists in the primary table.

5. Click this button in the Query Setup group in the Query Tools Design tab to add a table to an existing query.

6. This is the term for a query in which two copies of the same table are added to the query window and joined by two fields in the same table that contain matching field values.

7. This is the term used to describe another name with which you reference a table in a query. _____

8. This is the term for a query in which two tables are used in the query window with no join established to connect one table to the other. _____

9. This term describes a query nested inside another query. _____

10. Add this entry to the end of a multiple-value field name in the *Field* box in the query design grid to display each field value in a separate row. _____

11. Queries that perform operations on selected records are referred to by this term. _____

12. Create this type of query to create a new table from existing records in the active database or in an archive database. _____

13. This query removes a group of records that meet specified criteria. _____

14. This query adds a group of records to the end of an existing table in the active database or in another database. _____

15. Create this type of query to increase the prices in all records by 10%. _____

# Skills Check  Assess Your Performance

## Assessment

### 1  EXTRACT RECORDS USING A FILTER AND PROMPTED QUERIES

1. Open the database named **AL2-C3-VantageVideos.accdb** and enable content.
2. Open the table named WebCustomers.
3. Using the Filter By Form feature, display only those customers who reside in Burlington with a ZIP code that begins with 05401. **Hint: Type** 05401* **in the ZIP field to specify only the first five characters in the ZIP code. The asterisk is a wildcard that allows you to filter by specifying only a portion of the field value**.
4. Save the filter as a query named *CustBurlington05401*.
5. Close the Filter By Form datasheet and close the table. Click No when prompted to save changes to the table design.
6. Open the CustBurlington05401 query.
7. Print the query results datasheet in landscape orientation and then close the query.

8. Create a new query in Design view using the following specifications:
   a. Add the tables WebOrderDetails, WebOrders, and WebProducts to the query.
   b. Add the fields *WebOrderID*, *DateOrd*, *Qty*, and *Product* to the query design grid. ***Note: Add*** **WebOrderID** ***from the WebOrders table***.
   c. Create a parameter query to prompt the user to type the title of the video in the *Product* column. You determine the message that should display in the Enter Parameter Value dialog box.
   d. Save the query, name it *PromptedVideo*, and then close the query.
9. Run the PromptedVideo query. Type The Longest Day at the Enter Parameter Value dialog box. Print the query results datasheet and then close the query.
10. Open the PromptedVideo query in Design view. Delete the prompt message in the *Product* column. Create a parameter query to prompt the user to type a beginning and ending date to view Web orders in the *DateOrd* column. Use Save As to name the revised query *PromptedOrderDates* and then close the query.
11. Run the PromptedOrderDates query. Type February 1, 2012 as the beginning date and February 29, 2012 as the ending date. Print the query results datasheet and then close the query.

## Assessment

### 2 MODIFY JOIN PROPERTIES

1. With the **AL2-C3-VantageVideos.accdb** database open, create a new query in Design view using the following specifications:
   a. Add the tables WebCustomers and WebOrders to the query.
   b. Add the fields *CustID*, *FirstName*, *LastName*, and *WebOrderID* to the query design grid.
   c. Modify the join type between the WebCustomers table and the WebOrders table to a left outer join.
   d. Save the query and name it *CustWebOrders*.
2. Run the query. Print the query results datasheet and then close the query.
3. Create a new query in Design view using the following specifications:
   a. Add the tables WebOrderDetails and WebProducts to the query.
   b. Add the fields *WebOrdID*, *WebProdID*, and *Product* to the query design grid. ***Note: Add*** **WebProdID** ***from the WebProducts table***.
   c. Modify the join type between the WebProducts table and the WebOrderDetails table to a left outer join.
   d. Save the query and name it *WebProductOrders*.
4. Run the query. Print the query results datasheet and then close the query.

## Assessment

### 3 ADD A TABLE TO A QUERY AND CREATE AND USE A SUBQUERY TO PERFORM CALCULATIONS

1. With the **AL2-C3-VantageVideos.accdb** database open, open the CustWebOrders query in Design view and modify the query as follows:
   a. Modify the join type between the WebCustomers table and the WebOrders table to an inner join.
   b. Add the WebOrderDetails table and the WebProducts table to the query.

c. Add the fields named *DateOrd*, *Qty*, *Product*, and *SellPrice* to the query design grid.

d. Delete the *CustID* field from the query.

e. Create a calculated field with the column label *Total Sale* that multiplies the quantity ordered times the selling price. Format the calculated column to *Currency*.

f. Use Save As to name the revised query *WebSalesWithTotal*.

2. Run the query. Print the query results datasheet in landscape orientation with a left and right margin set to 0.5 inch and then close the query.

3. Create a new query in Design view that calculates the total sale with tax as follows:

a. Nest the WebSalesWithTotal query in the new query.

b. Add the fields *WebOrdID*, *DateOrd*, and *Total Sale* to the query design grid.

c. Create a calculated field with the column label *Tax* that multiples the value in the *Total Sale* column times .06 (decimal equivalent of 6%). Format the calculated column to *Standard*.

d. Create a second calculated column with the column label *Total Sale with Tax* that adds the *Total Sale* column to the *Tax* column.

e. Save the query and name it *WebSalesWithTotalAndTax*.

4. Run the query. Double-click the right column boundary for the last column in the query results datasheet to display the entire field heading and then print the query results datasheet. Close the query saving changes.

## Assessment

## 4    USE ACTION QUERIES TO ARCHIVE RECORDS AND UPDATE SELLING PRICES

1. With the **AL2-C3-VantageVideos.accdb** database open, open the WebSalesWithTotal query in Design view and modify the query as follows:

a. Delete the *SellPrice* and *Total Sale* columns from the query design grid.

b. Add a criterion to select the records for sales during the month of February 2012.

c. Run the query to make sure the correct records are being selected.

d. Change the query to a make-table query, name the new table *Feb2012WebSales*, and store the table in the database named **AL2-C3-VantageVideosArchive.accdb** on your storage medium.

e. Use Save As to name the revised query *Feb2012SalesMakeTable*.

f. Run the query.

2. Close the query and then close the **AL2-C3-VantageVideos.accdb** database.

3. Open the **AL2-C3-VantageVideosArchive.accdb** and then open the Feb2012WebSales table.

4. Adjust column widths as necessary and then print the datasheet. Close the table saving changes to the layout and then close the **AL2-C3-VantageVideosArchive.accdb** database.

5. Open the **AL2-C3-VantageVideos.accdb** database and enable content if necessary.

6. Open the Feb2012SalesMakeTable query in Design view and modify the query as follows:

a. Change the query to a delete query.

b. Remove the WebCustomers, WebOrderDetails, and WebProducts tables from the query.

c. Use Save As to name the revised query *Feb2012SalesDelete*.

d. Run the query and then close the query window.

7. Open the WebSalesWithTotal query. Print the query results datasheet in landscape orientation with left and right margins of 0.5 inch and then close the query.
8. Create a new query in Design view to update the selling prices of all videos as follows:
   a. Add the WebProducts table to the query.
   b. Add the *SellPrice* field to the query design grid.
   c. Change the query to an update query and add a formula that will add $1.05 to the selling price of all videos.
   d. Save the query and name it *PriceUpdate*.
   e. Run the query and then close the query window.
9. Open the WebProducts table. Print the datasheet and then close the table.
10. Close the **AL2-C3-VantageVideos.accdb** database.

# Visual Benchmark Demonstrate Your Proficiency

## CALCULATE DAYS BOARDED AND AMOUNT DUE USING NESTED QUERIES

1. Open **AL2-C3-PawsParadise.accdb**.
2. Review the query results datasheet shown in Figure 3.12. This query is the result of nesting a query within a query. Create the calculations as follows:
   a. Create the first query to calculate the number of days a dog is boarded in the kennel. Show in the query results the reservation ID, the customer's name, the dog's name, and the two date fields. Calculate the days the dog was boarded. Save the query and name it *DaysBoarded*.
   b. Nest DaysBoarded in a new query. Add the Dogs and the KennelCategories tables to the query. Join the DaysBoarded query to the Dogs table on the common *DogName* field. Add the fields to the query design grid as shown in Figure 3.12 and then calculate the amount due for each reservation.
   c. Sort and format the query results as shown in Figure 3.12. The font used is Cambria 11-point. The alternate row color used is Maroon 1 in the *Standard Colors* section of the color palette. ***Note: The first row is not formatted differently from the remainder of the datasheet; the row displays with a different row color because the first row is selected.*** Save the query and name it ReservationTotals.
3. Print the ReservationTotals query results datasheet in landscape orientation with left and right margins set to 0.5 inch.
4. Close the query.
5. Close the **AL2-C3-PawsParadise.accdb** database.

**Figure 3.12** Visual Benchmark

| Reservation | First Name | Last Name | Dog's Name | Date Out | Days Boarded | Kennel Type | Daily Rate | Amount Due |
|---|---|---|---|---|---|---|---|---|
| 1 | Shawn | Jenkins | Abby | 11/12/2012 | 3 | V.I.P. Suite | $38.50 | $115.50 |
| 2 | Shawn | Jenkins | Winnie | 11/12/2012 | 3 | V.I.P. Suite | $38.50 | $115.50 |
| 3 | Sean | Gallagher | Tank | 11/13/2012 | 3 | V.I.P. Suite | $38.50 | $115.50 |
| 4 | Sofia | Ramos | Apollo | 11/18/2012 | 7 | Indoor/Outdoor Suite | $25.50 | $178.50 |
| 5 | Sofia | Ramos | Murphy | 11/18/2012 | 7 | Indoor/Outdoor Suite | $25.50 | $178.50 |
| 6 | Dina | Lombardi | Niko | 11/16/2012 | 4 | Indoor/Outdoor Suite | $25.50 | $102.00 |
| 7 | Natale | Rizzo | Dallas | 11/14/2012 | 2 | Indoor/Outdoor Suite | $25.50 | $51.00 |
| 8 | James | Chung | Lassie | 11/13/2012 | 1 | Deluxe Suite | $29.50 | $29.50 |
| 9 | Bernard | Jedicke | Kosmo | 11/13/2012 | 1 | Day Care Boarding | $16.50 | $16.50 |
| 10 | Bernard | Jedicke | Sierra | 11/13/2012 | 1 | Day Care Boarding | $16.50 | $16.50 |
| 11 | Bernard | Jedicke | Emma | 11/13/2012 | 1 | Day Care Boarding | $16.50 | $16.50 |
| 12 | Carlotta | Sanchez | Scrappy | 11/19/2012 | 6 | Deluxe Suite | $29.50 | $177.00 |
| 13 | Michael | Mancini | Harley | 11/23/2012 | 10 | Indoor/Outdoor Suite | $25.50 | $255.00 |
| 14 | Glen | Waters | Barney | 11/29/2012 | 15 | Indoor/Outdoor Suite | $25.50 | $382.50 |
| 15 | Lenora | Diaz | Zack | 11/17/2012 | 3 | Indoor/Outdoor Suite | $25.50 | $76.50 |
| 16 | Maeve | Murphy | King | 11/19/2012 | 4 | V.I.P. Suite | $38.50 | $154.00 |
| 17 | Valerie | McTague | Chloe | 11/19/2012 | 3 | Deluxe Suite | $29.50 | $88.50 |
| 18 | Nadia | Costa | Bailey | 11/24/2012 | 7 | Deluxe Suite | $29.50 | $206.50 |
| 19 | Juan | Torres | Taffy | 11/21/2012 | 4 | V.I.P. Suite | $38.50 | $154.00 |
| 20 | Liam | Doherty | Zeus | 11/23/2012 | 5 | V.I.P. Suite | $38.50 | $192.50 |
| 21 | Dillon | Farrell | Chico | 11/22/2012 | 4 | Indoor/Outdoor Suite | $25.50 | $102.00 |
| 22 | Diane | Ye | Elvis | 11/25/2012 | 5 | Indoor/Outdoor Suite | $25.50 | $127.50 |
| 23 | Lorenzo | Rivera | Fifi | 11/27/2012 | 5 | V.I.P. Suite | $38.50 | $192.50 |
| 24 | Lorenzo | Rivera | Lucky | 11/27/2012 | 5 | Indoor/Outdoor Suite | $25.50 | $127.50 |
| 25 | Bernard | Jedicke | Kosmo | 11/27/2012 | 1 | Day Care Boarding | $16.50 | $16.50 |
| 26 | Bernard | Jedicke | Sierra | 11/27/2012 | 1 | Day Care Boarding | $16.50 | $16.50 |
| 27 | Bernard | Jedicke | Emma | 11/27/2012 | 1 | Day Care Boarding | $16.50 | $16.50 |

# Case Study  Apply Your Skills

**Part 1**

You are continuing your work as an intern at Hillsdale Realty. The office manager has requested a series of printouts with information from the database. Open the database named **AL2-C3-HillsdaleRealty.accdb** and enable content. Design, create, save, run, and print query results to provide the required information. You determine appropriate descriptive names for each query.

- A list of sales by agent that includes the date of sale, address, sale price, and commission rate. Sort the query results by the agent's last name and then by the date of sale with both fields sorted in ascending order.

- Modify the first query to allow the office manager to type the agent's name when she runs the query so that she can view individual sales reports by agent. To test your query, run the query using the agent name *Cecilia Ortega*. Save the revised query using a new name.

- A list that shows all of the agents and each agent's clients. Show the client ID, client first name, and client last name next to each agent's name. The manager wants to see which agents have not yet signed a client so you need to make sure the query results show all agents.

- A list of agents that shows his or her co-broker agent. The Agents table contains a field named *CoBroker*. This field is the agent ID for the person assigned to co-broker listings. The office manager has requested a list that shows the agent's last name instead of his or her ID number in the *CoBroker* field. Sort the list in ascending order by AgentLName. ***Hint: Create a self-join query and remember to use the alias and caption properties to rename the table and the column that will display the co-broker agent last name.***

- Modify the first query to add a column to calculate the amount of commission that will be owed on the sale by multiplying the sale price times the commission rate. Save the revised query using a new name.

- Use a query to update all commission quota values to add 15% to the existing quotas. After updating the values, create a new query to show each agent and his or her respective commission quota. Sort the list in ascending order by agent last name.

**Part 2**

**Help**

The office manager would like to see the five highest sale prices to date. Research in Help how to create a top values query. Using the information you learned in Help, modify the first query created in Part 1 to produce the top 5 list. Save the revised query using a new name and print the query results. ***Hint: Remove the sorting from the original query and then sort by the sale prices in descending order before converting the query to a top 5 values query.***

**Part 3**

The office manager would like to review the client preferences for each listing with each preference on a separate line. Include in the list the date of the listing, the street address, the client's name, and the client's telephone number. Add criteria to select only those records where the client has requested a pre-sale inspection or a staging service for his or her listing. Save and print the query.

# Access

# Creating and Using Custom Forms

## PERFORMANCE OBJECTIVES

**Upon successful completion of Chapter 4, you will be able to:**

- **Create a custom form in Design view using all three form sections**
- **Add fields individually and as a group**
- **Move, size, and format control objects**
- **Change the tab order of fields**
- **Create tabbed pages in a form and insert a subform on each page**
- **Add and format a calculation to a custom form**
- **Group and ungroup multiple controls**
- **Adjust the alignment and spacing of controls**
- **Add graphics to a form**
- **Anchor a control to a position in the form**
- **Create a datasheet form**
- **Modify form properties to restrict actions allowed in records**
- **Create a blank form**
- **Add list boxes to a form**
- **Sort records in a form and locate a record using a wildcard character**

**Tutorials**

4.1 Creating Custom Forms Using Design View

4.2 Binding a Table to a Form and Adding Fields

4.3 Moving, Resizing, and Formatting Control Objects

4.4 Changing the Tab Order of Fields

4.5 Adding a Tab Control and a Subform

4.6 Adding Subforms and a New Page to the Tab Control

4.7 Adding Calculations to a Form in Design View

4.8 Grouping, Aligning, and Spacing Controls

4.9 Creating a Datasheet Form and Modifying Form Properties

4.10 Sorting and Finding Records in a Form

Forms provide an interface for data entry and maintenance that allows end users to work with data stored in the underlying tables more efficiently. For example, forms can be designed using a layout that uses the screen space more effectively than the tabular layout of a datasheet. Forms can include fields from multiple tables allowing data to be entered in one object that updates several tables. Generally, database designers provide forms for end users to use to perform data maintenance and restrict access to tables to protect the structure and integrity of the database. In this chapter you will learn how to build custom forms. Model answers for this chapter's projects appear on the following page.

*Note: Before beginning the projects, copy to your storage medium the Access2010L2C4 subfolder from the Access2010L2 folder on the CD that accompanies this textbook and then make Access2010L2C4 the active folder.*

Access2010L2C4

103

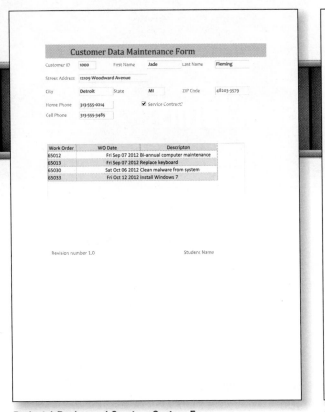

**Project 1 Design and Create a Custom Form**

Customer Data Maintenance Form

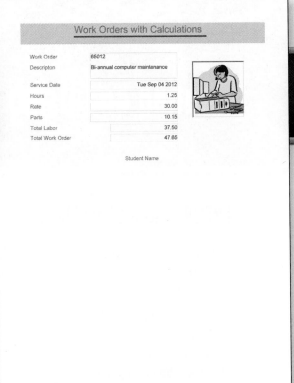

**Project 2 Create a Form with Calculations and Graphics**

Work Orders with Calculations Form

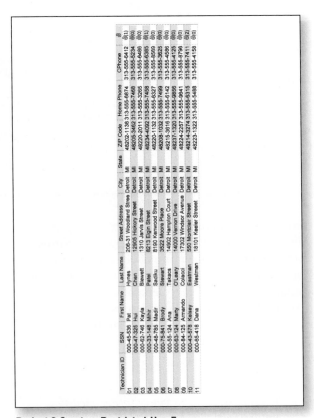

**Project 3 Create a Restricted-Use Form**

Technicians Form

**Project 4 Create a Blank Form with Lists**

SCPlans Form

You will create a custom form in Design view that includes subforms in tabbed pages to provide a single object in which data stored in four tables can be entered, viewed, and printed.

# Creating Custom Forms Using Design View ▪▪▪▪▪▪▪▪

Access provides several tools with which you can create forms such as the Form tool, the Split Form tool, and the Form Wizard. These features allow you to build a form quickly. A form generated using one of these tools can be modified in Layout view or Design view to customize the content, format, or layout. If you require a form with several custom options, you can begin in Design view and build the form from scratch. Click the Create tab and click the Form Design button in the Forms group to begin a new form using the Design view window shown in Figure 4.1.

**▼ Quick Steps**

**Start New Form in Design View**
1. Click Create tab.
2. Click Form Design button.

Form Design

**Figure 4.1** Form Design View

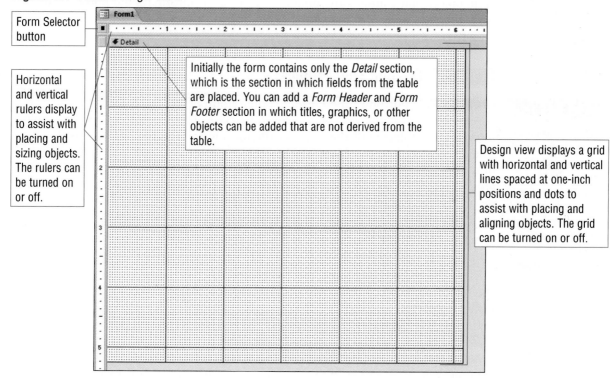

Form Selector button

Horizontal and vertical rulers display to assist with placing and sizing objects. The rulers can be turned on or off.

Initially the form contains only the *Detail* section, which is the section in which fields from the table are placed. You can add a *Form Header* and *Form Footer* section in which titles, graphics, or other objects can be added that are not derived from the table.

Design view displays a grid with horizontal and vertical lines spaced at one-inch positions and dots to assist with placing and aligning objects. The grid can be turned on or off.

**Figure 4.2** Controls, Header/Footer, and Tools Groups in Form Design Tools Design Tab

The form displays the *Detail* section, which is used to display fields from the table associated with the form. Objects are added to the form using buttons in the Controls, Header/Footer, and Tools groups in the Form Design Tools Design tab shown in Figure 4.2.

▼ **Quick Steps**

**Add Form Title**
1. Open form in Design view.
2. Click Title button.
3. Type title text.
4. Press Enter.

**Add Label Object**
1. Open form in Design view.
2. Click Label button.
3. Drag to create object the desired height and width.
4. Type label text.
5. Press Enter.

## Bound, Unbound, and Calculated Control Objects

As you begin to build a custom form, understanding the three types of objects that can be created in a form is important. A form is comprised of a series of control objects. A ***control object*** in a form is bound, unbound, or calculated. ***Bound objects*** draw data displayed in the control from the field in the table to which the control is associated. In other words, the content that is displayed in the control object in Form view is drawn from a field in a record in a table. ***Unbound objects*** are used to display text or graphics and do not rely on the table for their content. For example, an object that contains a clip art image to enhance the visual appearance or an object that contains the hours of business for informational purposes are both unbound objects. A ***calculated object*** displays the result of a mathematical formula.

## Creating Titles and Label Objects

Click the Title button in the Header/Footer group of the Form Design Tools Design tab to display the *Form Header* and *Form Footer* sections and automatically insert a label object with the name of the form inside the *Form Header* section. The text inside the title object is selected in order to type new text, delete, or otherwise modify the default title text. Click the Label button in the Controls group to draw a label control object within any section in the form and type descriptive or explanatory text inside the object.

Once a title or label control object has been created, the text can be formatted using buttons in the Font group in the Form Design Tools Format tab. You can also move and resize the control object to reposition it on the form.

The *Form Header* section is used to create objects that you want to display at the top of the form while scrolling records in Form view and is printed at the top of the page when a record or group of records is printed from Form view. Titles and company logos are generally placed in the *Form Header* section. The *Form Footer* section is used to create objects that you want to display at the bottom of the form while scrolling records in Form view and is printed at the end of a printout when a record or group of records is printed from Form view. Consider adding a creation date and/or revision number in the *Form Footer* section.

**HINT**

Before starting a new custom form in Design view it is a good idea to draw a sketch on a piece of paper that indicates the rough layout of the form. This will help you place the fields and determine other objects you need to create.

Label

Title

1. Open **AL2-C4-RSRCompServ.accdb** and enable content.
2. Click the Create tab and then click the Form Design button in the Forms group.

3. Add a title in the *Form Header* section of the form and center the text within the object by completing the following steps:
    a. With the Form Design Tools Design tab active, click the Title button in the Header/Footer group. Access displays the *Form Header* section above the *Detail* section and places a title object with the text *Form1* selected.

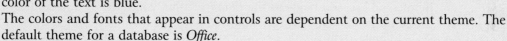

    b. Type Customer Data Maintenance Form. Notice the background behind the title object is shaded blue and the color of the text is blue.
    The colors and fonts that appear in controls are dependent on the current theme. The default theme for a database is *Office*.
    c. Press the Enter key.
    d. With the title object selected as indicated by the orange border around the title text, click the Form Design Tools Format tab and then click the Center button in the Font group.

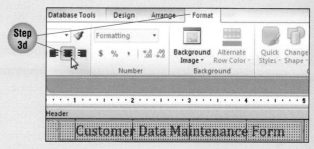

4. Scroll down the form until you can see the *Form Footer* section.
5. Position the mouse pointer at the bottom border of the form's grid until the pointer changes to a horizontal line with an up- and down-pointing arrow and then drag the bottom of the form down to the 0.5-inch position in the vertical ruler.

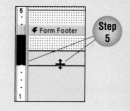

6. Add a label control object at the left edge of the form footer that contains a revision number and another label control object at the right edge of the form footer that contains your name by completing the following steps:
    a. Click the Form Design Tools Design tab and then click the Label button in the Controls group.
    b. Position the crosshairs with the label icon attached at the left side of the *Form Footer* section and drag to draw a label control object the approximate height and width shown. When you release the mouse, an insertion point appears inside the label control object.

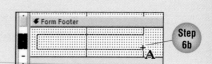

    c. Type Revision number 1.0 and press Enter.

d. Create another label control object at the right side of the *Form Footer* section similar in height and width to the one shown, type your first and last names inside the label control object, and press Enter. If necessary, refer to Steps 6a through 6c if you need help with this step.

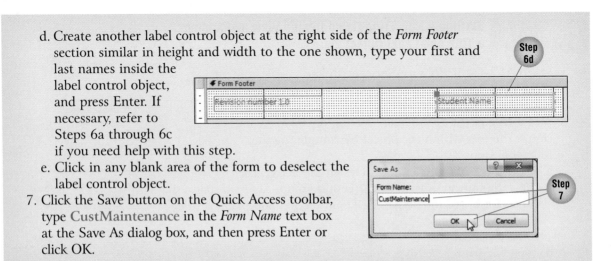

e. Click in any blank area of the form to deselect the label control object.

7. Click the Save button on the Quick Access toolbar, type CustMaintenance in the *Form Name* text box at the Save As dialog box, and then press Enter or click OK.

**Quick Steps**

**Connect Table to Form**
1. Open form in Design view.
2. Double-click Form Selector button.
3. Click Data tab in Property Sheet.
4. Click down-pointing arrow in *Record Source* property box.
5. Click desired table.
6. Close Property Sheet.

**Add Fields to Form**
1. Click Add Existing Fields button.
2. Drag field name from Field List pane to desired location in *Detail* section.
OR
1. Click first field name in Field List pane.
2. Hold down Shift key.
3. Click last field name in Field List pane.
4. Drag selected fields from Field List pane to desired location in *Detail* section.

Form Selector

Add Existing Fields

## Adding Fields to a Form

Before you can add fields to the *Detail* section, you need to first connect a table to the form. The table to be connected with the form is specified in the Record Source property in the Data tab of the Form Property Sheet. Double-click the Form Selector button located above the vertical ruler and left of the horizontal ruler to open the form's Property Sheet at the right side of the work area. Click the Data tab, click the down-pointing arrow in the *Record Source* property box, click the desired table at the drop-down list, and then close the Property Sheet.

Click the Add Existing Fields button in the Tools group in the Form Design Tools Design tab to open the Field List pane. Select and drag a group of field names or an individual field name from the Field List pane to the *Detail* section of the form. Release the pointer in the *Detail* section near the location at which you want to display the data. For each field added to the form, two control objects are inserted. A label control object containing the field name or Caption property text is placed at the left of where you release the mouse pointer, and a text box control object that is bound to the field is placed at the right of where you release the mouse. The text box control object is the object that displays table data from the record in Form view. Figure 4.3 displays the fields from the Customers table that you will add to the CustMaintenance form in Project 1b.

**Figure 4.3** Fields from Customer Table Added to Form in Project 1b

1. With the **AL2-C4-RSRCompServ.accdb** database open and the CustMaintenance form open in Design view, scroll up to the top of the form in the work area.
2. Connect the Customers table to the form by completing the following steps:
   a. Double-click the Form Selector button (displays as a black or blue square) located at the top of the vertical ruler and left of the horizontal ruler to open the form's Property Sheet.
   b. Click the Data tab in the Property Sheet.
   c. Click the down-pointing arrow in the *Record Source* property box and then click *Customers* at the drop-down list.
   d. Close the Property Sheet.

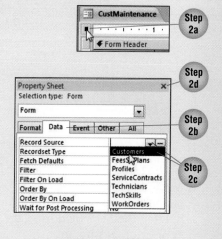

3. Add fields individually from the Customers table to the *Detail* section of the form by completing the following steps:
   a. Click the Add Existing Fields button in the Tools group in the Form Design Tools Design tab. The Field List pane opens at the right side of the work area.
   b. Position the mouse pointer at the right border of the form's grid until the pointer changes to a vertical line with a left- and right-pointing arrow and then drag the right edge of the form to the 6.5-inch position in the horizontal ruler.

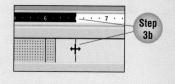

   c. If necessary, click *CustID* in the Field List pane to select the field and then drag the field name to the *Detail* section, releasing the mouse with the pointer near the top of the section at the 1-inch position in the horizontal ruler.

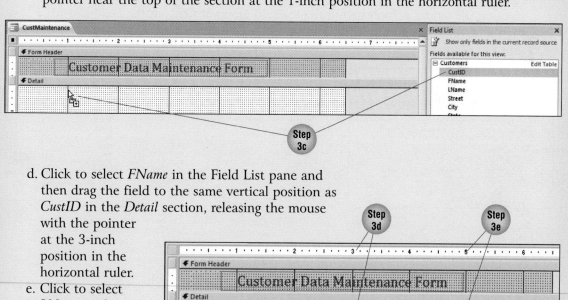

   d. Click to select *FName* in the Field List pane and then drag the field to the same vertical position as *CustID* in the *Detail* section, releasing the mouse with the pointer at the 3-inch position in the horizontal ruler.
   e. Click to select *LName* in the Field List pane and then drag the field to the same vertical position as *CustID* in the *Detail* section, releasing the mouse with the pointer at the 5-inch position in the horizontal ruler.

f. Drag the *Street* field from the Field List pane to the *Detail* section below *CustID*, releasing the mouse at the 1-inch position in the horizontal ruler and approximately 3 rows of grid dots below *CustID*.

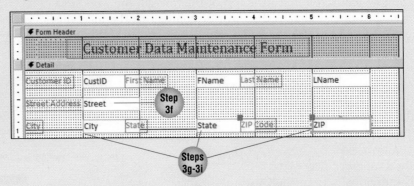

g. Drag the *City* field from the Field List pane to the *Detail* section below *Street*, releasing the mouse at approximately the 1-inch position in the horizontal ruler and approximately 3 rows of grid dots below *Street*.

h. Drag the *State* field from the Field List pane to the *Detail* section at the same horizontal position as *City*, releasing the mouse at the 3-inch position in the horizontal ruler.

i. Drag the *ZIP* field from the Field List pane to the *Detail* section at the same horizontal position as *City*, releasing the mouse at the 5-inch position in the horizontal ruler.

4. Add a group of fields from the Customers table to the *Detail* section of the form by completing the following steps:

a. Click the *HPhone* field name in the Field List pane.

b. Hold down the Shift key and click the *ServCont* field name in the Field List pane. Access selects all fields from the first field name clicked to the last field name clicked when the Shift key is used.

c. Position the mouse pointer within the selected group of fields in the Field List pane and then drag the group to the *Detail* section below *City*, releasing the mouse at the 1-inch position in the horizontal ruler approximately 3 rows of grid dots below *City*.

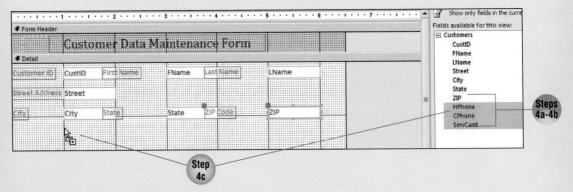

5. Click in any blank area to deselect the group of fields.
6. Compare your form with the one shown in Figure 4.3 on page 108.
7. Click the Save button on the Quick Access toolbar.
8. Close the Field List pane.

# Moving and Resizing Control Objects

Once fields are placed on the form, move or resize objects to change the layout. In Project 1b, you saw that Access places two control objects for each field on the form. A label control object, which contains the caption or field name, is placed left of a text box control object, which displays the field value from the record or a blank entry box when adding a new record. Click the label control object or the text box control object for the field you want to move or resize to display an orange border with eight handles. Access displays a large dark gray square (called the move handle) at the top left of the selected field's label control object or text box control object.

Point to the orange border of the selected control object until the pointer displays with the four-headed arrow move icon and then drag the field to the new position on the form. Access moves the connected label control or text box control along with the object you drag to the new location. If you want to move a selected label control or text box control independently from its connected object, point to the large dark gray handle at the top left of the selected control and drag using the move handle to the new position as described in Figure 4.4.

To resize a selected control object, point to one of the sizing handles (small orange squares) in the border of the selected object until the pointer displays with an up- and down-pointing arrow, a left- and right-pointing arrow, or a two-headed diagonal arrow to resize the height and/or width.

By default, the Snap to Grid feature is turned on in Design view. This feature pulls a control to the nearest grid point when moving or resizing objects. If you want to move or resize an object very precisely in small increments, you may want to turn the feature off. To do this, click the Form Design Tools Arrange tab, click the Size/Space button in the Sizing & Ordering group, and then click *Snap to Grid* at the drop-down list. Snap to Grid is a toggle feature which is turned on or off by clicking the button.

▼ **Quick Steps**

**Move Objects in Design View**
1. Select control object.
2. Drag using orange border or move handle to desired location.

**Resize Objects in Design View**
1. Select control object.
2. Drag middle top, bottom, left, or right sizing handle to resize the height or width.
OR
1. Select control object.
2. Drag corner sizing handle to resize the height and width at the same time.

**H I N T**

Do not be overly concerned with exact placement and alignment as you initially add fields to the form. You will learn how to use alignment and spacing tools in the Form Design Tools Arrange tab to assist with layout.

Size/Space

**Figure 4.4** Moving a Control Object in Design View

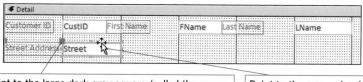

Point to the large dark gray square (called the move handle) at the top left of the selected control object to move the selected *Street* text box control object independently of the *Street Address* label control object.

Point to the orange border and drag the object to the desired location when you see this icon. The label control object containing the caption *Street Address* will move as well as the selected *Street* text box control object.

# Formatting Controls

**Format Controls Using Selection Rectangle**
1. In Design view, position pointer above top left control to be formatted.
2. Drag down and right to draw a rectangle around controls.
3. Release mouse.
4. Click desired formatting options.
5. Deselect controls.

**Format Multiple Controls Using Shift**
1. In Design view, click to select first control object.
2. Shift + click remaining control objects.
3. Click desired formatting options.
4. Deselect controls.

Use the buttons in the Font group in the Form Design Tools Format tab to change the font, font size, font color, background color, alignment, or apply bold, italic, or underline formatting to the selected control object. Use the Conditional Formatting button in the Control Formatting group to apply conditional formatting to the selected object.

Multiple control objects can be formatted at the same time by holding down the Shift key while clicking individual controls. You can also use the mouse pointer to draw a selection rectangle around a group of controls to select multiple objects inside the rectangle.

Apply a Theme to the form at the Form Design Tools Design tab. The Theme controls the default colors and fonts for objects on the form.

Themes

Form View

Design View

---

**Project 1c**   **Moving and Resizing Controls**                     Part 3 of 7

1. With the **AL2-C4-RSRCompServ.accdb** database open and the CustMaintenance form open in Design view, preview the form to determine the controls that need to be moved or resized by clicking the View button in the Views group of the Form Design Tools Design tab. (Do not click the down-pointing arrow on the button.)
2. The form is displayed in Form view with data from the first record displayed in the text box control objects. Notice that some label control objects are overlapping text box control objects and that the street address in the first record is not entirely displayed.
3. Click the Design View button located at the right end of the Status bar (last button in View buttons group).
4. Move the controls for those objects that are overlapping other objects by completing the following steps:
    a. Click the *First Name* label control object.
    b. Point to the large dark gray square (move handle) at the top left of the selected label control object until the pointer displays with the four-headed arrow attached and then drag right to the 2-inch position in the horizontal ruler. Notice the connected *FName* text box control object does not move because you are dragging using the move handle.

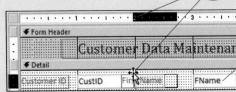

Step 4b

Connected *FName* text box control does not move when you drag using the move handle.

c. Click the *Last Name* label control object and then drag right using the move handle to the 4-inch position in the horizontal ruler.

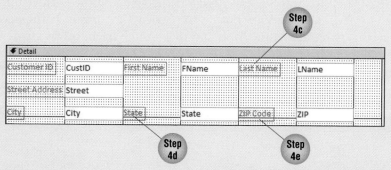

d. Move the *State* label control object right to the 2-inch position in the horizontal ruler.

e. Move the *ZIP Code* label control object right to the 4-inch position in the horizontal ruler.

f. Click in any blank area to deselect the *ZIP Code* label control.

5. Click the *Street* text box control object. Drag the right middle sizing handle to the right to the 3-inch position in the horizontal ruler.

6. Click the *State* text box control object and then drag the right middle sizing handle to the left to the 3.5-inch position in the horizontal ruler. (Since the *State* field displays only two characters, this control object can be resized smaller.)

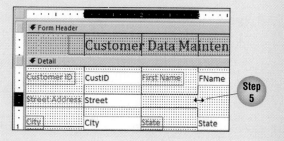

7. Resize the *CustID* text box control so that the right edge of the control is at the 1.5-inch position in the horizontal ruler.

8. Click the *Service Contract?* label control object. Point to any side of the selected object's orange border (not on a sizing handle) and then drag the object until the left edge is at the 3-inch position in the horizontal ruler adjacent to the *HPhone* field. Notice that both the label control object and the text box control object moved since you dragged the border (not the move handle).

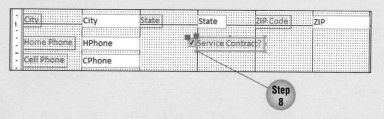

9. Deselect the *Service Contract?* control object.
10. Save the form.

1. With the **AL2-C4-RSRCompServ.accdb** database open and the CustMaintenance form open in Design view, click the View button to preview the form in Form view.
2. Scroll through a few records in the form and then switch back to Design view.
3. Format multiple controls using a selection rectangle by completing the following steps:
   a. Position the arrow pointer at the top left corner in the *Detail* section above the *Customer ID* label control object and then drag down and right until you have drawn a rectangle around all of the controls in the section as shown below and then release the mouse.

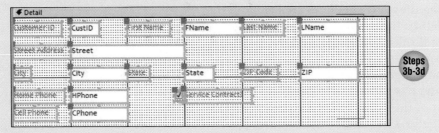

   b. Notice all objects contained within the rectangle are selected.
   c. Use the Font button in the Font group in the Form Design Tools Format tab to change the font to Candara.
   d. Use the Font Size button to change the font size to 10.

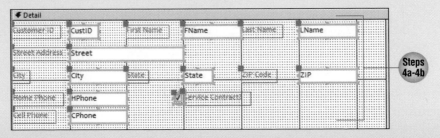

   e. Click in any blank area to deselect the controls.
4. Format by selecting multiple controls using the Shift key by completing the following steps:
   a. Click the *CustID* text box control object.
   b. Hold down the Shift key and click each of the other text box control objects in the *Detail* section.

c. Click the down-pointing arrow on the Font Color button and then click *Dark Red* at the color palette (first option in last row).

d. Click the Bold button.

5. Click in any blank area to deselect the controls.

6. Click the Form Design Tools Design tab and then switch to Form view to view the formatting changes applied to the form.

7. Switch to Design view and then save the form.

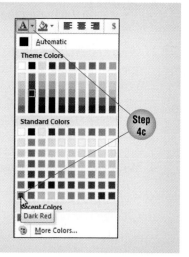

Step 4c

## Changing the Tab Order of Fields

Tab order refers to the order in which fields are selected when you press the Tab key while entering data in Form view. You do not have to enter data into a record in the order in which the fields are presented. Click the Tab Order button in the Tools group of the Form Design Tools Design tab to open the Tab Order dialog box shown in Figure 4.5.

Position the pointer in the gray field selector bar next to the field name that you want to move until the pointer displays as a right-pointing black arrow and click to select the field. Drag the selected field up or down to the desired position. The order of fields in the *Custom Order* list box in the Tab Order dialog box is the order in which the fields will be selected as the Tab key is pressed in a record in Form view. Click OK when you have finished relocating the fields.

**▼ Quick Steps**

**Change Tab Order of Fields**

1. Open form in Design view.
2. Click Tab Order button.
3. Click in gray field selector bar next to field name.
4. Drag field to desired location.
5. Repeat Steps 3–4 as required.
6. Click OK.

Tab Order

**Figure 4.5** Tab Order Dialog Box

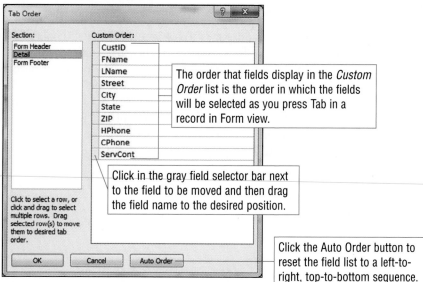

The order that fields display in the *Custom Order* list is the order in which the fields will be selected as you press Tab in a record in Form view.

Click in the gray field selector bar next to the field to be moved and then drag the field name to the desired position.

Click the Auto Order button to reset the field list to a left-to-right, top-to-bottom sequence.

1. With the **AL2-C4-RSRCompServ.accdb** database open and the CustMaintenance form open in Design view, click the View button to display the form in Form view.
2. With the insertion point positioned in the *CustID* field in the first record in the table, press the Tab key seven times. As you press Tab, notice that the order in which the fields are selected is a left-to-right, top-to-bottom sequence.
3. With the insertion point in the *HPhone* field, press Tab. Notice the selected field moves down to the *CPhone* field instead of moving right to the *ServCont* field.
4. With the insertion point in the *CPhone* field, press Tab to move to the *ServCont* field.
5. Switch to Design view.
6. Change the tab order of the fields so that the *ServCont* field is selected after the *HPhone* field by completing the following steps:
   a. Click the Tab Order button in the Tools group of the Form Design Tools Design tab.
   b. At the Tab Order dialog box, move the pointer to the gray field selector bar next to *ServCont* until the pointer displays as a right-pointing black arrow.
   c. Click to select the field.
   d. With the pointer now displayed as a white arrow in the field selector bar, drag *ServCont* up until the horizontal black line indicating the location at which the field will be moved is positioned between *HPhone* and *CPhone* in the *Custom Order* list and then release the mouse.
   e. Click OK.
7. Switch to Form view.
8. Press the Tab key nine times to move through the fields in the first record. Notice when you reach the *HPhone* field and press Tab, the *ServCont* field is active next instead of the *CPhone* field.
9. Switch to Design view.
10. Save the form.

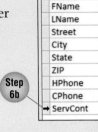

Step 6b

Step 6d

---

## Adding a Tab Control to a Form

A tab control is an object used to add pages to a form. Each page displays with a tab at the top. When viewing the form, you click the page tab to display the contents of the page within the tab control object. Add a tab control to a form to organize fields in a large table into smaller related groups or to insert multiple subforms that display on separate pages within the tab control object. Examine the tab control shown in Figure 4.6. You will create this object in Projects 1f–1g. The tab control contains three pages. The tabs across the top of the control display the caption assigned to each page.

**Figure 4.6** Tab Control with Three Pages Created in Projects 1f–1g

A tab displays at the top of each page added to a tab control object. Click the tab to change the contents in the tab control to the fields or subform added to the page.

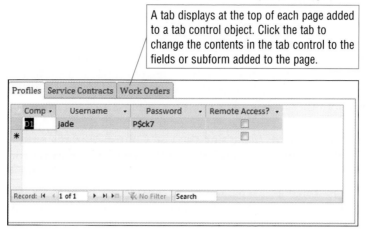

In Projects 1f–1g you will create a subform on each page within the tab control to display fields from a related table. When completed, the CustMaintenance form can be used to enter or view data related to customers that includes fields from four tables.

Tab Control

To add a tab control object to a form, click the Tab Control button in the Controls group in the Form Design Tools Design tab. Position the crosshairs with the tab control icon attached at the top left of the area in the *Detail* section where you want to begin the tab control and then drag down and right to draw the control the size that you want to make the tabbed pages. When you release the mouse, the tab control object initially displays with two pages as shown in Figure 4.7.

Change the text displayed in the tab at the top of the page by changing the Caption property in the page's Property Sheet. Add fields or create a subform on each page as needed. Add an additional page to the tab control by right-clicking an existing tab in the tab control object and then clicking *Insert Page* at the shortcut menu. To remove a page from the tab control, right-click the tab to be deleted and then click *Delete Page* at the shortcut menu.

▼ **Quick Steps**

**Change Page Caption**
1. Click desired tab in tab control.
2. Click Property Sheet button.
3. Click in *Caption* property box.
4. Type desired text.
5. Close Property Sheet.

**Add New Page to Tab Control**
1. Right-click existing tab in tab control.
2. Click *Insert Page* at shortcut menu.

**Figure 4.7** New Tab Control Object with Two Pages

Your page numbers may vary.

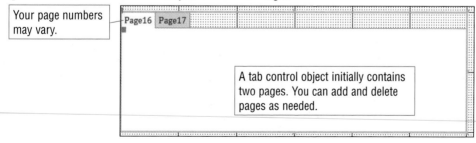

A tab control object initially contains two pages. You can add and delete pages as needed.

**Quick Steps**

**Add Subform to Page**
1. Click desired page tab in tab control.
2. Make sure Use Control Wizards is active.
3. Click More button in Controls scroll bar.
4. Click Subform/ Subreport button.
5. Click crosshairs inside selected page.
6. Click Next.
7. Choose table and fields.
8. Click Next.
9. Click Next.
10. Click Finish.
11. Delete subform label control object.
12. Move and resize subform object as required.

**H I N T**

Do not delete a subform object in the Navigation pane. If the subform object is deleted, the main form will no longer display the fields from the related table in the tab control.

Subform/Subreport

Control Wizard

# Creating a Subform

The Subform/Subreport button in the Controls group of the Form Design Tools Design tab is used to add a subform to a form. Create a subform to display fields from another related table within the existing form. The form in which a subform is created is called the main form. Adding a related table as a subform creates a control object within the main form that can be moved, formatted, and resized independently of other objects. The subform displays as a datasheet within the main form in Form view. Data can be entered or updated in the subform while the main form is being viewed. Make sure the Use Control Wizards button is toggled on in the Controls group before clicking the Subform/Subreport button so that you can add the subform using the Subform Wizard shown in Figure 4.8.

A subform is stored as a separate object outside the main form. You will notice an additional form name added in the Navigation pane with *subform* at the end of the name when you finish the steps in the Subform Wizard.

**Figure 4.8** First Dialog Box in Subform Wizard

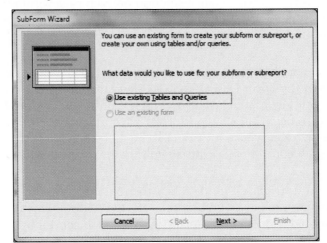

1. With the **AL2-C4-RSRCompServ.accdb** database open and the CustMaintenance form open in Design view, add a tab control object to the form by completing the following steps:
   a. Click the Tab Control button in the Controls group of the Form Design Tools Design tab.
   b. Position the crosshairs with the tab control icon attached at the left edge of the grid in the *Detail* section at the 2-inch position in the vertical ruler, drag down to the 4-inch position in the vertical ruler and right to the 6-inch position in the horizontal ruler, and then release the mouse.

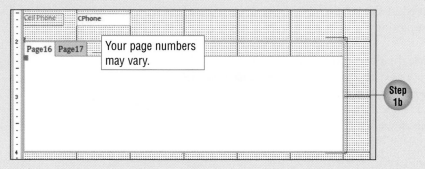

2. Change the page caption and add a subform to the first page within the tab control by completing the following steps:
   a. Click the first tab in the tab control that displays *Pagexx* where *xx* is the page number to select the page. (For example, click *Page16* in the image shown above.)
   b. Click the Property Sheet button in the Tools group.
   c. Click the Format tab in the Property Sheet, click in the *Caption* property box, type **Profiles**, and then close the Property Sheet. The tab displays the caption text in place of *Pagexx*.

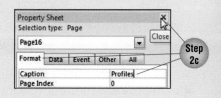

   d. By default, the Use Control Wizards feature is toggled on in the Controls group. Click the More button at the bottom of the Controls scroll bar to expand the Controls and view two rows of buttons and the Controls drop-down list. View the current status of the *Use Control Wizards* option. The button at the left of the option displays with an orange background when the feature is active. If the button is orange, click in a blank area to remove the expanded Controls list. If the feature is not active (displays with a white background), click the Use Control Wizards option to turn the feature on.

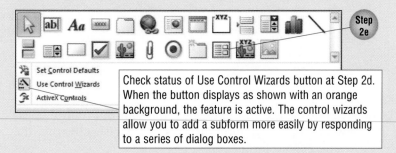

Check status of Use Control Wizards button at Step 2d. When the button displays as shown with an orange background, the feature is active. The control wizards allow you to add a subform more easily by responding to a series of dialog boxes.

   e. Click the More button at the bottom of the Controls scroll bar and then click the Subform/Subreport button at the expanded Controls list.

f. Move the crosshairs with the subform icon attached to the Profiles page in the tab control. The background of the page turns black. Click the mouse to start the Subform Wizard.

Step 2f

g. Click Next at the first Subform Wizard dialog box with *Use existing Tables and Queries* already selected.

h. At the second Subform Wizard dialog box, select the table and fields to be displayed in the subform by completing the following steps:

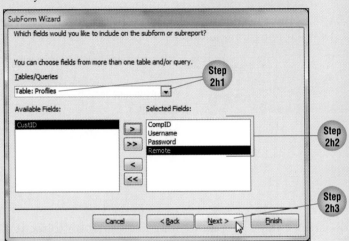

1) Click the down-pointing arrow next to the *Tables/Queries* list box and then click *Table: Profiles* at the drop-down list.

2) Move all of the fields except *CustID* from the *Available Fields* list box to the *Selected Fields* list box.

3) Click Next.

i. Click Next at the third Subform Wizard dialog box with *Show Profiles for each record in Customers using CustID* selected. Since the two tables have a relationship created with *CustID* as the joined field, Access knows the field that links records in the main form with the subform.

j. Click Finish at the last Subform Wizard dialog box to accept the default subform name *Profiles subform*.

3. Access creates the subform within the active page in the tab control with a label control object above the subform control. Click the label control object displaying the text *Profiles subform* to select the object and then press the Delete key.

4. Click the border of the subform control object to display the orange border and sizing handles and then move and resize the object as shown using the techniques you learned in Project 1c.

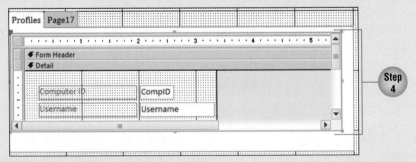

Step 4

5. Click in a blank area outside the grid to deselect the subform control object and then switch to Form view. Notice the subform displays as a datasheet within the tab control object in the CustMaintenance form.

6. Position the pointer on the column boundary line in the field names row in the datasheet between each column and then double-click to adjust each column's width to Best Fit.

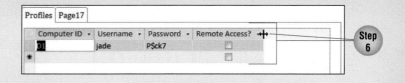

7. Notice that two sets of navigation buttons are displayed — one set at the bottom of the main form (just above the Status bar) and another set at the bottom of the datasheet in the subform. Use the navigation bar at the bottom of the main form to scroll a few records and watch the fields update in both the main form and the subform as you move to the next customer record.
8. Switch to Design view.
9. Save the form.
10. Notice in the Navigation pane a form object exists with the name *Profiles subform.* Subforms are separate objects within the database. If the main form is closed, you can open the subform individually to edit data.

In Design view the controls within the subform display one below another; however in Form view, the subform displays using a datasheet layout. If desired, you can change the Default View property in the subform's Property Sheet to *Single Form*. This view matches the layout of the controls in Design view to the layout of the fields in Form view. The fields display one below another in a single column in Form view. To do this, open the subform Property Sheet by double-clicking the Form Selector button at the top of the vertical ruler and left of the horizontal ruler in the subform control object in Design view. Click the down-pointing arrow in the Default View property in the Format tab and click *Single Form* at the drop-down list.

## Project 1g  Adding More Subforms and Adding a New Page to the Tab Control    Part 7 of 7

1. With the **AL2-C4-RSRCompServ.accdb** database open and the CustMaintenance form open in Design view, change the caption for the second page in the tab control to Service Contracts by completing steps similar to those in Steps 2a–2c of Project 1f.
2. With the Service Contracts page selected in the tab control, add a subform to display the fields from the ServiceContracts table on the page by completing the following steps:
   a. Click the More button at the bottom of the Controls scroll bar and then click the Subform/Subreport button at the expanded Controls list.
   b. Click inside the selected Service Contracts page in the tab control.
   c. Click Next at the first Subform Wizard dialog box.
   d. At the second Subform Wizard dialog box change the table displayed in the *Tables/Queries* list box to *Table: ServiceContracts*.
   e. Move all fields from the table except the *CustID* field to the *Selected Fields* list box.
   f. Click Next.
   g. Click Next at the third Subform Wizard dialog box with *Show ServiceContracts for each record in Customers using CustID* selected.
   h. Click Finish at the last Subform Wizard dialog box to accept the default subform name *ServiceContracts subform*.

3. Select and then delete the label control object above the subform displaying the text *ServiceContracts subform*.

4. Click the subform control object to display the orange border and sizing handles and move and resize the form as shown.

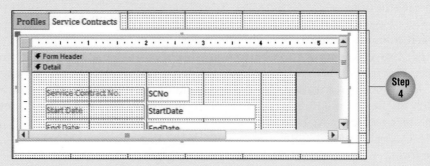

Step 4

5. Deselect the subform control object and then switch to Form view.

6. Click the Service Contracts tab and adjust the column width for each column in the datasheet to Best Fit.

7. Switch to Design view and save the form.

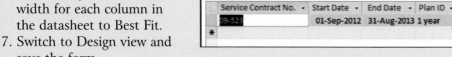

Step 6

8. Add a new page to the tab control and add a subform to display selected fields from the WorkOrders table in the new page by completing the following steps:

   a. Right-click the Service Contracts tab and then click *Insert Page* at the shortcut menu.

   b. With the new page already selected, display the Property Sheet, change the page caption to **Work Orders**, and then close the Property Sheet.

   c. Click the More button at the bottom of the Controls scroll bar and then click the Subform/Subreport button. Click inside the selected Work Orders page. Create a subform to display selected fields from the WorkOrders table by completing the following steps:

   1) Click Next at the first Subform Wizard dialog box.

   2) At the second Subform Wizard dialog box, change the table displayed in the *Tables/Queries* list box to *Table: WorkOrders*.

   3) Move the following fields from the *Available Fields* list box to the *Selected Fields* list box.

   *WO*
   *WODate*
   *Descr*

   4) Click Next.

   5) Click Next at the third Subform Wizard dialog box.

   6) Click Finish at the last Subform Wizard dialog box to accept the default subform name.

9. Select and then delete the label control object above the subform displaying the text *WorkOrders subform*.

10. Click the subform control object to display the orange border and sizing handles and move and resize the form as shown.

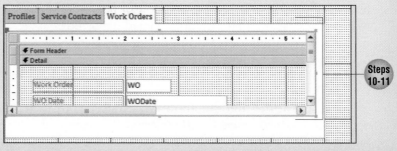

Steps 10-11

11. Access automatically extends a form's width and widens the tab control object if a table with many fields is added in a subform. If necessary, select the tab control object and decrease the width so that the right edge of the tab control is at the 6-inch position in the horizontal ruler. If necessary, decrease the width of the form so that the right edge of the grid is at the 6.5-inch position in the horizontal ruler. *Hint: If Access resizes the tab control to the edge of the form, you may have to temporarily widen the grid in order to see the middle sizing handle at the right edge of the tab control object.*

12. Deselect the subform control object and then switch to Form view.

13. While viewing the form, you decide the title would look better if it was not centered. Switch to Design view, click the Title control object in the *Form Header* section, click the Form Design Tools Format tab, and then click the Align Text Left button in the Font group.

14. Click the Form Design Tools Design tab and then switch to Form view.

15. Click the Work Orders tab and adjust the column width for each column in the datasheet to Best Fit. Compare your CustMaintenance form with the one shown in Figure 4.9.

16. Print the selected record only. To do this, open the Print dialog box, click *Selected Record(s)* in the *Print Range* section and then click OK.

17. Save and then close the CustMaintenance form.

**Figure 4.9** Completed CustMaintenance Form

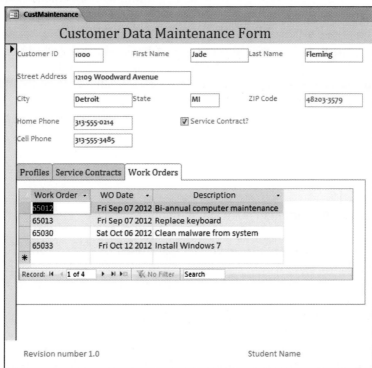

Adding the tab control with a separate page displaying a subform for each table related to the Customers table in the CustMaintenance form allowed you to create one object that can be used to view and update fields in multiple tables.

You will create a new form using the Form Wizard, add two calculations to the form, use features that assist with alignment and spacing of multiple control objects, and add graphics to the form.

### ▼ Quick Steps

**Add Calculated Control to Form**
1. Open form in Design view.
2. Click Text Box button.
3. Position crosshairs in *Detail* section at desired location.
4. Drag to create control object the required height and width.
5. Release mouse.
6. Click in text box control.
7. Type formula.
8. Press Enter.
9. Delete text in label control object.
10. Type label text and press Enter.

Text Box

## Adding Calculations to a Form in Design View ■■■■■■□□

To display a calculated value in a form, you can create a query that includes a calculated column and then create a new form based on the query. Alternatively, you can create a calculated control object in an existing form using Design view. To do this, click the Text Box button in the Controls group in the Form Design Tools Design tab and then drag the crosshairs in the *Detail* section to create a control object the approximate height and width required to show the calculation. Access displays a text box control with *Unbound* displayed inside the object and a label control to the left displaying *Textxx* inside the object (where *xx* is the text box object number). A calculated control is considered an unbound object since the data displayed in the control is not drawn from a stored field value in a record. Click inside the text box control object (*Unbound* disappears when you click inside the control) and type the formula beginning with an equals sign. For example, the formula *=[Hours]\*[Rate]* multiplies the value in the *Hours* field times the value in the *Rate* field. Field names in a formula are encased in square brackets.

Open the Property Sheet for the calculated control object to format the calculated values to *Fixed*, *Standard*, or *Currency* depending on the calculated value. Edit the label control object next to the calculated control to add a descriptive label that describes the calculated value.

---

### Project 2a **Adding and Formatting Calculated Control Objects** Part 1 of 4

1. With the **AL2-C4-RSRCompServ.accdb** database open, create a new form based on the WorkOrders table using the Form Wizard by completing the following steps:
   a. Click to select the WorkOrders table in the Navigation pane and then click the Create tab.
   b. Click the Form Wizard button in the Forms group.
   c. With *Table: WorkOrders* selected in the *Table/Queries* list box, complete the steps in the Form Wizard as follows:
      1) Move the following fields from the *Available Fields* list box to the *Selected Fields* list box and then click Next.
         *WO, Descr, ServDate, Hours, Rate, Parts*
      2) With *Columnar* layout selected, click Next.
      3) With *WorkOrders* the default text in the *What title do you want for your form?* text box, click *Modify the form's design* at the last dialog box and click Finish.

2. With the WorkOrders form displayed in Design view, change the theme and add a calculated control object to display the total labor for the work order by completing the following steps:

a. Click the Themes button in the Themes group of the Form Design Tools Design tab and then click *Clarity* (second option in third row) at the drop-down gallery.

b. Position the pointer on the top border of the gray *Form Footer* section bar until the pointer displays as a horizontal line with an up- and down-pointing arrow and then drag down just below the 3-inch position in the vertical ruler. This creates more grid space in the *Detail* section in which you can add controls.

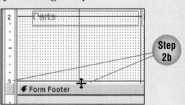

c. Click the Text Box button in the Controls group.

d. Position the crosshairs with the text box icon attached below the *Parts* text box control, drag to create an object the approximate height and width shown, and then release the mouse.

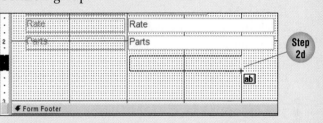

e. Click in the text box control (displays *Unbound*) and type =[Hours]*[Rate].

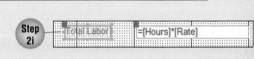

f. Press the Enter key.

g. With the calculated control object selected, click the Property Sheet button in the Tools group. With the Format tab in the Property Sheet active, click the down-pointing arrow in the *Format* property box, click *Standard* at the drop-down list, and then close the Property Sheet.

h. With the calculated control object still selected, click the Form Design Tools Format tab and then click the Align Text Left button in the Font group. (By default, calculated values display right-aligned in Form view.)

i. Click to select the label control object to the left of the calculated control object (displays *Textxx* [where *xx* is the text box label number]). Click inside the selected label control object a second time to display an insertion point. Delete *Textxx:*, type **Total Labor**, and press Enter. Notice the label control automatically expands to accommodate the width of the typed text.

3. Click the Form Design Tools Design tab. Click the View button to display the form in Form view and scroll a few records to view the calculated field. Do not be concerned with the size, position, alignment, and/or spacing of the controls since this will be fixed in a later project.

4. Switch to Design view and save the form.

5. A calculated control object can be used as a field in another formula. To do this, reference the calculated object in the formula by its *Name* property encased in square brackets. Change the name for the calculated object created in Step 2 to a more descriptive name by completing the following steps:

a. Click the calculated control object (displays the formula *=[Hours]*[Rate]*).

b. Click the Property Sheet button in the Tools group.

c. Click the Other tab in the Property Sheet.

d. Select and delete the existing text (displays *Textxx* [where *xx* is the text box number]) in the *Name* property box.

e. Type **LaborCalc** and then close the Property Sheet.

6. Add another calculated control object to the form to add the labor and parts to display the total value for the work order by completing the following steps:

a. Click the Text Box button.

b. Position the crosshairs with the text box icon attached below the calculated control created in Step 2, drag to create an object the approximate height and width as the first calculated control, and then release the mouse.

c. Click in the text box control (displays *Unbound*), type **=[LaborCalc]+[Parts]**, and press the Enter key.

d. Format the calculated control to *Currency* and align the text at the left side of the control. Refer to Steps 2g through 2h if you need assistance with this step.

e. Change the entry in the label control object to Total Work Order. Refer to Step 2i if you need assistance with this step.

7. Save the form. Display the form in Form view and scroll a few records to view the calculations.

8. Switch to Design view.

Step 5e

Step 6e

Steps 6a-6d

▼ **Quick Steps**

**Align Multiple Objects**

1. In Design view, select desired control objects.
2. Click Form Design Tools Arrange tab.
3. Click Align button.
4. Click desired option at drop-down list.
5. Deselect controls.

Align

# Adjusting Objects for Consistency in Appearance ■ ■ ■ ■ ■

When working in Design view, Access provides tools to assist with positioning, aligning, sizing, and spacing multiple controls to create a uniform and consistent appearance. Access these tools from the Size/Space and Align buttons in the Sizing & Ordering group of the Form Design Tools Arrange tab.

## Aligning Multiple Controls at the Same Position

The Align button options in the Sizing & Ordering group of the Form Design Tools Arrange tab shown in Figure 4.10 can be used to align multiple selected controls at the same horizontal or vertical position. Using the Align button options saves the work of adjusting each control individually to the same position on the form.

**Figure 4.10** Alignment Options in Align Button Drop-down List

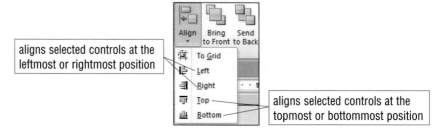

aligns selected controls at the leftmost or rightmost position

aligns selected controls at the topmost or bottommost position

# Adjusting the Sizing and Spacing between Controls

The Size/Space button drop-down list in the Sizing & Ordering group of the Form Design Tools Arrange tab shown in Figure 4.11 contains options to assist with consistent sizing of controls and spacing between controls. Use options in the *Size* section of the drop-down list to adjust the height or width to the tallest, shortest, widest, or narrowest of the selected control objects. Use options in the *Spacing* section to adjust the horizontal and vertical spacing between controls, to increase the space, decrease the space, or make all of the spaces between selected objects equal.

These tools are helpful when creating a new form by adding controls manually to the grid or after editing an existing form since the space between controls can easily change after adding or deleting objects. To precisely move individual control objects to adjust the spacing would be time-consuming.

▼ **Quick Steps**

**Adjust Spacing between Objects**
1. In Design view, select desired control objects.
2. Click Form Design Tools Arrange tab.
3. Click Size/Space button.
4. Click desired option in *Spacing* section.
5. Deselect controls.

Size/Space

**Figure 4.11** Size and Spacing Options in Size/Space Button Drop-Down List

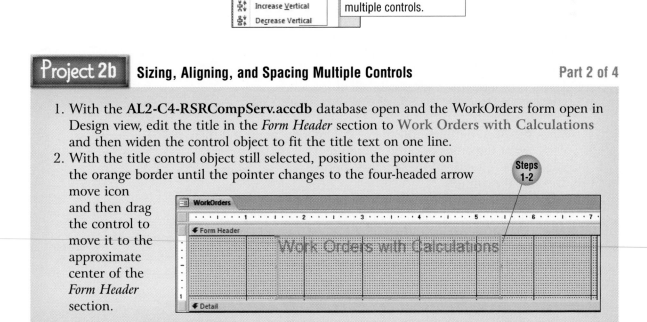

Use these options to adjust the height or width of multiple controls.

Use these options to adjust the space between multiple controls.

**Project 2b**  **Sizing, Aligning, and Spacing Multiple Controls**  Part 2 of 4

1. With the **AL2-C4-RSRCompServ.accdb** database open and the WorkOrders form open in Design view, edit the title in the *Form Header* section to Work Orders with Calculations and then widen the control object to fit the title text on one line.
2. With the title control object still selected, position the pointer on the orange border until the pointer changes to the four-headed arrow move icon and then drag the control to move it to the approximate center of the *Form Header* section.

Steps 1-2

3. Point to the bottom gray border in the *Form Footer* section bar until the pointer displays as a horizontal line with an up- and down-pointing arrow and then drag down approximately 0.5 inch to create space in the *Form Footer* section. Create a label control object with your name in the center of the *Form Footer* section.

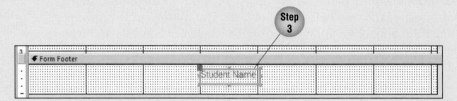

4. Click to select the *Descr* text box control object and then drag the right middle sizing handle left until the control is resized to approximately the 4.5-inch position in the horizontal ruler.
5. Shift + click to select the six text box control objects for the fields above the two calculated controls. Click the Form Design Tools Arrange tab, click the Size/Space button in the Sizing & Ordering group, and then click *To Widest* at the drop-down list. The six text box control objects are now all the same width, with the width set to the length of the widest selected object.

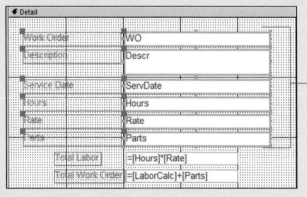

Six selected text box control objects resized to the same width at Step 5

6. Click in any blank area to deselect the controls.
7. Use the Align button to align multiple controls by completing the following steps:
   a. Draw a selection rectangle around all of the label control objects at the left side of the form to select all eight label controls.
   b. Click the Align button in the Sizing & Ordering group and then click *Left* at the drop-down list. All of the label control objects align at the left edge of the leftmost control.
   c. Deselect the controls.
   d. Draw a selection rectangle around all of the text box control objects at the right of the form to select all eight text box controls.
   e. Click the Align button in the Sizing & Ordering group and then click *Right* at the drop-down list. All of the control objects align at the right edge of the rightmost control.
   f. Deselect the controls.

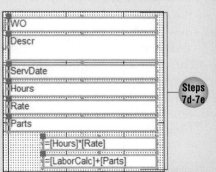

Steps 7a-7b

Steps 7d-7e

8. Adjust the vertical space between controls to make all of the control objects equally spaced in the *Detail* section by completing the following steps:

    a. Draw a selection rectangle around all of the control objects in the *Detail* section.

    b. Click the Size/Space button and then click *Equal Vertical* in the *Spacing* section of the drop-down list. All of the control objects now have the same amount of vertical space between each object.

    c. Deselect the controls.

9. Save the form.

10. Display the form in Form view and scroll a few records to view the revised alignment and spacing options.

11. Switch to Design view.

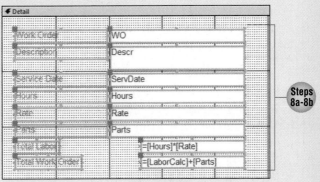

Steps 8a-8b

# Adding Graphics to a Form in Design View

A picture that is saved in a graphic file format can be added to a form using the Logo button or the Insert Image button in the Controls group in the Form Design Tools Design tab. Click the Logo button and Access opens the Insert Picture dialog box. Navigate to the drive and/or folder in which the graphic file is stored and then double-click the image file name. Access automatically adds the image to the left side of the *Form Header* section. Move and/or resize the image as needed. Access supports these popular graphic file formats for a logo control object: *bmp, gif, jpeg, jpg,* and *png.*

Use the Insert Image button when you want to place the picture in another section or prefer to draw a larger control object to hold the picture at the start. Click the Insert Image button and then click *Browse* at the drop-down list to open the Insert Picture dialog box. Navigate to the drive and/or folder in which the graphic file is stored and then double-click the image file name. Next, position the crosshairs pointer with the image icon attached at the desired location in the form where you want to place the image, and then drag the crosshairs to draw a control object the approximate height and width desired. Access supports these popular graphic file formats for an image control object: *gif, jpeg, jpg,* and *png.*

Use the Line button in the Controls group to draw horizontal or vertical lines in the form. Hold down the Shift key while dragging to draw a straight line. Once the line is drawn, use the Shape Outline button in the Control Formatting group of the Form Design Tools Format tab to modify the line thickness, line type, and line color.

You can also add clip art images to a form. Access does not provide a clip art button in the Controls group; however, you can use Microsoft Word to insert a clip art image in a document and use standard Windows commands to copy the image to the clipboard and paste the clip art into a form. Access inserts the clip art in an unbound OLE control object.

▼ **Quick Steps**

**Add Clip Art to Form**

1. Open form in Design view.
2. Start Microsoft Word.
3. Click Insert, Clip Art.
4. Locate and insert desired clip art into document.
5. Copy clip art image to clipboard.
6. Switch to Microsoft Access.
7. Paste image into desired form section.
8. Move and resize as required.
9. If necessary, display Property Sheet and change Size Mode property.
10. Switch to Microsoft Word.
11. Exit Word without saving.

Logo

Line

Insert Image

1. With the **AL2-C4-RSRCompServ.accdb** database open and the WorkOrders form open in Design view, start Microsoft Word.
2. Locate and insert a clip art image in a new document and copy and paste the image to the form in Microsoft Access by completing the following steps:

Step 2c

   a. At a blank Word document screen, click the Insert tab and then click the Clip Art button in the Illustrations group to open the Clip Art task pane.
   b. Select and delete existing text in the *Search for* text box, type computer repairs, and then press the Enter key.
   c. Scroll down the results list box and click the image shown to insert the clip art in the current document. If the image shown is not available, select a suitable alternative image.
   d. Right-click the clip art image in the Word document and click *Copy* at the shortcut menu.

Step 2f

   e. Click the button on the Taskbar representing Microsoft Access.
   f. Right-click in the *Detail* section of the form and click *Paste* at the shortcut menu. Access inserts the image overlapping existing controls and displays the orange border with selection handles.
   g. Move and resize the image to the approximate position and size shown below (your size and image may vary). You will notice when you resize the control object that Access cuts off parts of the image as you make the control object smaller. This action reflects the default *Clip* property for the object. You will correct this in Step 3.

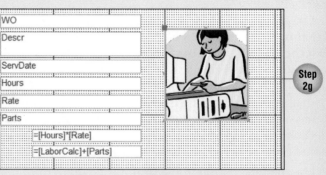

Step 2g

   h. Click the button on the Taskbar representing Microsoft Word and exit Word. Click Don't Save when prompted to save the document. Click No if prompted to make the Clipboard contents available for other applications.

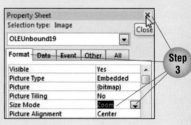

Step 3

3. Right-click the clip art image pasted at the right side of the *Detail* section in the form and click *Properties* at the shortcut menu. With Format the active tab in the Property Sheet, click in the *Size Mode* property box, click the down-pointing arrow that appears, and then click *Zoom* at the drop-down list. Close the Property Sheet.
   Changing *Size Mode* to *Zoom* instructs Access to resize the image within the control object maintaining the original proportions to height and width. The *Size Mode* drop-down list also contains the *Stretch* option. Use this option to stretch the image to fit the height and width of the control object. Using *Stretch* may cause a skewed appearance to the image.

4. Deselect the control object containing the clip art image and display the form in Form view. You decide a line below the title would help improve the form's appearance. Draw and modify the line by completing the following steps:
   a. Switch to Design view and click the Line button in the Controls group.
   b. Position the crosshairs with the line icon attached below the title in the *Form Header* section beginning a few rows of grid dots below the first letter in the title, hold down the Shift key, drag right releasing the mouse below the last letter in the title, and then release the Shift key.

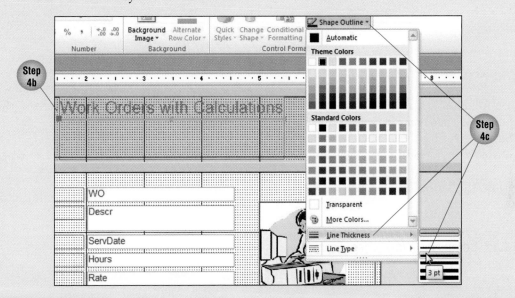

   c. Click the Form Design Tools Format tab, click the Shape Outline button in the Control Formatting group, point to *Line Thickness* at the drop-down list, and then click *3 pt* (fourth thickness option).
   d. With the line object still selected, click the Shape Outline button and then click the *Dark Red* color square (first option in last row of *Standard Colors*).
   e. Deselect the line object.
5. Display the form in Form view to view the line under the title.
6. Switch to Design view. If necessary, adjust the length and/or position of the line as desired.
7. Adjust alignment and formatting options of numeric fields by completing the following steps:
   a. Shift + click to select the *Hours*, *Rate*, *Parts*, and both calculated text box control objects.
   b. Click the Form Design Tools Format tab and then click the Align Text Right button in the Font group.
   c. Deselect the controls.
   d. Shift + click the *Parts* text box control and the bottom calculated control object that displays the formula *=[LaborCalc]+[Parts]*.
   e. Click the Form Design Tools Design tab and then click the Property Sheet button in the Tools group. Change the Format property to *Standard* and then close the Property Sheet.
   f. Deselect the controls.

8. Click to select the title text in the *Form Header* section and then drag the bottom middle sizing handle up to decrease the height of the control object to approximately 0.5 inch in the vertical ruler.

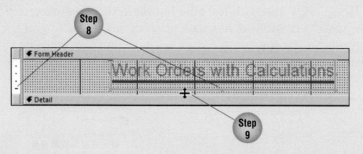

9. Position the pointer on the top of the gray *Detail* section bar until the pointer displays as a horizontal line with an up- and down-pointing arrow and then drag up to decrease the height of the *Form Header* section to approximately 0.6 inch in the vertical ruler.
10. Save the form.
11. Display the form in Form view and compare your form with the one shown in Figure 4.12.
12. Print the selected record only with the left and right margins set to 0.5 inch.
13. Close the form.

**Figure 4.12** Completed WorkOrders Form

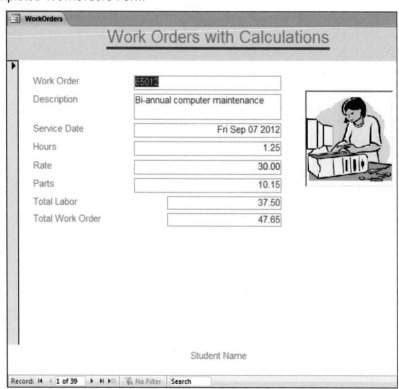

# Anchoring Controls to a Form ▪▪▪▪▪▪▪▪▪▪▪▪▪▪▪▪▪▪

A control object in a form can be anchored to a section or to another control object using the Anchoring button in the Position group in the Form Design Tools Arrange tab. When a control object is anchored, the object's position is maintained when the form is resized. For example, if a clip art image is anchored to the top right of the *Detail* section, when the form is resized in Form view, the image automatically moves in conjunction with the new form size so that the original distance between the image and the top right of the *Detail* section is maintained. If an image is not anchored and the form is resized, the position of the image relative to the edges of the form can change.

By default, *Top Left* is selected as the anchor position for each control object in a form. To change the anchor position, select the object(s), click the Form Design Tools Arrange tab, click the Anchoring button, and then click *Stretch Down*, *Bottom Left*, *Stretch Across Top*, *Stretch Down and Across*, *Stretch Across Bottom*, *Top Right*, *Stretch Down and Right*, or *Bottom Right*. Click the option that represents how you want the object to dynamically move as a form is resized. Some options will cause a control object to resize as well as move when the form is changed.

▼ **Quick Steps**

**Anchor Control in Form**
1. Open form in Design view.
2. Select control object(s) to be anchored.
3. Click Form Design Tools Arrange tab.
4. Click Anchoring button.
5. Click desired anchor position.
6. Deselect object.
7. Save form.

Anchoring

**Project 2d**    **Anchoring an Image to a Position within a Section**      Part 4 of 4

1. With the **AL2-C4-RSRCompServ.accdb** database open, open the WorkOrders form in Form view.
2. Switch to Design view.
3. Anchor the clip art image to the top of the *Detail* section of the form by completing the following steps:
   a. Click to select the clip art image.
   b. Click the Form Design Tools Arrange tab.
   c. Click the Anchoring button in the Position group.

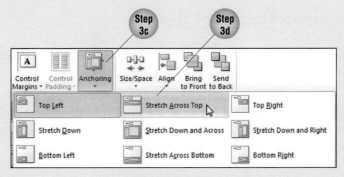

   d. Click *Stretch Across Top* at the drop-down list.
   e. Take note of the distance between the top border of the selected clip art image and the top of the *Detail* section.

4. Display the form in Form view. Notice the image has shifted up and become stretched across the top of the *Detail* section maintaining the distance between the top of the control object's boundary and the top of the *Detail* section.

Clip art image is shifted up and stretched across top of *Detail* section. The distance between the top of the image and the top of the *Detail* section is maintained when the form is resized.

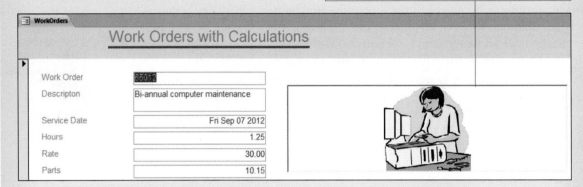

5. Click the File tab and then click Save Object As. Type WorkOrdersAnchored at the Save As dialog box and then press the Enter key or click OK.
6. Click the Home tab and then close the form.

---

# Project 3 Create a Restricted-Use Form 1 Part

You will create a datasheet form to be used to enter information into a table and set the form's properties to prevent records from being deleted in the form.

▼ **Quick Steps**

**Create Datasheet Form**
1. Select table in Navigation pane.
2. Click Create tab.
3. Click More Forms button.
4. Click *Datasheet*.
5. Save form.

**Restrict Record Actions for Form**
1. Open form in Design view.
2. Double-click Form Selector button.
3. Click Data tab.
4. Change *Allow Additions*, *Allow Deletions*, *Allow Edits*, or *Allow Filters* to *No*.
5. Close Property Sheet.
6. Save form.

## Creating a Datasheet Form and Restricting Form Actions

A form can be created that looks just like a table's datasheet. Click the table for which you want to create the datasheet form in the Navigation pane, click the Create tab, click the More Forms button in the Forms group, and then click *Datasheet* at the drop-down list. Access creates a form including all fields from the selected table presented in a datasheet layout.

Although the datasheet form has the look and feel of a table datasheet, the form object prevents end users from accessing and modifying the underlying table's structure.

Using options available in the Data tab of a form's Property Sheet shown in Figure 4.13, you can restrict actions that can be performed while a form is displayed in Form view. For example, you can prevent new records from being added and/or existing records from being deleted and/or edited and/or filtered. Setting the Data Entry property to *Yes* means the end user will see a blank form only when the form is opened. A data entry form is intended to be used to add new records only; the user is prevented from scrolling through existing records in the form.

**Figure 4.13** Form Property Sheet with Data Tab Selected

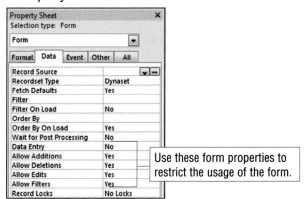

Use these form properties to restrict the usage of the form.

## Project 3 · Creating a Datasheet Form and Preventing Record Deletions · Part 1 of 1

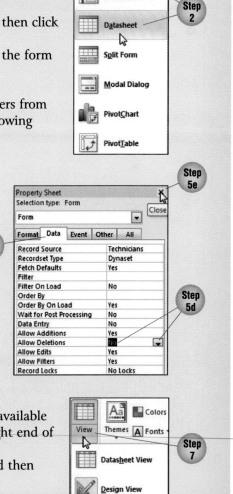

1. With the **AL2-C4-RSRCompServ.accdb** database open, click the Technicians table in the Navigation pane, and then click the Create tab.

2. Click the More Forms button in the Forms group and then click *Datasheet* at the drop-down list.

3. Review the Technicians form in the work area. Notice the form resembles a table datasheet.

4. Switch to Design view.

5. Modify the Technician's form properties to prevent users from deleting records using the form by completing the following steps:
   a. Click in a blank area to deselect the controls.
   b. Double-click the Form Selector button (displays as a black square) located at the top of the vertical ruler and left of the horizontal ruler to open the form's Property Sheet.
   c. Click the Data tab.
   d. Click in the *Allow Deletions* property box, click the down-pointing arrow that appears, and then click *No* at the drop-down list.
   e. Close the Property Sheet.

6. Click the Save button and then click OK to accept *Technicians* as the *Form Name*.

7. Click the down-pointing arrow on the View button in the Views group in the Form Design Tools Design tab. Notice that *Datasheet View* and *Design View* are the only views available. The *Form View* option is not available in the drop-down list or in the View buttons at the right end of the Status bar.

8. Click in a blank area to remove the drop-down list and then close the form.

9. Double-click the Technicians form object in the Navigation pane. Be careful to open the form object and not the table object.
10. Click in the record selector bar next to the first row in the datasheet for Technician ID 01 to select the record.

11. Click the Home tab and then look at the Delete button in the Records group. Notice the Delete button is dimmed. The feature is unavailable since the *Allow Deletions* form property was set to *No*.
12. Print the first page only of the Technicians form in landscape orientation and then close the form.
13. Right-click the Technicians form object in the Navigation pane and then click *Layout View* at the shortcut menu. Notice the datasheet form displays in a columnar layout in Layout view. The Technicians table includes a field named *Attachments*. In this field in the first record a picture of the technician has been attached to the record. In Layout View, Access automatically opens the image file and displays the contents.

In Layout view the datasheet form displays in a columnar layout.

The *Attachments* field automatically displays an attached image file if one has been added to the *Attachments* field.

14. Close the form.

roject **4** **Create a Blank Form with Lists**                    **1 Part**

You will use the Blank Form tool to create a new form for maintaining the service plan fees table named FeesSCPlans. In the form, you will create list boxes to provide an easy way to enter data for new service contract plans.

# Creating a Form Using the Blank Form Tool ■■■■■■■■■

When you need to create a form that contains a small number of fields you can use the Blank Form tool in Access to quickly build the form. A blank form begins with no controls or format and displays as a blank white page in Layout view. Click the Create tab and then click the Blank Form button in the Forms group to begin a new form. Access opens the Field List pane at the right side of the work area. Expand the list for the desired table and then add fields to the form as needed. If the Field List pane displays with no table names, click the hyperlink to <u>Show all tables</u> at the top of the pane.

## Adding a List Box to a Form

A list box displays a list of values for a field within the control object. In Form view, the user can easily see the entire list for the field. You can create the list of values when you create the control object or instruct Access to populate the list using values from a table or query. When you add a list box control to the form, the List Box Wizard begins as long as *Use Control Wizards* is active. Within the List Box Wizard you specify the values to be shown within the list box.

## Adding a Combo Box to a Form

A combo box is similar to a list box; however, a combo box includes a text box within the control object so that the user can either type the value for the field or click the down-pointing arrow to display field values in a drop-down list and click the desired value. As with a list box, when you add a combo box control to the form, the Combo Box Wizard begins as long as *Use Control Wizards* is active. Within the Combo Box Wizard you specify the values to be shown within the drop-down list.

▼ **Quick Steps**

**Create Blank Form**
1. Click Create tab.
2. Click Blank Form button.
3. Expand field list for desired table.
4. Drag fields to form as needed.
5. Add a title, format, or make other design changes as needed.
6. Save form.

**Create List Box**
1. Open form in Layout or Design view.
2. Click List Box button in Controls group.
3. Click within form at desired location.
4. Create values within List Box Wizard.
5. Save form.

**Create Combo Box**
1. Open form in Layout or Design view.
2. Click Combo Box button in Controls group.
3. Click within form at desired location.
4. Create values within Combo Box Wizard.
5. Save form.

Blank
Form

List
Box

Combo
Box

---

**Project 4** | **Creating a Blank Form with List Boxes** | Part 1 of 1

1. With the **AL2-C4-RSRCompServ.accdb** database open, click the Create tab and then click the Blank Form button in the Forms group.
2. If the Field List pane at the right side of the work area does not display the table names, click the <u>Show all tables</u> hyperlink; otherwise, proceed to Step 3.
3. Add fields from the FeesSCPlans table to the form by completing the following steps:
   a. Click the plus symbol next to the table named *FeesSCPlans* to expand the field list.

b. Click the first field named *ID* in the Field List pane and then drag the field to the top left of the form.

c. Click the second field named *Term* in the Field List pane, hold down the Shift key, and then click the last field named *Rate* in the Field List pane to select the remaining fields in the FeesSCPlans table.

d. Position the mouse pointer within the selected field names and then drag the group of fields to the form below the *ID* field. Release the mouse when you see the gold bar displayed below *ID*.

e. With the four fields selected that were added to the table, hold down the Shift key and click the *ID* field.

f. Position the mouse pointer on the orange border at the right of any of the selected label control objects until the pointer changes to a left- and right-pointing arrow and then drag the right edge of the label control objects to the right until you can read all of the label text as shown below.

Step
3f

4. Add a List Box control object to show the plan letters in a list by completing the following steps:

Step
4a

a. Click the List Box control in the Controls group of the Form Layout Tools Design tab.

b. Position the pointer with the List Box icon attached below the *Plan* field text box control object in the form. Click the mouse when you see the gold bar displayed between *A* and *1* in the right column. The List Box Wizard starts when you release the mouse.

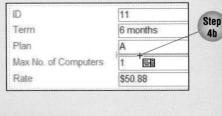

Step
4b

c. At the first List Box Wizard dialog box, click *I will type in the values that I want* and then click Next.

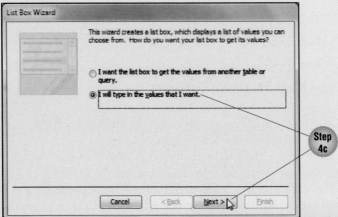

Step
4c

d. At the second List Box Wizard dialog box, click in the first cell below *Col1*, type **A**, and then press the Tab key.

e. Type **B**, press Tab, type **C**, press Tab, type **D**, and then click Next.

f. At the third List Box Wizard dialog box, click *Store that value in this field*, click the down-pointing arrow at the right of the list box, and then click *Plan* at the drop down list.

g. Click Next.

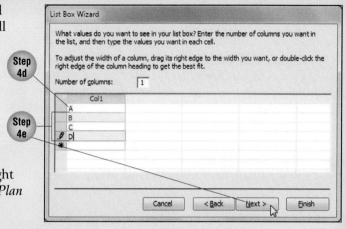

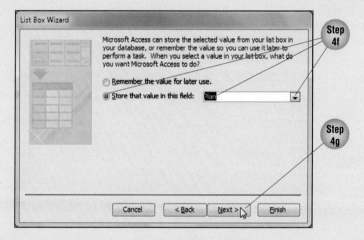

h. At the last List Box Wizard dialog box, with the current text already selected in the *What label would you like for your list box?* text box, type **PlanList** and then click Finish. Access adds the list box to the form displaying all of the values you entered in the list.

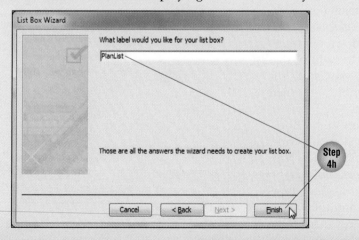

5. Add a Combo Box control object to enter the maximum number of computers in a plan by completing the following steps:

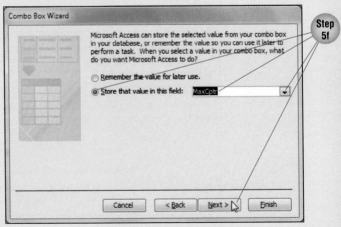

a. Click the Combo Box control in the Controls group of the Form Layout Tools Design tab.

b. Position the pointer with the Combo Box icon attached below the *Max No. of Computers* text box control object in the form. Click the mouse when you see the gold bar displayed between *1* and *$50.88* in the right column. The Combo Box Wizard starts when you release the mouse.

c. At the first Combo Box Wizard dialog box, click *I will type in the values that I want* and then click Next.

d. At the second Combo Box Wizard dialog box, click in the first cell below *Col1*, type 1, and then press Tab.

e. Type 2, press Tab, type 3, press Tab, type 4, press Tab, type 5, and then click Next.

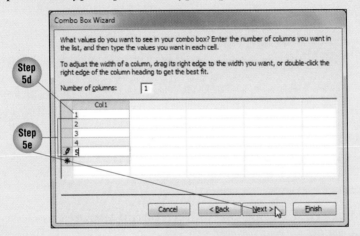

f. At the third Combo Box Wizard dialog box, click *Store that value in this field*, click the down-pointing arrow at the right of the list box, click *MaxCptr* at the drop down list, and then click Next.

g. At the last Combo Box Wizard dialog box, with the current text already selected in the *What label would you like for your list box?*, type CptrList and then click Finish. Access adds the combo box to the form displaying a value and a drop-down arrow at the right end of the text box.

6. Double-click the label for the combo box added in Step 5 (currently reads *CptrList*) and then type **Maximum Computers**. Edit the label for the list box added in Step 4 (currently reads *PlanList*) to add a space between *Plan* and *List*.

7. Right-click the label control object above the combo box that displays the text *Max No. of Computers* and then click *Select Entire Row* at the shortcut menu. Press Delete to remove the selected row from the form.

8. Click the Title button in the Header/Footer group of the Form Layout Tools Design tab and then type the title text **Service Contract Plans**.

9. Save the form and name it *SCPlans*.

10. Switch to Form view and scroll through the records in the form.

11. Add a new form to the table by completing the following steps:
    a. Click the New button in the Records group in the Home tab.
    b. Press Tab to move past the *ID* field since this field is an AutoNumber field.
    c. Click the down-pointing arrow at the *Term* field and then click *2 years* at the drop-down list.
    d. Click *C* in the *Plan List* list box that displays below *Plan*. Notice that *C* is entered into the *Plan* field text box control object when you click the letter *C* in the list box.
    e. Click the down-pointing arrow at the *Maximum Computers* field combo list box and then click *3* at the drop-down list.
    f. Click in the *Rate* text box and then type 236.50.

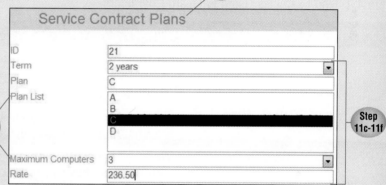

12. Print the selected record and then close the form.

---

**P**roject **5** **Sort and Find Records within a Form**            **1 Part**

You will open a custom-built form and use the form to sort and find records using a wildcard character and by searching backwards by date.

---

# Sorting and Finding Records in Forms ■■■■■■■■■■■■

One of the advantages to using a form for data entry and maintenance is that the form displays a single record at a time within the work area. This prevents distractions from viewing records other than the one on which you need to focus at the moment, reducing the likelihood of editing the wrong record. In a table with many records, quickly finding the specific record that you need to maintain or view is important. Use the Sort and Find features to move to the desired record quickly.

The Find feature allows you to search for records without specifying the entire field value. To do this, you substitute wildcard characters in the position(s) where you do not want to specify the exact text. Two commonly used wildcard characters are the asterisk (*) and the question mark (?). For example, you may want to search for a record by a person's last name but you are not sure of the correct spelling. The asterisk wildcard character is used in a position where there may be one or more characters that can vary. The question mark wildcard character is used in a fixed-width word where you want to view all records with the same number of characters in the field. In this case, substitute one question mark for each character not specified. Table 4.1 provides examples of the usage of the asterisk and question mark wildcard characters.

In Project 4, you will use the asterisk wildcard character to locate customer records for a specified street.

Ascending

Find

Descending

**Table 4.1** Find Examples Using Wildcard Characters

| Find What Entry | In This Field | Will Find |
|---|---|---|
| 104? | Customer ID | Customer records with a customer ID that begins with 104 and has one more character such as 1041, 1042, 1043 and so on up to 1049. |
| 4820? | ZIP Code | Customer records with a zip code that begins with 4820 and has one more character such as 48201, 48202, and so on. |
| 650?? | Work Order | Work order records with a work order number that begins with 650 and has two more characters such as 65023, 65035, 65055 and so on. |
| 313* | Home Phone | Customer records with a telephone number that begins with the 313 area code. |
| Peter* | Last Name | Customer records with a last name that begins with Peter and has any number of characters following such as Peters, Peterson, Petersen, Peterovski. |
| 4820* | ZIP Code | Customer records with a zip code that begins with 4820 and has any number of characters after such as 48201 or 48203-4841. |
| *oak* | Street Address | Customer records with any street address that has oak in the middle such as 1755 Oak Drive, 12-234 Oak Street, or 9 Oak Boulevard. |

1. With the **AL2-C4-RSRCompServ.accdb** database open, open the CustMaintenance form in Form view.
2. Click in the *Last Name* field to place an insertion point in the field and then click the Ascending button in the Sort & Filter group in the Home tab. The records are now arranged in alphabetic order by the customer's last name in ascending order. Scroll through a few records in the form watching the last names to confirm the new sorted order.

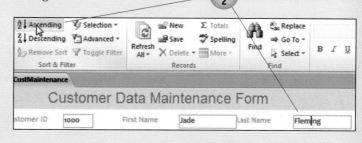

3. Assume that you now need to locate the name of the customer that resides on Roselawn Street. You do not know the exact house number or the customer's name. Complete the following steps to find the record using a wildcard character in the criterion:
   a. Click the First Record button in the Record Navigation bar to return to record 1 and then click the insertion point in the *Street Address* field to activate the field by which you want to search records.
   b. Click the Find button in the Find group.
   c. With the insertion point positioned in the *Find What* text box, type *roselawn* and then click the Find Next button. Access displays the first record in the form in which a match was made. The entry *roselawn* means "Find any record in which any number of characters before roselawn and any number of characters after roselawn exist in the active field."

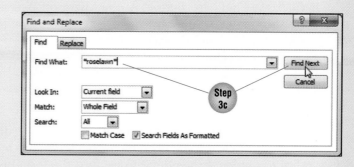

   d. Click the Find Next button a second time to see if any other records exist for customers on Roselawn Street.
   e. At the Microsoft Access message box indicating that Access has finished searching records, click OK.
   f. Close the Find and Replace dialog box.
4. Close the CustMaintenance form.
5. Open the WorkOrders form in Form view.
6. Click in the *Service Date* field and then click the Descending button in the Sort & Filter group to sort the records from the most recent service date to the oldest service date. Scroll through a few records in the form watching the service dates to confirm the new sorted order.
7. Find the records for work orders completed on October 19, 2012 by completing the following steps:
   a. Click the First Record button in the Record Navigation bar to return to record 1 and then click the Find button with the insertion point still active in the *Service Date* field.

b. With the existing text in the *Find What* text box already selected, press Delete to remove the entry and then type 10/19/2012.

c. Click the down-pointing arrow next to the *Search* list box and click *Down* at the drop-down list. Since the records are arranged in descending order, you need Access to search in a downward direction.

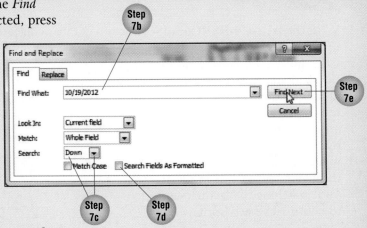

d. Click the *Search Fields As Formatted* check box to clear the check mark.
Since the date entered in the *Find What* text box does not match the date format in the *Service Date* field, this check box must be cleared or Access will not match any records.

e. Click the Find Next button. Access moves to the first record for the specified date (Work Order 65039). If necessary, drag the Find and Replace dialog box down towards the bottom of the work area so that you can view the record details.

f. Click the Find Next button. Access moves to the next record (Work Order 65038).

g. Click the Find Next button. Access moves to the next record (Work Order 65037).

h. Click the Find Next button. At the Microsoft Access message box indicating Access has finished searching records, click OK.

i. Close the Find and Replace dialog box.

8. Close the WorkOrders form.

9. Close the **AL2-C4-RSRCompServ.accdb** database.

Remove Sort

Once a form has been sorted, Access displays the records in the sorted order whenever you open the form. To remove a sort and have the order revert to the order of the primary key, open the form in Form view and then click the Remove Sort (displays the ScreenTip *Clear All Sorts*) button in the Sort & Filter group in the Home tab. Access clears the sort order and the table's records are rearranged in ascending order by the primary key field value.

In this chapter you have learned techniques for building a custom form using Design view. As you learned in Project 2, you can create a form using one of the form tools such as the Form Wizard and then make changes to the form in Design view. As you become more experienced with Access, you will likely use a combination of three methods to build custom forms: a form tool to build the basic table and field structure of the form; Layout view to apply formatting options, add a title and logo, and make other appearance changes; and Design view to add advanced control objects such as tab controls, subforms, and calculations.

# Chapter Summary

- A new form in Design view initially displays only the *Detail* section, which is the section in which fields are placed to display record data.

- A *Form Header* and *Form Footer* section can be added to the form. Objects placed in the Form Header display at the top of the form or print at the beginning of a printout of records from Form view. Objects placed in the *Form Footer* section display at the bottom of the form or print at the end of the printout of records from Form view.

- A form can contain three types of control objects: bound, unbound, and calculated.

- Click the Title button to display the *Form Header* and *Form Footer* sections and add a label control object in the Form Header that contains the form name.

- Click the Label button in the Controls group to add a label control object containing unbound text to any section within the form.

- Double-click the Form Selector button in Design view to open the form's Property Sheet and specify the table to be bound to the form in the Record Source property.

- Once a table has been associated with a form, click the Add Existing Fields button to open the Field List pane.

- Drag individual field names or a group of selected field names from the Field List pane to the *Detail* section in the form to add fields to the form.

- Use the move handle (large dark gray square at top left of selected control) to move a selected object independently of the control's associated label control or text box control.

- Use buttons in the Font group in the Form Design Tools Format tab to apply formatting options to selected controls.

- Multiple control objects can be selected in Design view by drawing a selection rectangle around a group of adjacent control objects or by holding down the Shift key while clicking controls.

- Open the Tab Order dialog box to change the order in which fields are selected as you press Tab to move from field to field in Form view.

- A tab control object in a form allows you to organize groups of related fields in pages.

- Click the Subform/Subreport button in the controls group to create a subform in a page within a tab control object.

- Create a calculated control object in a form using the Text Box button in the Controls group.

- Type a formula in the text box control object (displays *Unbound*) beginning with an equals sign (=). Field names within the formula are encased in square brackets.

- Use the Size/Space and Align buttons in the Sizing & Ordering group in the Form Design Tools Arrange tab to resize, align, or adjust spacing between multiple selected control objects.

- Images can be added to a form in Design view using the Logo button in the Header/Footer group or the Insert Image button in the Controls group.

- Draw a horizontal or vertical line in a form using the Line button in the Controls group. Hold down the Shift key while dragging to draw a straight line.

- Use the Shape Outline button in the Form Design Tools Format tab to adjust a line's thickness, type, or color.

- Clip art images can be copied to the clipboard from another Microsoft Office program such as Microsoft Word and then pasted to a form in Design view.

- Change a control object's Size Mode property if a clip art image has become truncated after resizing to *Zoom* or *Stretch*.

- A control object can be anchored to a position in a form so that the object's position relative to the edges of the form is maintained when the form is resized.

- A datasheet form is a form that looks like a table datasheet.

- Modify properties in the Data tab of a form's Property Sheet to restrict the actions a user can perform when viewing records in Form view.

- The Blank Form tool in the Forms group of the Create tab creates a new form with no controls or format applied. The form opens as a blank white page in Layout view with the Field List pane opened at the right of the work area.

- A list box control object displays all of the list values inside a rectangular-shaped control object in the form. Field values can be added to the list within the List Box Wizard by typing the values or by selecting a field from a table or query.

- A combo box control object displays a text box as well as a down-pointing arrow to a drop-down list of field values. The end user can type the field value into the text box or click the down-pointing arrow to pick the field value from a list. Field values are added within the Combo Box Wizard by typing the values or by selecting a field from a table or query.

- Sort a form in Form view by clicking in the field by which to sort records and then clicking the Ascending button or the Descending button.

- Click in a field by which to search records in Form view, click the Find button, and then enter the search criterion in the *Find What* text box. Typing an asterisk or question mark in the criterion allows you to search records using a wildcard character inserted for variable data.

# Commands Review

| FEATURE | RIBBON TAB, GROUP | BUTTON | KEYBOARD SHORTCUT |
|---|---|---|---|
| Add existing fields | Form Design Tools Design, Tools | | |
| Adjust size of multiple controls | Form Design Tools Arrange, Sizing & Ordering | | |
| Align multiple controls at same position | Form Design Tools Arrange, Sizing & Ordering | | |
| Anchor controls to form | Form Design Tools Arrange, Position | | |
| Blank Form | Create, Forms | | |
| Change tab order of fields | Form Design Tools Design, Tools | | |
| Combo Box control object | Form Layout Tools Design, Controls | | |
| Create datasheet form | Create, Forms | | |
| Design view | Home, Views | | |
| Equal spacing between controls | Form Design Tools Arrange, Sizing & Ordering | | |
| Find | Home, Find | | Ctrl + F |
| Form view | Form Design Tools Design, Views | | |
| Insert Image | Form Design Tools Design, Controls | | |
| Label control object | Form Design Tools Design, Controls | | |
| List Box control object | Form Layout Tools Design, Controls | | |
| Line | Form Design Tools Design, Controls | | |
| Property Sheet | Form Design Tools Design, Tools | | |
| Sort ascending order | Home, Sort & Filter | | |
| Sort descending order | Home, Sort & Filter | | |
| Subform | Form Design Tools Design, Controls | | |
| Tab control object | Form Design Tools Design, Controls | | |
| Text box control object | Form Design Tools Design, Controls | | |
| Title | Form Design Tools Design, Header/Footer | | |

# Concepts Check Test Your Knowledge

**Completion:** In the space provided at the right, indicate the correct term, command, or number.

1. A new form in Design view initially displays only this section in the form.

2. These are the three types of control objects found in a form.

3. Use this button from the Controls group to create an object in the *Form Footer* section in which to display a form's version number.

4. Before you can add fields to the table you must first connect a table to the form in this property box in the form's Property Sheet.

5. The large dark gray handle at the top left of a selected control is referred to by this name.

6. Hold down this key while clicking controls to select multiple control objects to be formatted.

7. Open this dialog box to change the order in which fields are selected when the Tab key is pressed in Form view.

8. Add this object to the bottom of a form to display subforms in individual pages.

9. Make sure this feature is active in the Controls group before clicking the Subform/Subreport button so that the Subform Wizard is available.

10. Click this button in the Controls group to add a calculation to a form.

11. The *Equal Vertical* option is located on this button's drop-down list in the Form Design Tools Arrange tab.

12. Change this property for a control object containing a clip art image to *Zoom* to proportionately adjust the image to the resized object's height and width.

13. The *Datasheet* form is available from this button's drop-down list in the Forms group in the Create tab.

14. Click this tab in a form's Property Sheet to locate the *Allow Deletions* property box.

15. This form tool opens as a blank white page in Layout view.

16. These two controls are used to add list boxes to a form.

17. Type this entry in the *Find What* text box to search for all records in the active field that begin with the zip code 48221 and have any four-character extension.

_____

# Skills Check  Assess Your Performance

## Assessment

## 1  CREATE A CUSTOM FORM USING DESIGN VIEW

1. Open the database named **AL2-C4-VantageVideos.accdb** and enable content.
2. Create a query named CustWebOrders using the following specifications:
   a. Add the WebOrderDetails, WebOrders, and WebProducts tables to the query.
   b. Add the following fields in order:

| WebOrders Table | WebOrderDetails Table | WebProducts Table |
|---|---|---|
| *WebOrdID* | *Qty* | *Product* |
| *CustID* | | *SellPrice* |
| *DateOrd* | | |

   c. Run the query and then close the query results datasheet.
3. Create a new form using Design view and build the form using the following specifications:
   a. Expand the width of the form in the grid to the 6.5-inch position in the horizontal ruler.
   b. Add a title in the *Form Header* section with the text *Web Customer Orders*. Use the move handle that displays at the top and left of the selected title control to move the title until the first letter in the title text (W) is at approximately the 1.5-inch position in the horizontal ruler.
   c. Add your name in a label control object centered in the *Form Footer* section.
   d. Apply the Flow theme.
   e. Connect the WebCustomers table to the form and add all of the fields to the *Detail* section in the layout shown in Figure 4.14. Adjust the width of the control objects as shown. Remember to use the Size/Space and Align buttons to help you position multiple controls at the same horizontal or vertical position and adjust spacing between controls.

**Figure 4.14** Assessment 1

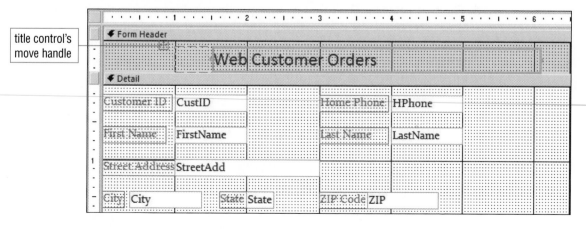

f. Change the tab order of the fields so that the *HPhone* field is selected after *CustID*.

g. Add a tab control object below the existing fields that is approximately two inches in height and with the width extended to the right edge of the form.

   1) On the first page, change the caption to *Web Orders* and add all fields from the CustWebOrders query in a subform. Delete the subform label control object. Delete the label control object and the text box control object for the CustID field in the subform and then move the remaining fields up to fill in the space. Move and resize the subform to fit the width of the page. Adjust column widths in Form view as needed to view all columns within the page.

   2) On the second page, change the caption to *Payment Information* and add all fields except *EmailAdd* from the WebCustPymnt table in a subform. Delete the subform label control object and move and resize the subform to fit the width of the page. Adjust column widths in Form view as needed.

4. Make any formatting changes you think would improve the appearance of the form.

5. Save the form and name it *WebCustOrders*.

6. Print the form in Form view with the first record displayed and the Web Orders page active.

7. Close the form.

## Assessment

### 2 CREATE A FORM USING THE FORM WIZARD; ADD A CALCULATION AND GRAPHICS

1. With the **AL2-C4-VantageVideos.accdb** database open, create a new form using the Form Wizard as follows:
   a. Select all fields from the WebProducts table.
   b. Select the *Columnar* style.
   c. Accept the default form name *WebProducts*.

2. View the completed form in Form view.

3. Switch to Design view and edit the form to resemble the form shown in Figure 4.15 using the following additional information:
   a. Apply the Solstice theme.
   b. *Retail Value* is a calculated field that uses a formula to multiply the quantity of videos that are in stock times the selling price.
   c. The clip art image can be found by searching using the keyword *Movies*. Choose a suitable alternative image if the image shown is not available on the computer you are using.
   d. The font color for the title text and the lines is *Maroon 5* in the *Standard Colors* section of the color palette.
   e. Use your best judgment for other formatting options to match as closely as possible the form shown in Figure 4.15.

4. Print the form in Form view with the first record displayed.

5. Save and close the form.

**Figure 4.15** Assessment 2

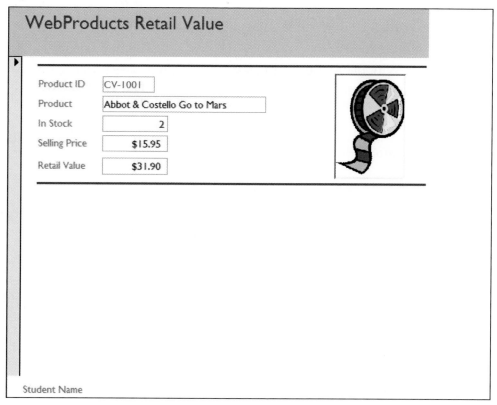

## Assessment

### 3 CREATE A RESTRICTED-USE FORM

1. With the **AL2-C4-VantageVideos.accdb** database open, create a datasheet form using the WebCustPymnt table.
2. Modify the form so that records cannot be deleted when using the form.
3. Display the form in Datasheet view with the Home tab active and a record selected.
4. Use the PrintScreen key or the Windows Snipping tool to capture an image of the screen with the Delete button dimmed while the record is selected.
5. Paste the screen image into a blank Word document. Type your name, the chapter number and assessment number and any other identification information required by your instructor above or below the screen image.
6. Print the document.
7. Save the Word document and name it **AL2-C4-VantageVideosForm.**
8. Exit Word.
9. Save the form using the default form name *WebCustPymnt* and then close the form.

## 4 CREATE A CUSTOM FORM USING THE BLANK FORM TOOL; ADD A LIST BOX

1. With the **AL2-C4-VantageVideos.accdb** database open, create a new form using the Blank Form tool that adds all of the fields from the WebCustomers table. Widen the labels column so that all of the label text is visible in the form.
2. Add a list box control object between the *City* and *State* fields. Type the values into the list as follows:

   > Burlington
   > Charlotte
   > Colchester

   Store the values in the field named *City* and accept the default label for the control object at the last List Box Wizard dialog box.
3. Delete the label control object for the list box.
4. Add a title to the form with the text *Customer Maintenance Form*.
5. Save the form and name it *WebCustomerMaintenance*.
6. Switch to Form view and add the following new record to the WebCustomers table:

   | | |
   |---|---|
   | *Customer ID* | 121 |
   | *First Name* | Morgan |
   | *Last Name* | Kalil |
   | *Street Address* | 29011 Greenbush Road |
   | *City* | Click *Charlotte* in the list box |
   | *State* | Accept default value of *VT* |
   | *ZIP Code* | 05445-9314 |
   | *Home Phone* | 802-555-9185 |

7. Print the selected record and then close the form.
8. Close the **AL2-C4-VantageVideos.accdb** database.

# Visual Benchmark  Demonstrate Your Proficiency

## CREATE CUSTOM RESERVATIONS FORM

1. Open **AL2-C4-PawsParadise.accdb**.
2. Review the form shown in Figure 4.16 and Figure 4.17. This form was created from scratch in Design view. Create the form using your best judgment for alignment, spacing, sizing, and position of controls as well as the following information:
   a. Connect the Reservations table to the main form.
   b. Apply the Slipstream theme.
   c. The line color is *Dark Blue* and the thickness is *3 pt*.
   d. The Days Boarded value is calculated by subtracting the two date fields.
   e. Each subform's Default View property (Format tab) was changed from Datasheet to *Single Form*. This view displays the fields one below the other instead of in a tabular arrangement. ***Hint: Create the subform by including the linked common field in the wizard dialog box so that the correct relationship between the main form and the subform is established. You can then delete extra controls while editing the subform object.***
3. Save the form naming it *Reservations*.
4. Display the form in Form view and then print the first record only.
5. Close the form and then close the **AL2-C4-PawsParadise.accdb** database.

**Figure 4.16** Visual Benchmark Custom Form with Dog Information Tab Displayed

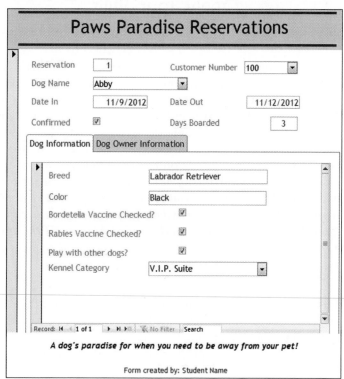

**Figure 4.17** Visual Benchmark Custom Form with Dog Owner Information Tab Displayed

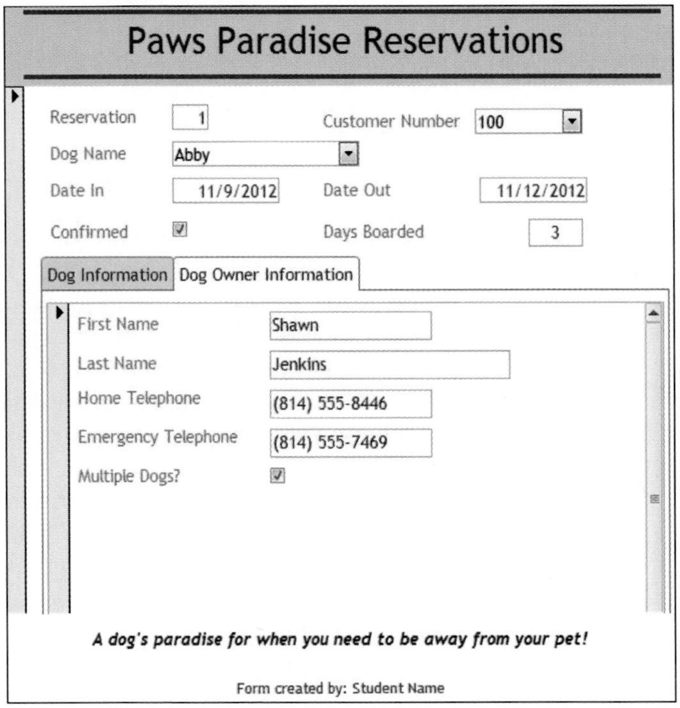

# Case Study Apply Your Skills

**Part 1**

You are continuing your work as an intern with Hillsdale Realty. The office manager has requested that you create a form for easier data entry and maintenance of the listings and sales information. Open the database named **AL2-C4-HillsdaleRealty.accdb** and enable content. Design and create the form similar to the one shown in Figure 4.18 using the Listings and SalesAndComm tables. Apply the Hardcover theme. Include the calculated field at the bottom of the subform. Modify the tab order of the fields to match the arrangement of the fields in Figure 4.18. ***Hints: Change the default view for the subform to Single Form and add a calculated control in the subform control object that multiplies the sale price times the commission rate. Search for the clip art image using the keywords "for sale"; choose another suitable image if the one shown is not available on the computer you are using.*** Save the form and name it appropriately. Print the first record in the form.

**Part 2**

The office manager would like another form created that displays the information from the Agents table along with the clients related to each agent. Design and create a form. You determine the form design, layout, and formatting options. Save the form and name it appropriately. Print the form with the first record displayed in the main form.

**Figure 4.18** Case Study Part 1 Form

**Part 3**

Open the main form created in Part 1. While viewing the form you realize that the Record Navigation bar at the bottom of the subform is not needed since a listing would only have one sale record. Remove the Record Navigation bar in the subform by opening the subform's Property sheet. At the Format tab, change the Navigation Buttons property to *No*. Close the Property sheet and then display the form in Form view. Notice the subform no longer displays a Record Navigation bar. Save the revised form. Capture a screen image of the revised form using the PrintScreen key or the Windows Snipping tool. Paste the screen image into a new Word document screen. Type your name, the chapter number, and any other identifying information required by your instructor above or below the screen image. Print the Word document. Save the Word document naming it **AL2-C4-CS-P3-HillsdaleRealty** and then exit Word.

# Access

Microsoft®

# Performance Assessment

Access2010L2U1

*Note: The Student Resources CD does not include an Access Level 2, Unit 1 subfolder of files because no data files are required for the Unit 1 assessments. You will create all of the files yourself. Before beginning the assessments, create a folder called Access2010L2U1 for the new files.*

# Assessing Proficiency

In this unit you have learned to design advanced tables that incorporate best practices in database design. You have created tables with multiple-field primary keys, multiple-value fields, attachment fields, and lookup fields to retrieve data from another table. You have learned to modify the join type in a relationship to achieve various query results and understand the concept of normalization as it applies to table design. You have created select queries, parameter queries, and action queries. Finally, you learned how to build a custom form using Design view that includes calculations, multiple pages, and subforms.

## Assessment 1 Create Tables for a Property Management Database

1. Create a new database named **AL2-U1-BenchmarkPropMgt.accdb**.
2. Create the tables shown in Figure U1.1 to store residential building management and tenant information including setting the primary key and assigning data types and field sizes. Leave field sizes at the default setting for those fields that do not have a field size specified in Figure U1.1.
3. Close any tables that have been left open.

**Figure U1.1** Assessment 1

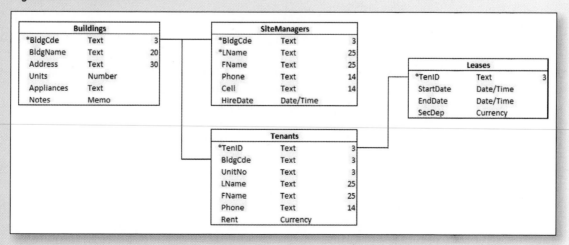

4. Open the Access Options dialog box and click the *Compact on Close* check box with the Current Database pane active to make sure the file size is optimized each time you close the database. Click OK at the message you must close and reopen the current database for the option to take effect.

5. Close **AL2-U1-BenchmarkPropMgt.accdb**.

### Assessment 2 Add Captions and Modify Field Properties

1. Open the **AL2-U1-BenchmarkPropMgt.accdb** database and then create captions for the fields as follows:

Buildings Table

| **Field Name** | **Caption** |
|---|---|
| *BldgCde* | Bldg Code |
| *BldgName* | Name |

Leases Table

| **Field Name** | **Caption** |
|---|---|
| *TenID* | Tenant ID |
| *StartDate* | Start Date |
| *EndDate* | End Date |
| *SecDep* | Security Deposit |

SiteManagers Table

| **Field Name** | **Caption** |
|---|---|
| *BldgCde* | Bldg Code |
| *LName* | Last Name |
| *FName* | First Name |
| *Phone* | Telephone |
| Cell | Cell Phone |
| *HireDate* | Hire Date |

Tenants Table

| **Field Name** | **Caption** |
|---|---|
| *TenID* | Tenant ID |
| *BldgCde* | Bldg Code |
| *UnitNo* | Unit No |
| *LName* | Last Name |
| *FName* | First Name |
| *Phone* | Telephone |

2. Make *UnitNo* in the Tenants table a required field including disallowing zero-length strings.

3. Create a custom format for all date fields that displays dates in the short date format with leading zeroes for months and days. Use a slash to separate each section in the date, for example, *01/05/2012*.

4. Create the following custom input masks:
   a. In *BldgCde* in the Buildings table, require three digits and display the underscore character as the placeholder.
   b. In *TenID* in the Tenants table, require three digits and display the underscore character as the placeholder.

c. In all of the date fields, create an input mask that will require dates to be entered using the short date format created in Step 3 with all digits required. *Hints: You can use the Input Mask Wizard to create the first input mask and then modify the code created by the wizard to change optional digits to required digits. Next, copy and paste the input mask codes to the other two date fields.*

d. Require all telephone numbers to include the area code with hyphens between each section of the number. Display the pound symbol (#) as the placeholder character. (Apply the same Hints for this step as provided for Step 4c.)

5. Enable rich text formatting in the *Notes* field in the Buildings table.
6. Make *995.00* the default value in the *Rent* field in the Tenants table.
7. Save and then close all tables.

## Assessment 3 **Add Records**

1. With the **AL2-U1-BenchmarkPropMgt.accdb** database open, add the following records:

Buildings Table

| Field | Record 1 | Record 2 | Record 3 |
|---|---|---|---|
| *Bldg Code* | 115 | 120 | 125 |
| *Name* | Coventry Park | Mornington Place | Bayview Towers |
| *Address* | 33 Westview Road | 1100 Forrester Lane | 12 Lakeview Circle |
| *Units* | 38 | 60 | 110 |
| *Appliances* | (leave blank) | (leave blank) | (leave blank) |
| *Notes* | New roof in 2010 | Furnace and air conditioning units under warranty until 2015 | Parking lot resurfaced in 2009 |

Leases Table

| Field | Record 1 | Record 2 | Record 3 |
|---|---|---|---|
| *Tenant ID* | 101 | 102 | 103 |
| *Start Date* | 01 01 2012 | 02 01 2012 | 02 01 2012 |
| *End Date* | 12 31 2012 | 01 31 2013 | 01 31 2013 |
| *Security Deposit* | 995 | 995 | 1125 |

SiteManagers Table

| Field | Record 1 | Record 2 | Record 3 |
|---|---|---|---|
| *Bldg Code* | 115 | 120 | 125 |
| *Last Name* | Jenkins | Hernandez | Doxtator |
| *First Name* | Blair | Maria | Cody |
| *Telephone* | 800 555 3485 | 800 555 8675 | 800 555 9677 |
| *Cell Phone* | 800 555 3748 | 800 555 3996 | 800 555 7795 |
| *Hire Date* | 02 08 2009 | 04 23 2010 | 09 15 2010 |

Tenants Table

| Field | Record 1 | Record 2 | Record 3 |
|---|---|---|---|
| *Tenant ID* | 101 | 102 | 103 |
| *Bldg Code* | 115 | 115 | 115 |
| *Unit No* | 110 | 215 | 320 |
| *Last Name* | Chen | Ayoub | Reiser |
| *First Name* | Wei | Mona | Helena |
| *Telephone* | 519 555 8776 | 519 555 2286 | 519 555 7668 |
| *Rent* | 995 | 995 | 1125 |

2. Apply bold and red font color to the years entered in the *Notes* field in each record.
3. For each table, adjust column widths until all data is entirely visible and print the table, adjusting print options as necessary to fit the table on one page.
4. Save and then close all tables.

### Assessment 4  Create Lookup Lists and Edit Relationships

1. With the **AL2-U1-BenchmarkPropMgt.accdb** database open, create the following lookup lists to display values from another table:
   a. In the SiteManagers table, create a lookup list for *BldgCde* that displays the building codes and names from the Buildings table. Sort the list by the building names and show the key column. Widen the column displaying the building names to accommodate longer names that may be added to the table in the future. Store the *BldgCde* value in the field.
   b. In the Tenants table, create a lookup list for *BldgCde* using the same specifications as Step 1a.
   c. In the Leases table, create a lookup list for *TenID* that displays the tenant IDs, first names, and last names from the Tenants table. Sort the list by the last names and show the key column. Store the *TenID* value in the field.
2. Create a multiple-value drop-down list for the *Appliances* field in the Buildings table with the following items.

   Refrigerator
   Stove
   Microwave
   Dishwasher
   Washer
   Dryer

3. Edit the three records to populate the *Appliances* field as follows:

   | Bldg Code | Appliances |
   | --- | --- |
   | 115 | Refrigerator, Stove, Microwave |
   | 120 | Refrigerator, Stove, Microwave, Dishwasher |
   | 125 | Refrigerator, Stove, Washer, Dryer |

4. Adjust the field width of the *Appliances* column to Best Fit, change the field width of the *Notes* column to 35 and the row height to 30, and then print the Buildings table in landscape orientation with left and right margins set to 0.25 inch.
5. Close the Buildings table, saving changes to the table layout.
6. Open the Relationships window. Edit all relationships to turn on referential integrity and the two cascade options.
7. Arrange the table field list boxes in the window to show the relationships with the primary tables on the left and the related tables on the right. Make sure no join lines are overlapping each other so that each relationship is easily distinguished from others. Create, save, and print a relationships report using the default report name.
8. Close the relationship report window and the relationships window.

## Assessment 5 Create Select Queries

1. With the **AL2-U1-BenchmarkPropMgt.accdb** database open, design and create the following select queries:

   a. A query named *PromptedTenant* that displays the *BldgCde* and *BldgName* fields from the Buildings table and the *UnitNo, FName, LName,* and *Phone* fields from the Tenants table. Include prompts to specify the building name and the unit number criteria when the query is run.

   b. A query named *PromptedLease* that displays the *TenID* from the Tenants table, the *BldgName* from the Buildings table, the *UnitNo, FName,* and *LName* fields from the Tenants table, and the *StartDate, EndDate,* and *SecDep* fields from the Leases table. Include prompts to specify the starting date and ending date criteria when the query is run.

   c. A query named *TenantsList* that displays the *BldgCde* and *BldgName* fields from the Buildings table and the *UnitNo, FName, LName* and *Rent* fields from the Tenants table. Sort in ascending order by the building names. Modify the join properties to show all records from the Buildings table in a left outer join.

   d. A query named *BuildingsList* that displays all of the fields in the Buildings table except the *Notes* field. Show each entry in the multiple-value *Appliances* field in a separate row in the query results datasheet and assign the field the caption *Supplied Appliances*.

2. Run the PromptedTenant query. Type **coventry park** when prompted for the building name and **110** when prompted for the unit number. Print the query results datasheet and then close the query.

3. Run the PromptedLease query. Type **02/01/2012** when prompted for the starting date and **01/31/2013** when prompted for the ending date. Print the query results datasheet in landscape orientation and then close the query.

4. Run the TenantsList query, print the query results datasheet, and then close the query.

5. Run the BuildingsList query, print the query results datasheet, and then close the query.

## Assessment 6 Calculate in a Query and Use an Update Query to Increase Rents

1. With the **AL2-U1-BenchmarkPropMgt.accdb** database open, create a query to calculate the total rental income from each unit as follows:

   a. Open the TenantsList query in Design view and use Save Object As to name the query *RentalIncome*.

   b. Modify the join properties to show records only when the joined fields are equal in both tables using an inner join.

   c. Add a calculated field to the query with the column heading *Annual Rent* that calculates twelve months of rental income.

   d. Run the query and add a total row in the query results datasheet with a sum function in the *Rent* and *Annual Rent* columns.

   e. Print the query results datasheet in landscape orientation and then close the query saving changes.

2. Create an update query named *RentIncrease* to increase all rents by 4%. Run the query.

3. Close the RentIncrease query.

4. Open the RentalIncome query, print the query results datasheet in landscape orientation, and then close the query.

## Assessment 7 Design and Create Forms

1. With the **AL2-U1-BenchmarkPropMgt.accdb** database open, design and create a form to enter data into the Buildings table as a main form with the SiteManagers table in a subform. Name the main form *BldgsAndMgrs*. You determine the form design, layout, and formatting options. Include an appropriate clip art image in the form. Add your name in the *Form Footer* section. Print the first record in the Buildings table displayed in Form view.

2. Design and create a form to enter data into the Tenants table as a main form with the Leases table in a subform similar to the one shown in Figure U1.2. Name the form *TenantsAndLeases*. Modify the tab order to move in the order *Tenant ID, Bldg Code, Unit No, Telephone, First Name, Last Name* and *Rent. Annual Rent* is a calculated control. Use your best judgment to match the color formatting as closely as possible within the theme colors. Add labels and graphics as shown. Note that the subform does not show a Record Navigation bar. Refer to Case Study Part 3 on page 149 in Chapter 4 if you need help turning off the bar.

3. Print all records using the TenantsAndLeases form and then close the form saving changes.

4. Close the **AL2-U1-BenchmarkPropMgt.accdb** database.

**Figure U1.2** Assessment 7, Step 2

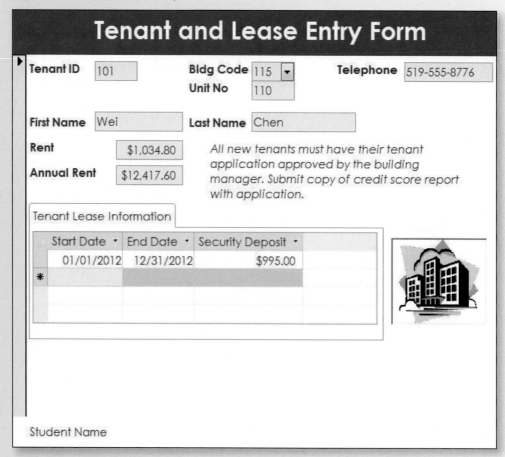

# Writing Activities

The following activities give you the opportunity to practice your writing skills along with demonstrating an understanding of some of the important Access features you have mastered in this unit. Use correct grammar, appropriate word choices, and clear sentence constructions when required.

## Activity 1 Design Tables for Parking Information in the Property Management Database

The office manager at Benchmark Property Management would like to add tables to the **AL2-U1-BenchmarkPropMgt.accdb** database to store information about assigned parking at each of the buildings. Design and create a table to store parking rates and another table to track rental information for each parking spot using the information provided below. Create two lookup lists in the assigned parking table, one to look up the correct parking rate in the rates table and another to look up the tenant's ID in the Tenants table. Add at least three records to test your tables.

Use the following information to assist you with the table design:

*Parking Rates*
- Coventry Park charges $30 per month for parking.
- Mornington Place charges $41 per month for parking.
- Bayview Towers charges $58 per month for parking.

*Assigned Parking Table*
- Include fields to store the vehicle make, model, color, and license plate number of the tenant's vehicle that will be parked in the spot.
- Include a field to store the date the tenant began renting the spot.

In Microsoft Word, document your table design by including each table's name and the fields created in each table including the data type and field properties that you set such as field size, caption, input mask, and so on. Indicate the primary key(s) in each table by typing an asterisk preceding the field name. Save the Word document and name it **AL2-U1-Act1-BenchmarkPropMgt**. Print the document and then exit Word.

## Activity 2 Design Tables for a Soccer League Database

You are assisting the volunteer registration coordinator for a local soccer league. The registration coordinator would like to create an Access database in which to store information about this season's soccer players so that he can extract reports by age category to develop team lists and generate financial reports for the league treasurer. Design and create tables in a new database named **AL2-U1-SoccerRegn.accdb**. The registration coordinator has given you a sample registration form to help you design the tables. Refer to the sample form shown in Figure U1.3.

**Figure U1.3** Activity 2

Create one data entry form to enter information into the tables and add at least five records to test your table and form design. Print all of the records using the form. Design and create a prompted query that will print a list of soccer players selecting records by age category. Design and create another query to print the soccer players registered for the current season including the registration fee paid. Add a total row in the query results datasheet to show the total registration fees collected. Run each query to test your query design and print the query results datasheets.

In Microsoft Word, create a one-page quick reference guide for the registration coordinator and the treasurer that provides instructions on how to open the database and use the data entry form, the prompted query, and the registration fee query. Include in your instructions how to print objects in the database, including how to print a selected form. Save the Word document and name it **AL2-U1-Act2-SoccerRegistration**. Print the document and exit Word.

# Internet Research ▪■■▪■■■■▪▪■■▪■■■

## Plan Your Volunteer Work

You want to volunteer each week after school but are not sure which organization would be a good fit with your skills and interests. As you begin to consider where you would like to donate your time and expertise you decide to use your newly learned Access skills to develop a volunteer organization database that you can share with your friends and relatives. Research five to eight organizations in your area that need volunteers on a regular basis. Pick a variety of organizations so that your database will have at least one organization that will appeal to most people. Design tables in Access in a new database named **AL2-U1-VolunteerOrg.accdb** to store the organization name, address, telephone number, and volunteer coordinator (if applicable). Include a field with notes about the organization's mission. Look for annual fundraising events at which volunteers are needed and include an Events table related to the organization. Design and create a form for data entry and use the form to input records for the organizations that you researched. Print all of the records using the form. Using Microsoft Word, create a brief document with instructions for your friends and relatives on how to open the database, browse records using the form, and print information. Save and print the document naming it **AL2-U1-VolunteerInfo**.

Microsoft®

# Access® Level 2

# Unit 2 ■ Advanced Reports, Access Tools, and Customizing Access

Chapter 5 ■ Creating and Using Custom Reports

Chapter 6 ■ Using Access Tools and Managing Objects

Chapter 7 ■ Automating, Customizing, and Securing Access

Chapter 8 ■ Integrating Access Data

Microsoft®

# Access®

# Creating and Using Custom Reports

## PERFORMANCE OBJECTIVES

**Upon successful completion of Chapter 5, you will be able to:**

- **Create a custom report in Design view using all five report sections**
- **Move, size, format, and align control objects**
- **Insert a subreport into a report**
- **Add page numbering, date and time controls**
- **Add graphics to a report**
- **Group records including adding functions and totals**
- **Modify section or group properties to control print options**
- **Create and modify charts in a report**
- **Create a blank report**
- **Add hyperlinks and list boxes to a report**
- **Change the shape of a tab control**
- **Change the tab order of fields**

**Tutorials**

**5.1** Creating Custom Reports Using Design View

**5.2** Connecting a Table or Query to a Report and Adding Fields

**5.3** Moving Control Objects to Another Section

**5.4** Inserting a Subreport

**5.5** Formatting Controls in a Report

**5.6** Grouping Records in a Report

**5.7** Creating a Report with a Grouping Level Using the Report Wizard

**5.8** Adding Functions to a Group; Keeping a Group Together

**5.9** Modifying Section Properties; Inserting a Chart

**5.10** Creating a Report Using the Blank Report Tool

Reports are used to generate printouts from the tables in a database. Although data can be printed from a table datasheet, query results datasheet, or form using the Print feature, these printouts do not allow you to customize the output and do not offer formatting options to present the data in a different manner. The Report feature provides tools and options that can be used to control the content and formatting in order to produce professional-quality reports that serve a particular purpose. In this chapter you will learn how to build custom reports. Model answers for this chapter's projects appear on the following pages.

Access2010L2C5

*Note: Before beginning the projects, copy to your storage medium the Access2010L2C5 subfolder from the Access2010L2 folder on the CD that accompanies this textbook and then make Access2010L2C5 the active folder.*

## RSR Computer Service Work Orders

| Work Order | Customer ID | First Name | Last Name | WO Date | Descripton |
|---|---|---|---|---|---|
| 65012 | 1000 | Jade | Fleming | Fri Sep 07 2012 | Bi-annual computer maintenance |

| Service Date | Total Labor | Parts | Total Work Order |
|---|---|---|---|
| Tue Sep 04 2012 | $37.50 | $10.15 | $47.65 |

| 65013 | 1000 | Jade | Fleming | Fri Sep 07 2012 | Replace keyboard |
|---|---|---|---|---|---|

| Service Date | Total Labor | Parts | Total Work Order |
|---|---|---|---|
| Mon Sep 10 2012 | $14.25 | $42.75 | $57.00 |

| 65030 | 1000 | Jade | Fleming | Sat Oct 06 2012 | Clean malware from system |
|---|---|---|---|---|---|

| Service Date | Total Labor | Parts | Total Work Order |
|---|---|---|---|
| Sat Oct 06 2012 | $15.50 | $0.00 | $15.50 |

| 65033 | 1000 | Jade | Fleming | Fri Oct 12 2012 | Install Windows 7 |
|---|---|---|---|---|---|

| Service Date | Total Labor | Parts | Total Work Order |
|---|---|---|---|
| Sat Oct 13 2012 | $97.50 | $335.75 | $433.25 |

| 65014 | 1005 | Cayla | Fahri | Mon Sep 10 2012 | Replace power supply |
|---|---|---|---|---|---|

| Service Date | Total Labor | Parts | Total Work Order |
|---|---|---|---|
| Mon Sep 10 2012 | $52.50 | $62.77 | $115.27 |

| 65024 | 1005 | Cayla | Fahri | Mon Sep 24 2012 | Install malware protection |
|---|---|---|---|---|---|

| Service Date | Total Labor | Parts | Total Work Order |
|---|---|---|---|
| Mon Sep 24 2012 | $15.50 | $75.50 | $91.00 |

| 65015 | 1008 | Leslie | Carmichael | Mon Sep 10 2012 | Restore operating system |
|---|---|---|---|---|---|

| Service Date | Total Labor | Parts | Total Work Order |
|---|---|---|---|
| Tue Sep 11 2012 | $67.50 | $0.00 | $67.50 |

| 65032 | 1008 | Leslie | Carmichael | Fri Oct 12 2012 | Install second hard drive |
|---|---|---|---|---|---|

| Service Date | Total Labor | Parts | Total Work Order |
|---|---|---|---|
| Sat Oct 13 2012 | $60.00 | $425.75 | $485.75 |

Page 1 of 5

| Work Order | Customer ID | First Name | Last Name | WO Date | Descripton |
|---|---|---|---|---|---|
| 65036 | 1008 | Leslie | Carmichael | Mon Oct 15 2012 | Set up home network |

| Service Date | Total Labor | Parts | Total Work Order |
|---|---|---|---|
| Tue Oct 16 2012 | $67.50 | $85.22 | $152.72 |

| 65044 | 1008 | Leslie | Carmichael | Tue Oct 23 2012 | DVD drive is not working |
|---|---|---|---|---|---|

| Service Date | Total Labor | Parts | Total Work Order |
|---|---|---|---|
| Tue Oct 23 2012 | $30.00 | $55.40 | $85.40 |

| 65016 | 1010 | Randall | Lemaire | Tue Sep 11 2012 | Install upgraded video card |
|---|---|---|---|---|---|

| Service Date | Total Labor | Parts | Total Work Order |
|---|---|---|---|
| Tue Sep 11 2012 | $30.00 | $48.75 | $78.75 |

| 65025 | 1010 | Randall | Lemaire | Fri Sep 28 2012 | Troubleshoot hard drive noise |
|---|---|---|---|---|---|

| Service Date | Total Labor | Parts | Total Work Order |
|---|---|---|---|
| Fri Sep 28 2012 | $45.00 | $0.00 | $45.00 |

| 65027 | 1010 | Randall | Lemaire | Sun Sep 30 2012 | Replace hard drive |
|---|---|---|---|---|---|

| Service Date | Total Labor | Parts | Total Work Order |
|---|---|---|---|
| Tue Oct 02 2012 | $45.00 | $375.50 | $420.50 |

| 65038 | 1010 | Randall | Lemaire | Fri Oct 19 2012 | Install Windows 7 |
|---|---|---|---|---|---|

| Service Date | Total Labor | Parts | Total Work Order |
|---|---|---|---|
| Fri Oct 19 2012 | $75.00 | $0.00 | $75.00 |

| 65046 | 1010 | Randall | Lemaire | Fri Oct 26 2012 | Windows 7 training |
|---|---|---|---|---|---|

| Service Date | Total Labor | Parts | Total Work Order |
|---|---|---|---|
| Fri Oct 26 2012 | $60.00 | $0.00 | $60.00 |

| 65017 | 1015 | Shauna | Friesen | Fri Sep 14 2012 | Replace DVD drive |
|---|---|---|---|---|---|

| Service Date | Total Labor | Parts | Total Work Order |
|---|---|---|---|
| Sat Sep 15 2012 | $16.88 | $55.87 | $72.75 |

| 65037 | 1015 | Shauna | Friesen | Fri Oct 19 2012 | Bi-annual computer maintenance |
|---|---|---|---|---|---|

| Service Date | Total Labor | Parts | Total Work Order |
|---|---|---|---|
| Fri Oct 19 2012 | $37.50 | $8.75 | $46.25 |

Page 2 of 5

## Projects 1 and 2 Design and Create a Custom Report, Add Features and Enhance a Report   Project 2b, WorkOrders Report

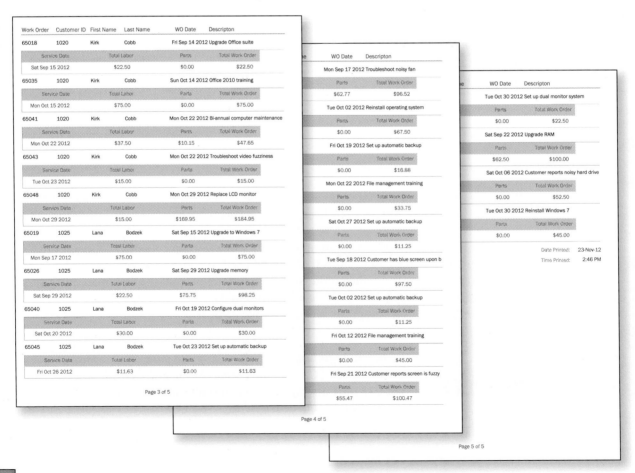

| Work Order | Customer ID | First Name | Last Name | WO Date | Descripton |
|---|---|---|---|---|---|
| 65018 | 1020 | Kirk | Cobb | Fri Sep 14 2012 | Upgrade Office suite |

| Service Date | Total Labor | Parts | Total Work Order |
|---|---|---|---|
| Sat Sep 15 2012 | $22.50 | $0.00 | $22.50 |

| 65035 | 1020 | Kirk | Cobb | Sun Oct 14 2012 | Office 2010 training |
|---|---|---|---|---|---|

| Service Date | Total Labor | Parts | Total Work Order |
|---|---|---|---|
| Mon Oct 15 2012 | $75.00 | $0.00 | $75.00 |

| 65041 | 1020 | Kirk | Cobb | Mon Oct 22 2012 | Bi-annual computer maintenance |
|---|---|---|---|---|---|

| Service Date | Total Labor | Parts | Total Work Order |
|---|---|---|---|
| Mon Oct 22 2012 | $37.50 | $10.15 | $47.65 |

| 65043 | 1020 | Kirk | Cobb | Mon Oct 22 2012 | Troubleshoot video fuzziness |
|---|---|---|---|---|---|

| Service Date | Total Labor | Parts | Total Work Order |
|---|---|---|---|
| Tue Oct 23 2012 | $15.00 | $0.00 | $15.00 |

| 65048 | 1020 | Kirk | Cobb | Mon Oct 29 2012 | Replace LCD monitor |
|---|---|---|---|---|---|

| Service Date | Total Labor | Parts | Total Work Order |
|---|---|---|---|
| Mon Oct 29 2012 | $15.00 | $169.95 | $184.95 |

| 65019 | 1025 | Lana | Bodzek | Sat Sep 15 2012 | Upgrade to Windows 7 |
|---|---|---|---|---|---|

| Service Date | Total Labor | Parts | Total Work Order |
|---|---|---|---|
| Mon Sep 17 2012 | $75.00 | $0.00 | $75.00 |

| 65026 | 1025 | Lana | Bodzek | Sat Sep 29 2012 | Upgrade memory |
|---|---|---|---|---|---|

| Service Date | Total Labor | Parts | Total Work Order |
|---|---|---|---|
| Sat Sep 29 2012 | $22.50 | $75.75 | $98.25 |

| 65040 | 1025 | Lana | Bodzek | Fri Oct 19 2012 | Configure dual monitors |
|---|---|---|---|---|---|

| Service Date | Total Labor | Parts | Total Work Order |
|---|---|---|---|
| Sat Oct 20 2012 | $30.00 | $0.00 | $30.00 |

| 65045 | 1025 | Lana | Bodzek | Tue Oct 23 2012 | Set up automatic backup |
|---|---|---|---|---|---|

| Service Date | Total Labor | Parts | Total Work Order |
|---|---|---|---|
| Fri Oct 26 2012 | $11.63 | $0.00 | $11.63 |

Page 3 of 5

| WO Date | Descripton |
|---|---|
| Mon Sep 17 2012 | Troubleshoot noisy fan |

| Parts | Total Work Order |
|---|---|
| $62.77 | $96.52 |

| Tue Oct 02 2012 | Reinstall operating system |
|---|---|

| Parts | Total Work Order |
|---|---|
| $0.00 | $67.50 |

| Fri Oct 19 2012 | Set up automatic backup |
|---|---|

| Parts | Total Work Order |
|---|---|
| $0.00 | $16.88 |

| Mon Oct 22 2012 | File management training |
|---|---|

| Parts | Total Work Order |
|---|---|
| $0.00 | $33.75 |

| Sat Oct 27 2012 | Set up automatic backup |
|---|---|

| Parts | Total Work Order |
|---|---|
| $0.00 | $11.25 |

| Tue Sep 18 2012 | Customer has blue screen upon b |
|---|---|

| Parts | Total Work Order |
|---|---|
| $0.00 | $97.50 |

| Tue Oct 02 2012 | Set up automatic backup |
|---|---|

| Parts | Total Work Order |
|---|---|
| $0.00 | $11.25 |

| Fri Oct 12 2012 | File management training |
|---|---|

| Parts | Total Work Order |
|---|---|
| $0.00 | $45.00 |

| Fri Sep 21 2012 | Customer reports screen is fuzzy |
|---|---|

| Parts | Total Work Order |
|---|---|
| $55.47 | $100.47 |

Page 4 of 5

| WO Date | Descripton |
|---|---|
| Tue Oct 30 2012 | Set up dual monitor system |

| Parts | Total Work Order |
|---|---|
| $0.00 | $22.50 |

| Sat Sep 22 2012 | Upgrade RAM |
|---|---|

| Parts | Total Work Order |
|---|---|
| $62.50 | $100.00 |

| Sat Oct 06 2012 | Customer reports noisy hard drive |
|---|---|

| Parts | Total Work Order |
|---|---|
| $0.00 | $52.50 |

| Tue Oct 30 2012 | Reinstall Windows 7 |
|---|---|

| Parts | Total Work Order |
|---|---|
| $0.00 | $45.00 |

| Date Printed: | 23-Nov-12 |
|---|---|
| Time Printed: | 2:46 PM |

Page 5 of 5

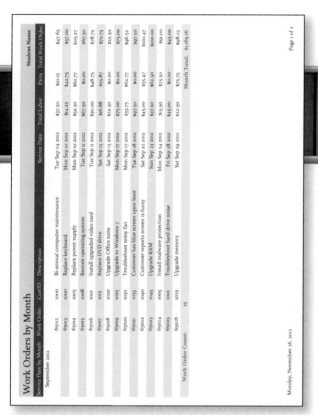
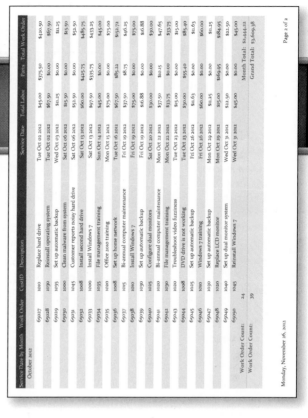

**Projects 3 and 4 Group Records and Add Functions to Count and Sum, Modify Section and Group Properties**

Project 4, WorkOrdersbyMonth Report

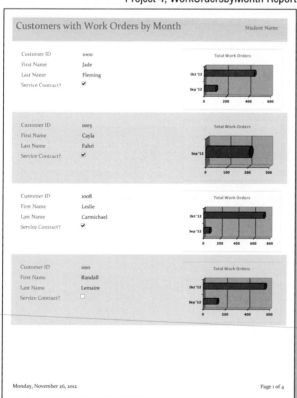

**Project 5 Create and Format a Chart**

Project 5b, CustomersWOChart Report

**Project 6 Create a Blank Report with Hyperlinks and a List**

TechCertifications Report

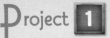

roject **1** **Design and Create a Custom Report** 5 Parts

You will create a custom report in Design view with fields from two tables and insert a subreport.

▼ **Quick Steps**

**Start New Report in Design View**
1. Click Create tab.
2. Click Report Design button.

**Add Report Title**
1. Open report in Design view.
2. Click Title button.
3. Type title text.
4. Press Enter.

**Add Label Object**
1. Open report in Design view.
2. Click Label button.
3. Drag to create object the desired height and width.
4. Type label text.
5. Press Enter.

Report Design

# Creating Custom Reports Using Design View ■■■■■■■■

Access provides the Report tool and the Report Wizard that can be used to create reports. These features allow you to build a report quickly that can be modified in Layout view or Design view to customize the content, format, or layout. In most cases, you will want to use one of the report tools to generate the report structure and then customize the report; however, if you require a report with several custom options, you can begin in Design view and build the report from scratch. Click the Create tab and click the Report Design button in the Reports group to begin a new report using the Design view window shown in Figure 5.1.

Creating a report in Design view involves using the same techniques that you learned in Chapter 4 for designing and building a custom form. You will add a title; connect a table or query to the report; add fields; and align, move, resize, and format controls the same way that you learned to do these tasks in a form.

A report can contain up to five sections, each of which is described in Table 5.1. You can also add a *Group Header* and a *Group Footer* section, which are used when you group records that contain repeating values in a field such as a department or city. You will learn how to use these additional sections in Project 3. A report that is grouped by more than one field can have multiple *Group Header* and *Group Footer* sections.

**Figure 5.1** Report Design View

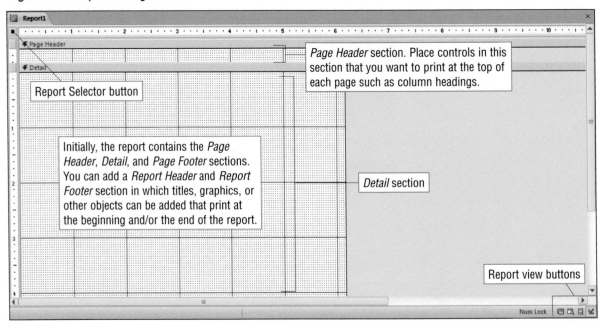

**Table 5.1** Report Sections

| Report Section | Description |
| --- | --- |
| Report Header | Content in the *Report Header* section prints at the beginning of the report and generally includes controls for the report title and company logo or other image. |
| Page Header | Content in the *Page Header* section prints at the top of each page in the report. Place controls for column headings in a tabular report format in the page header. |
| Detail | Similar to a form, controls for the fields from the table or query that make up the body of the report are placed in the *Detail* section. |
| Page Footer | Content in the *Page Footer* section prints at the bottom of each page in the report. Add a control to this section to print a page number at the bottom of each page. |
| Report Footer | Content in the *Report Footer* section prints at the end of the report. Add controls in this section to print grand totals or perform another function such as average, max, min, or count. |

**Project 1a** Starting a New Report Using Design View and Adding a Title and Label Object

1. Open **AL2-C5-RSRCompServ.accdb** and enable content.
2. Click the Create tab and then click the Report Design button in the Reports group.
3. Add a title in the *Report Header* section of the report by completing the following steps:
   a. With the Report Design Tools Design tab active, click the Title button in the Header/Footer group. Access adds the *Report Header* section above the *Page Header* section and places a title object with the text *Report1* selected.
   b. Type **RSR Computer Service Work Orders** and press Enter.

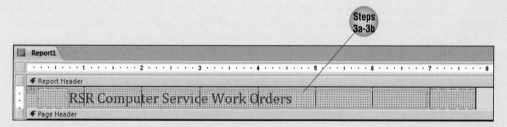

4. With the title control object still selected, click the Report Design Tools Format tab and then click the Center button in the Font group.
5. Drag the right edge of the report grid until the width is aligned at the 8-inch position in the horizontal ruler.
6. Scroll down the report until you can see the *Page Footer* and *Report Footer* sections. The *Report Footer* section was added to the design grid at the same time the *Report Header* section was added when the title was created in Step 3.

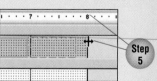

7. Drag the bottom edge of the report grid down until the bottom of the report is at the 0.5-inch position in the vertical ruler.
8. Click the Report Design Tools Design tab and then click the Label button in the Controls group. Add a label control object at the left edge of the *Report Footer* section that contains your first and last names.
9. Click in any blank area of the report to deselect the label control object.
10. Save the report and name it *WorkOrders*.

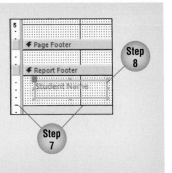

Step 8

Step 7

## Connecting a Table or Query to the Report and Adding Fields

A new report started in Design view does not have a table or query associated with it. In order to view data in the report, Access needs to know from which table the data should be gathered. Similar to a form, you connect a table or query to the report using the Record Source property in the report's Property Sheet. This step must be completed first before fields can be added to the *Detail* section. The steps to connect a table or query to the report are the same as the steps you learned to connect a table to a form. Double-click the Report Selector button located above the vertical ruler and left of the horizontal ruler to open the report's Property Sheet. Click the Data tab and then select the table or query name in the drop-down list in the *Record Source* property box.

Display the Field List pane and drag individual fields from the table or query or a group of fields to the *Detail* section. After fields have been added you can move and resize the control objects as needed.

The Field List pane displays in one of two states: with one section only with the fields from the table or query associated with the report, or with two additional sections with fields from other tables in the database. If the Field List pane contains only the fields from the associated table or query, you can add fields from other tables by displaying other table names from the database within the Field List pane. At the top of the pane, Access displays a hyperlink with the text Show all tables. Click the hyperlink to display two additional sections within the pane: *Fields available in related tables* and *Fields available in other tables*. Next to each table name is an expand button (displays as a plus symbol). Click the expand button next to a table name to display the fields stored within the table and then drag the field name to the *Detail* section of the report. You will perform these steps in Project1b.

### ▼ Quick Steps

**Connect Table or Query to Report**
1. Open report in Design view.
2. Double-click Report Selector button.
3. Click Data tab in Property Sheet.
4. Click down-pointing arrow in *Record Source* property box.
5. Click desired table or query.
6. Close Property Sheet.

**Add Fields to Report**
1. Click Add Existing Fields button.
2. Drag field name(s) from Field List pane to *Detail* section.

**Add Fields from Related Table**
1. Open Field List pane.
2. Click Show all tables hyperlink.
3. Click expand button next to desired table name in *Fields available in related tables* section.
4. Drag field name from related table list to *Detail* section.

Report Selector

Add Existing Fields

1. With the **AL2-C5-RSRCompServ.accdb** database open and the WorkOrders report open in Design view, scroll up to the top of the report in the work area.
2. Connect the WorkOrders table to the report so that Access knows which fields to display in the Field List pane by completing the following steps:
   a. Double-click the Report Selector button located at the top of the vertical ruler and left of the horizontal ruler to open the report's Property Sheet.
   b. Click the Data tab in the Property Sheet, click the down-pointing arrow in the *Record Source* property box, and then click *WorkOrders* at the drop-down list.
   c. Close the Property Sheet.
3. Click the Add Existing Fields button in the Tools group in the Report Design Tools Design tab to open the Field List pane.
4. Add fields from the WorkOrders table and related fields from the Customers table by completing the following steps:
   a. Click the <u>Show all tables</u> hyperlink at the top of the Field List pane. Access adds two sections to the pane. One section contains related tables and the other section contains other tables in the database which do not have an established relationship with the report's table. Next to each table name is an expand button (displays as a plus symbol) which is used to display field names for the table. *Note: Skip this step if the hyperlink at the top of the Field List pane displays <u>Show only fields in the current record source</u> since the additional sections are already added to the pane.*
   b. Click the expand button next to *Customers* in the *Fields available in related tables* section of the Field List pane. Access expands the list to display the field names in the Customers table below the Customers table name.

   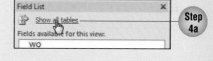

   c. Drag the *WO*, *CustID*, *WODate*, and *Descr* fields from the WorkOrders table to the design grid as shown.
   d. Drag the *FName* and *LName* fields from the Customers table to the design grid as shown. Notice the Customer table and field names move to the *Fields available for this view* section in the Field List pane once you add the first field from the Customers table to the *Detail* section.
5. Close the Field List pane.
6. Save the report.

**Move Controls to Another Section**
1. Open report in Design view.
2. Select controls to be moved.
3. Click Home tab.
4. Click Cut button.
5. Click section bar in which to move controls.
6. Click Paste button.
7. Deselect controls.

# Moving Control Objects to Another Section

As with a form, when a field is added to the *Detail* section in a report, a label control object containing the caption or field name is placed left of a text box control object that displays the field value from the record when the report is viewed or printed. In the WorkOrders report, the label control object for each field needs to be moved to the *Page Header* section so that the field names or captions print at the top of each page as column headings. To do this, you will cut and paste the controls from the *Detail* section to the *Page Header* section in Project 1c.

**Project 1c**　**Moving Controls to Another Section**　　　　　　　　**Part 3 of 5**

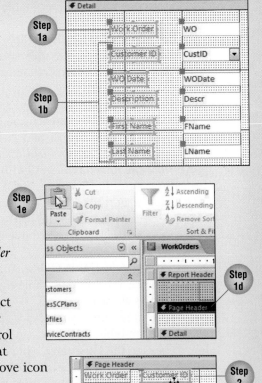

1. With the **AL2-C5-RSRCompServ.accdb** database open and the WorkOrders report open in Design view, move the label control objects from the *Detail* section to the *Page Header* section by completing the following steps:
   a. Click to select the *Work Order* label control object.
   b. Shift + click to select each of the other label control objects.
   c. Click the Home tab and then click the Cut button in the Clipboard group.
   d. Click the gray *Page Header* section bar.
   e. Click the Paste button in the Clipboard group. (Do not click the down-pointing arrow on the button.) Access pastes the label control objects and expands the *Page Header* section.
   f. Deselect the controls.
2. Click to select the *Customer ID* label control object and then move the control to the top of the *Page Header* section next to the *Work Order* label control as shown by dragging the object while pointing at the orange border with the four-headed arrow move icon displayed (not on a sizing handle).
3. Move the remaining four label control objects to the top of the *Page Header* section in the order shown in the image at the top of the next page by completing a step similar to Step 2.

4. Drag the top of the gray *Detail* section bar up until the top of the bar is aligned at the bottom edge of the label control objects in the *Page Header* section as shown below.

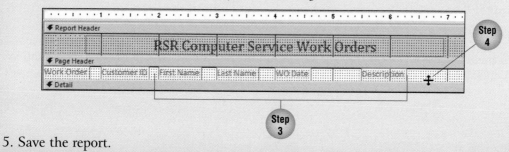

Step 4

Step 3

5. Save the report.

## Applying a Theme

Apply a theme to the report using the Themes button at the Report Design Tools Design tab. The theme controls the default colors and fonts for the report. The Themes options align with the themes available in Word, Excel, and PowerPoint so that you can maintain a consistent look for Access reports that you use for other documents, worksheets, or presentations. Note that changing a theme for one report automatically changes the theme for all reports in the database.

▼ **Quick Steps**

**Apply Theme**
1. Open report in Design view.
2. Click Report Design Tools Design tab.
3. Click Themes button.
4. Click desired theme.

Themes

---

**Project 1d**    **Moving Controls, Resizing Controls, and Applying a Theme**      Part 4 of 5

1. With the **AL2-C5-RSRCompServ.accdb** database open and the WorkOrders report open in Design view, move each text box control object in the *Detail* section below the object's associated label control object in the *Page Header* section so that the field values will align below the correct column headings in the report as shown below.

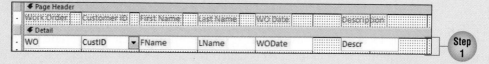

Step 1

2. Click the Report Design Tools Design tab, click the View button arrow in the Views group, and then click *Print Preview* at the drop-down list. (Note that there is also a Print Preview button in the Views group at the right end of the Status bar.) Notice the field value in the *WO Date* column is displaying pound symbols indicating the field's text box control object needs to be widened.

3. Click the Design View button in the View group located at the right end of the Status bar next to the Zoom slider to return to Design view.

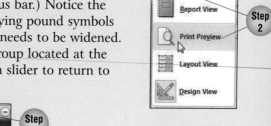

Step 2

Step 3

4. Resize the *WODate* text box control in the *Detail* section until the right edge of the control meets the left edge of the *Descr* text box control object.
5. Resize the *Descr* text box control in the *Detail* section until the right edge of the control is aligned approximately at the 7.75-inch position in the horizontal ruler.
6. Deselect the *Descr* control object.
7. Click the Themes button in the Themes group of the Report Design Tools Arrange tab and then click *Angles* at the drop-down gallery (third option in first row).

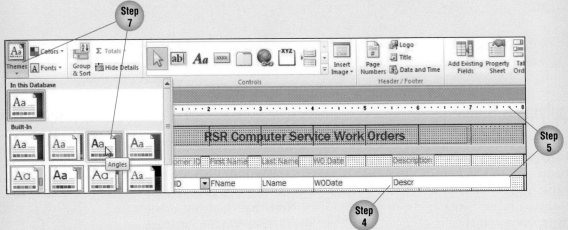

8. Save the report.
9. Display the report in Print Preview to review the changes made in this project. Switch back to Design view when finished previewing the report. ***Note: Do not be concerned if you only see one record in the report. Currently, the*** Detail ***section is sized such that only one record can fit on a page. This will be corrected in the next project.***

## Inserting a Subreport

Subform/ Subreport

A ***subreport*** is a report that is inserted inside another report. Similar to a nested query, using a subreport allows you to reuse a group of fields, formatting, and calculations in more than one report without having to recreate the setup each time. The Subform/Subreport button in the Controls group of the Report Design Tools Design tab is used to insert a subreport into a report. The report into which the subreport is embedded is called the main report. Adding a related table or query as a subreport creates a control object within the main report that can be moved, formatted, and resized independently of the other control objects. Make sure the Use Control Wizards button is toggled on in the expanded Controls group before clicking the Subform/Subreport button so that you can add the subreport using the SubReport Wizard shown in Figure 5.2.

A subreport is stored as a separate object outside the main report. You will notice an additional report name added in the Navigation pane with *subreport* at the end of the name when you finish the steps in the SubReport Wizard. Do not delete a subreport object in the Navigation pane. If the subreport object is deleted, the main report will no longer be able to display the fields from the related table or query in the report.

**Figure 5.2** First Dialog Box in SubReport Wizard

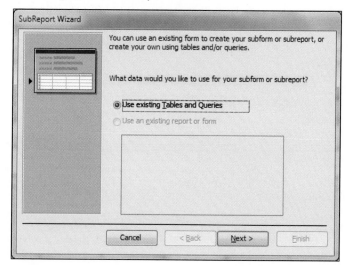

▼ **Quick Steps**

**Insert Subreport**
1. Open report in Design view.
2. Make sure Use Control Wizards is active.
3. Click Subform/Subreport button.
4. Drag crosshairs desired height and width in *Detail* section.
5. Click Next.
6. Choose table or query and fields.
7. Click Next.
8. Choose field by which to link main report with subreport.
9. Click Next.
10. Click Finish.
11. If desired, delete subreport label control object.
12. Move and/or resize subreport object as required.

**Project 1e**  **Inserting a Subreport**    Part 5 of 5

1. With the **AL2-C5-RSRCompServ.accdb** database open and the WorkOrders report open in Design view, insert a subreport into the WorkOrders report with fields from a query for the service date, labor, and parts for each work order by completing the following steps:

   a. By default, the *Use Control Wizards* option is toggled on in the Controls group. Click the More button at the bottom of the Controls scroll bar to expand the Controls and view three rows of buttons and the Controls drop-down list. View the current status of the *Use Control Wizards* option. The button at the left of the option displays with an orange background when the feature is active. If the button is orange, click in a blank area to remove the expanded Controls list. If the feature is not active (displays with a white background), click *Use Control Wizards* to turn the feature on.

   b. Click the More button at the bottom of the Controls scroll bar and then click the Subform/Subreport button at the expanded Controls list.

   > An orange background means the *Use Control Wizards* option is active. Check status and turn the feature on if necessary at Step 1a.

   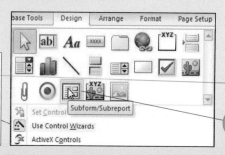

   Step 1b

c. Move the crosshairs with the subreport icon attached to the *Detail* section below the *WO* text box control object and drag down and right to create a subreport object the approximate height and width shown below. When you release the mouse, the SubReport Wizard begins.

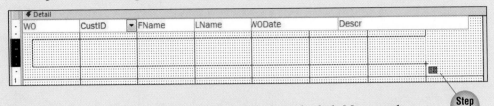

Step
1c

d. With *Use existing Tables and Queries* already selected, click Next at the first SubReport Wizard dialog box.

e. At the second SubReport Wizard dialog box, select the query fields to be displayed in the subreport by completing the following steps:

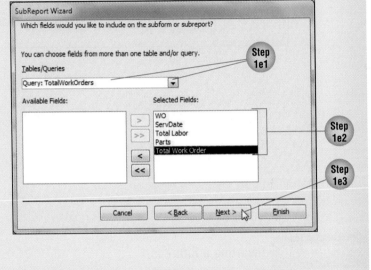

Step
1e1

Step
1e2

Step
1e3

1) Click the down-pointing arrow next to the *Tables/Queries* list box and then click *Query: TotalWorkOrders* at the drop-down list.

2) Move all of the fields from the *Available Fields* list box to the *Selected Fields* list box.

3) Click Next.

f. At the third SubReport Wizard dialog box, choose the field by which to link the main report with the subreport by completing the following steps:

1) With *Choose from a list* and the first option in the list box selected, read the text that displays below the list box describing the linked field. The text indicates that the main report will be linked to the subreport using the *CustID* field. This is not the correct field since you want your report to show the service date, labor, and parts based on the work order number.

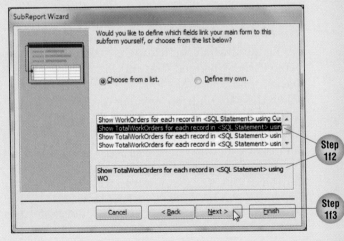

Step
1f2

Step
1f3

2) Click the second option in the list box and then read the text below the list box.

3) Since the second option indicates the two reports will be linked using the *WO field*, click Next.

g. Click Finish at the last SubReport Wizard dialog box to accept the default subreport name *TotalWorkOrders subreport*.

2. Access inserts the subreport with a label control object above the subreport control that contains the name of the subreport. Click the label control displaying the text *TotalWorkOrders subreport* to select the object and then press the Delete key.

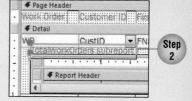

Step 2

3. Click the Report View button in the Views group of the Report Design Tools Design tab. Note that a Report View button is also located in the View group at the right end of the Status bar (first button). Report view is not the same as Print Preview. Report view will display the report with data in the fields and is useful for viewing reports within the database; however, this view does not show how the report will paginate when printed. For printing purposes, always use Print Preview to resize and adjust control objects.

4. Notice the work order number in the subreport is the same work order number that is displayed in the first record in the main report.

The main report and the subreport are correctly linked by the *WO* field.

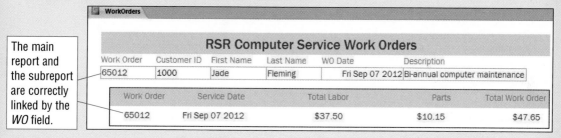

5. Switch back to Design view.

6. Now that you know the subreport is linked correctly to the main report, you do not need to display the work order number in the subreport. Delete the work order number control objects in the subreport by completing the following steps:

   a. Click to select the subreport control object and then drag the bottom middle sizing handle down to increase the height of the subreport until you can see all of the controls in the *Report Header* and *Detail* sections.

   b. Click to select the *Work Order* label control object in the *Report Header* section and then Shift + click the *WO* text box control object in the *Detail* section in the subreport.

   c. Press Delete.

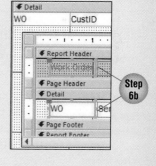

Step 6b

7. Click to select the subreport control object and then drag the bottom middle sizing handle of the control up until the height of the subreport is approximately 0.5 inch.

8. Scroll down the report until you can see the gray *Page Footer* section bar.

9. Drag the top of the *Page Footer* section bar up until the section bar is just below the subreport control object in the *Detail* section as shown below.

Height of subreport control object decreased at Step 7.

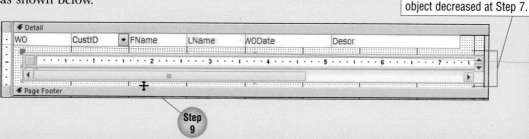

Step 9

10. Save the report and then switch to Report view to view the revised report. Resizing the *Detail* section at Step 9 allowed the report to show more records and related subreport records on the page since the spacing between sections was reduced.

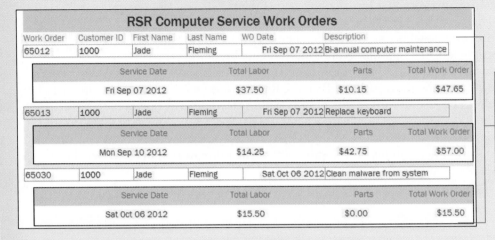

| RSR Computer Service Work Orders | | | | | |
| --- | --- | --- | --- | --- | --- |
| Work Order | Customer ID | First Name | Last Name | WO Date | Description |
| 65012 | 1000 | Jade | Fleming | Fri Sep 07 2012 | Bi-annual computer maintenance |

| Service Date | Total Labor | Parts | Total Work Order |
| --- | --- | --- | --- |
| Fri Sep 07 2012 | $37.50 | $10.15 | $47.65 |

| 65013 | 1000 | Jade | Fleming | Fri Sep 07 2012 | Replace keyboard |
| --- | --- | --- | --- | --- | --- |

| Service Date | Total Labor | Parts | Total Work Order |
| --- | --- | --- | --- |
| Mon Sep 10 2012 | $14.25 | $42.75 | $57.00 |

| 65030 | 1000 | Jade | Fleming | Sat Oct 06 2012 | Clean malware from system |
| --- | --- | --- | --- | --- | --- |

| Service Date | Total Labor | Parts | Total Work Order |
| --- | --- | --- | --- |
| Sat Oct 06 2012 | $15.50 | $0.00 | $15.50 |

Reducing the height of the *Detail* section allows Access to display more records on the page.

11. Close the report.

---

## Project 2   Add Features and Enhance a Report    2 Parts

You will modify the WorkOrders report to add page numbering, date and time controls, and graphics.

# Adding Page Numbering and Date and Time Controls

**▼ Quick Steps**

**Add Page Numbers**
1. Open Report in Design view.
2. Click Page Numbers button.
3. Select desired format, position, and alignment options.
4. Click OK.

Page Numbers

When you create a report using the Report tool, page numbering and the current date and time are automatically added to the top right of a report. The Report wizard automatically inserts the current date at the bottom left and page numbering at the bottom right of the report. In Design view, you can add page numbering to a report using the Page Numbers button in the Header/Footer group of the Report Design Tools Design tab. Clicking the button opens the Page Numbers dialog box

**Figure 5.3** Page Numbers Dialog Box

shown in Figure 5.3. Choose the desired format, position, and alignment for the page number and click OK. Access inserts a control object in either the Page Header or the *Page Footer* section depending on the *Position* option selected in the dialog box. Including the page number in a report is a good idea in case the pages become shuffled and need to be reorganized back into sequential order.

Add the current date and/or time in the *Report Header* section by clicking the Date and Time button in the Header/Footer group to open the Date and Time dialog box shown in Figure 5.4. By default both the *Include Date* and *Include Time* check boxes are selected. Access creates one control object for the desired date format and a separate control object for the desired time format. Access places the control objects with the date above the time aligned at the right edge of the *Report Header* section. Once inserted, you can move the controls to another section in the report. Adding a date and/or time control means that the current date and/or time the report is printed are included on the printout. This information is important for the reader of a report to know the currency of the data he or she is reading. Always include a date control as a minimum. Depending on the end user's needs, the time control may or may not be required.

**▼ Quick Steps**

**Add Date and/or Time**
1. Open report in Design view.
2. Click Date and Time button.
3. Select desired date and/or time options.
4. Click OK.
5. If necessary, move and/or resize controls as required.

Date and Time

**Figure 5.4** Date and Time Dialog Box

---

**Project 2a**  Adding Page Numbering and the Date and Time to a Report        Part 1 of 2

1. With the **AL2-C5-RSRCompServ.accdb** database open, right-click the WorkOrders report in the Navigation pane and click *Design View* at the shortcut menu.
2. When the subreport was inserted in Project 1e, the width of the report may have been automatically extended beyond the page width. Look at the Report Selector button. If a green diagonal triangle displays in the upper left corner of the button, correct the page width by completing the following steps; otherwise, skip this step if your Report Selector button does not display with a green diagonal triangle.
   a. Click the subreport control object to display the orange border and sizing handles. Point to the orange border and then drag the subreport control object left until the left edge of the control object is at the left edge of the *Detail* section. Next, drag the right middle sizing handle left to decrease the subreport width until the right edge of the subreport control object is aligned with the right edge of the *Descr* text box control object above it.

b. Click the green triangle to display the error checking options button and then click the error checking options button to display the drop-down list of options.

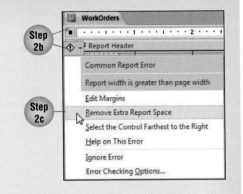

c. Click *Remove Extra Report Space* at the drop-down list to automatically decrease the width of the report. Notice the green diagonal triangle is removed from the Report Selector button once the report width has been corrected.

3. Add page numbering at the bottom center of each page by completing the following steps:

a. Click the Page Numbers button in the Header/Footer group of the Report Design Tools Design tab.

b. Click *Page N of M* in the *Format* section of the Page Numbers dialog box.

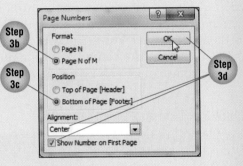

c. Click *Bottom of Page [Footer]* in the *Position* section.

d. With *Alignment* set to *Center* and a check mark in the *Show Number on First Page* check box, click OK. Access adds a control object in the center of the *Page Footer* section with the codes required to print the page numbers in the desired format.

4. Add the current date and time to the end of the report along with a label control object containing the text *Date and Time Printed:* by completing the following steps:

a. Click the Date and Time button in the Controls group.

b. Click the second option in the *Include Date* section in the Date and Time dialog box that displays the date in the format *dd-mmm-yy*. For example, *23-Nov-12*.

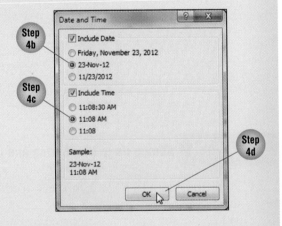

c. Click the second option in the *Include Time* section that displays the time in the format *hh:mm AM/PM*. For example, *11:08 AM*.

d. Click OK. Access adds two control objects one above the other at the right end of the *Report Header* section with the date code *=Date()* and the time code *=Time()*.

e. Select both control objects added to the *Report Header* section containing the date and time codes. Click the Home tab and then click the Cut button in the Clipboard group.

f. Click the *Report Footer* section bar and then click the Paste button in the Clipboard group. Access pastes the two objects at the left side of the *Report Footer* section. With the date and time control objects still selected, position the mouse pointer on the orange border until the pointer displays with the four-headed arrow move icon and then drag the controls to the right side of the *Report Footer* section, aligning the right edge of the controls near the right edge of the report grid.

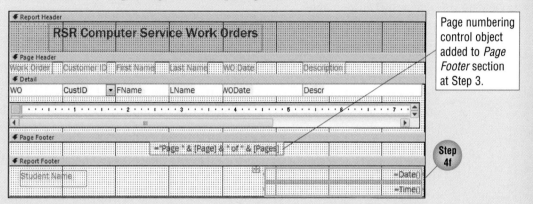

Page numbering control object added to *Page Footer* section at Step 3.

Step 4f

g. Resize and then move the date and time controls to arrange them as shown.

h. Create the two label control objects, type the text **Date Printed:** and **Time Printed:**, and position them left of the date control object and time control object as shown.

Steps 4g-4h

5. Save the report and then display Print Preview.

6. Scroll to the bottom of the first page to view the page numbering at the bottom center of the page.

7. Click the Last Page button in the Page Navigation bar to scroll to the last page in the report and view the date and time at the end of the report.

8. Notice in Print Preview the subreport data is being cut off at the right edge of the report, meaning that the total work order value is not visible. Exit Print Preview to switch back to Design view.

9. Adjust the size and placement of the subreport control objects by completing the following steps:

a. Since the subreport's control objects are not visible within the WorkOrders report, making changes to the contents of the subreport is more easily completed by working within the separate TotalWorkOrders subreport. Close the WorkOrders report.

b. Right-click the TotalWorkOrders subreport in the Navigation pane and then click Design View at the shortcut menu.

c. Press Ctrl + A to select all objects (Ctrl + A is the shortcut for Select All).

d. Position the mouse pointer on the edge of any selected control until the four-headed arrow move icon appears and then drag the controls to the left edge of the report grid.

e. Click in any blank area to deselect the controls and then drag the right edge of the grid left to approximately the 7-inch position in the horizontal ruler.

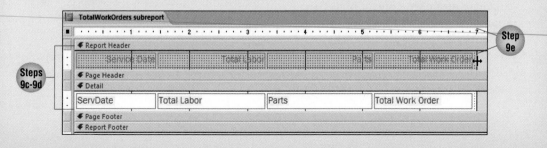

Step 9e

Steps 9c-9d

    f. Click to select the *Parts* label control object in the *Page Header* section and then drag the right middle sizing handle left until the right edge of the control aligns at the 5-inch position in the horizontal ruler.

10. Save and close the TotalWorkOrders subreport.
11. Open the WorkOrders report. Notice the subreport data is no longer truncated at the right side of the report.
12. Display the report in Design view.

# Adding Graphics to a Report ■■■■■■■■■■■■■■■■■■■■■

The same techniques that you learned in Chapter 4 to add pictures or clip art or to draw lines in a form in Design view can be applied to a report. Recall from Chapter 4 that clip art when resized is truncated to fit within the resized control object. Display the Property Sheet for the clip art object and change the Size Mode property to *Zoom* or *Stretch* to resize the image to the height and width of the control object.

Insert Image

    A company logo or other company artwork that is available in a standard picture file format such as .gif, .jpg, or .png can be inserted in an image control object. Click the Insert Image button in the Controls group of the Report Design Tools Design tab, browse to the image file's drive and folder, double-click the image file name, and then drag to create the image control object the desired height and width within the report.

---

**Project 2b**     **Adding Graphics and Formatting Controls**          Part 2 of 2

1. With the **AL2-C5-RSRCompServ.accdb** database open, insert a company logo in the report by completing the following steps:
    a. Position the mouse pointer on the top of the gray *Page Header* section bar until the pointer displays as a horizontal line with an up- and down-pointing arrow and then drag the section bar down approximately 0.5 inch to increase the height of the *Report Header* section.
    b. Click the Insert Image button in the Controls group of the Report Design Tools Design tab and then click *Browse* at the drop-down list.
    c. At the Insert Picture dialog box, navigate to the drive and or folder for the Access2010L2C5 data files on your storage medium and then double-click the file named **RSRLogo.jpg**.
    d. Position the crosshairs with the image icon attached at the top of the *Report Header* section near the 6-inch position in the horizontal ruler and then drag to create an image control object the approximate height and width shown at the right.

Steps
1b-1d

2. Draw and format a horizontal line below the title by completing the following steps:
    a. Click the More button at the bottom of the Controls scroll bar and then click the Line button in the expanded Controls group.

b. Position the crosshairs with the line icon attached below the first letter in the title in the *Report Header* section, hold down the Shift key, drag right releasing the mouse below the last letter in the title, and then release the Shift key.

c. Click the Report Design Tools Format tab and then click the Shape Outline button.

d. Point to *Line Thickness* and then click *3 pt* (fourth option).

e. With the line still selected, click the Shape Outline button, click *Turquoise, Accent 3* (seventh option in first row in *Theme Colors* section of color palette) and then deselect the line.

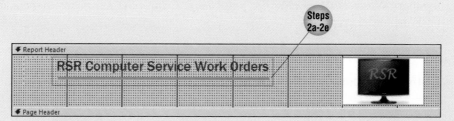

3. Draw and format a horizontal line below the report's column headings by completing the following steps:

a. Drag the top of the *Detail* section bar down approximately 0.25 inch to add grid space in the *Page Header* section.

b. Click the Report Design Tools Design tab, click the More button at the bottom of the Controls scroll bar, and then click the Line button in the expanded Controls group.

c. Draw a straight horizontal line that extends the width of the report along the bottom of the label control objects in the *Page Header* section.

d. Change the Line Thickness to *1 pt* and change the line color to the same turquoise applied to the line below the report title.

e. Deselect the line.

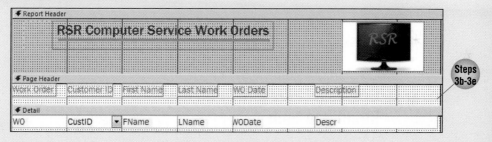

4. Format, move, and resize control objects as follows:

a. Select all of the label control objects in the *Page Header* section, change the font size to *12* and the font color to *Turquoise, Accent 3, Darker 50%* (seventh option in last row of *Theme Colors* section).

b. Resize the controls as needed to show all of the label text after increasing the font size.

c. Move the report title and the line below the title until the first *R* in the title is aligned at the 1-inch position in the horizontal ruler.

d. Move the *WO Date* label control object in the Page Header section until the left edge of the object is aligned at the 4.5-inch position in the horizontal ruler.

e. Click the *Report Header* section bar, click the Shape Fill button in the Control Formatting group of the Report Design Tools Format tab, and then click *White, Background 1* (first option in first row in *Theme Colors* section).

f. Select all of the text box control objects in the *Detail* section. Open the Property Sheet, click the Format tab, click in the *Border Style* property box, click the down-pointing arrow that appears, click *Transparent* at the drop-down list, and then close the Property Sheet. This removes the border around the data in the fields.

g. With all of the text box control objects still selected, change the font color to *Black, Text 1* (second option in first row of *Theme Colors* section).
5. Display the report in Report view.
6. Compare your report with the partial report shown in Figure 5.5. If necessary, return to Design view, make adjustments to formats, alignment, or position of control objects, and then redisplay the report in Report view.
7. Save the report.
8. Print the report. *Note: This report is five pages long. Print only if required by your instructor.*
9. Close the WorkOrders report.

**Figure 5.5** Partial View of Completed WorkOrders Report

| Work Order | Customer ID | First Name | Last Name | WO Date | Description |
|---|---|---|---|---|---|
| 65012 | 1000 | Jade | Fleming | Fri Sep 07 2012 | Bi-annual computer maintenance |

| Service Date | Total Labor | Parts | Total Work Order |
|---|---|---|---|
| Fri Sep 07 2012 | $37.50 | $10.15 | $47.65 |

| Work Order | Customer ID | First Name | Last Name | WO Date | Description |
|---|---|---|---|---|---|
| 65013 | 1000 | Jade | Fleming | Fri Sep 07 2012 | Replace keyboard |

| Service Date | Total Labor | Parts | Total Work Order |
|---|---|---|---|
| Mon Sep 10 2012 | $14.25 | $42.75 | $57.00 |

| Work Order | Customer ID | First Name | Last Name | WO Date | Description |
|---|---|---|---|---|---|
| 65030 | 1000 | Jade | Fleming | Sat Oct 06 2012 | Clean malware from system |

| Service Date | Total Labor | Parts | Total Work Order |
|---|---|---|---|
| Sat Oct 06 2012 | $15.50 | $0.00 | $15.50 |

## Project ③ Group Records and Add Functions to Count and Sum    2 Parts

You will create a new report using the Report Wizard and then modify the report in Design view to add sum and count functions.

# Grouping Records and Adding Functions in a Report

A field included in a report that contains repeating field values such as a department, city, or name, is a suitable field by which to group records. For example, a report could be organized to show all records together for the same department or the same city. By summarizing the records by a common field value, you can add totals using functions to calculate the sum, average, max, min, or count for each group. For example, a report similar to the partial report shown in

**Figure 5.6** Example Report with Work Order Records Grouped by Customer

### Work Orders by Customer

11/30/2012
9:39:45 PM

| Customer ID | First Name | Last Name | Work Order | Description | Service Date | Total Work Order |
|---|---|---|---|---|---|---|
| 1000 | Jade | Fleming | | | | |
| | | | 65012 | Bi-annual computer maintenance | Fri Sep 07 2012 | $47.65 |
| | | | 65013 | Replace keyboard | Mon Sep 10 2012 | $57.00 |
| | | | 65030 | Clean malware from system | Sat Oct 06 2012 | $15.50 |
| | | | 65033 | Install Windows 7 | Sat Oct 13 2012 | $433.25 |
| | | | | | Customer Total: | $553.40 |
| 1005 | Cayla | Fahri | | | | |
| | | | 65014 | Replace power supply | Mon Sep 10 2012 | $115.27 |
| | | | 65024 | Install malware protection | Mon Sep 24 2012 | $91.00 |
| | | | | | Customer Total: | $206.27 |
| 1008 | Leslie | Carmichael | | | | |
| | | | 65015 | Restore operating system | Tue Sep 11 2012 | $67.50 |
| | | | 65032 | Install second hard drive | Sat Oct 13 2012 | $485.75 |
| | | | 65036 | Set up home network | Tue Oct 16 2012 | $152.72 |
| | | | 65044 | DVD drive is not working | Tue Oct 23 2012 | $85.40 |
| | | | | | Customer Total: | $791.37 |

> Report is grouped on *CustID* field (displays with column heading *Customer ID*) allowing owners to easily see how many calls were made to each customer and how much revenue each customer generated.

Figure 5.6 that organizes the work orders by customer allows the owners of RSR Computer Service to easily see which customer has provided the most revenue to their service business. In this report, the *CustID* field (column heading *Customer ID*) is used to group the records and a sum function has been added to each group.

As you learned in Level 1, Chapter 6, you can group records in a report using the Report Wizard. At the Report Wizard dialog box shown in Figure 5.7, you can specify how you want to group the report. Double-click a field name in the field list box to add a grouping level. The preview window updates to display the grouped field in blue. More than one grouping level can be added to a report. If you change your mind after adding a grouping level, use the Remove Field button (button with left-pointing arrow) to remove the grouped level. Use the Priority buttons (buttons with up- and down-pointing arrows) to change the grouping order when you have multiple grouped fields.

If you created a report using the wizard and did not specify a grouping level, you can group records after the report has been generated using Layout view or

### ▼ Quick Steps

**Group Records Using Report Wizard**
1. Click Create tab.
2. Click Report Wizard button.
3. Choose table or query and fields.
4. Click Next.
5. If necessary, remove default grouped field name.
6. Double-click field name by which to group records.
7. Click Next.
8. Choose field(s) by which to sort.
9. Click Next.
10. Choose layout options.
11. Click Next.
12. Enter title for report.
13. Click Finish.

**Figure 5.7** Grouping by a Field Using the Report Wizard

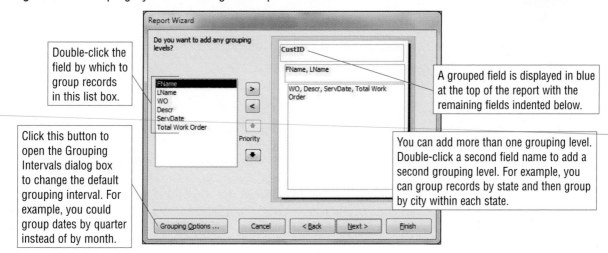

Double-click the field by which to group records in this list box.

Click this button to open the Grouping Intervals dialog box to change the default grouping interval. For example, you could group dates by quarter instead of by month.

A grouped field is displayed in blue at the top of the report with the remaining fields indented below.

You can add more than one grouping level. Double-click a second field name to add a second grouping level. For example, you can group records by state and then group by city within each state.

**Use Layout view to group records using the Group, Sort, and Total pane since Access does all of the work for you after you select the group field. In Design view, Access creates the *Group Header* section but does not automatically place the field's text box control within the group section—you have to do this manually.**

Design view. In Layout view, click the Group & Sort button in the Grouping & Totals group of the Report Layout Tools Design tab. In Design view, click the Group & Sort button in the Grouping & Totals group in the Report Design Tools Design tab. Clicking the button in either view opens the Group, Sort, and Total pane shown in Figure 5.8 at the bottom of the work area. Click the Add a group button and then click the field name by which to group records in the pop-up list.

**Figure 5.8** Group, Sort, and Total Pane

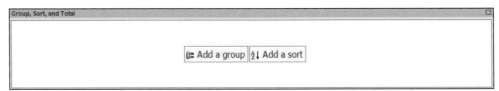

Group & Sort

---

**Project 3a**     **Creating a Report with a Grouping Level Using the Report Wizard**     Part 1 of 2

1. With the **AL2-C5-RSRCompServ.accdb** database open, modify the TotalWorkOrders query to add two fields you want to include in a report by completing the following steps:
   a. Open the TotalWorkOrders query in Design view.
   b. Drag the *CustID* field from the WorkOrders field list box to the *Field* box in the second column in the design grid. The existing *ServDate* and other fields will shift right to accommodate the new field.
   c. Drag the *Descr* field from the WorkOrders table to the *Field* box in the third column in the design grid.
   d. Save the revised query.
   e. Run the query.

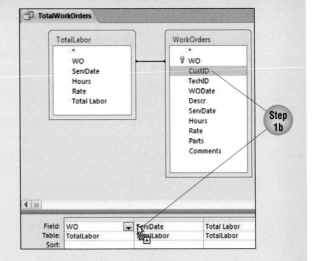

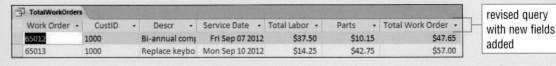

revised query with new fields added

   f. Close the query.
2. Create a report based on the TotalWorkOrders query that is grouped by the service dates by month using the Report Wizard by completing the following steps:
   a. Click the Create tab and then click the Report Wizard button in the Reports group.
   b. At the first Report Wizard dialog box with *Query: TotalWorkOrders* already selected in the *Tables/Queries* list box, move all of the fields from the *Available Fields* list box to the *Selected Fields* list box and then click Next.

c. At the second Report Wizard dialog box, specify the grouping level by the *ServDate* field by completing the following steps:

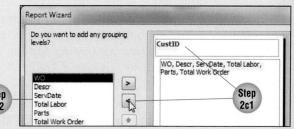

1) With *CustID* displayed in blue in the preview section indicating the report will be grouped by customer number, click the Remove field button (displays as a left-pointing arrow) to remove the grouping level.

2) Double-click *ServDate* in the field list box to add a grouping level by the service date field. By default, Access groups the date field by month.

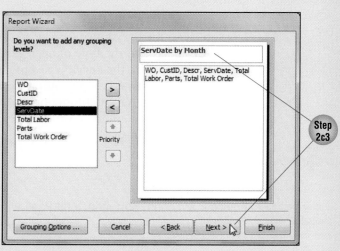

3) With the preview section now displaying that the report will be grouped by *ServDate by Month*, click Next.

d. At the third Report Wizard dialog box, click the down-pointing arrow at the right of the first sort list box, click *WO* at the drop-down list to sort within each group by the work order numbers in ascending order, and then click Next.

e. At the fourth Report Wizard dialog box, click *Landscape* in the *Orientation* section and then click Next.

f. At the last Report Wizard dialog box, select the existing text in the *What title do you want for your report?* text box, type **WorkOrdersbyMonth**, and click Finish.

3. Minimize the Navigation pane.

4. Preview the report and then switch to Layout view or Design view. Edit text in the report title and column heading labels and adjust widths as necessary until the report looks similar to the one shown below. Change the theme to *Flow* and modify the colors for the *Report Header* and *Page Header* sections using your best judgment to match the theme colors as shown.

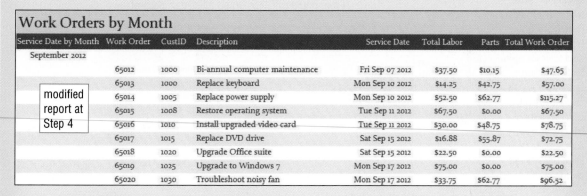

## Work Orders by Month

| Service Date by Month | Work Order | CustID | Description | Service Date | Total Labor | Parts | Total Work Order |
|---|---|---|---|---|---|---|---|
| September 2012 | | | | | | | |
| | 65012 | 1000 | Bi-annual computer maintenance | Fri Sep 07 2012 | $37.50 | $10.15 | $47.65 |
| | 65013 | 1000 | Replace keyboard | Mon Sep 10 2012 | $14.25 | $42.75 | $57.00 |
| | 65014 | 1005 | Replace power supply | Mon Sep 10 2012 | $52.50 | $62.77 | $115.27 |
| | 65015 | 1008 | Restore operating system | Tue Sep 11 2012 | $67.50 | $0.00 | $67.50 |
| | 65016 | 1010 | Install upgraded video card | Tue Sep 11 2012 | $30.00 | $48.75 | $78.75 |
| | 65017 | 1015 | Replace DVD drive | Sat Sep 15 2012 | $16.88 | $55.87 | $72.75 |
| | 65018 | 1020 | Upgrade Office suite | Sat Sep 15 2012 | $22.50 | $0.00 | $22.50 |
| | 65019 | 1025 | Upgrade to Windows 7 | Mon Sep 17 2012 | $75.00 | $0.00 | $75.00 |
| | 65020 | 1030 | Troubleshoot noisy fan | Mon Sep 17 2012 | $33.75 | $62.77 | $96.52 |

modified report at Step 4

5. Save the report.

When a report is grouped, the Group, Sort, and Total pane can be used to add a calculation below a numeric field at the end of each group. You can add a function to more than one field within the group. For example you can calculate a Sum function on a sales field and a Count function on an invoice field. The following functions are available for numeric fields: Sum, Average, Count Records, Count Values, Maximum, Minimum, Standard Deviation, and Variance. A non-numeric field can have a Count Records or Count Values function added.

The Group, Sort, and Total pane for a report with an existing grouping level displays similar to the one shown in Figure 5.9. Click the More Options button next to the group level to which a total is to be added to expand the available group options.

Click the down-pointing arrow next to *with no totals* to open the *Totals* option box similar to the one shown in Figure 5.10. Select the field to which a function should be added and the type of aggregate function to calculate using the drop-down list boxes. Use the check boxes to choose to add a grand total to the end of the report, calculate group subtotals as a percentage of the grand total, and whether to add the subtotal function to the *Group Header* or *Group Footer* section. Continue adding functions to other fields as needed and click outside the *Totals* option box when finished to close the box.

**Figure 5.9** Group, Sort, and Total Pane with a Grouping Level Added

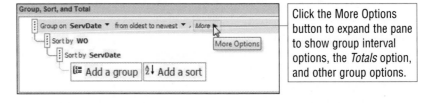

Click the More Options button to expand the pane to show group interval options, the *Totals* option, and other group options.

**Figure 5.10** *Totals* Option Box in Group, Sort, and Total Pane

Click here in the expanded options list to open the *Totals* option box in which you specify the field(s) and function(s) to add to the report. You can also add functions to calculate a grand total at the end of the report and calculate group totals as a percentage of the grand total.

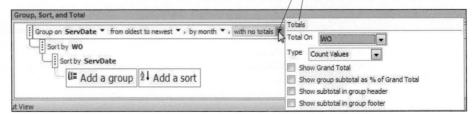

1. With the **AL2-C5-RSRCompServ.accdb** database open, display the WorkOrdersbyMonth report in Design view.

2. Add two functions at the end of each month to show the number of work orders and the total value of work orders by completing the following steps:

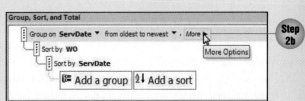

a. In the Grouping & Totals group of the Report Design Tools Design tab, click the Group & Sort button.

b. At the Group, Sort, and Total pane located at the bottom of the work area, click the More Options button located next to *from oldest to newest* in the *Group on ServDate* group options.

c. Click the down-pointing arrow next to *with no totals* in the expanded group options.

d. At the *Totals* option box, with *WO* in the *Total On* list box, specify the type of function and the placement of the result by completing the following steps:

1) Click the down-pointing arrow next to *Type* and then click *Count Records* at the drop-down list.

2) Click the *Show Grand Total* check box to insert a check mark. Access adds a count function in a control object in the *Report Footer* section below the *WO* column.

3) Click the *Show subtotal in group footer* check box to insert a check mark. Access displays a new section with the title *ServDate Footer* in the gray section bar below the *Detail* section and inserts a count function in a control object below the *WO* column.

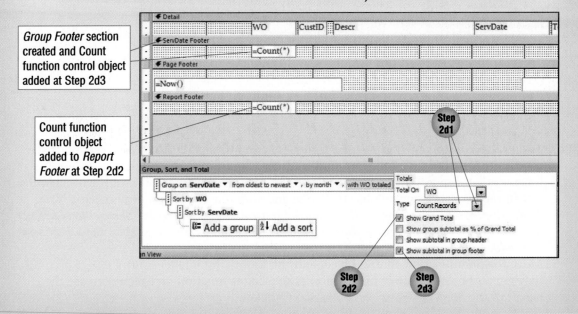

Group Footer section created and Count function control object added at Step 2d3

Count function control object added to *Report Footer* at Step 2d2

e. With the Totals option box still open, click the down-pointing arrow next to *Total On* and select *Total Work Order* at the drop-down list. The *Type* option defaults to *Sum* for a numeric field.

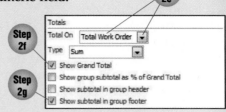

f. Click the *Show Grand Total* check box to insert a check mark. Access adds a Sum function in a control object in the *Report Footer* section.

g. Click the *Show subtotal in group footer* check box to insert a check mark. Access adds a Sum function in a control object in the *ServDate Footer* section.

h. Click outside the *Totals* option box to close the box.

3. Click the Group & Sort button to close the Group, Sort, and Total pane.

4. Review the two Count functions and the two Sum functions added to the report in Design view.

5. Display the report in Print Preview to view the calculated results. Notice the printout requires two pages with the report's grand totals printing on page 2. Also notice that Access added the Sum function below the Count function rather than at the bottom of the *Total Work Order* column.

6. Close Print preview to switch back to Design view.

7. Click to select the Sum function control object in the *ServDate Footer* section, Shift + click to select the Sum function control object in the *Report Footer* section. Position the mouse pointer on the orange border of either one of the selected control objects and then drag to move the two objects simultaneously to the right below the Total Work Order object in the *Detail* section.

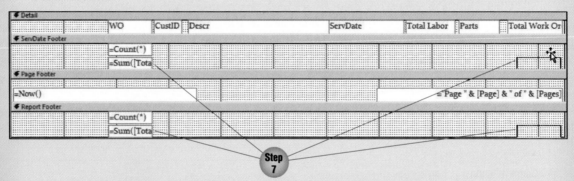

8. Add a label control object left of the Count function in the *ServDate Footer* section that displays the text *Work Order Count:* and another label control object left of the Sum function that displays the text *Month Total:*. Apply bold, red font color, and right-align the text in the two label control objects. Resize and align the two labels as necessary. ***Note: Access displays an error flag on the two label control objects indicating these objects are not associated with another control object. You can ignore these error flags since the labels have been added for descriptive text only.***

9. Move the Sum function control object and the Month Total label control object up until they are at the same horizontal position as the Count function and then decrease the height of the *ServDate Footer* section as shown below.

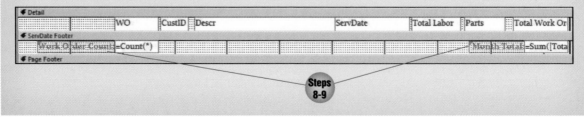

10. Display the report in Print Preview to view the labels. If necessary, return to Design view to make further size and alignment adjustments.

partial report displayed in Print Preview with labels and functions added

| Service Date by Month | Work Order | CustID | Description | Service Date | Total Labor | Parts | Total Work Order |
|---|---|---|---|---|---|---|---|
| September 2012 | | | | | | | |
| | 65012 | 1000 | Bi-annual computer maintenance | Fri Sep 07 2012 | $37.50 | $10.15 | $47.65 |
| | 65013 | 1000 | Replace keyboard | Mon Sep 10 2012 | $14.25 | $42.75 | $57.00 |
| | 65014 | 1005 | Replace power supply | Mon Sep 10 2012 | $52.50 | $62.77 | $115.27 |
| | 65015 | 1008 | Restore operating system | Tue Sep 11 2012 | $67.50 | $0.00 | $67.50 |
| | 65016 | 1010 | Install upgraded video card | Tue Sep 11 2012 | $30.00 | $48.75 | $78.75 |
| | 65017 | 1015 | Replace DVD drive | Sat Sep 15 2012 | $16.88 | $55.87 | $72.75 |
| | 65018 | 1020 | Upgrade Office suite | Sat Sep 15 2012 | $22.50 | $0.00 | $22.50 |
| | 65019 | 1025 | Upgrade to Windows 7 | Mon Sep 17 2012 | $75.00 | $0.00 | $75.00 |
| | 65020 | 1030 | Troubleshoot noisy fan | Mon Sep 17 2012 | $33.75 | $62.77 | $96.52 |
| | 65021 | 1035 | Customer has blue screen upon boot | Tue Sep 18 2012 | $97.50 | $0.00 | $97.50 |
| | 65022 | 1040 | Customer reports screen is fuzzy | Sat Sep 22 2012 | $45.00 | $55.47 | $100.47 |
| | 65023 | 1045 | Upgrade RAM | Sun Sep 23 2012 | $37.50 | $62.50 | $100.00 |
| | 65024 | 1005 | Install malware protection | Mon Sep 24 2012 | $15.50 | $75.50 | $91.00 |
| | 65025 | 1010 | Troubleshoot hard drive noise | Fri Sep 28 2012 | $45.00 | $0.00 | $45.00 |
| | 65026 | 1025 | Upgrade memory | Sat Sep 29 2012 | $22.50 | $75.75 | $98.25 |
| Work Order Count: | | 15 | | | | Month Total: | $1,165.16 |

11. With the report displayed in Design view, select the Sum function control object in the *Report Footer* section and move the control up until it is positioned at the same horizontal position as the Count function below the *WO* column.
12. Click to select the *Work Order Count*: label control object, Shift + click to select the *Month Total*: label control object, click the Home tab, and then click the Copy button in the Clipboard group. Click the *Report Footer* section bar and then click the Paste button in the Clipboard group. Move and align the copied labels as shown below. Edit the *Month Total*: label control object to *Grand Total*: as shown.

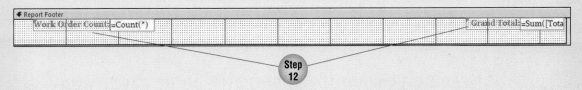

Step 12

13. Display the report in Report view. Scroll to the bottom of the page to view the labels next to the grand totals. If necessary, return to Design view to make further size and alignment adjustments and then save and close the report.
14. Redisplay the Navigation pane.

---

Project **4** **Modify Section and Group Properties**          **1 Part**

You will change a report's page setup and then modify section and group properties to control print options.

## Modifying Section Properties ■■■■■■■■■■■■■■■■■■

A report has a Property Sheet, each control object within the report has a Property Sheet, and each section within the report has a Property Sheet. Section properties control whether the section is visible when printed, the section's height, background color, special effects, and so on. Figure 5.11 displays the Format tab in the Property Sheet for the *Report Header* section. Some of the options can be

**Figure 5.11** *Report Header* Section Property Sheet with Format Tab Selected

▼ **Quick Steps**

**Modify Section Properties**
1. Open report in Design view.
2. Double-click gray section bar.
3. Change desired properties.
4. Close Property Sheet.

**Keep Group Together on One Page**
1. Open report in Design view or Layout view.
2. Click Group & Sort button.
3. Click More Options button.
4. Click down-pointing arrow next to *do not keep group together on one page.*
5. Click desired print option.
6. Close Group, Sort, and Total pane.

changed without opening the Property Sheet. For example, you can increase or decrease the height of a section by dragging the top or bottom of a gray section bar in Design view. You can also set the background color using the Fill/Back Color button in the Font group of the Report Design Tools Format tab.

Use the Keep Together property to ensure that a section is not split over two pages by a page break. If necessary, Access starts printing the section at the top of the next page; however, if the section is longer than can fit on one page, Access continues printing the section on the following page. In that case, you can decrease margins and/or apply a smaller font size to fit the text for the section all on one page.

Use the Force New Page property to insert a page break before a section begins *(Before Section)*, after a section is finished *(After Section)*, or before and after a section *(Before & After)*.

# Keeping a Group Together on the Same Page ▪▪▪▪▪▪▪▪

Open the Group, Sort, and Total pane and click the More Options button for a group to specify whether you want to keep an entire group together on the same page. By default, Access does not keep a group together. Click the down-pointing arrow next to *do not keep group together on one page* and then click the desired option as shown in Figure 5.12.

**Figure 5.12** Group, Sort, and Total Pane with Keep Group Together Print Options

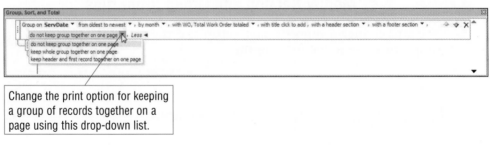

Change the print option for keeping a group of records together on a page using this drop-down list.

1. With the **AL2-C5-RSRCompServ.accdb** database open, display the WorkOrdersbyMonth report in Print Preview, click the Zoom button (do not click the down-pointing arrow on the button) in the Zoom group to change the zoom to view an entire page within the window.
2. Click the Next Page button in the Page Navigation bar to view page 2 of the report with the grand totals.
3. Switch to Design view and minimize the Navigation pane.
4. Change the section properties for the *Group Footer* and the *Report Footer* sections displaying the Count and Sum functions by completing the following steps:
   a. Double-click the gray *ServDate Footer* section bar to open the section's Property Sheet.
   b. Click in the *Back Color* property box and click the Build button to open the color palette.
   c. Click *Light Turquoise, Background 2* (third option in first row of *Theme Colors* section).
   d. Close the Property Sheet.
   e. Select the Count function control object and the Sum function control object in the *ServDate Footer* section and change the font color to red and apply bold.

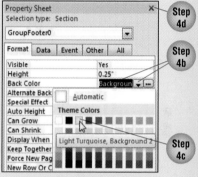

   f. With the Count and Sum function control objects still selected, right-click either one of the selected controls, point to *Fill/Back Color* at the shortcut menu, and then click *Transparent*. The controls by default displayed with a white fill color in the background. Changing to *Transparent* means the background color applied at Step 4c will now display behind the calculations.
   g. Double-click the gray *Report Footer* section bar and then change the *Back Color* to the same color as the ServDate footer (see Steps 4b through 4c) and then close the Property Sheet.
   h. Apply the same formatting in Steps 4e through 4f to the Count and Sum function control objects in the *Report Footer* section.
5. Print each month's work orders on a separate page by completing the following steps:
   a. Click the Group & Sort button in the Report Design Tools Design tab.
   b. Click the More Options button in the Group, Sort, and Total pane.
   c. Click the down-pointing arrow next to *do not keep group together on one page* and then click *keep whole group together on one page* at the drop-down list.
   d. Close the Group, Sort, and Total pane.
6. Create a label control object at the top right of the *Report Header* section with your first and last name. Bold the label control object and apply dark blue font color.
7. Display the report in Print Preview and zoom to One Page. Compare your report with the one shown in Figure 5.13. Scroll to page 2 to view all of October's work orders together on the same page.
8. Save, print, and then close the report.
9. Redisplay the Navigation pane.

**Figure 5.13** Page 1 of Completed Report in Project 4

| Service Date by Month | Work Order | CustID | Description | Service Date | Total Labor | Parts | Total Work Order |
|---|---|---|---|---|---|---|---|
| **Work Orders by Month** | | | | | | | **Student Name** |
| September 2012 | | | | | | | |
| | 65012 | 1000 | Bi-annual computer maintenance | Fri Sep 07 2012 | $37.50 | $10.15 | $47.65 |
| | 65013 | 1000 | Replace keyboard | Mon Sep 10 2012 | $14.25 | $42.75 | $57.00 |
| | 65014 | 1005 | Replace power supply | Mon Sep 10 2012 | $52.50 | $62.77 | $115.27 |
| | 65015 | 1008 | Restore operating system | Tue Sep 11 2012 | $67.50 | $0.00 | $67.50 |
| | 65016 | 1010 | Install upgraded video card | Tue Sep 11 2012 | $30.00 | $48.75 | $78.75 |
| | 65017 | 1015 | Replace DVD drive | Sat Sep 15 2012 | $16.88 | $55.87 | $72.75 |
| | 65018 | 1020 | Upgrade Office suite | Sat Sep 15 2012 | $22.50 | $0.00 | $22.50 |
| | 65019 | 1025 | Upgrade to Windows 7 | Mon Sep 17 2012 | $75.00 | $0.00 | $75.00 |
| | 65020 | 1030 | Troubleshoot noisy fan | Mon Sep 17 2012 | $33.75 | $62.77 | $96.52 |
| | 65021 | 1035 | Customer has blue screen upon boot | Tue Sep 18 2012 | $97.50 | $0.00 | $97.50 |
| | 65022 | 1040 | Customer reports screen is fuzzy | Sat Sep 22 2012 | $45.00 | $55.47 | $100.47 |
| | 65023 | 1045 | Upgrade RAM | Sun Sep 23 2012 | $37.50 | $62.50 | $100.00 |
| | 65024 | 1005 | Install malware protection | Mon Sep 24 2012 | $15.50 | $75.50 | $91.00 |
| | 65025 | 1010 | Troubleshoot hard drive noise | Fri Sep 28 2012 | $45.00 | $0.00 | $45.00 |
| | 65026 | 1025 | Upgrade memory | Sat Sep 29 2012 | $22.50 | $75.75 | $98.25 |
| Work Order Count: | | 15 | | | | Month Total: | $1,165.16 |

Friday, November 30, 2012

Page 1 of 2

---

## Project 5 — Create and Format a Chart — 2 Parts

You will create and format a chart in a customers report to show the total parts and labor on work orders by month.

## Inserting, Editing, and Formatting a Chart into a Report

**HINT**

The chart feature in Access is not the same Chart tool that is included with Word, Excel, and PowerPoint.

Insert Chart

A chart can be added to a report to graphically display numerical data from another table or query. The chart is linked to a field in the report that is common to both objects. Access summarizes and graphs the data from the charted table or query based on the fields you select for each record in the report.

With a report open in Design view, increase the height or width of the *Detail* section to make room for the chart, click the Insert Chart button in the Controls group of the Report Design Tools Design tab and drag the crosshairs with the chart icon attached the approximate height and width for the chart. When you release the mouse, Access launches the Chart Wizard with the first of six dialog boxes shown in Figure 5.14 that guide you through the steps of creating a chart.

**Figure 5.14  First Dialog Box in Chart Wizard**

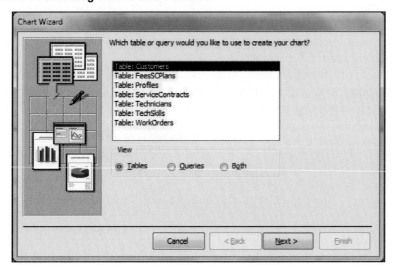

In Project 5 you will use the Chart Wizard to insert a chart in a customer report that depicts the total value of work orders for each customer by month. The data for the chart will be drawn from a related query. A chart can also be inserted into a form and formatted by completing steps similar to those in Projects 5a and 5b.

▼ **Quick Steps**

**Insert Chart in Report**
1. Open report in Design view.
2. Click Insert Chart button.
3. Drag to create control object the height and width desired.
4. Select table or query for chart data.
5. Click Next.
6. Add fields to use in chart.
7. Click Next.
8. Click desired chart type.
9. Click Next.
10. Add fields as needed to chart layout.
11. Click Preview Chart.
12. Close Sample Preview window.
13. Click Next.
14. Select field to link report with chart.
15. Click Next.
16. Type chart name.
17. Click Finish.

---

**Project 5a**  **Creating a Report and Inserting a Chart**  Part 1 of 2

1. With the **AL2-C5-RSRCompServ.accdb** database open, create a new report using the Report Wizard by completing the following steps:
   a. Select the Customers table in the Navigation pane, click the Create tab and then click the Report Wizard button.
   b. At the first Report Wizard dialog box with *Table: Customers* selected in the *Tables/Queries* list box, move *CustID, FName, LName,* and *ServCont* from the *Available Fields* list box to the *Selected Fields* list box and then click Next.
   c. Click Next at the second Report Wizard dialog box with no group field selected.
   d. Click Next at the third Report Wizard dialog to choose not to sort the report.
   e. Click *Columnar* at the fourth Report Wizard dialog box and then click Next.
   f. Click at the end of the current text in the *What title do you want for your report?* text box, type WOChart so that the report title is *CustomersWOChart*, and then click Finish.
2. Minimize the Navigation pane and display the report in Design view.
3. Edit the report title in the *Report Header* section to *Customers with Work Orders by Month*.
4. Drag the top of the *Page Footer* section bar down until the *Detail* section ends at the 2-inch position in the vertical ruler.

5. Insert a chart at the right side of the report to show the value of the work orders for each customer by month by completing the following steps:
   a. Click the More button at the bottom of the Controls scroll bar and then click the Chart button in the second row of the Controls.
   b. Position the crosshairs with the chart icon attached in the *Detail* section at the 5-inch position in the horizontal ruler aligned near the top of the *CustID* control object and drag down and right to create a chart object the approximate height and width shown.

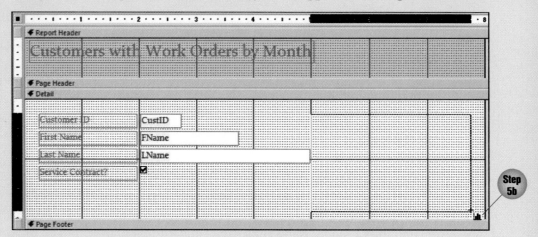

c. At the first Chart Wizard dialog box, click *Queries* in the *View* section, click *Query: TotalWorkOrders* in the list box, and then click Next.

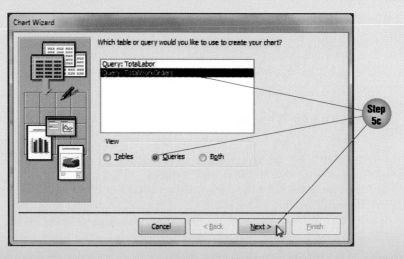

d. At the second Chart Wizard dialog box, double-click *ServDate* and *Total Work Order* in the *Available Fields* list box to move the fields to the *Fields for Chart* list box and then click Next.

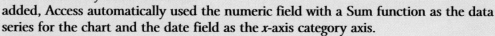

e. At the third Chart Wizard dialog box, click the second chart type in the first row (3-D Column Chart) and then click Next.

f. At the fourth Chart Wizard dialog box, look at the fields that Access has already placed to lay out the chart. Since only two fields were added, Access automatically used the numeric field with a Sum function as the data series for the chart and the date field as the *x*-axis category axis.

g. Click Next.

h. At the fifth Chart Wizard dialog box notice that Access has correctly detected the field to link records in the Customers report with the chart (based on the TotalWorkOrders query) as *CustID*. Click Next.

i. At the last Chart Wizard dialog box, click Finish. Access inserts a chart within the height and width of the chart control. The chart displayed in the control in Design view is not the actual chart based on the query data—it is only a sample to show the chart elements.

6. Display the report in Print Preview and scroll through the four pages in the report. Customers for which an empty chart displays have no work order data to be graphed.

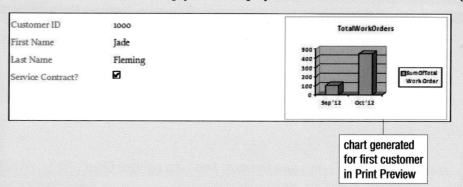

chart generated for first customer in Print Preview

7. Save and close the report and then redisplay the Navigation pane.

The chart application within Access is not the same chart feature that is available in Microsoft Word, Microsoft Excel, and Microsoft PowerPoint. Access uses the Microsoft Graph application for charts. Open a report in Design view and double-click a chart object to edit the chart. In chart editing mode, a Menu bar and a toolbar display at the top of the Access window as well as a datasheet for the chart in the work area. You can change the chart type, add, remove, or change chart options, and format chart elements.

**Change Chart Type**
1. Open report in Design view.
2. Double-click chart.
3. Click Chart on Menu bar.
4. Click *Chart Type*.
5. Click desired chart type in list box.
6. Click desired chart subtype.
7. Click OK.

**Change Chart Options**
1. Open report in Design view.
2. Double-click chart.
3. Click Chart on Menu bar.
4. Click *Chart Options*.
5. Click tab for options to be changed.
6. Change options as required.
7. Click OK.

**Format Chart Element**
1. Open report in Design view.
2. Double-click chart.
3. Right-click chart element.
4. Click *Format* for selected chart element.
5. Change format options as required.
6. Click OK.

Click Chart on the Menu bar and click *Chart Options* to add, delete, or edit text in chart titles, to add or remove chart axes, gridlines, the legend, data labels, or a data table at the Chart Options dialog box. Click Chart and click *Chart Type* to open the Chart Type dialog box and choose a different chart such as a bar chart or a pie chart.

Right-click an object within the chart such as the chart title, legend, chart area, or data series and a format option displays in the shortcut menu for the selected chart element. Click the Format option to open a Format dialog box for the selected element. Make the desired changes and click OK.

When you have finished editing the chart, click outside the chart object to exit chart editing mode. Sometimes Access displays a sample chart within the control object in chart editing mode instead of the actual chart which can make editing specific chart elements difficult if your actual chart does not match the sample. If this occurs, exit chart editing mode, close and reopen the report in Design view, or switch views to cause Access to update the chart displayed in the control object.

---

**Project 5b** | **Changing the Chart Type, Chart Options, and Formatting a Chart** | Part 2 of 2

1. With the **AL2-C5-RSRCompServ.accdb** database open, display the CustomersWOChart report in Design view.
2. Change the chart type, edit the chart title, and remove the legend in the chart by completing the following steps:
   a. Double-click within the chart to open the chart in chart editing mode. Access displays a datasheet with the chart and opens the Microsoft Graph application in which you edit charts.
   b. Click Chart on the Menu bar and then click *Chart Type*.

c. At the Chart Type dialog box with the Standard Types tab selected, click *Bar* in the *Chart type* list box and click the first chart in the second row in the *Chart sub-type* section.

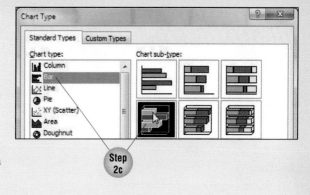

d. Click OK.
e. Click Chart on the Menu bar and then click *Chart Options*.
f. At the Chart Options dialog box with the Titles tab selected, edit the text in the *Chart title* text box by inserting a space between the words so that the title text reads *Total Work Orders*.
g. Click the Legend tab.
h. Click the *Show legend* check box to clear the check mark. Since there is only one data series, the chart title sufficiently describes the data and the legend can be removed from the chart.
i. Click OK.

3. Format the bars in the chart to change the shape and colors by completing the following steps. *Note: If the chart shown is not the actual chart but the sample chart showing multiple data bars, click outside the chart object to exit chart editing mode, save, and then close the report. Reopen the report in Report view, switch to Design view, and then double-click the chart to open Microsoft Graph.*

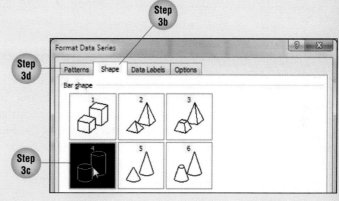

a. Right-click the bar in the chart and click *Format Data Series* at the shortcut menu.
b. At the Format Data Series dialog box, click the Shape tab.
c. Click *4* in the *Bar shape* section (cylinder shape).
d. Click the Patterns tab.
e. Click the bright blue color square (last option in last row).
f. Click OK.

4. Right-click the chart title, click *Format Chart Title* at the shortcut menu, click the Font tab, change the *Color* to red (first option in third row at drop-down list), and then click OK.
5. Click outside the chart object to exit Microsoft Graph.
6. Create a label control object with your first and last names in the *Report Header* section with the right edge of the control aligned with the right edge of the chart.

7. Display the report in Print Preview.

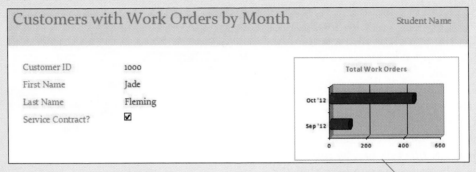

Customers with Work Orders by Month                    Student Name

| Customer ID | 1000 |
| First Name | Jade |
| Last Name | Fleming |
| Service Contract? | ☑ |

Total Work Orders

edited and formatted chart for first customer record displayed in Print Preview

8. Print the first page only of the report.
9. Save and close the report.

---

## Project 6 · Create a Blank Report with Hyperlinks and a List    1 Part

You will use the Blank Report tool to create a new report for viewing technician certifications. In the report, you will reorder the tab fields, create a list box inside a tab control, change the shape of the tab control, and add hyperlinks.

## Creating a Report Using the Blank Report Tool ▪■■■▪▪■■

**▼ Quick Steps**

**Create Blank Report**
1. Click Create tab.
2. Click Blank Report button.
3. Expand field list for desired table.
4. Drag fields to report as needed.
5. Add a title, control objects, format, or make other design changes as needed.
6. Save report.

A blank report begins with no controls or format and displays as a blank white page in Layout view similar to the blank form tool you learned about in Chapter 4. Click the Create tab and then click the Blank Report button in the Reports group to begin a new report. Access opens the Field List pane at the right side of the work area. Expand the list for the desired table and then add fields to the report as needed. If the Field List pane displays with no table names, click the hyperlink to Show all tables at the top of the pane.

### Adding a Tab Control to a Report

You learned how to add a tab control to a form in Chapter 4 in which you were able to display fields from different tables in pages. In Form view, you displayed a page by clicking the page tab. Similarly, a tab control can be used in a report to display fields from the same table or a different table in pages. To create a tab control in a report, follow the same steps you learned in Chapter 4 to add a tab control to a form.

### Adding a List Box or a Combo Box to a Report

Blank Report

Tab Control

List Box

As with a form, a list box in a report displays a list of values for a field within the control object. In Report view, one can easily see the entire list for the field. If a list is too long for the size of the list box control, scroll bars display with which you can scroll up or down the list when viewing the report. Although you cannot edit data in a report, you can use a list box to view all of the field values and see which value has been selected for the current record.

A combo box added to a report does not display as a list; however, the field value that was entered into the field from the associated table, query, or form is shown in the combo box control object. Since you cannot edit data in a report, the combo box field is not shown as a drop-down list. A combo box can be changed to display as a list box within the report. In this case, the list box displays all of the field values with the value stored in the current record shown selected within the list.

A list box or a combo box can be added to a report by following the same steps as you learned in Chapter 4 to add a list box or a combo box to a form.

## Adding Hyperlinks to a Report

With the Hyperlink button in the Controls group of the Report Layout Tools Design tab you can create a link in a report to a web page, a picture, an email address, or a program. Click the Hyperlink button and then click within the report at the desired location to open the Insert Hyperlink dialog box in which you provide the text to display in the control object and the address to which the object should be linked. Use the Places bar at the left of the Insert Hyperlink dialog box to choose to link to an existing file or web page, another object within the database, or an email address.

## Changing the Shape of a Control Object

The Change Shape button in the Control Formatting group of the Report Layout Tools Format tab contains eight shape options in a drop-down list. You can use the shape options to modify the appearance of a command button, a toggle button, a navigation button, or a tab control. Select the control object you want to modify, click the Change Shape button and then click the desired shape at the drop-down list.

## Changing the Tab Order of Fields

In Chapter 4 you learned how to open the Tab Order dialog box and change the order in which the tab key moves from field to field. In a report, you can also change the order in which the tab key moves from field to field in Report view. Although you do not add, delete, or edit data in Report view, you may want to use the tab key to move within a report. Display the report in Design view, click the Tab Order button in the Tools group of the Report Design Tools Design tab, and drag the fields up or down the *Custom Order* list as desired.

Combo Box

▼ **Quick Steps**

**Add Hyperlink to Report**
1. Open report in Layout view or Design view.
2. Click Hyperlink button in Controls group.
3. Click in desired location with report.
4. Type text to display in control in *Text to display* text box.
5. Type URL in *Address* text box.
6. Click OK.

**Change Shape of Control Object**
1. Open report in Layout view.
2. Click to select control object.
3. Click Report Layout Tools Format tab.
4. Click Change Shape button.
5. Click desired shape.

Hyperlink

Change Shape

Tab Order

---

**Project 6**  Creating a Blank Report with Hyperlinks and a List   Part 1 of 1

1. With the **AL2-C5-RSRCompServ.accdb** database open, click the Create tab and then click the Blank Report button in the Reports group.
2. If the Field List pane at the right side of the work area does not display the table names, click the Show all tables hyperlink; otherwise, proceed to Step 3.

3. Add fields from the Technicians table and a tab control object to the report by completing the following steps:
   a. Click the plus symbol next to the table named Technicians to expand the field list.
   b. Click the first field named *TechID* in the Field List pane and then drag the field to the top left of the report.
   c. Right-click the *Technician ID* column, point to *Layout* at the shortcut menu, and then click *Stacked*. A stacked layout is better suited to this report where you want to show each technician's certifications next to their name in a tab control object.
   d. Drag the *FName* field from the Field List pane below the first *Technician ID* text box control object. Release the mouse when you see the gold bar below the *01* text box control object next to *Technician ID*.
   e. Drag the *LName* field from the Field List pane below the first *First Name* text box control object. Release the mouse when the gold bar displays below *Pat*.
   f. Click the Tab Control button in the Controls group of the Report Layout Tools Design tab.
   g. Position the mouse pointer with the Tab Control icon attached at the right of the first *Technician ID* text box control in the report. Click the mouse when you see the gold bar displayed at the right of the *01* text box control object.
   h. Right-click the selected tab control object, point to *Layout*, and then click *Remove Layout* at the shortcut menu.
   i. Select the *HPhone* and *CPhone* fields in the Field List pane and then drag the two fields below the *Last Name* text box control object. Release the mouse when the gold bar displays below *Hynes*.
   j. Double-click over the first *Pagexx* tab (where *xx* is the page number) in the tab control object at the right of the report to select the tab control object. Point to the bottom orange border of the selected tab control object until the pointer displays as an up- and down-pointing arrow and then drag the bottom of the object down until the bottom aligns with the bottom of the *Cell Phone* control objects.

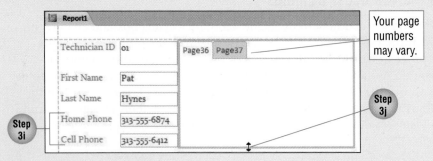

4. Add a field from the TechSkills table to the tab control object and change the control to a list box by completing the following steps:
   a. Click the plus symbol next to the TechSkills table name in the *Fields available in related tables* section of the Field List pane to expand the list.
   b. Click to select the *Certifications* field name and then drag the field to the first page in the tab control next to *Technician ID 01*.

c. Access inserts the field in the page with both the label control object and the text box control object selected. To change the field to display as a list box you need to select only the text box control object. Click to select the text box control object (displays *Cisco CCNP, CompTIA A+,* and *Microsoft MCTS* in the first record.

d. Right-click the selected text box control object, point to *Change To,* and then click *List Box* at the shortcut menu.

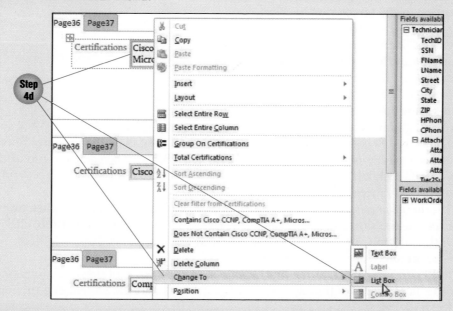

5. Add hyperlinks to the bottom of the tab control by completing the following steps:

a. Click the Hyperlink button in the Controls group of the Report Layout Tools Design tab.

b. Position the mouse pointer with the Hyperlink icon attached below *Certifications* in the tab control object. Release the mouse when the gold bar displays.

c. At the Insert Hyperlink dialog box, click in the *Text to display* text box and then type Cisco Certifications.

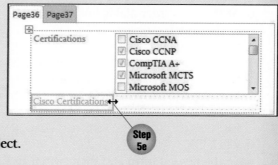

d. Click in the *Address* text box, type www.cisco.com/web/learning/ netacad/course_catalog/index.html, and then click OK.

e. Drag the right orange border of the hyperlink control object right until the entire text displays within the control object.

f. Add a second hyperlink control object below the list box in the tab control object that displays the text *Microsoft Certifications* and links to the address *www.microsoft .com/learning/en/us/certification/cert-overview.aspx* by completing steps similar to those in Steps 5a to 5d.

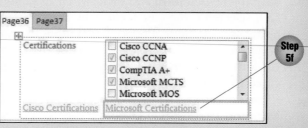

6. Right-click the second page in the tab control and then click *Delete Page* at the shortcut menu. Do not be concerned if Access displays the first page with an empty list box. The screen will refresh at the next step.

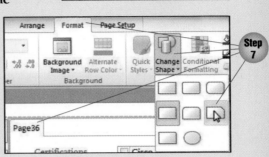

Step 6

7. Double-click over *Pagexx* (where *xx* is the page number) in the tab control to select the entire tab control object. Click the Report Layout Tools Format tab, click the Change Shape button in the Control Formatting group, and then click *Snip Single Corner Rectangle* at the drop-down list (last option in second row of shapes).

Step 7

8. Click to select *Pagexx* (where *xx* is the page number), click the Report Layout Tools Design tab, and then click the Property Sheet button to open the Property Sheet. With *Selection Type: Page* displayed at the top of the Property Sheet, click in the *Caption* property, type Technician's Certifications, and then close the Property Sheet.

9. Right-click the *Technician ID* text box control object (displays *01*) and then click *Select Entire Column* at the shortcut menu. Click the Report Layout Tools Format tab, click the Shape Outline button, and then click *Transparent* at the drop-down list.

10. Save the report and name it *TechCertifications*.

11. Switch to Report view. Click in the first *Technician ID* text box and press Tab four times to see how the Tab key moves through the first fields in order at the left edge of the report.

12. Switch to Design view. Assume that you want the Tab key to move to the technician's last name first and then to the technician's first name. Change the tab order of the fields by completing the following steps:

   a. Click the Tab Order button in the Tools group of the Report Design Tools Design tab.

   b. At the Tab Order dialog box, click in the gray bar next to *LName* in the *Custom Order* section to select the field and then drag the field to the top of the list until the black line displays above *TechID*.

   c. Drag *TechID* to the bottom of the list.

   d. Click OK.

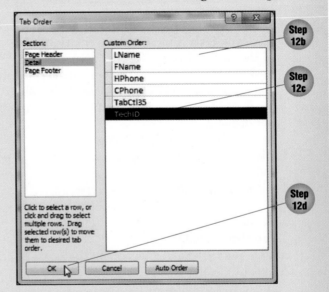

Step 12b

Step 12c

Step 12d

13. Save the revised form and then switch to Report view. Press the Tab key. Notice the first field selected is the *Last Name* field. Press Tab a second time. Notice the selected field moves to *First Name*. Press Tab two more times to watch the selected fields move to the *Home Phone* and *Cell Phone* fields below the *Last Name* field.

14. Click the *Cisco Certifications* hyperlink to open an Internet Explorer window and display the Cisco Courses & Certificatioins web page.

15. Close the browser window and then click the *Microsoft Certifications* hyperlink to display the Microsoft Certification Overview page in a browser window.

16. Close the browser window and then display the report in Print Preview.
17. Print the first page only of the report and then close Print Preview.
18. Close the TechCertifications report and then close the **AL2-C5-RSRCompServ.accdb** database.

In this chapter you have learned how to build a custom report from scratch using Design view. You have also created reports using the Report Wizard and the Blank Report tool and used options in Design view and Layout view to customize the reports. As you become more comfortable with reports, explore other tools available in Layout View and Design view using the Design, Arrange, Format, and Page Setup tabs. More features are available to assist you with creating professional-quality reports.

# Chapter Summary

- A report generally contains five sections: *Report Header, Page Header, Detail, Page Footer,* and *Report Footer*.

- Drag a field or group of fields from the Field List pane to the *Detail* section of the report, which represents the body of the report.

- An additional *Group Header* and *Group Footer* section can be added if the report is grouped by a field containing repeating values such as a department or city.

- Click the Create tab and click the Report Design button to build a custom report from scratch.

- Connect a table or query to a report using the *Record Source* property box in the Data tab of the report's Property Sheet.

- Place label control objects to be used as column headings in a tabular report within the *Page Header* section in Design view.

- A related table or query can be inserted as a subreport within a main report. A subreport is stored as a separate object outside the main report.

- Click the Page Numbers button in the Header/Footer group to open the Page Numbers Dialog box in which you specify the format, position, and alignment options for page numbering in a report.

- The current date and/or time can be added as a control object within the *Report Header* section using the Date and Time button in the Header/Footer group.

- Add pictures, clip art images, or draw lines in a report using the same techniques that you learned for adding graphics to forms.

- A report can be grouped by a field at the Report Wizard or by opening the Group, Sort, and Total pane.

- Functions such as Sum, Average or Count can be added to each group within a report and grand totals added to the end of a report by expanding the group options in the Group, Sort, and Total pane.

- Each section within a report has a set of properties that can be viewed or changed by opening the section's Property Sheet.
- The Keep Together property for a section is used to prevent a section from being split by a page break.
- The Force New Page property in a section Property Sheet can be used to automatically insert a page break before a section begins, after the section ends, or before and after a section.
- At the Group, Sort, and Total pane, you can specify to keep an entire group together on the same page.
- A chart can be added to a report to graphically display numerical data from another table or query related to the report.
- Open a report in Design view, click the Chart button in the Controls group to create a chart control object in a report or form, and use the Chart Wizard to generate the chart.
- Double-click a chart control object in Design view to edit the chart using Microsoft Graph by changing the chart type; adding, removing, or changing chart options; and formatting chart elements.
- The Blank Report tool in the Reports group in the Create tab creates a new report with no controls or format applied. The report opens as a blank white page in Layout view with the Field List pane opened at the right of the work area.
- A tab control and a list box can be added to a blank report using the same techniques as you learned for adding these controls to a form.
- Use the Hyperlink button to create a link in a report to a web page, a picture, an email address, or a program.
- The shape of a command button, a toggle button, a navigation button, or a tab control can be modified using the Change Shape button in the Control Formatting group of the Report Layout Tools Format tab.
- You can alter the order of the fields in which the Tab key will move within a report at the Tab Order dialog box. Display a report in Design view to access the Tab Order button in the Tools group of the Report Design Tools Design tab.

# Commands Review

| FEATURE | RIBBON TAB, GROUP | BUTTON |
|---|---|---|
| Add existing fields | Report Design Tools Design, Tools | |
| Blank report | Create, Reports | |
| Change Shape of selected control | Report Layout Tools Format, Control Formatting | |
| Date and Time | Report Design Tools Design, Header/Footer | |
| Design view | Report Design Tools Design, Views | |
| Group & Sort | Report Design Tools Design, Grouping & Totals | |
| Insert a chart | Report Design Tools Design, Controls | |
| Insert a Hyperlink | Report Layout Tools Design, Controls | |
| Insert image | Report Design Tools Design, Controls | |
| Page numbering | Report Design Tools Design, Header/Footer | |
| Property Sheet | Report Design Tools Design, Tools | |
| Report Design | Create, Reports | |
| Report Wizard | Create, Reports | |
| Report view | Report Design Tools Design, Views | |
| Subreport | Report Design Tools Design, Controls | |
| Tab Control | Report Layout Tools Design, Controls | |
| Tab Order | Report Design Tools Design, Tools | |
| Theme | Report Design Tools Design, Themes | |
| Title | Report Design Tools Design, Header/Footer | |

# Concepts Check Test Your Knowledge

**Completion:** In the space provided at the right, indicate the correct term, command, or number.

1. Add controls in this section to print grand totals at the end of a report.

   _____

2. Double-click this button to open the Property Sheet for a report.

   _____

3. The Subform/Subreport button is found in this group within the Report Design Tools Design tab.

   _____

4. The Page Numbers button is located in this group in the Report Design Tools Design tab.

   _____

5. If the date and time are added to a report using the Date and Time dialog box, Access creates the control objects in this report section.

   _____

6. At the Report Wizard dialog box, Access displays a grouped field in this color in the preview section.

   _____

7. An existing report can have grouping added by opening this pane.

   _____

8. Click this button to expand the group options for a grouped field in order to add a Sum function to each group.

   _____

9. Modify this section property to instruct Access to insert a page break after the section is finished printing.

   _____

10. Double-click this element in report Design view to open the Property Sheet for a section.

   _____

11. Use this button in the expanded Controls group to insert a bar chart into a report.

   _____

12. Launch the Microsoft Graph application to edit a chart by doing this action with the mouse.

   _____

13. When finished editing a chart, exit Microsoft Graph by doing this action with the mouse.

   _____

14. This report tool opens as a blank white page in Layout view.

   _____

15. Click this button to create a control object within a report that will display a web page when clicked.

   _____

16. This button in the Control Formatting group of the Report Layout Tools Format tab can be used to change the shape of a selected control.

   _____

# Skills Check  Assess Your Performance

## Assessment

### 1 | CREATE A CUSTOM REPORT USING DESIGN VIEW

1. Open the database named **AL2-C5-VantageVideos.accdb** and enable content.
2. Create a new report using the Report Design button and build the report using the following specifications:
   a. Add a title in the *Report Header* section with the text Web Products and Sales.
   b. Add your name in a label control object in the center of the *Report Footer* section.
   c. Connect the WebProducts table to the report. Add all of the fields from the table to the report.
   d. Move the label control objects for each field from the *Detail* section to the *Page Header* section arranging the controls horizontally in the order the fields appeared in the table. You determine the amount of space to leave between controls. Resize the *Page Header* section when finished so that the extra space is removed.
   e. Align each text box control object in the *Detail* section below the object's associated label control object in the *Page Header* section.
   f. Use Report view to check alignment and width of controls to make sure data is not truncated in any of the control objects. Make adjustments as needed in Design view or Layout View.
   g. Apply the Opulent theme.
   h. Insert a subreport into the *Detail* section using the following specifications. *Hint: You may need to first adjust the height of the* Detail *section to make room for the subreport if you have been using Layout view.*
      1) Use the WebSaleswithTotal query and add the fields in order *CustID, WebOrdID, DateOrd, WebProdID,* and *Qty* to the subreport.
      2) Accept the default link option to link the main report to the subreport on the *WebProdID* field.
      3) Accept the default subreport name.
      4) Edit the text in the subreport label control object to *Web Sales.*
      5) View the report to ensure the data is properly linked.
      6) Remove the *WebProdID* field (including the associated label control object) from the subreport since this data is duplicated in the main report and then move the *Qty* field (including the associated label control object) left to fill in the space.
      7) Move and/or resize the subreport control object as desired.
   i. Resize the *Detail* section so that the section ends just below the subreport.
   j. Format the *WebProdID, Product, InStock,* and *SellPrice* fields in the *Detail* section to 12-point bold.
   k. Make any additional adjustments to the position, height, width, alignment, or formatting of any control objects you think would improve the appearance of the report; however, do not add any further elements as you will continue work on this report in the next assessment.
3. Save the report and name it *WebProductsWithSales.*
4. Print and then close the report.

## Assessment

### 2 ENHANCE THE REPORT

1. With the **AL2-C5-VantageVideos.accdb** database open, display the WebProductsWithSales report in Design view.
2. Add page numbering using the *Page N of M* format to the bottom left of each page.
3. Add the current date to the bottom right of each page aligning the right edge of the control in the *Page Footer* section at the 7-inch position in the horizontal ruler. You determine the date format.
4. Insert an appropriate clip art image to the top right of the report resized to a suitable height and width and with the right edge of the image aligned at the 7-inch position in the horizontal ruler. Adjust the position of the report title to center it vertically left of the clip art image and horizontally within the title control object.
5. Draw a horizontal line under the report title. You determine the line thickness, line type, and line color.
6. Change all four margins for the report to 0.5 inch.
7. The diagonal green triangle appears on the Report Selector button after changing the margins. Click the Error Checking button and then click *Select the Control Farthest to the Right*. This will remove the drop-down list and select the control object that is at the right edge of the report that would prevent you from resizing the grid to remove extra space. The control selected is part of the date and time controls that were added within the title placeholder at Step 3. Drag the right middle sizing handle of the selected control left to decrease the control's width aligning the control at the right edge of the clip art image. Click the Error Checking button again and then click *Remove Extra Report Space* at the drop-down list.
8. Save the report.
9. Print page 1 only of the revised report and then close the report.

## Assessment

### 3 CREATE A NEW REPORT WITH GROUPING AND TOTALS

1. With the **AL2-C5-VantageVideos.accdb** database open, create a new report using the Report Wizard as follows:
   a. Use the WebSalesWithTotal query and add all fields to the report except *CustID* and *WebProdID*.
   b. Group by the *DateOrd* field by month.
   c. Click Next to leave the sort field blank.
   d. Use a *Stepped* layout in *Landscape* orientation.
   e. Edit the report title to *WebSalesByDate*.
2. Preview both pages of the report and then switch to Design view.
3. Add your name in a label control object at the left edge of the *Report Footer* section.
4. Open the Group, Sort, and Total pane and make the following changes:
   a. Add a Sum function to each month's *Total Sale* column. Show a grand total at the end of the report as well as the subtotal in the group footer.
   b. Add a sort by the *LastName* field.
5. Add an appropriate label next to the Sum function in the *DateOrd Footer* section and next to the Sum function in the *Report Footer* section.

6. Edit the report title to *Web Sales by Date* and edit the *DateOrd by Month* label to *Month*.
7. Display the report in Print Preview and note any column widths that need to be adjusted or labels that need to be edited in order to display the entire entry. Switch to Design view or Layout view and adjust column widths as necessary so that all data is entirely visible. If necessary, abbreviate long column labels. For example, *Quantity* could be abbreviated to *Qty*.
8. Change the top and bottom margin to 0.75 inch and then print the report.
9. Save and then close the report.

## Assessment

### 4 CREATE AND FORMAT A NEW REPORT WITH A CHART

1. With the **AL2-C5-VantageVideos.accdb** database open, create a new report using the Report Wizard as follows:
   a. Use the WebCustomers table and add the customer number, customer name, and home telephone fields to the report.
   b. Do not group or sort the report.
   c. Use a *Columnar* layout in *Portrait* orientation.
   d. Edit the report title to *WebCustomersWithChart*.
2. Preview the report.
3. Switch to Design view.
4. Insert a chart at the right side of the page next to each customer record using the following information:
   a. Use the WebSalesWithTotal query.
   b. Add the *DateOrd* and *Total Sale* fields to the chart field list.
   c. Select a bar chart style. You determine which style to use.
   d. Accept the default chart layout that Access creates with *DateOrd by month* as the *x*-axis labels and *SumOfTotal Sale* as the value axis.
   e. Accept *CustID* as the linked field for the report and the chart.
   f. Edit the title for the chart to *Web Sales*.
5. Preview the report with the bar chart and then switch to Design view.
6. Edit the chart as follows:
   a. Change the chart type to a column chart. You determine the sub-type.
   b. Delete the legend.
   c. Change the color of the bar to dark purple.
7. Edit the report title to *Customers with Web Sales Chart*.
8. Add your name in a label control object at the bottom left of the report.
9. Make any other formatting changes you think would improve the appearance of the report.
10. Print page 1 only of the report.
11. Save and then close the report.

## Assessment

### 5 CREATE A CUSTOM REPORT USING THE BLANK REPORT TOOL

1. With the **AL2-C5-VantageVideos.accdb** database open, create a new report using the Blank Report tool.
2. Add the first field named *CustID* from the WebCustomers table and then change the layout of the report to *Stacked*.

3. Add the remaining fields from the WebCustomers table below the *Customer ID* field. Make sure you release the mouse with the gold bar displayed below *101* for the first *Customer ID*.
4. Widen the labels column so that *Street Address* does not wrap to a second line in the label column.
5. Insert a tab control object at the right of the *Customer ID* field. Make sure you click the mouse when the gold bar displays at the right of *101*.
6. Remove the layout from the tab control column and then lengthen the tab control object to align with the bottom of the *Home Phone* field.
7. Expand the field list for the *WebCustPymnt* table and then add the following fields to the tab control object.
    *CCType*
    *CCNumber*
    *CCExpMonth*
    *CCExpYear*
8. Select all of the label control objects in the tab control and widen the objects so that all of the label text is visible.
9. Save the report and name it *CustomersWithCreditCards*.
10. Delete the second page in the tab control and then change the shape of the selected tab control object. You choose the shape.
11. Change the caption of the page in the tab control to *Credit Card Details*.
12. Insert a title at the top of the report with the text *Customers with Payment Information*.
13. Print the first page only of the report.
14. Save and close the report and then close the **AL2-C5-VantageVideos.accdb** database.

# Visual Benchmark Demonstrate Your Proficiency

## CREATE CUSTOM RESERVATIONS REPORT WITH TOTALS

1. Open **AL2-C5-PawsParadise.accdb** and enable content.
2. Review the partial report shown in Figure 5.15. This report was created based on the Dog Owners table with the Dogs table added as a subreport. Create the report with subreport with the following specifications and using your best judgment for formatting options as well as alignment, spacing, sizing, and position of controls:
   a. Apply the Austin theme.
   b. Substitute another suitable clip art image if the one shown is not available on the computer you are using.
   c. Add the current date and page numbering to the bottom of each page.
   d. Edit the labels in the subreport as shown in Figure 5.15.
   e. Add your name in the *Report Footer* section.
3. Save the report naming it *DogOwnersWithDogs*.
4. Preview the report. If necessary return to Layout view or Design view to make adjustments as needed. When finished, save and print the report.
5. Close the report and then close the **AL2-C5-PawsParadise.accdb** database.

**Figure 5.15 Partial View of Completed Visual Benchmark Report**

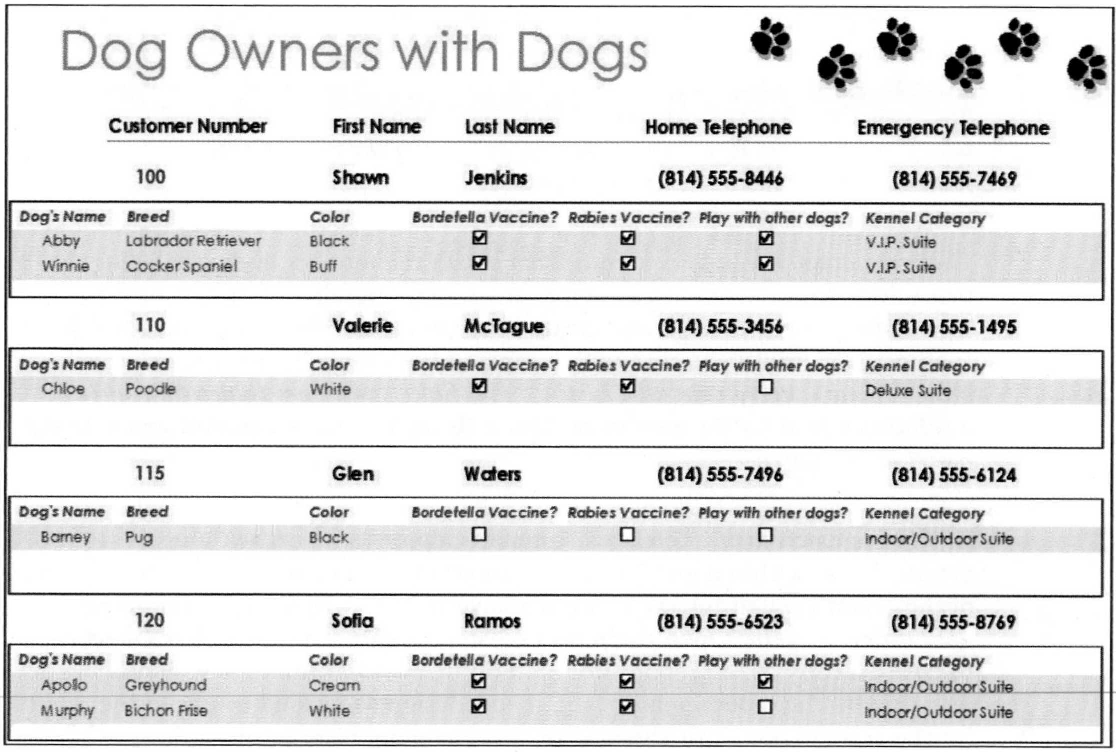

Dog Owners with Dogs

| Customer Number | First Name | Last Name | Home Telephone | Emergency Telephone |
|---|---|---|---|---|
| 100 | Shawn | Jenkins | (814) 555-8446 | (814) 555-7469 |

| Dog's Name | Breed | Color | Bordetella Vaccine? | Rabies Vaccine? | Play with other dogs? | Kennel Category |
|---|---|---|---|---|---|---|
| Abby | Labrador Retriever | Black | ☑ | ☑ | ☑ | V.I.P. Suite |
| Winnie | Cocker Spaniel | Buff | ☑ | ☑ | ☑ | V.I.P. Suite |

| | | | | |
|---|---|---|---|---|
| 110 | Valerie | McTague | (814) 555-3456 | (814) 555-1495 |

| Dog's Name | Breed | Color | Bordetella Vaccine? | Rabies Vaccine? | Play with other dogs? | Kennel Category |
|---|---|---|---|---|---|---|
| Chloe | Poodle | White | ☑ | ☑ | ☐ | Deluxe Suite |

| | | | | |
|---|---|---|---|---|
| 115 | Glen | Waters | (814) 555-7496 | (814) 555-6124 |

| Dog's Name | Breed | Color | Bordetella Vaccine? | Rabies Vaccine? | Play with other dogs? | Kennel Category |
|---|---|---|---|---|---|---|
| Barney | Pug | Black | ☐ | ☐ | ☐ | Indoor/Outdoor Suite |

| | | | | |
|---|---|---|---|---|
| 120 | Sofia | Ramos | (814) 555-6523 | (814) 555-8769 |

| Dog's Name | Breed | Color | Bordetella Vaccine? | Rabies Vaccine? | Play with other dogs? | Kennel Category |
|---|---|---|---|---|---|---|
| Apollo | Greyhound | Cream | ☑ | ☑ | ☑ | Indoor/Outdoor Suite |
| Murphy | Bichon Frise | White | ☑ | ☑ | ☐ | Indoor/Outdoor Suite |

# Case Study  Apply Your Skills

**Part 1**

Continuing your work as an intern at Hillsdale Realty, your next task is to create reports for management. Open the database named **AL2-C5-HillsdaleRealty.accdb** and enable content. For each report created, add your name in a label control object in the Report Footer. The first report has been requested by the office manager. The office manager uses the SalesByAgentWithComm query frequently but has asked for a report that provides the information in a more useful format. Specifically, the office manager would like the report to be organized with each individual agent's sales together showing the total value of sales and commissions earned for that agent and sorted by the date the listing sold. The office manager would also like to see grand totals and the percentage of the grand total that each agent has achieved for the sale prices and commissions earned. Design and create the report including features such as page numbering, date and time controls, and graphics. Save the report and name it appropriately. Print the report with top and bottom margins set to 0.5 inch and making sure that an entire group is kept together on the same page.

**Part 2**

The office manager would like a printout of the listings with the client's preferences and the agent attached to the listing grouped by the city. (Note that not all listings have a preferences record but the office manager wants to see all listings on the report.) You determine an appropriate sort order within each city's group of records. Design and create the report. Save the report and name it appropriately. Print the report with a top margin of 0.75 inch and make sure that an entire group is kept together on the same page. *Hint: Consider creating a query first with the relevant fields needed from the Listings, Preferences, and Agents tables and base the report on the query. For one of the relationships in the query you will need to modify the join properties.*

**Part 3**

The accountant would like a report that shows the number of days a listing that sold was on the market as well as the average number of days it took to sell a listing by city. Design and create the report. Save the report and name it appropriately. Print the report with a top and bottom margins set to 0.75 inch. *Hint: Create a query using the Listings and SalesAndComm tables that includes a calculated field for the number of days a listing was on the market and base the report on the query.*

**Part 4**

In Help research how to create a summary report (a report without the record details shown within a group). The accountant would like a compacted version of the report created for the office manager in Part 1 that shows the totals only for each agent. Open the report created in Part 1 and use *Save Object As* to create a copy of the report. You determine an appropriate new name. In the new copy of the report, modify the report design as needed to create the report for the accountant. Print the new report, changing page setup options as needed to fit the entire report on one page. Save and close the report. Close the **AL2-C5-HillsdaleRealty.accdb** database.

# Microsoft® Access®

# Using Access Tools and Managing Objects

## PERFORMANCE OBJECTIVES

Upon successful completion of Chapter 6, you will be able to:

- Create a new database using a template
- Add a group of objects to a database using an Application Parts template
- Create a new form using an Application Parts Blank Form
- Create a form to be used as a template in a database
- Create a table by copying the structure of another table
- Evaluate a table using the Table Analyzer Wizard
- Evaluate a database using the Performance Analyzer
- Split a database
- Print documentation about a database using the Database Documenter
- Rename and delete objects

**Tutorials**

**6.1** Creating a Database Using a Template

**6.2** Creating a Table Using a Table Template

**6.3** Copying a Table Structure to a New Table

**6.4** Modifying a Table Using the Table Analyzer Wizard

**6.5** Optimizing Performance Using the Performance Analyzer

**6.6** Splitting a Database

**6.7** Documenting a Database

**6.8** Renaming and Deleting Objects

Access provides tools to assist you with creating and managing databases and objects within databases. Templates are provided that can be used to create a new database or create a new table and/or related group of objects. Blank form templates provide you with a predefined layout and may include a form title and command buttons. If none of the predefined templates suit your needs, you can create your own template. Access provides wizards to assist with analyzing a table and a database in order to improve performance. A database can be split into two files to store the tables separate from the queries, forms, and reports. The Database Documenter can be used to print a report that provides details about objects and object properties. In this chapter you will learn how to use these Access tools and how to rename and delete objects in the Navigation pane. Model answers for this chapter's projects appear on the following pages.

Access2010L2C6

*Note: Before beginning the projects, copy to your storage medium the Access2010L2C6 subfolder from the Access2010L2 folder on the CD that accompanies this textbook and then make Access2010L2C6 the active folder.*

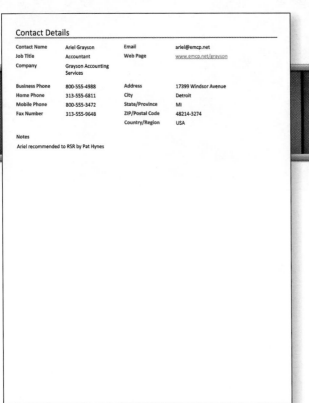

**Contact Details**

| | | | | |
|---|---|---|---|---|
| Contact Name | Ariel Grayson | Email | | ariel@emcp.net |
| Job Title | Accountant | Web Page | | www.emcp.net/grayson |
| Company | Grayson Accounting Services | | | |
| Business Phone | 800-555-4988 | Address | | 17399 Windsor Avenue |
| Home Phone | 313-555-6811 | City | | Detroit |
| Mobile Phone | 800-555-3472 | State/Province | | MI |
| Fax Number | 313-555-9648 | ZIP/Postal Code | | 48214-3274 |
| | | Country/Region | | USA |

Notes

Ariel recommended to RSR by Pat Hynes

**Project 1 Create a New Database Using a Template**

Project 1b, ContactDetails Report

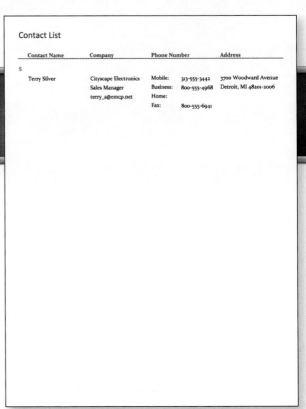

**Contact List**

| Contact Name | Company | Phone Number | | Address |
|---|---|---|---|---|
| **S** | | | | |
| Terry Silver | Cityscape Electronics | Mobile: | 313-555-3442 | 3700 Woodward Avenue |
| | Sales Manager | Business: | 800-555-4968 | Detroit, MI 48201-2006 |
| | terry_s@emcp.net | Home: | | |
| | | Fax: | 800-555-6941 | |

**Project 2 Create Objects Using a Template**

Project 2a, ContactList Report

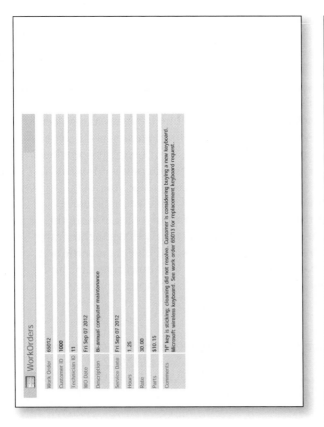

Project 2c, WorkOrders Form

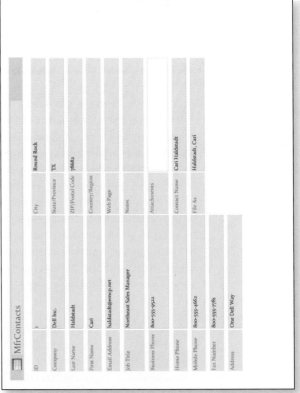

**Project 3 Copy Table Structure**

MfrContacts Form

12/4/2012

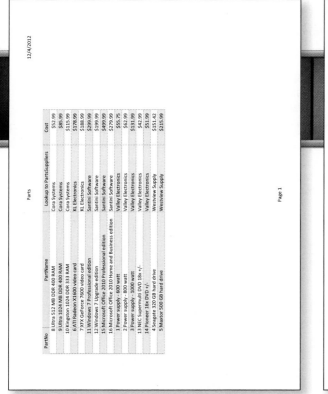

Parts     Page 1

| PartNo | PartName | Lookup to PartsSuppliers | Cost |
|---|---|---|---|
| 8 | Ultra 512 MB DDR 400 RAM | Cora Systems | $52.99 |
| 9 | Ultra 1024 MB DDR 400 RAM | Cora Systems | $85.99 |
| 10 | Kingston 1024 DDR 333 RAM | Cora Systems | $115.99 |
| 6 | ATI Radeon X1600 video card | KL Electronics | $178.99 |
| 7 | XFX GeForce 7600 video card | KL Electronics | $188.99 |
| 11 | Windows 7 Professional edition | Santini Software | $299.99 |
| 12 | Windows 7 Upgrade edition | Santini Software | $199.99 |
| 15 | Microsoft Office 2010 Professional edition | Santini Software | $499.99 |
| 16 | Microsoft Office 2010 Home and Business edition | Santini Software | $279.99 |
| 1 | Power supply - 600 watt | Valley Electronics | $55.75 |
| 2 | Power supply - 800 watt | Valley Electronics | $62.99 |
| 3 | Power supply - 1000 watt | Valley Electronics | $131.99 |
| 13 | NEC Supermulti DVD 18x +/- | Valley Electronics | $42.99 |
| 14 | Pioneer 16x DVD +/- | Valley Electronics | $51.99 |
| 4 | Seagate 320 GB hard drive | Westview Supply | $151.42 |
| 5 | Maxtor 500 GB hard drive | Westview Supply | $215.99 |

G:\Access2010L2C6\AL2-C6-RSRCompServ_be.accdb     Tuesday, December 04, 2012
Table: PartsSuppliers     Page: 1

**Properties**

| | | | |
|---|---|---|---|
| DateCreated: | 12/4/2012 1:59:48 PM | LastUpdated: | 12/4/2012 1:59:48 PM |
| RecordCount: | 5 | Updatable: | True |

**Columns**

| Name | | Type | Size |
|---|---|---|---|
| Supplier | | Text | 255 |
| | AllowZeroLength: | False | |
| | AppendOnly: | False | |
| | Attributes: | Variable Length | |
| | CollatingOrder: | General | |
| | DataUpdatable: | False | |
| | OrdinalPosition: | 0 | |
| | Required: | False | |
| | SourceField: | Supplier | |
| | SourceTable: | PartsSuppliers | |
| ID | | Long Integer | 4 |
| | AllowZeroLength: | False | |
| | AppendOnly: | False | |
| | Attributes: | Fixed Size, Auto-Increment | |
| | CollatingOrder: | General | |
| | DataUpdatable: | False | |
| | OrdinalPosition: | 1 | |
| | Required: | False | |
| | SourceField: | ID | |
| | SourceTable: | PartsSuppliers | |

**Relationships**

PartsSuppliersPartsAndCosts

| PartsSuppliers | | PartsAndCosts |
|---|---|---|
| ID | 1   ∞ | PartsSuppliers_ID |

Attributes:     Enforced, Cascade Updates
RelationshipType:     One-To-Many

**Project 4 Use Access Tools to Optimize and Document a Database**

              Project 4a, Parts Query            Project 4d, PartsSuppliers Definition Report

---

# Project 1   Create a New Database Using a Template    2 Parts

You will create a new database using one of the database templates supplied with Access.

---

# Creating a New Database Using a Template ■■■■■■■

At the New tab Backstage view, you can create a new database using one of the professionally designed templates provided by Microsoft. The database templates provide a complete series of objects including predefined tables, forms, reports, queries, and relationships. You can use a template as provided and immediately start entering data or you can base a new database on a template and modify the objects to suit your needs. If a template exists for a database application that you need, you can save time by creating the database based on one of the template designs.

To create a new database using a template, start Access and click *Sample Templates* in the Available Templates category in the center pane at the New tab Backstage view. The available template designs display in the center pane. Click a template name in the center pane, click the Browse button to navigate to the drive and/or folder in which you want to store the database, and then type a file name at the File New Database dialog box. This returns you to the previous screen with the new database file name entered below the *File Name* text box in the right pane of the New tab Backstage view. Click the Create button to create the database as shown in Figure 6.1.

### ▼ Quick Steps

**Create Database from Template**
1. Start Access.
2. Click *Sample Templates*.
3. Click desired template.
4. Click Browse button.
5. Navigate to drive and/or folder.
6. Edit file name as required.
7. Click OK.
8. Click Create button.

**Figure 6.1** AvailableTemplates in the *Sample Templates* Section of the New Tab
Backstage View

Templates Navigation bar. Click the Back button to return to the previous list in the center pane.

Step 1: Click the template design for the type of database you want to create.

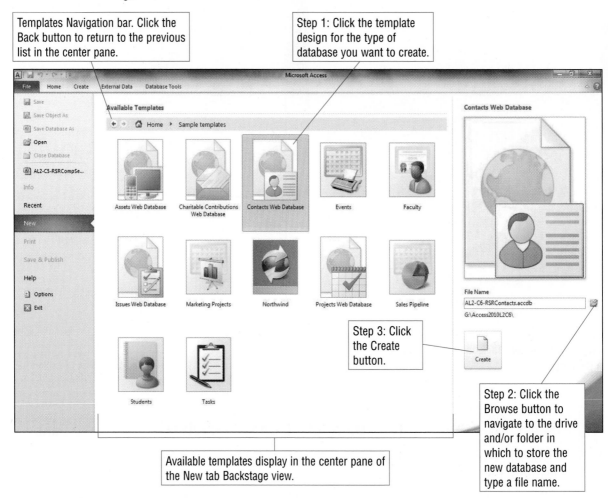

Step 3: Click the Create button.

Step 2: Click the Browse button to navigate to the drive and/or folder in which to store the new database and type a file name.

Available templates display in the center pane of the New tab Backstage view.

If one of the sample templates does not provide the type of application that you need, click the Back button in the Navigation bar below Available Templates and then click one of the categories below *Office.com Templates* to view a list of database templates that can be downloaded from the Microsoft Office Online website to your computer.

**Project 1a**  **Creating a New Contacts Database Using a Template**  Part 1 of 2

1. Start Microsoft Access 2010.
2. At the New tab Backstage view, click *Sample Templates* in the center pane.

3. Click *Contacts Web Database* in the center pane and then click the Browse button (displays as a file folder icon) next to the *File Name* text box in the right pane.

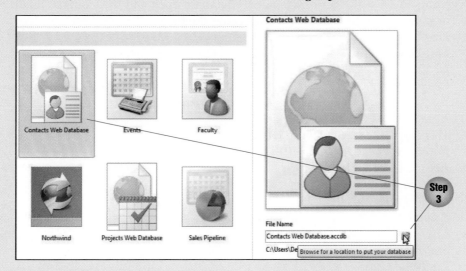

4. At the File New Database dialog box, navigate to the Access2010L2C6 folder on your storage medium, select and delete the current entry in the *File name* text box, and then type **AL2-C6-RSRContacts**.
5. Click OK.

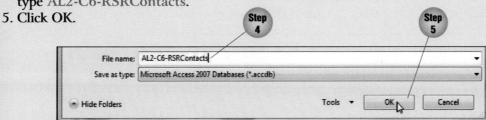

6. Click the Create button.
7. The database is created with all objects from the template loaded into the current window and the Main form opened with a *Welcome to the Contacts web database* page with links to Help information. Click the Enable Content button in the Security Warning message bar.
8. Click the Shutter Bar Open/Close button to display the Navigation pane.

9. Review the list of objects created for you by Access in the Navigation pane and then double-click to open the Contacts table.
10. Scroll right to view all of the fields in the Contacts table and then close the table.
11. Double-click *ContactDetails* in the *Forms* section of the Navigation pane and review the form in the work area.

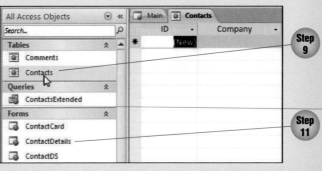

1. With the **AL2-C6-RSRContacts.accdb** database open and the ContactDetails form open in Form view, add the following record using the form:

| | |
|---|---|
| *First Name* | Ariel |
| *Last Name* | Grayson |
| *Job Title* | Accountant |
| *Company* | Grayson Accounting Services ***Note: Press Tab or Enter twice after this field to move to the E-mail field.*** |
| *E-mail* | ariel@emcp.net |
| *Web Page* | www.emcp.net/grayson |
| *Business Phone* | 800-555-4988 |
| *Fax* | 313-555-9648 |
| *Home Phone* | 313-555-6811 |
| *Mobile Phone* | 800-555-3472 |
| *Address* | 17399 Windsor Avenue |
| *City* | Detroit |
| *State/Province* | MI |
| *Zip/Postal Code* | 48214-3274 |
| *Country/Region* | USA |
| *Notes* | Ariel recommended to RSR by Pat Hynes |

2. Add a picture of the contact using the *Attachments* field by completing the following steps:
   a. Double-click the gray empty picture in the *Attachments* box at the top left of the form.

b. At the Attachments dialog box, click the Add button.

c. At the Choose File dialog box, navigate to the Access2010L2C6 folder on your storage medium.

d. Double-click *ArielGrayson.jpg* to add the file to the Attachments dialog box.

e. Click OK.

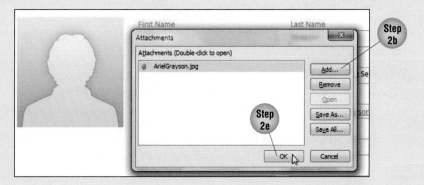

3. Click the Save & Close button located at the top right of the form.

4. Click the Address Book tab located at the top left of the Main form and review the contact information for Ariel Grayson in the Address Book.

5. Click the Report Center tab in the Main form and then click the <u>Contact Details</u> hyperlink in the Select a Report pane at the right side of the work area.

6. Click each of the other report hyperlinks in the Select a Report pane.

7. Close the Main form.

8. Double-click *ContactDetails* in the *Reports* section of the Navigation pane. Display the report in Print Preview and then print the report.

9. Close Print Preview, close the Contact Details report, and then close the **AL2-C6-RSRContacts.accdb** database.

Picture displays in form after adding a .jpg file to Attachments dialog box. If you add a Word document in the *Attachments* box, a Word icon displays.

---

P roject **2** **Create Objects Using a Template**   **3 Parts**

You will create a series of objects in an existing database using Application Parts templates. You will also define a form as a template for all new forms in a database.

# Creating Objects Using an Application Parts Template

**▼ Quick Steps**

**Create Objects Using an Application Parts Template**
1. Open database.
2. Click Create tab.
3. Click Application Parts button.
4. Click desired template.
5. Choose relationship options.
6. Add data or modify objects as required.

**H I N T**

You can create your own Application Parts template by copying an object you will reuse in other databases to a new database and then save the database as a template at the Save & Publish tab Backstage view.

Application Parts

Access 2010 provides templates that include prebuilt objects that can be inserted into an existing database using the Application Parts button in the Create tab. The *Quick Start* section of the Application Parts button drop-down list includes *Comments*, which creates a table; *Contacts*, which creates a table, query, forms and reports; and *Issues, Tasks,* and *Users*, which each create a table and two forms.

If you need to add a table about one of these topics to an existing database, consider creating the table using the Application Parts template since related objects such as forms and reports are also automatically generated. Once the application part is added, you can modify any of the object designs to suit your needs. To create a group of objects based on a template, click the Create tab and click the Application Parts button in the Templates group. Click the desired template in the *Quick Start* section of the drop-down list shown in Figure 6.2.

Access opens the Create Relationship Wizard to guide you through creating the relationship for the new table. Decide in advance of creating the new table what relationship, if any, will exist between the new table and an existing table in the database. At the first Create Relationship Wizard dialog box shown in Figure 6.3, click the first option if the new table will be the "many" table in a one-to-many relationship. Use the Tables drop-down list to choose the "one" table and click Next. Click the second option if the new table will be the "one" table in a one-to-many relationship, choose the "many" table from the Tables drop-down list, and choose Next. At the second Create Relationship Wizard dialog box you enter the settings for the lookup column between the two tables. Choose the field to be used to join the tables, choose a sort order if desired, assign the name for the lookup column, and then click the Create button. If the new table will not be related to any of the existing tables in the database, choose the *There is no relationship* option and click the Create button at the first Create Relationship Wizard dialog box.

**Figure 6.2** Application Parts Button Drop-Down List

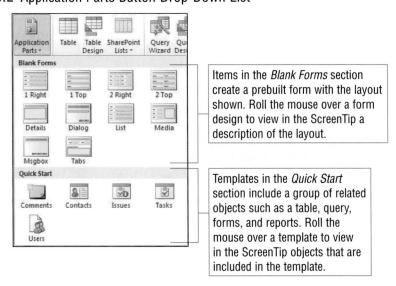

**Figure 6.3** Create Relationship Wizard Dialog Box

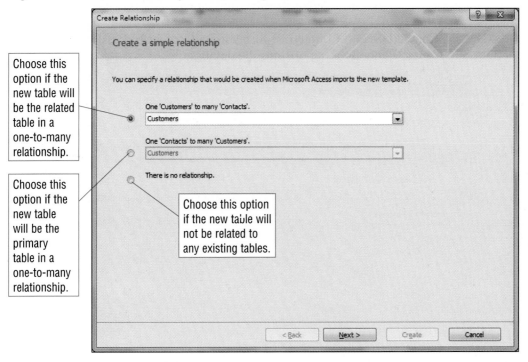

Choose this option if the new table will be the related table in a one-to-many relationship.

Choose this option if the new table will be the primary table in a one-to-many relationship.

Choose this option if the new table will not be related to any existing tables.

**Project 2a**  **Creating a Contacts Table, Query, Forms, and Reports Using a Template**    Part 1 of 3

1. Open **AL2-C6-RSRCompServ.accdb** and enable content.
2. Create a new table, query, forms, and reports related to contacts using a template by completing the following steps:
   a. Click the Create tab.
   b. Click the Application Parts button in the Templates group and click *Contacts* in the *Quick Start* section of the drop-down list.

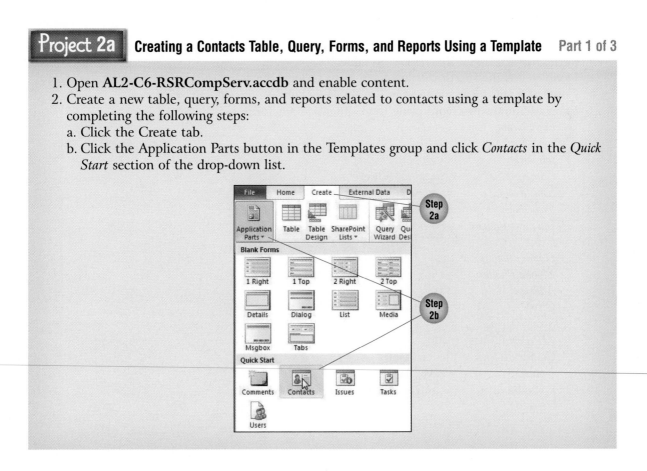

c. At the Create Relationship Wizard dialog box, click the *There is no relationship* option and then click Create. Access imports a Contacts table; a ContactsExtended query; a ContactDetails, ContactDS, and ContactList form; and a ContactAddressBook, ContactList, and ContactPhoneBook report into the database.

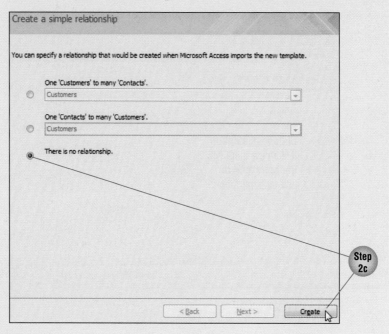

3. Double-click the Contacts table in the Navigation pane. Scroll right to view all of the fields in the new table and then close the table.
4. Double-click the ContactDetails form in the Navigation pane. Notice the form is the same ContactDetails form you used in Project 1b in the Contacts database.
5. Enter the following record using the ContactDetails form:

| | |
|---|---|
| *First Name* | Terry |
| *Last Name* | Silver |
| *Job Title* | Sales Manager |
| *Company* | Cityscape Electronics |
| *E-mail* | terry_s@emcp.net |
| *Web Page* | www.emcp.net/cityscape |
| *Business Phone* | 800-555-4968 |
| *Fax* | 800-555-6941 |
| *Home Phone* | (leave blank) |
| *Mobile Phone* | 313-555-3442 |
| *Address* | 3700 Woodward Avenue |
| *City* | Detroit |
| *State/Province* | MI |
| *ZIP/Postal Code* | 48201-2006 |
| *Country/Region* | (leave blank) |
| *Notes* | (leave blank) |

6. Click the Save & Close button at the top right of the form.

**Contact Details**   [Save & New]   [Save & Close]   ← Step 6

First Name: Terry
Last Name: Silver

Job Title: Sales Manager
Company: Cityscape Electronics

E-mail: terry_s@emcp.net
Web Page: www.emcp.net/cityscape

Business Phone: 800-555-4968
Fax: 800-555-6941   ← Step 5

Home Phone:
Mobile Phone: 313-555-3442

Address: 3700 Woodward Avenue

City: Detroit
State/Province: MI
ZIP/Postal Code: 48201-2006
Country/Region:

Notes

7. Open the ContactList report.
8. Display the report in Print Preview and then print the report.
9. Close Print Preview and then close the ContactList report.

Application Parts also includes various blank form layouts to make the task of creating a new form easier by allowing you to pick a layout that has already been defined. The *Blank Forms* section of the Application Parts button drop-down list contains 10 prebuilt blank forms. Most of the forms contain command buttons that perform actions such as saving changes or saving and closing the form. Resting the mouse pointer over a blank form option at the Application Parts button drop-down list displays a description of the form's layout in a ScreenTip. When you click a blank form option, Access creates the form object using a predefined form name. For example, if you click *1 Right*, Access creates a form named *SingleOneColumnRightLabels*. Locate the form name in the Navigation pane and open the form in Layout view or Design view to customize the form as needed.

Application Parts forms have a control layout applied so that all of the form's controls will move and resize together. Remove the control layout to make individual size adjustments. In Design view, select all of the controls and click the Remove Layout button in the Table group of the Arrange tab.

### ▼ Quick Steps

**Create Form Using Blank Form Application Parts**
1. Click Create tab.
2. Click Application Parts button.
3. Click desired blank form layout.
4. Add fields to form.
5. Customize form as needed.
6. Save form.

1. With the **AL2-C6-RSRCompServ.accdb** database open, create a new form for maintaining records in the Parts table using an Application Parts blank form by completing the following steps:

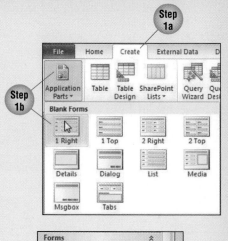

   Step 1a

   Step 1b

   a. If necessary, click the Create tab.
   b. Click the Applications Parts button in the Templates group and then click *1 Right* in the *Blank Forms* section at the drop-down list. Access creates a form named *SingleOneColumnRightLabels*.
   c. If necessary, position the mouse pointer on the right border of the Navigation pane until the pointer changes to a left- and right-pointing arrow and then drag right to widen the Navigation pane until you can read all of the object names.
   d. Double-click the form named *SingleOneColumnRightLabels* in the Navigation pane.

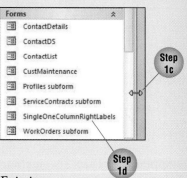

   Step 1c

   Step 1d

2. Switch to Layout view.
3. Click to select the *Field1* label control object. Shift + click to select the *Field2*, *Field3*, and *Field4* label control objects and then press Delete.
4. Associate the Parts table with the form and add fields from the Parts table by completing the following steps:
   a. If the Field List pane is not currently open, click the Add Existing Fields button in the Tools group of the Form Layout Tools Design tab.
   b. Click the Show all tables hyperlink at the top of the pane. Skip this step if your Field List pane already displays all of the table names in the database.
   c. Click the plus symbol next to *Parts* in the Field List pane to expand the list and show all of the fields in the Parts table.
   d. Drag the *PartNo* field to the second column in the row shown at the right.

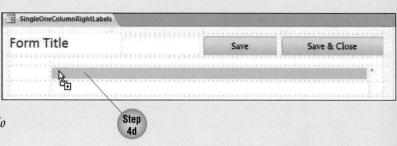

   Step 4d

   e. Drag the remaining fields *PartName*, *Supplier*, and *Cost* below *PartNo* as shown below.

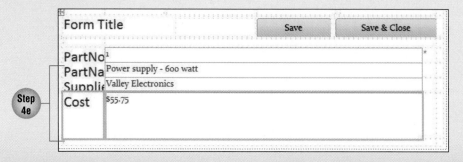

   Step 4e

5. With the *Cost* field selected, drag the bottom orange border of the control up to decrease the height of the control object so that the bottom border is approximately 0.5 inch below the label text.

6. Select the four label control objects and drag the right orange border of the selected controls right to widen the labels until you can read all of the label text.

7. With the four label control objects still selected, click the Form Layout Tools Arrange tab, click the Control Padding button in the Position group, and then click *Wide* at the drop-down list.

8. Double-click the form title to place an insertion point inside the title text, delete *Form Title*, type **Repair Parts**, and then press Enter.

9. Apply formatting changes to the form as follows:

   a. Select the two command buttons at the top right of the form (Save and Save & Close), click the Form Layout Tools Format tab, click the Quick Styles button, and then click *Intense Effect - Blue, Accent 1* at the drop-down list.

   b. Select the *Repair Parts* title control object and change the font color to *Blue, Accent 1* (fifth color option in first row of *Theme Colors* section).

   c. Apply *Blue, Accent 1* font color to the four label control objects.

   d. Apply *Light Turquoise, Background 2* (third color option in first row of *Theme Colors* section) background color to the four text box control objects adjacent to the labels.

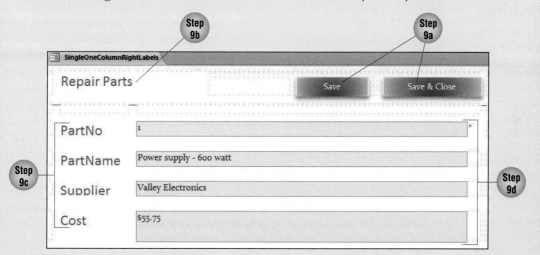

   e. Click in a blank area of the form to deselect the four text box control objects.

10. Click the File tab, click Save Object As, type **PartsForm** in the *Save 'SingleOneColumnRightLabels' to* text box at the Save As dialog box, and then click OK.

11. Click the Home tab and then switch to Form view.

12. Scroll through a few records in the PartsForm and then click the Save & Close button at the top right of the form to close the PartsForm.

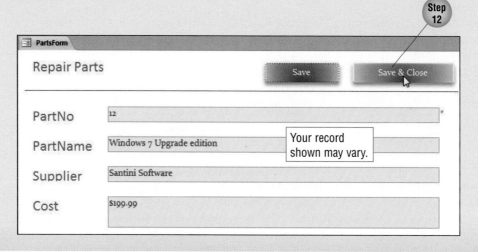

Step 12

Repair Parts

Save    Save & Close

PartNo          12

PartName        Windows 7 Upgrade edition

Your record shown may vary.

Supplier        Santini Software

Cost            $199.99

# Setting Form Control Defaults and Creating a User-Defined Form Template ▪▪▪▪▪▪▪▪▪▪▪▪▪▪▪▪▪

▼ **Quick Steps**

**Create User-Defined Form Template**
1. Create new form in Design view.
2. Add control object to form.
3. Format control object as desired.
4. Click More button at bottom of Control group.
5. Click *Set Control Defaults.*
6. Repeat Steps 2 to 5 for each type of control to be used.
7. Save form naming it *Normal.*

Delete the Normal form if you want to go back to using the standard default options for control objects in forms.

A standard design for all forms in a database is a good practice to portray a professional image and ensure consistency. You may wish to use different settings from the default control object settings. For example, you may want all label control objects to be 14-point blue text on a gray background. To manually change these options in each form is time-consuming and may lead to inconsistencies. The *Set Control Defaults* option at the Controls drop-down list allows you to change the defaults for all new labels in a form. To do this, open the form in Design view, format one label control object with the desired settings, click the More button at the bottom of the Controls vertical scroll bar, and then click *Set Control Defaults* at the drop-down list. All new labels added to the form will have the format options already defined that you want to use.

To further customize the database, you can create a form template that will set the desired control defaults for each type of control object that you place on a form. To do this, open a new form in Design view and create one control object for each type of control that you want to specify a default setting. For example, add a label control object, a text box control object, a command button, a list box control object, and so on making sure you format each control object with the desired colors and backgrounds. As you finish each control, use the *Set Control Defaults* option to change the default settings or select all controls after you have finished the form and perform one *Set Control Defaults* command. When finished, save the form using the form name *Normal*. The Normal form becomes the template for all new forms in the database. Existing forms retain their initial format unless you manually change them.

1. With the **AL2-C6-RSRCompServ.accdb** database open, create a form to be used as the form template for the database for all new forms by completing the following steps:
   a. Click the Create tab and then click the Form Design button in the Forms group.
   b. Click the Themes button in the Themes group and then click *Opulent* at the drop-down list.
   c. Click the Label button in the Controls group of the Form Design Tools Design tab, draw a label in the *Detail* section, type **Sample Label Text**, and then press Enter. The position and size of the label object is not of concern at this time since you are using this control object only to set new default formatting options.
   d. Click the Form Design Tools Format tab. Change the font color to *Purple, Accent 2* (sixth color option in first row of *Theme Colors* section) and the background color to *Lavender, Background 2* (third color option in first row of *Theme Colors* section).

   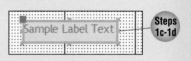

   f. Click the Form Design Tools Design tab, click the Text Box button in the Controls group, and then draw a text box control object in the *Detail* section. Format the text box control object and its associated label control object as follows:
      1) Apply the same font color and background color to the label control object attached to the text box as you applied to the label control object in Step 1d.
      2) Select the text box control object (displays *Unbound*) and apply the same background color as you applied to the label control object in Step 1d.
   g. Click the Form Design Tools Design tab, click the Combo Box button in the Controls group, and then draw a combo box control object in the *Detail* section. If the Combo Box Wizard begins, click the Cancel button. Format the combo box control object using the same format options as you applied to the text box control object in Steps 1f1 to 1f2.
   h. Press Ctrl + A to select all of the control objects in the form.
   i. Click the Form Design Tools Design tab, click the More button at the bottom of the Controls scroll bar, and then click *Set Control Defaults* at the drop-down list.

   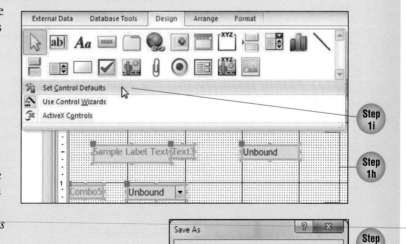

2. Save the form and name it *Normal*.

3. Close the Normal form. Normal becomes the form template for the *AL2-C6-RSRCompServ.accdb* database. Any new form created will have labels, text boxes, and combo boxes formatted as specified in Step 1.
4. Click the WorkOrders table name in the Navigation pane, click the Create tab, and then click the Form button in the Forms group. The new WorkOrders form uses the formatting applied to the labels, text boxes, and combo boxes in the Normal form template.
5. With the first record displayed in the WorkOrders form in Form view, open the Print dialog box. Click the Setup button and then click the Columns tab at the Page Setup dialog box. Select the current value in the *Width* text box in the *Column Size* section, type 8, and then click OK. Click *Selected Record(s)* in the *Print Range* section of the Print dialog box and then click OK.
6. Close the WorkOrders form. Click Yes when prompted to save changes to the design of the form and then click OK to accept the default form name *WorkOrders*.

---

## Project 3   Copy Table Structure     1 Part

You will create a new table to store contact information for manufacturer sales representatives by copying an existing table's field names and field properties.

---

▼ **Quick Steps**

**Copy Table Structure**
1. Select table.
2. Click Copy button.
3. Click Paste button.
4. Type new table name.
5. Click *Structure Only*.
6. Click OK.

**HINT**

If a new table that is needed is similar to an existing table's fields and/or field properties, you can save time by copying the existing table's structure and then adding, deleting, and modifying fields in Design view.

## Copying Table Structure to Create a New Table ■■■■■■■

Using copy and paste commands you can copy an existing table's structure if you need to create a new table that uses the same or similar fields as an existing table. For example, in Project 3 you will copy the Contacts table structure to create a new table for manufacturer contacts that you want to maintain separately from other contact records. Since the fields needed for manufacturer contact records are the same as those that already exist for the other contact records, you can base the new table on the existing table.

To copy a table's structure, click the existing table name in the Navigation pane and click the Copy button in the Clipboard group in the Home tab. Next, click the Paste button in the Clipboard group. When a table has been copied to the clipboard, clicking the Paste button causes the Paste Table As dialog box shown in Figure 6.4 to appear.

Type the desired name for the new table in the *Table Name* text box, click *Structure Only* in the *Paste Options* section, and then click OK. Once the table is created you can add, delete, or modify fields as needed.

**Figure 6.4** Paste Table As Dialog Box

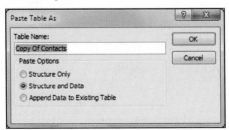

1. With the **AL2-C6-RSRCompServ.accdb** database open, click to select the Contacts table in the Navigation pane.
2. Click the Home tab and then click the Copy button in the Clipboard group.
3. Click the Paste button in the Clipboard group. (Do not click the down-pointing arrow on the button.)
4. At the Paste Table As dialog box, type MfrContacts in the *Table Name* text box, click *Structure Only* in the *Paste Options* section, and then press Enter or click OK.

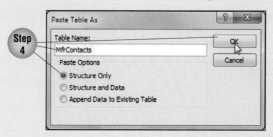

5. Open the MfrContacts table. The table structure contains the same fields as the Contacts table.
6. Enter the following data in a new record using Datasheet view. Press Tab or Enter past the remaining fields after *ZIP/Postal Code* to finish the record.

| | |
|---|---|
| *Company* | Dell Inc. |
| *Last Name* | Haldstadt |
| *First Name* | Cari |
| *Email Address* | haldstadt@emcp.net |
| *Job Title* | Northeast Sales Manager |
| *Business Phone* | 800-555-9522 |
| *Home Phone* | (leave blank) |
| *Mobile Phone* | 800-555-4662 |
| *Fax Number* | 800-555-7781 |
| *Address* | One Dell Way |
| *City* | Round Rock |
| *State/Province* | TX |
| *ZIP/Postal Code* | 78682 |

7. Close the table.

8. With MfrContacts selected in the Navigation pane, click the Create tab and then click the Form button in the Forms group to create a new form based on the table.

MfrContacts form created at Step 8.

9. Click the File tab, click Print, and then click Print Preview to display the form in Print Preview. Change the page orientation to landscape and then close Print Preview.
10. Save the form using the default name *MfrContacts*.
11. Print the selected record and then close the form.

Project 4 Use Access Tools to Optimize and Document a Database    5 Parts

You will use the Table Analyzer Wizard to improve a table's design, the Performance Analyzer to optimize database design, and split a database by separating tables from queries, forms, and reports. Finally, you will use the Database Documenter to print a report documenting table structure.

## Modifying a Table Using the Table Analyzer Wizard ■■■■

The Table Analyzer Wizard helps you normalize a table.

The Table Analyzer Wizard is used to examine a table and determine if duplicate information in the table can be split into smaller related tables to improve the table design. Repeated information in tables can result in inconsistencies and wasted storage space. The wizard presents a solution with fields that can be separated into a new table related to the original table with a lookup field. You can accept the proposed solution or modify the suggestion. In Project 4a you will use the Table Analyzer Wizard in a new Parts table. The table was created to store information about parts that are commonly used by the technicians at RSR Computer Service. Access will examine the table and propose that the *Supplier* field be moved to a separate table. The reason this solution is a better design is that several parts records can be associated with the same supplier. In the current table design, the supplier name is typed into a field in each record. With several parts associated with the same supplier name, the field contains many duplicated entries that use disk space. Furthermore, the potential exists for a typing mistake in a record, which could result in a query not producing the correct list.

To begin the Table Analyzer Wizard, click the Database Tools tab and then click the Analyze Table button in the Analyze group. This presents the first Table Analyzer Wizard dialog box shown in Figure 6.5. The first two dialog boxes in the wizard explain what the Table Analyzer does to improve the table design. At the third dialog box in the wizard, you select the table to be analyzed. At the fourth dialog box, you choose to let the wizard decide which fields to group together in the smaller tables or manually split the tables by dragging and dropping fields.

The wizard looks for fields with repetitive data and suggests a solution. You confirm the grouping of fields and the primary keys in the new tables and, at the final step in the wizard, you can elect to have Access create a query so that the fields in the split tables are presented together in a datasheet that resembles the original table.

**▼ Quick Steps**

**Evaluate Table with Table Analyzer Wizard**
1. Click Database Tools tab.
2. Click Analyze Table button.
3. Click Next.
4. Click Next.
5. Click table name.
6. Click Next.
7. If necessary, click *Yes, let wizard decide.*
8. Click Next.
9. Confirm grouping of fields in proposed tables.
10. Rename each table.
11. Click Next.
12. Confirm and/or set primary key in each table.
13. Click Next.
14. If necessary, click *Yes, create the query.*
15. Click Finish.
16. Close Help window.
17. Close query.

**Figure 6.5** First Table Analyzer Wizard Dialog Box

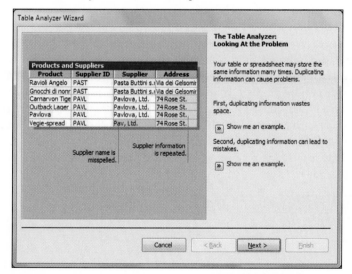

Analyze Table

---

**Project 4a**  **Splitting a Table Using the Table Analyzer Wizard**   Part 1 of 5

1. With the **AL2-C6-RSRCompServ.accdb** database open, open the Parts table in Datasheet view and review the table structure and data. Notice the table includes four fields: *PartNo, PartName, Supplier,* and *Cost.* Also notice that supplier names are repeated in the *Supplier* field.
2. Close the Parts table.
3. Use the Table Analyzer Wizard to evaluate the Parts table design to determine if the table can be improved by completing the following steps:
   a. Click the Database Tools tab.

b. Click the Analyze Table button in the Analyze group.
c. Read the information at the first Table Analyzer Wizard dialog box and click Next.
d. Read the information at the second Table Analyzer Wizard dialog box and click Next.
e. With *Parts* selected in the *Tables* list box at the third Table Analyzer Wizard dialog box, click Next.

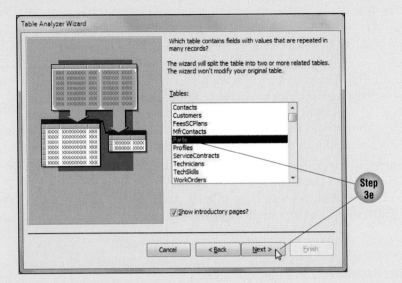

f. With *Yes, let the wizard decide* selected for *Do you want the wizard to decide what fields go in what tables?* at the fourth Table Analyzer Wizard dialog box, click Next.
g. At the fifth Table Analyzer Wizard dialog box, look at the two tables the wizard is proposing. Notice that the *Supplier* field has been moved to a new table with a one-to-many relationship created between the table with the supplier names ("one" table) and a new table with the remaining fields ("many" table). Access names the new tables *Table1* and *Table2* and asks two questions: *Is the wizard grouping information correctly?* and *What name do you want for each table?* **Note: If necessary, resize the table list boxes in order to see the proposed fields.**
h. The proposed tables have the fields grouped correctly. Rename the first table by double-clicking the Table1 title bar.

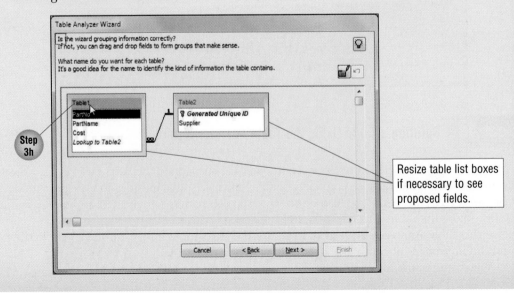

i. Type **PartsAndCosts** in the *Table Name* text box and press Enter or click OK.

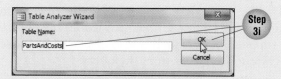

j. Click the Table2 title bar and click the Rename Table button located near the top right of the dialog box above the table list boxes. Type **PartsSuppliers** in the *Table Name* text box and press Enter or click OK.

k. Click Next.

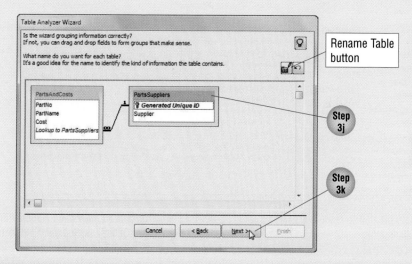

l. At the sixth Table Analyzer Wizard dialog box, the primary key fields for each table are set and/or confirmed. The primary key fields are displayed in bold in the table list boxes. Notice the PartsAndCosts table does not have a primary key defined. Click *PartNo* in the *PartsAndCosts table* list box and click the Primary Key button located near the top right of the dialog box. Access sets *PartNo* as the primary key field, displays a key icon, and applies bold to the field name.

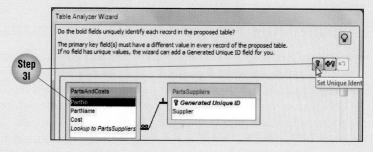

m. Click Next.

n. At the last Table Analyzer Wizard dialog box, you can choose to have Access create a query with the original table name that includes the fields from the new tables. Creating the query means existing forms or reports that were based on the original table will still operate. With *Yes, create the query* selected, click Finish. Access renames the original table *Parts_OLD*, creates the query with the name *Parts*, and opens the Parts query results datasheet with the Access Help window in the foreground.

o. Close the Help window.

4. Examine the Parts query datasheet and the object names added in the Navigation pane including the new tables PartsAndCosts and PartsSuppliers along with the original table named Parts_OLD. The Parts query looks just like the original table you opened at Step 1 with the exception of the additional field named *Lookup to PartsSupplier*. The lookup field displays the supplier name, which is also displayed in the original *Supplier* field. The second *Supplier* field can be deleted from the query.
5. Switch to Design view and delete the *Supplier* field.

| PartNo | PartName | Lookup to PartsSuppliers | Supplier | Cost |
|---|---|---|---|---|
| 8 | Ultra 512 MB DDR 400 RAM | Cora Systems | Cora Systems | $52.99 |
| 9 | Ultra 1024 MB DDR 400 RAM | Cora Systems | Cora Systems | $85.99 |
| 10 | Kingston 1024 DDR 333 RAM | Cora Systems | Cora Systems | $115.99 |
| 6 | ATI Radeon X1600 video card | KL Electronics | KL Electronics | $178.99 |
| 7 | XFX GeForce 7600 video card | KL Electronics | KL Electronics | $188.99 |
| 11 | Windows 7 Professional edition | Santini Software | Santini Software | $299.99 |
| 12 | Windows 7 Upgrade edition | Santini Software | Santini Software | $199.99 |
| 15 | Microsoft Office 2010 Professional edition | Santini Software | Santini Software | $499.99 |
| 16 | Microsoft Office 2010 Home and Business edition | Santini Software | Santini Software | $279.99 |
| 1 | Power supply - 600 watt | Valley Electronics | Valley Electronics | $55.75 |
| 2 | Power supply - 800 watt | Valley Electronics | Valley Electronics | $62.99 |
| 3 | Power supply - 1000 watt | Valley Electronics | Valley Electronics | $131.99 |
| 13 | NEC Supermulti DVD 18x +/- | Valley Electronics | Valley Electronics | $42.99 |
| 14 | Pioneer 16x DVD +/- | Valley Electronics | Valley Electronics | $51.99 |
| 4 | Seagate 320 GB hard drive | Westview Supply | Westview Supply | $151.42 |
| 5 | Maxtor 500 GB hard drive | Westview Supply | Westview Supply | $215.99 |
| * | (New) | | | |

All Access Objects
Search...
Tables
- Contacts
- Customers
- FeesSCPlans
- MfrContacts
- Parts_OLD
- PartsAndCosts
- PartsSuppliers
- Profiles
- ServiceContracts
- Technicians
- TechSkills
- WorkOrders
Queries
- ContactsExtended
- Parts

renamed original table and new tables created through Table Analyzer Wizard

query created to resemble original table

*Lookup to PartsSuppliers* and *Supplier* display the same information. Delete the *Supplier* field from the query at Step 5.

6. Save the revised query. Switch to Datasheet view, adjust all column widths to Best Fit, and print the query results datasheet in landscape orientation.
7. Close the query saving changes to the layout.

▼ **Quick Steps**

**Optimize Database Performance**
1. Click the Database Tools tab.
2. Click Analyze Performance button.
3. Click All Object Types tab.
4. Click Select All button.
5. Click OK.
6. Review *Analysis Results* items.
7. Optimize desired *Recommendation* or *Suggestion* items.
8. Click Close button.

Analyze Performance

# Optimizing Performance Using the Performance Analyzer ■■■■■■■■■■■■■■■■■■■

The Performance Analyzer can evaluate an individual object, a group of objects, or the entire database for ways that objects can be modified to optimize the use of system resources such as memory and improve the speed of data access. If you find the database seems to run slowly, consider running tables, queries, forms, reports, or the entire database through the Performance Analyzer. To do this, click the Database Tools tab and click the Analyze Performance button in the Analyze group to open the Performance Analyzer dialog box shown in Figure 6.6. Select a tab for the object type, click the check box next to an object to have the object analyzed, and click OK. You can select multiple objects or click the Select All button to select all objects in the current tab for analysis. To evaluate the entire database, click the All Object Types tab and then click the Select All button. Click OK to begin the analysis.

**Figure 6.6** Performance Analyzer Dialog Box

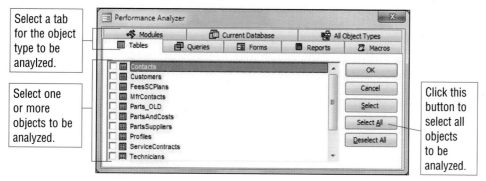

Select a tab for the object type to be anaylzed.

Select one or more objects to be analyzed.

Click this button to select all objects to be analyzed.

Three types of results are presented to optimize the selected objects: *Recommendation, Suggestion,* and *Idea.* Click an item in the *Analysis Results* list to read a description of the proposed optimization method in the *Analysis Notes* section. Click a recommendation or suggestion in the *Analysis Results* list box and then click the Optimize button to instruct Access to carry out the recommendation or suggestion. Access will modify the object and mark the item as *Fixed* when completed. The Performance Analyzer may provide items to improve the design such as assigning a different data type for a field based on the type of data that has been entered into records or creating relationships between tables that are not related.

Make sure objects are closed that will be evaluated using the Performance Analyzer—open objects are skipped when the evaluation is run.

**Project 4b** | **Analyzing a Database to Improve Performance** | Part 2 of 5

1. With the **AL2-C6-RSRCompServ.accdb** database open, use the Performance Analyzer to evaluate the database for optimization techniques by completing the following steps:
   a. If necessary, click the Database Tools tab.
   b. Click the Analyze Performance button in the Analyze group.
   c. At the Performance Analyzer dialog box, click the All Object Types tab.
   d. Click the Select All button.

   e. Click OK. The Performance Analyzer displays the name of each object as the object is evaluated and presents the *Analysis Results* when completed.

2. Review the items in *Analysis Results* and optimize a relationship by completing the following steps:
   a. Click the first entry in the *Analysis Results* list with the text *Application: Save your application as an MDE file* and read the description of the idea in the *Analysis Notes* section. You will learn about saving the application as an MDE file in the next chapter.

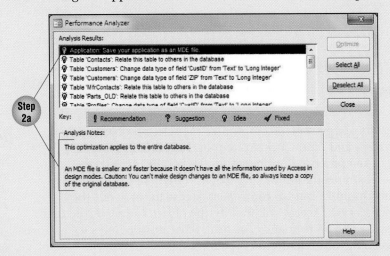

   b. Click the fifth entry in the *Analysis Results* with the text *Table MfrContacts: Relate this table to others in the database* and read the description of the idea in the *Analysis Notes* section. The contact information stored in this table is for manufacturer sales representatives and cannot be related to any other tables.
   c. Scroll down the *Analysis Results* list box and click the item with the green question mark representing a suggestion with the text *Table WorkOrders: Relate to table WorkOrders*. Read the description of the suggestion in the *Analysis Notes* section. Note that the optimization will benefit the TotalWorkOrders query. This optimization refers to a query that contains a subquery with two levels of calculations. The suggestion is referring to creating a relationship to speed up the query calculations.
   d. Click the Optimize button.

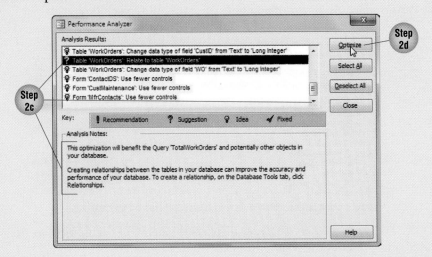

   e. Access creates the relationship and changes the question mark next to the item in the *Analysis Results* list box to a check mark. The check mark indicates the item has been fixed.

f. Click the second to the last item in the *Analysis Results* list box with the text *Form CustMaintenance: Use fewer controls* and read the description of the idea. Note that the idea is to break the form into multiple forms with information used often retained in the existing form. Information viewed less often should be split out into individual forms. To implement this optimization idea, you would need to redesign the form.

3. Click the Close button to close the Performance Analyzer dialog box.

Check mark indicates the suggestion was implemented at Step 2e.

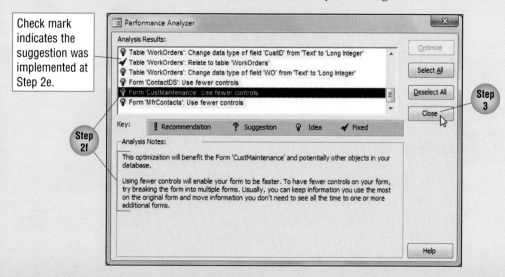

## Splitting a Database ■■■■■■■■■■■■■■■■■■■■■■■■■■

If a database is placed in a network where multiple users access the database simultaneously, the speed with which the data is accessed may decrease. One solution to improve the performance of the database is to split the database into two files: one file containing the tables (called the ***back-end***) is stored in the network share folder, and the other file containing the queries, forms, and reports (called the ***front-end***) is stored on the individual end-user computers. The individual end users can create and/or customize their own queries, forms, and reports to serve their individual purposes. The front-end database contains tables linked to the back-end data, so that each user is updating a single data source.

To split an existing database into a back-end and a front-end database, Access provides the Database Splitter Wizard. Click the Database Tools tab and click the Access Database button in the Move Data group to begin the Database Splitter Wizard shown in Figure 6.7.

Click the Split Database button to open the Create Back-end Database dialog box where you navigate to the drive and/or folder in which to store the database file containing the original tables. By default, Access uses the original database file name with _be appended to the end of the name before the file extension. Change the file name if desired and then click the Split button. Access moves the table objects to the back-end file, creates links to the back-end tables in the front-end file, and displays a message when the process is complete that the database was successfully split.

▼ **Quick Steps**

**Split a Database**
1. Click Database Tools tab.
2. Click Access Database button.
3. Click Split Database button.
4. If necessary, navigate to desired drive and/ or folder.
5. If necessary, edit the *File name.*
6. Click Split button.
7. Click OK.

**H I N T**

Consider making a backup copy of the database before you split the file, in case you need to restore the database back to its original state.

Access Database

**Figure 6.7** First Database Splitter Wizard Dialog Box

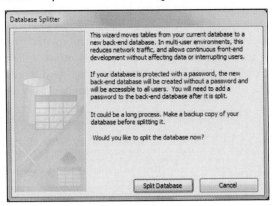

**Project 4c** | **Splitting a Database** |

1. With the **AL2-C6-RSRCompServ.accdb** database open, split the database to create a back-end and a front-end database by completing the following steps:
   a. If necessary, click the Database Tools tab.
   b. Click the Access Database button in the Move Data group.
   c. Click the Split Database button at the first Database Splitter Wizard dialog box.
   d. At the Create Back-end Database dialog box with the default option to save the back-end database in the same folder from which the original database originated (Access2010L2C6) and the file name *AL2-C6-RSRCompServ_be.accdb* in the *File name* text box, click the Split button.

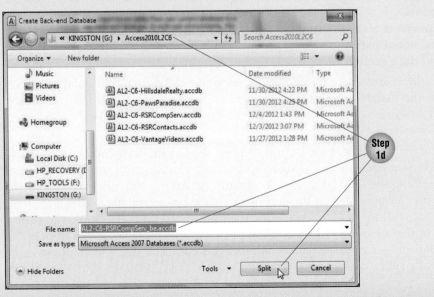

e. Click OK at the Database Splitter message box indicating the database was successfully split.

Step 1e

2. When the database was split, Access moved the tables to the back-end file and created links to the tables in the front-end file. Notice the table names in the Navigation pane are all preceded with a right-pointing arrow. The arrow indicates the table is a linked object. Opening a linked table causes Access to retrieve the records from the back-end database to display in the table datasheet. Open the linked Contacts table datasheet and review the data.

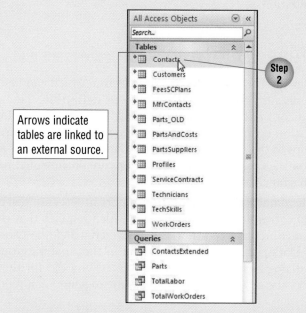

Arrows indicate tables are linked to an external source.

Step 2

3. Switch to Design view. Since the table is linked to an external source, Access displays a message indicating the table design cannot be modified; changes to fields or field properties have to be made in the source database. Click No at the Microsoft Access message box asking if you want to open the table anyway.

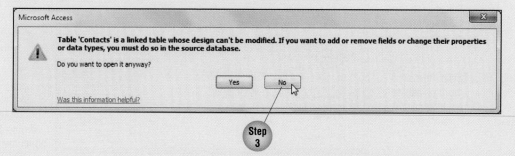

Step 3

4. Close the table and then close the **AL2-C6-RSRCompServ.accdb** database.
5. Open the **AL2-C6-RSRCompServ_be.accdb** database and enable content.

6. Notice the back-end database file contains only the tables. Open the Customers table in Datasheet view and review the data.
7. Switch to Design view. Notice that in the back-end database you can switch to Design view to make changes without receiving the message box you saw at Step 3 since this database contains the original source table.
8. Close the table.

Another reason to split a database may be to overcome the file size restriction in Access 2010. Database specifications for Access 2010 place the maximum file size at 2 gigabytes. This size includes any space needed by Access to open system objects while working with the database; therefore, the actual maximum file size is less than 2 gigabytes. However, the size restriction does not include links to external data sources. By splitting a database you can extend the size beyond the 2-gigabyte limitation.

▼ **Quick Steps**

**Print Object Documentation**
1. Click Database Tools tab.
2. Click Database Documenter button.
3. Click Options button.
4. Choose desired report options.
5. Click OK.
6. Click desired object name.
7. Click OK.
8. Print report.
9. Close report.

Database Documenter

# Documenting a Database ■■■■■■■■■■■■■■■■■■■■■

Access provides the Database Documenter feature which can be used to print a report with details about a database object's definition. The report is used to obtain hard copy documentation of a table's structure with field properties or documentation regarding a query, form, or report definition. You can add the relationships to the report to include relationship diagrams for all defined relationships for the table. Relationship options are documented below each relationship diagram.

Storing the database documentation report in a secure place is a good idea in case of data corruption or other disaster which requires that the database be manually repaired, rebuilt, or otherwise recovered. Click the Database Tools tab and click the Database Documenter button in the Analyze group to open the Documenter dialog box shown in Figure 6.8. As you did for the Performance Analyzer, select the object for which you want to generate a report and then click OK.

**Figure 6.8** Documenter Dialog Box

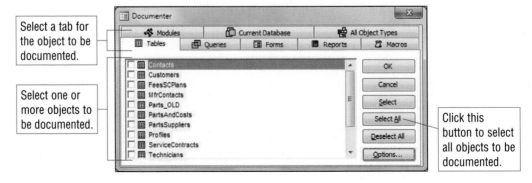

1. With the **AL2-C6-RSRCompServ_be.accdb** database open, generate a report providing details of the table structure, field properties, and relationships for an individual table by completing the following steps:
   a. Click the Database Tools tab.
   b. In the Analyze group, click the Database Documenter button.
   c. At the Documenter dialog box, click the Options button.
   d. At the Print Table Definition dialog box, click the *Permissions by User and Group* check box in the *Include for Table* section to clear the check mark.
   e. Make sure *Names, Data Types, Sizes, and Properties* is selected in the *Include for Fields* section.
   f. Click *Nothing* in the *Include for Indexes* section.
   g. Click OK.
   h. With Tables the active tab in the Documenter dialog box, click the *PartsSuppliers* check box to select the object.
   i. Click OK.

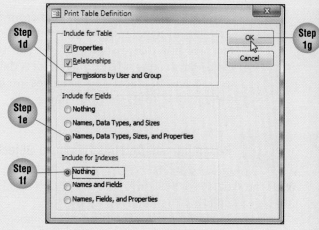

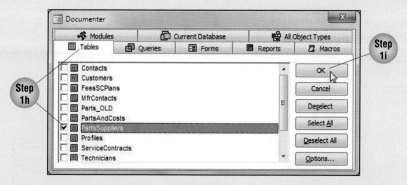

2. Access generates the table definition report and displays the report in Print Preview. Print the report.
3. Notice the Save option is dimmed. You cannot save a report generated by the Documenter.
4. Click the Close Print Preview button in the Close Preview group in the Print Preview tab.
5. Generate another report providing details of all of the tables and view the report by completing the following steps:
   a. Click the Database Documenter button.
   b. With Tables the active tab at the Documenter dialog box, click the Select All button to select all table objects and then click OK to generate the report.
   c. Change the Zoom to 100% and maximize the report window.
   d. Scroll down the first page of the report and review the data.
   e. Click the Last Page button in the Page navigation bar to navigate to the last page in the report. Review the relationship diagrams and relationship options documented on the last page of the report. Notice the page number is 55.
6. Close the report.

# Renaming and Deleting Objects ■■■■■■■■■■■■■■■

**▼ Quick Steps**

**Rename Object**
1. Right-click object in Navigation pane.
2. Click *Rename*.
3. Type new name.
4. Press Enter.

**Delete Object**
1. Right-click object in Navigation pane.
2. Click *Delete*.
3. Click Yes.

As part of managing a database you may decide to rename or delete objects within the database file. To do this, right-click the object name in the Navigation pane and click *Rename* or *Delete* at the shortcut menu. Be cautious with renaming or deleting objects which have dependencies to other objects. For example if you delete a table and a query exists which is dependent on fields within the table deleted, the query will no longer run. You will need to edit in Design view queries, forms, or reports that reference a table that was renamed for those objects that include fields from the renamed table.

You can also delete an object from the database by selecting the object in the Navigation pane and pressing the Delete key. Click Yes at the Microsoft Access message box that displays asking you to confirm you want to delete the object. Consider making a backup copy of a database before renaming or deleting objects in case several object dependencies are broken afterwards and you want to restore the database to its previous state.

| Project 4e | Renaming and Deleting Database Objects | Part 5 of 5 |
|---|---|---|

1. With the **AL2-C6-RSRCompServ_be.accdb** database open, rename the MfrContacts table by completing the following steps:
   a. Right-click *MfrContacts* in the Navigation pane.
   b. Click *Rename* at the shortcut menu.
   c. Type **ManufacturerContacts** and press Enter.
2. Delete the original table that was split using the Table Analyzer Wizard in Project 4a by completing the following steps:
   a. Right-click *Parts_OLD* in the Navigation pane.
   b. Click *Delete* at the shortcut menu.
   c. Click Yes at the Microsoft Access message box asking if you want to delete the table Parts_OLD.

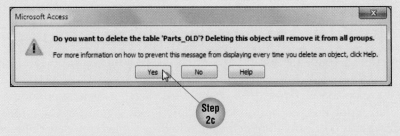

3. Close the **AL2-C6-RSRCompServ_be.accdb** database.
4. Open the **AL2-C6-RSRCompServ.accdb** front-end database and enable content.
5. When the database was split in Project 4c, Access created links to the existing table objects at the time the database was split. Since you have now renamed and deleted a table object in the back-end database, the linked objects will no longer work.

6. Double-click the link to MfrContacts in the Navigation pane. Since the table was renamed at Step 1, Access can no longer find the source data. At the Microsoft Access message box informing you that the database engine cannot find the input table, click OK. The link would have to be recreated to establish a new connection to the renamed table. You will learn how to link to external tables in Chapter 8.

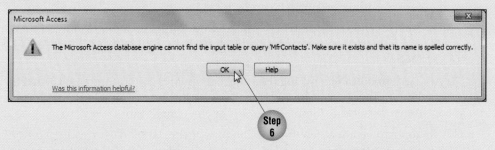

Step 6

7. Double-click the link to Parts_OLD. Since this table was deleted, the same message appears. Click OK to close the message box.

8. Right-click *Parts_OLD* in the Navigation pane and click *Delete* at the shortcut menu. Click Yes at the Microsoft Access message asking if you want to remove the link.

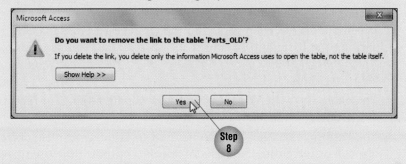

Step 8

9. Close the **AL2-C6-RSRCompServ.accdb** database.

In this chapter you have learned to use some of the tools that Access provides to create a new database, create new tables and related objects, improve database or individual object design and performance, and document the database. You have also learned how to rename and delete objects.

# Chapter Summary

- Access includes predefined database templates that include tables, queries, forms, and reports which can be used to create a new database.

- You can choose a database template from sample templates stored on your computer or you can download a database template from Microsoft Office Online.

- Predefined table and related object templates for Comments; Contacts; and Issues, Tasks, and Users are available from the Application Parts button drop-down list in the Templates group in the Create tab.

- You can create a new form using one of the 10 blank forms in the Application Parts button drop-down list. Most of the blank forms include command buttons that perform actions such as saving changes or saving and closing the form.

- Define your own form template by creating a form named *Normal* which includes a sample of each control object with the formatting options applied that you want to use for future forms. Select all of the controls and use the *Set Control Defaults* option to save the new settings.

- When a table has been copied to the clipboard from the Navigation pane, clicking the Paste button causes the Paste Table As dialog box to open in which you choose to paste *Structure Only*, *Structure and Data*, or *Append Data to Existing Table*.

- The Table Analyzer Wizard is used to evaluate a table for repeated data and determine if the table can be split into smaller related tables.

- The Performance Analyzer can be used to evaluate a single object, a group of objects, or the entire database for ways to optimize the use of system resources or disk space.

- The Performance Analyzer provides three types of results in the *Analysis Results* list: *Recommendation*, *Suggestion*, or *Idea*.

- Click an item in the *Analysis Results* list box that is a recommendation or suggestion and click the Optimize button to instruct Access to carry out the modification.

- A database can be split into two individual files, a back-end database and a front-end database, to improve performance for a multi-user database or to overcome the maximum database file size restriction.

- Split a database using the Database Splitter Wizard, which is started from the Access Database button in the Move Data group of the Database Tools tab.

- Access provides the Database Documenter feature, which is used to obtain hard copy reports providing object definition and field or control properties.

- Rename an object by right-clicking the object name in the Navigation pane, clicking *Rename* at the shortcut menu, typing a new name, and then pressing Enter.

- Delete an object by right-clicking the object name in the Navigation pane, clicking *Delete* at the shortcut menu, and then clicking Yes at the message box asking if you want to delete the object.

# Commands Review

| FEATURE | RIBBON TAB, GROUP | BUTTON | KEYBOARD SHORTCUT |
|---|---|---|---|
| Application Parts | Create, Templates | | |
| Documenter | Database Tools, Analyze | | |
| Paste Table As | Home, Clipboard | | Ctrl + V |
| Performance Analyzer | Database Tools, Analyze | | |
| Split database | Database Tools, Move Data | | |
| Table Analyzer Wizard | Database Tools, Analyze | | |

# Concepts Check  Test Your Knowledge

**Completion:** In the space provided at the right, indicate the correct term, command, or number.

1. Click this option in the Available Templates category to view the database templates stored on the computer you are using.

2. A predefined table with related objects to store information about Contacts can be imported into the current database using this button in the Templates group in the Create tab.

3. Access provides 10 prebuilt forms with a defined layout and with most including titles and command buttons in this section of the Application Parts button drop-down list.

4. Name a form with this name to use the form as a template for all new forms.

5. Clicking the Paste button after copying a table in the Navigation pane causes this dialog box to open.

6. This wizard analyzes a table for repeated information and proposes a solution where the table can be split into smaller related tables.

7. Optimize a database using this button in the Analyze group in the Database Tools tab.

8. List the three types of solutions the Performance Analyzer provides to optimize the selected objects.

   _____

9. Click an item in the *Analysis Results* list and read a description of the optimization method in this section of the Performance Analyzer dialog box.

   _____

10. A database can be split into a front-end database file and a back-end database file using this button in the Move Data group in the Database Tools tab.

   _____

11. When a database has been split, the back-end database file contains these objects.

   _____

12. When a database has been split, the front-end database file contains links to these objects.

   _____

13. Open this dialog box to print a report with a table's definition and field properties.

   _____

14. Rename a database object in the Navigation pane by performing this action.

   _____

15. Remove a selected object from the database by pressing this key.

   _____

# Skills Check   Assess Your Performance

## Assessment

### 1   CREATE A NEW DATABASE USING A TEMPLATE

1. Create a new database named **AL2-C6-VantageAssets.accdb** using the Assets Web Database template. At the Login dialog box that appears, click *New User* located at the bottom left of the dialog box. Type your name in the *Full Name* text box, your email address in the *E-mail* text box, and then click the Save & Close button. At the Login dialog box with your name added to the *Users* list, click the Close button in the dialog box title bar to close the dialog box and finish importing the database elements.
2. Click Enable Content in the Security Warning message bar. If necessary, at the Login dialog box, click your name in the *Users* list box and then click the Login button.
3. Display the Navigation pane and then spend a few moments opening and viewing various objects within the database. Close all objects when you are finished including the Main form.

4. Open the AssetDetails form, add the following records using the form and then close the form.

| | |
|---|---|
| *Asset* | Web Server |
| *Owner* | (click your name in the drop-down list) |
| *Location* | Head office |
| *Model* | TrueEdge 6500 |
| *Attachments* | (attach the data file named *WebServer.jpg*) |
| *Manufacturer* | Edge Industries |
| *Condition* | New |
| *Acquired Date* | (enter the current date) |
| *Category* | Servers |
| *Current Value* | 1850.00 |
| *Retired Date* | (leave blank) |
| *Comments* | (leave blank) |

| | |
|---|---|
| *Asset* | Workstation |
| *Owner* | (click your name in the drop-down list) |
| *Location* | Head office |
| *Model* | EdgeConnect 100 |
| *Attachments* | (attach the data file named *Workstation1.jpg*) |
| *Manufacturer* | Edge Industries |
| *Condition* | New |
| *Acquired Date* | (enter the current date) |
| *Category* | Desktop Computers |
| *Current Value* | 985.00 |
| *Retired Date* | (leave blank) |
| *Comments* | (leave blank) |

5. Print the two records as displayed in the AssetDetails form.
6. Close the form and then close the **AL2-C6-VantageAssets.accdb** database.

## Assessment

### 2   CREATE TABLE USING AN APPLICATIONS PARTS TEMPLATE

1. Open **AL2-C6-VantageVideos.accdb** and enable content.
2. Create a new group of objects related to Tasks using the Tasks Application Part. Specify no relationship at the Create Relationship Wizard.
3. Using the TaskDetails form, add a record using the following information. Substitute your name for *Student Name* in the *Description* field.

| | |
|---|---|
| *Task* | Set up backup Web server |
| *Status* | Not started |
| *Priority* | (1) High |
| *Start Date* | Enter the current date |
| *Due Date* | Enter a due date that is one week from the current date |
| *Attachments* | (leave blank) |
| *% Complete* | (leave at default value of 0%) |
| *Description* | Configure hot server to be on standby in event of failover. Assigned to *Student Name*. |

4. Open the Tasks table to view the record added to the table using the form at Step 3. Close the table.
5. Print the selected record using the TaskDetails form.
6. Close the form.

## 3 USE ACCESS TOOLS TO IMPROVE DESIGN AND PERFORMANCE

1. With the **AL2-C6-VantageVideos.accdb** database open, use the Table Analyzer Wizard to analyze the WebCustPymnt table using the following information.
   a. Rename the new table with all of the fields except the *CCType* field to *WebCustCreditCards*.
   b. Rename the new table with the *CCType* field to *CreditCardTypes*.
   c. Choose an appropriate field for the primary key in the WebCustCreditCards table.
   d. If the wizard determines that the Discover card is a typographical error, choose (*Leave as is*) at the *Correction* drop-down list and click Next.
   e. Create the query.
2. Close the Help window.
3. Delete the *CCType* field in the WebCustPymnt query. Adjust all column widths to Best Fit and print the query results datasheet using left and right margins of 0.25 inch.
4. Close the query saving the layout changes.
5. Delete the WebCustPymnt_OLD table.
6. Split the database to create a front-end database and a back-end database file. Accept the default file name for the back-end database.
7. Close the **AL2-C6-VantageVideos.accdb** database.
8. Open the **AL2-C6-VantageVideos_be.accdb** database and enable content.
9. Generate and print a report that provides the table and field property definitions for the CreditCardTypes table. Include the relationships in the report.
10. Close the **AL2-C6-VantageVideos_be.accdb** database.

# Visual Benchmark Demonstrate Your Proficiency

## 1 CREATE TABLE TO STORE GROOMERS INFORMATION

1. Open **AL2-C6-PawsParadise.accdb** and enable content.
2. Review the table shown in Figure 6.9 and create the new table in the database by copying the structure of the DogOwners table.
3. Modify the table design as needed, add the records shown in the figure, and rename the table as shown.
4. Adjust all column widths and print the table.
5. Close the table.

**Figure 6.9** Visual Benchmark 1

| Groomer ID | First Name | Last Name | Street Address | City | State | ZIP Code | Home Telephone | Hourly Rate |
|---|---|---|---|---|---|---|---|---|
| 01 | Max | Lahey | 715 Irish Hollow | Smethport | PA | 16749- | (814) 555-6253 | $28.50 |
| 02 | Juan | Modesta | 117 Spring Drive | Bradford | PA | 16701- | (814) 555-3845 | $28.50 |
| 03 | Pat | O'Connor | 147 Lamont Drive | Bradford | PA | 16701- | (814) 555-2118 | $31.50 |
| 04 | Greg | Walczak | 22 Foster Square | Allegheny | PA | 15212- | (814) 555-7448 | $35.50 |
| 05 | Melissa | Cochrane | 140 Congress Street | Bradford | PA | 16701- | (814) 555-6489 | $28.50 |
| * | | | | Bradford | PA | | | |

## 2 CREATE FORM TEMPLATE

1. With the **AL2-C6-PawsParadise.accdb** database open, examine the control objects shown in the form named *Normal* in Figure 6.10. Create a Normal form to be used as a template with the three control objects shown. Use font color *Green, Accent 1, Darker 50%* and background color *Green, Accent 1, Lighter 80%* for the formatting.
2. Create a new form for the Groomers table using the Form button in the Forms group of the Create tab. Decrease the width of the form title and text box control objects in the form so that one form will fit on one page and then print the first form only.
3. Save the Groomers form accepting the default name *Groomers*.
4. Close the form and then close the **AL2-C6-PawsParadise.accdb** database.

**Figure 6.10** Visual Benchmark 2

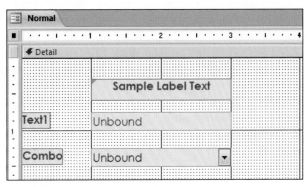

# Case Study  Apply Your Skills

**Part 1**

As an intern at Hillsdale Realty, you have been building a listings, sales, and commission database over the past weeks. You decide to create a new database to store information about home shows and conferences that Hillsdale Realty attends as an exhibitor. To save time developing new objects, use the Events sample template to create a new database in the Access2010L2C6 folder on your storage medium named **AL2-C6-HillsdaleShows.accdb**. Enable content and then add the following two trade show events to the database using the Event List form.

- The three-day Homebuilders Association Trade Show begins April 15, 2012 at the Phoenix Convention Center.
- The four-day Green Home Design Conference begins October 11, 2012 at the University of Phoenix Hohokam Campus.

The office manager likes the idea of tracking the trade shows in the database and would like you to create a similar table to keep track of conferences that agents attend as visitors. Close the Event List form and display the Navigation pane. Change the Navigation pane view to display objects by *Object Type*. Next, copy the structure of the Events table to create a new table named *AgentConferences*. Modify the AgentConferences table to delete the *Attachments* field and add a new field to store the number of people the company will send to the show. Create a form for the AgentConferences table using the Form button and add the following record.

- Five employees will attend the three-day Window and Door Manufacturers Association Annual Conference beginning November 7, 2012 at the Georgia International Convention Center.

Preview the AgentConferences form in Print Preview. If necessary, make adjustments to fit the form on one page. Print the AgentConferences form with the first record displayed. Save and close the form. Open the Event Details report. Print and then close the report. Close the **AL2-C6-HillsdaleShows.accdb** database.

**Part 2**

You want to see if Access tools can help you improve the database design of the database you have been building over the past weeks. Open the database named **AL2-C6-HillsdaleRealty.accdb** and enable content. Use the Table Analyzer Wizard to analyze the Listings table. Accept the proposed table split, create appropriate table names, assign primary key fields, and create the query. Modify the query as needed to remove duplicate columns. Sort the query in ascending order by the *ListDate* field. Print the query results datasheet with all column widths adjusted to Best Fit. Delete the original table with _OLD in the name. When changes are made to tables after other objects are created that are dependent on the table, errors can occur. Open the ListingsAndSales form. Notice the error in the control object named *City*. Since the Table Analyzer Wizard split the original Listings table on the *City* field, the original field added to the form no longer exists. Display the form in Design view and delete the *City* control object. Display the Field List task pane and add the appropriate field to the form. Size and align the controls as needed and then save and close the form.

**Part 3**

Use the Performance Analyzer to analyze the entire database. When the Listings table was split in Part 2, the relationships between the original Listings table and other objects were removed, leaving the new split table not related to other tables. Select and optimize entries in the *Analysis Results* list that will create the relationships for you between the new Listings table and other objects. Next, notice that all of the fields that store identification numbers such as *AgentID*, *ClientID*, *ListingNo*, and *QuotaID* have the idea proposed that the data type should be changed from Text to Long Integer. Long Integer is not actually a data type but a field size setting for a numeric field. Research data types in Help. Specifically find out the difference between assigning a field the Text data type and the Number data type. Using Microsoft Word, compose a memo to your instructor with the following information:

- An explanation of the use of the Text data type
- An explanation of the use of the Number data type
- Your recommendation of which data type should be used for the four *ID* fields in the database and why

Save the memo and name it **AL2-C6-HillsdaleDBAnalysisMemo.docx**. Print the memo and exit Word. In the database, open the Relationships window. Delete the original Listings table from the window and display the new Listings table name to show the relationships created when the database was optimized. Rearrange the table field list boxes so that the join lines are easy to follow and generate a relationship report. Print the relationships report. Save and close the relationships report and then close the **AL2-C6-HillsdaleRealty.accdb** database.

# Access®

# Automating, Customizing, and Securing Access

## PERFORMANCE OBJECTIVES

**Upon successful completion of Chapter 7, you will be able to:**

- Create, run, edit, and delete a macro
- Assign a macro to a command button on a form
- View macro code created in a form's Property Sheet for a command button
- Convert macros to Visual Basic
- Create and edit a Navigation form
- Change database startup options
- Show and hide the Navigation pane
- Customize the Navigation pane by hiding objects
- Define error checking options
- Customize the ribbon
- Create an ACCDE database file
- View trust center settings

**Tutorials**

7.1   Creating and Editing a Macro

7.2   Creating a Command Button to Run a Macro

7.3   Creating a Navigation Form

7.4   Adding a Command Button to a Navigation Form

7.5   Limiting Ribbon Tabs and Menus in a Database

7.6   Customizing the Navigation Pane

7.7   Configuring Error Checking Options

7.8   Customizing the Ribbon

7.9   Creating an ACCDE Database File

7.10   Viewing Trust Center Settings

Macros are used to automate repetitive tasks or to store actions that can be executed by clicking a button in a form. A Navigaton form is a form used as a menu that provides an interface between the end user and the objects within the database file. In this chapter you will learn how to automate a database using macros and a Navigation form. You will also learn methods to secure and customize the Access environment to prevent changes to the design of objects. Model answers for this chapter's projects appear on the following page.

Access2010L2C7

*Note: Before beginning the projects, copy to your storage medium the Access2010L2C7 subfolder from the Access2010L2 folder on the CD that accompanies this textbook and then make Access2010L2C7 the active folder.*

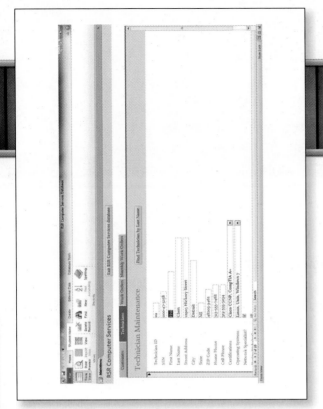

**Project 3 Configure Database Options**
Project 3d, Customized Database Startup Options,
Navigation Pane, and Custom Ribbon Tab

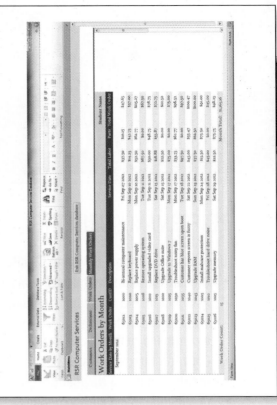

**Project 4 Secure a Database**
Project 4a, ACCDE Database Window

## Project 1  Create Macros and Assign Macros to Command Buttons    8 Parts

You will create macros to automate routine tasks and add macros to command buttons in forms that run the macros.

## Creating a Macro

A *macro* is a series of instructions stored in sequence that can be recalled and carried out whenever the need arises. Macros are generally created when a task that is never varied is repeated frequently. For example, a macro could be created to open a query, form, or report. The macro object stores a series of instructions (called *actions*) in the sequence in which the actions are to be performed. Macros appear as objects within the Navigation pane. Double-clicking the macro name causes Access to perform the instructions. A macro can also be assigned to a command button to enable the macro to be run using a single mouse click. For example, you could create a macro in a form that automates the process of finding a record by the last name field and assign the macro to a button. The macro would contain two instructions, the first instruction to move to the field in which the last name is stored, and the second instruction to open the Find dialog box.

To create a macro, click the Create tab and then click the Macro button in the Macros & Code group. This opens the Macro Builder Window shown in Figure 7.1. Click the down-pointing arrow at the right end of the *Add New Action* list box and click the desired instruction at the drop-down list. As an alternative, you can add an action using the Action Catalog pane as described in Figure 7.1.

Each new action entered into the Macro Builder window is associated with a set of **arguments** that displays once the action has been added. Similar to field properties in Table Design view, the arguments displayed in the *Action Arguments* section vary depending on the active action that has been expanded in the Macro Builder window. For example, Figure 7.2 displays the action arguments for the OpenForm action.

The OpenForm action is used to open a form similar to double-clicking a form name in the Navigation pane. Within the *Action Arguments* section you specify the name of the form to open and the view in which the form is to be presented. You can choose to open the form in Form view, Design view, Print Preview, Datasheet view, PivotTable view, PivotChart view, or Layout view. Use the *Filter Name* or *Where Condition* arguments to restrict the records displayed in the report. The Data Mode argument is used to place editing restrictions on records while the form is open. You can open the form in *Add* mode to allow adding new records only (users cannot view existing records), *Edit* mode to allow records to be added, edited, or deleted, or *Read Only* mode to allow records to be viewed only. The *Window Mode* argument is used to instruct Access to open the form in *Normal* mode (as you normally view forms in the work area), *Hidden* mode (form is hidden), *Icon* mode (form opens minimized), or *Dialog* mode (form opens in a separate window similar to a dialog box).

▼ **Quick Steps**

**Create Macro**
1. Click Create tab.
2. Click Macro button.
3. Click *Add New Action* list arrow.
4. Click desired action.
5. Enter arguments as required in *Action Arguments* section.
6. Click Save button.
7. Type name for macro.
8. Press Enter or click OK.
9. Repeat Steps 3–6 as needed.

**Run Macro**
Double-click macro name in Navigation pane.
OR
1. Right-click macro name.
2. Click *Run*.

Macro

**Figure 7.1** Macro Builder Window

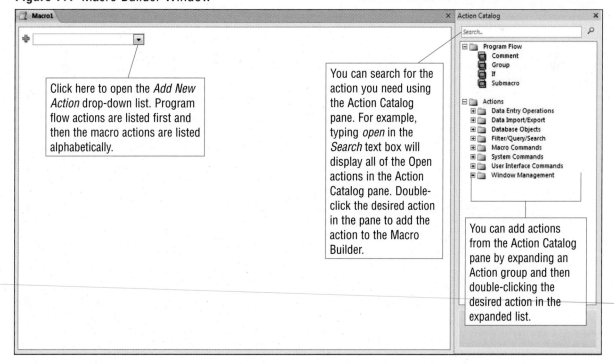

**Hovering the mouse over an argument's entry box allows you to read a description of the argument and the available parameters in a ScreenTip.**

To create a macro with multiple actions, add the second instruction in the *Add New Action* list box that appears below the first action. Access executes each action in the order they appear in the Macro Builder window. In Project 1a you will create a macro with multiple actions that will instruct Access to open a form, make active a control within the form, and then open the Find dialog box in order to search for a record. The *GoToControl* action is used to make active a control within a form or report and the *RunMenuCommand* action is used to execute an Access command. For each of these actions, a single argument specifies the name of the control to move to and the name of the command you want to run. As you add actions to the Macro Builder window, you can expand and collapse the *Action Arguments* section for actions as needed. When several actions are added to the Macro Builder window, collapsing arguments allows you to focus on only the current action you are editing.

**Figure 7.2** Macro Builder Window with Action Arguments for *OpenForm* Action

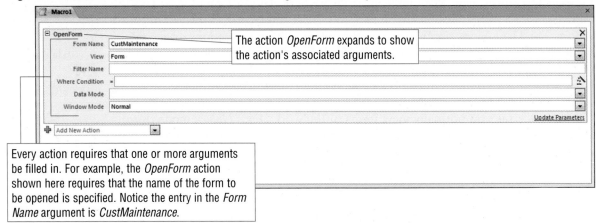

The action *OpenForm* expands to show the action's associated arguments.

Every action requires that one or more arguments be filled in. For example, the *OpenForm* action shown here requires that the name of the form to be opened is specified. Notice the entry in the *Form Name* argument is *CustMaintenance*.

---

**Project 1a**  **Creating a Macro to Open a Form and Find a Record**    Part 1 of 8

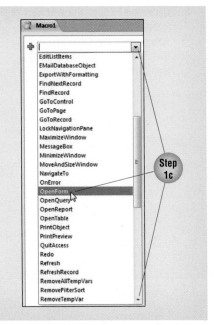

1. Open the **AL2-C7-RSRCompServ.accdb** database and enable content. Create a macro to open the TechMaintenance form by completing the following steps:
   a. Click the Create tab.
   b. Click the Macro button in the Macros & Code group.
   c. At the Macro Builder window, click the down-pointing arrow at the right of the *Add New Action* list box, scroll down the list, and then click *OpenForm*. Access adds the action and opens the *Action Arguments* section. Most actions require at least one action argument as a minimum.

Step 1c

d. Click the down-pointing arrow at the right of the *Form Name* argument box in the *Action Arguments* section and then click *TechMaintenance* at the drop-down list.

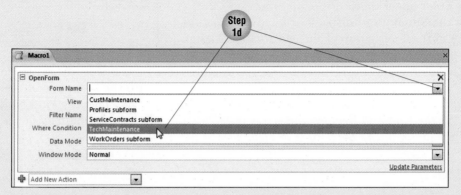

2. Add additional instructions to move to the technician's last name field and then open the Find dialog box by completing the following steps:

   a. Click the down-pointing arrow at the right of the *Add New Action* list box, scroll down the list, and then click *GoToControl*. Notice that only one action argument is required for the *GoToControl* action.

   b. Click in the *Control Name* argument box in the *Action Arguments* section and then type **LName**. (At the *Control Name* argument box, the name of the field that you want to make active in the form is required.)

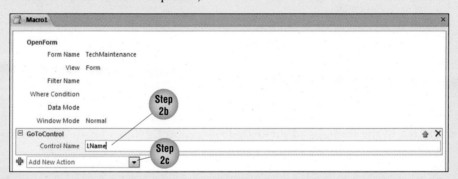

   c. Click the down-pointing arrow at the right of the *Add New Action* list box, scroll down the list box, and then click *RunMenuCommand* at the drop-down list.

   d. Click the down-pointing arrow at the right of the *Command* argument box, scroll down the list box, and then click *Find*.

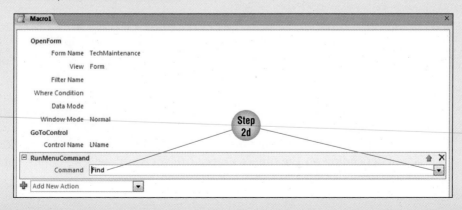

3. Click the Save button, type FormFindTech in the *Macro Name* text box at the Save As dialog box, and press Enter or click OK.

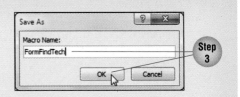

4. Click the Run button (displays as a red exclamation mark) in the Tools group of the Macro Tools Design tab. The Run button instructs Access to carry out the instructions in the macro. The TechMaintenance form opens, the active field is *Last Name,* and the Find and Replace dialog box appears with the last name of the first technician entered in the *Find What* text box. Type Sadiku and click the Find Next button. ***Note: If the Find and Replace dialog box is overlapping the* Last Name *field in the form, drag the dialog box to the bottom or right edge of the work area.***

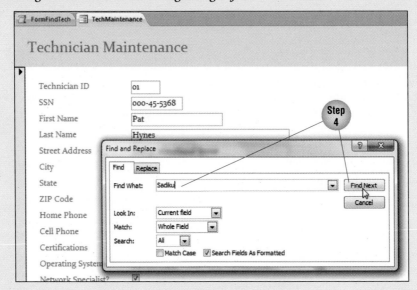

5. Access moves to record 5. Close the Find and Replace dialog box. Notice the last name text is selected in the form. Read the data displayed in the form for the technician named *Madir Sadiku.*

6. Close the form.

7. At the Macro Builder window, click the Close button located at the top right of the work area and left of the Action Catalog pane. This closes the FormTechFind macro. Notice a new category named Macros has been added to the Navigation pane and the FormTechFind macro name appears as an object below Macros.

A macro can also be created by dragging and dropping an object name from the Navigation pane to the *Add New Action* list box in a Macro Builder window. By default, Access creates an *OpenTable, OpenQuery, OpenForm,* or *OpenReport* action depending on the object dragged to the window. The object name is also automatically entered in the *Action Arguments* section.

1. With the **AL2-C7-RSRCompServ.accdb** database open, create a macro to open the CustMaintenance form using the drag and drop method by completing the following steps:

    a. Click the Create tab.

    b. Click the Macro button in the Macros & Code group.

    c. Position the mouse pointer on the CustMaintenance form name in the Navigation pane, hold down the left mouse button, drag the object name to the *Add New Action* list box in the Macro Builder window, and then release the mouse. Access inserts an OpenForm action with *CustMaintenance* entered in the *Form Name* argument box.

    *Drag CustMaintenance form name in Navigation pane to Add New Action list box at Step 1c.*

2. Click the Save button, type FormCustMaint, and then press the Enter key or click OK.

3. Click the Run button in the Tools group of the Macro Tools Design tab.

4. Close the form.

5. Click the Close button located at the top right of the work area and left of the Action Catalog pane to close the macro.

---

1. With the **AL2-C7-RSRCompServ.accdb** database open, create a macro using the Action Catalog pane to find a record in a form by making active the home telephone field, opening the Find dialog box, and then completing the following steps:

    a. Click the Create tab.

    b. Click the Macro button in the Macros & Code group.

    c. Click the Expand button (displays as a plus symbol) next to *Database Objects* in the *Actions* list in the Action Catalog pane to expand the category and display the actions available for changing controls or objects in the database. ***Note: If you accidentally closed the Action Catalog pane in a previous Macro Builder window and the pane does not redisplay in the new Macro Builder window, click the Action Catalog button in the Show/Hide group of the Macro Tools Design tab to restore the pane.***

    d. Double-click *GoToControl* at the expanded *Database Objects* actions list in the Action Catalog pane to add the action to the Macro Builder window.

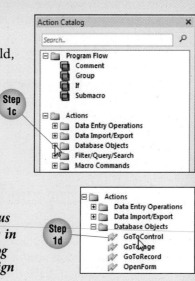

e. With the insertion point positioned in the *Control Name* argument box in the Macro Builder window, type **HPhone**.

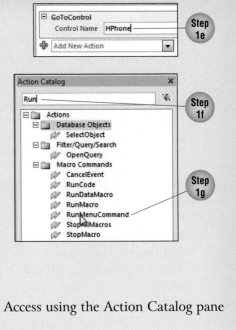

f. Click in the Search text box at the top of the Action Catalog pane and then type **Run**. As you type text in the Search text box, Access displays in the Action Catalog pane the available actions that begin with the same text as the text you typed.

g. Double-click *RunMenuCommand* in the *Macro Commands* list in the Action Catalog pane.

h. With the insertion point positioned in the *Command* argument box in the Macro Builder window, type **Find**.

i. Click the Save button on the Quick Access toolbar.

j. At the Save As dialog box, type **HPhoneFind** and then press Enter or click OK.

k. Close the HPhoneFind macro.

2. Create a macro to close the current database and exit Access using the Action Catalog pane by completing the following steps:

a. Click the Create tab and then click the Macro button.

b. Click the Clear Filter button (displays as a red x over a funnel) at the right of the Search text box in the Action Catalog pane to clear *Run* from the Search text box and redisplay all action catalog categories.

c. Click the Expand button (displays as a plus symbol) next to *System Commands* in the *Actions* list in the Action Catalog pane.

d. Double-click *QuitAccess* in the expanded *System Commands* actions list.

e. With *Save All* the default argument in the *Options* argument box, click the Save button on the Quick Access toolbar.

f. Type **ExitRSRdb** at the Save As dialog box and then press Enter or click OK.

3. Close the ExitRSRdb macro.

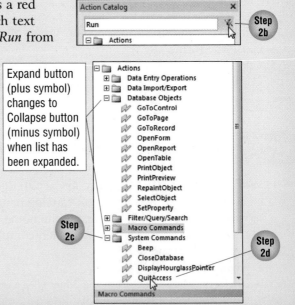

Expand button (plus symbol) changes to Collapse button (minus symbol) when list has been expanded.

## Editing and Deleting a Macro ■■■■■■■■■■■■■■■■■■

To edit a macro, right-click the macro name in the Navigation pane and click *Design View* at the shortcut menu. The macro opens in the Macro Builder window. Edit an action and/or the action's arguments, insert new actions, or delete actions as required. Save the revised macro and close the Macro Builder window when finished.

To delete a macro, right-click the macro name in the Navigation pane and then click *Delete* at the shortcut menu. At the Microsoft Access dialog box asking if you want to delete the macro, click Yes.

1. With the **AL2-C7-RSRCompServ.accdb** database open, assume you decide that the macro to find a technician record will begin with the TechMaintenance form already opened. This means you have to delete the first macro instruction to open the TechMaintenance form in the FormFindTech macro. To do this, complete the following steps:
   a. If necessary, scroll down the Navigation pane to view the macro object names.
   b. Right-click the macro named FormFindTech and then click *Design View* at the shortcut menu. The macro opens in the Macro Builder window.
   c. Position the mouse pointer over the *OpenForm* action in the Macro Builder window. As you point to an action in the Macro Builder window Access displays a collapse button at the left of the action to allow you to collapse the *Arguments* section, a down-pointing green arrow at the right side of the Macro Builder window to allow you to move the action, and a black x to delete the action.

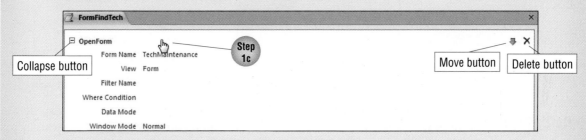

   d. Click the Delete button located at the right side of the Macro Builder window next to *OpenForm*. The action is removed from the Macro Builder window. ***Note: If the buttons at the right side of the Macro Builder window disappear as you move the mouse right, move the pointer up so that the pointer is on the same line as OpenForm to redisplay the buttons.***

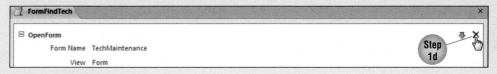

2. Save the revised macro.
3. Close the macro.
4. The revised macro contains two instructions that activate the *LName* control and then open the Find dialog box. This macro could be used in any form that contains a field named *LName*; therefore, you decide to rename the macro. To begin, right-click FormFindTech in the Navigation pane, click *Rename* at the shortcut menu, type **LNameFind**, and then press Enter.

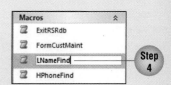

5. Delete the FormCustMaint macro by completing the following steps:
   a. Right-click *FormCustMaint* in the Navigation pane and then click *Delete* at the shortcut menu.
   b. At the Microsoft Access dialog box asking if you want to delete the macro, click Yes.

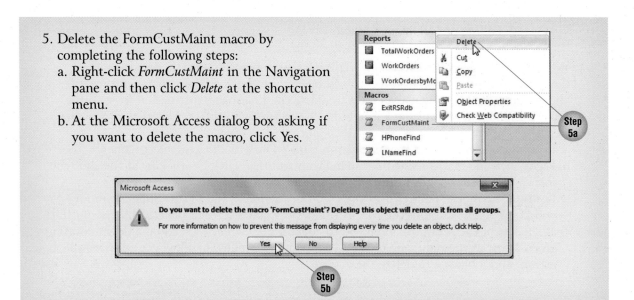

# Creating a Command Button to Run a Macro ■■■■■■■■

### ▼ Quick Steps

**Create Command Button in Form**
1. Open form in Design view.
2. Click Button button.
3. Drag to create button desired height and width.
4. Click *Miscellaneous.*
5. Click *Run Macro.*
6. Click Next.
7. Click desired macro name.
8. Click Next.
9. Click *Text.*
10. Select current text in *Text* text box.
11. Type desired text to appear on button.
12. Click Next.
13. Type name for command button.
14. Click Finish.

A macro can be assigned to a button added to a form so that the macro can be executed with a single mouse click. This method of running a macro makes macros more accessible and efficient. Open a form in Design view to add a button to the form to be used to run a macro. Click the Button button in the Controls group in the Form Design Tools Design tab and drag to create the button the approximate height and width in the desired form section. When you release the mouse, the Command Button Wizard launches if the Use Control Wizards feature is active. At the first Command Button Wizard dialog box shown in Figure 7.3, you begin by choosing the type of command to assign to the button.

Click *Miscellaneous* in the *Categories* list box and *Run Macro* in the *Actions* list box and click Next. At the second Command Button Wizard dialog box you choose the name of the macro to assign to the button. At the third dialog box, shown in Figure 7.4, specify text to display on the face of the button or choose to

**Figure 7.3** First Command Button Wizard Dialog Box

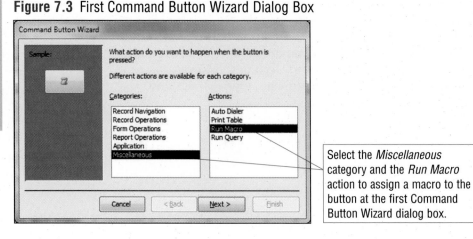

Select the *Miscellaneous* category and the *Run Macro* action to assign a macro to the button at the first Command Button Wizard dialog box.

**Figure 7.4** Third Command Button Wizard Dialog Box

Click to display *Text* or *Picture* on the face of the button.

Click the Browse button to locate a picture you want to display on the face of the button.

Button

Control Wizard

display a picture as an icon. The button in the *Sample* section of the dialog box updates to show how the button will appear as you enter text or select a picture file. At the last Command Button Wizard dialog box, assign a name to associate with the command button and click Finish.

---

**Project 1e** Creating a Button and Assigning a Macro to the Button in a Form    **Part 5 of 8**

1. With the **AL2-C7-RSRCompServ.accdb** database open, create a command button to run the macro to locate a technician record by last name in the TechMaintenance form by completing the following steps:

   a. Open the TechMaintenance form in Design view. To make room for the new button in the *Form Header* section, click to select the control object with the title text and then drag the right middle sizing handle left until the right edge is at approximately 3.5 inches in the horizontal ruler.

   b. By default, the Use Control Wizards feature is toggled on in the Controls group. Click the More button at the bottom of the Controls scroll bar to expand the Controls and display the *Controls* drop-down list. View the current status of the *Use Control Wizards* option. The button at the left of the option displays with an orange background when the feature is active. If the button is orange, click in a blank area to remove the expanded Controls list. If the feature is not active (displays with a white background), click *Use Control Wizards* to turn the feature on.

   c. Click the Button button in the Controls group in the Form Design Tools Design tab.

   d. Position the crosshairs with the button icon attached in the *Form Header* section, drag to create a button the approximate height and width shown, and then release the mouse.

   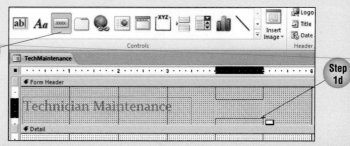

   Step 1c

   Step 1d

e. At the first Command Button Wizard dialog box, click *Miscellaneous* in the *Categories* list box.

f. Click *Run Macro* in the *Actions* list box and then click Next.

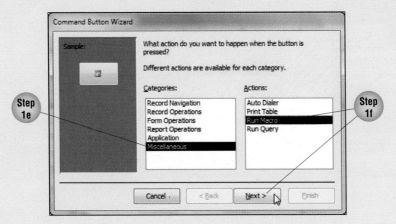

g. Click *LNameFind* in the *What macro would you like the command button to run?* list box at the second Command Button Wizard dialog box and then click Next.

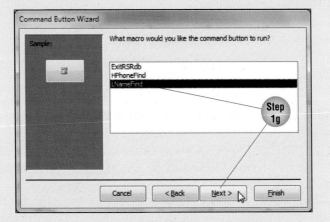

h. At the third Command Button Wizard dialog box, click *Text*.

i. Select the current text in the *Text* text box, type **Find Technician by Last Name**, and click Next.

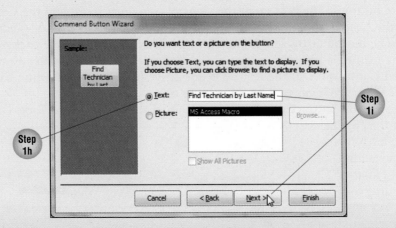

j. With *Command##* (where ## is the number of the command button) already selected in the *What do you want to name the button?* text box, type **FindTechRec** and then click Finish. Access automatically resizes the width of the button to accommodate the text to be displayed on the face of the button.

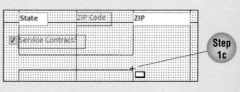

**Command Button Wizard**

Sample:

Find Technician by Last

What do you want to name the button?

A meaningful name will help you to refer to the button later.

FindTechRec

That's all the information the wizard needs to create your command button. Note: This wizard creates embedded macros that cannot run or be edited in Access 2003 and earlier versions.

**Step 1j**

Cancel      < Back      Next >      Finish

2. Save the revised form.
3. Switch to Form view.
4. Click the Find Technician by Last Name button to run the macro.
5. Type **Colacci** in the *Find What* text box at the Find and Replace dialog box and press Enter or click the Find Next button. Access moves the active record to record 9.
6. Close the Find and Replace dialog box.
7. Close the form.

**TechMaintenance**

Technician Maintenance      Find Technician by Last Name

**Step 4**

---

**Project 1f**   **Creating Two Command Buttons and Assigning Macros to the Buttons**   **Part 6 of 8**

1. With the **AL2-C7-RSRCompServ.accdb** database open, create a command button to run the macro to find a record by the home telephone number field in the CustMaintenance form by completing the following steps:
   a. Open the CustMaintenance form in Design view.
   b. Click the Button button in the Controls group in the Form Design Tools Design tab.
   c. Position the crosshairs with the button icon attached in the *Detail* section below the *Service Contract?* label control object, drag to create a button the approximate height and width shown, and then release the mouse.

State      ZIP Code      ZIP

☑ Service Contract?

**Step 1c**

   d. Click *Miscellaneous* in the *Categories* list box, click *Run Macro* in the *Actions* list box, and then click Next.
   e. Click *HPhoneFind* and click Next.
   f. Click *Text*, select the current text in the *Text* text box, type **Find Customer by Home Phone**, and click Next.
   g. Type **FindByPhone** and then click Finish.

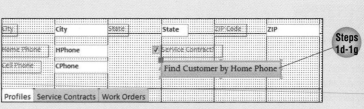

City      City      State      State      ZIP Code      ZIP

Home Phone      HPhone      ☑ Service Contract?

Cell Phone      CPhone      Find Customer by Home Phone

Profiles   Service Contracts   Work Orders

**Steps 1d-1g**

2. Save the revised form.
3. Create a second button below the button you created in Step 1 to run the macro to find a record by the last name by completing steps similar to those in Steps 1b through 1g and with the following additional information:
   - Select *LNameFind* as the macro to assign to the button.
   - Display the text *Find Customer by Last Name* on the button.
   - Name the button *FindByLName*.
4. Resize, align, and position the two buttons as shown.

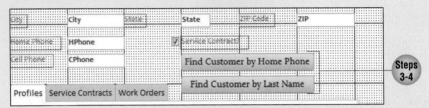

5. Save the revised form.
6. Switch to Form view.
7. Click the Find Customer by Home Phone button, type 313-555-7486 at the Find and Replace dialog box, and then press Enter or click Find Next. Close the dialog box and review the record for *Customer ID* 1025.
8. Click the Find Customer by Last Name button, type Antone at the Find and Replace dialog box, and then press Enter or click Find Next. Close the dialog box and review the record for *Customer ID* 1075.
9. Close the CustMaintenance form.

▼ **Quick Steps**

**View Macro Code for Command Button**
1. Open form in Design view.
2. Click to select command button.
3. Display the Property Sheet.
4. Click the Event tab.
5. Click the Build button in the *On Click* property box.

**H I N T**

To delete an embedded macro, open the Property Sheet, select *[Embedded Macro]* in the *On Click* property box and then press Delete. Close the Property Sheet and then save the form.

The Command Button Wizard used in Project 1e and 1f created an embedded macro in the Property Sheet of the button. An **embedded macro** is a macro that is stored within a form, report, or control that is run when a specific event occurs. For example, when the user clicks the button the macro is run. Clicking the button is the *event* that causes the macro action to be performed. You can view the embedded macro by opening the command button's Property Sheet and clicking the Event tab. In the *On Click* property box, you will see *[Embedded Macro]*. Click the Build button (button with three dots) at the right end of the *On Click* property box to open the Macro Builder window with the macro actions displayed. The macro and the macro actions were created for you by the Command Button Wizard. Embedded macros are not objects that you can see in the Navigation pane. To view or edit an embedded macro you need to open the form, report, or control Property Sheet.

1. With the **AL2-C7-RSRCompServ.accdb** database open, view the macro actions embedded in a command button when you used the Command Button Wizard by completing the following steps:

   a. Open the CustMaintenance form in Design view.

   b. Click to select the Find Customer by Home Phone command button.

   c. Click the Property Sheet button in the Tools group of the Form Design Tools Design tab or press function key F4.

   d. Click the Event tab in the Command Button Property Sheet.

   e. Notice the text in the *On Click* property box reads *[Embedded Macro]*.

   f. Click the Build button (button with three dots) in the *On Click* property box. When you click the Build button, Access opens the Macro Builder window for the macro that was embedded in the command button.

   g. Notice the name of the macro created for you by the Command Button Wizard is *CustMaintenance: FindByPhone: On Click*. The form name, followed by the button name to which the macro is associated and then the event that causes the macro to run (*On Click*), comprise the embedded macro's name.

   h. Review the macro actions in the Macro Builder window. Notice the macro action is *RunMacro* with the name of the macro you selected at the second Command Button Wizard dialog box, *HPhoneFind*, entered in the *Macro Name* argument.

   i. Click the Close button in the Close group of the Macro Tools Design tab.

2. With the Property Sheet still open, click to select the Find Customer by Last Name command button and then click the Build button in the *On Click* property box of the Event tab in the Property Sheet. Review the embedded macro name and macro actions in the Macro Builder window and then click the Close button in the Close group of the Macro Tools Design tab.

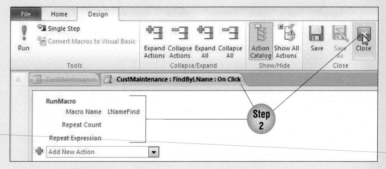

3. Close the CustMaintenance form.

## Quick Steps

**Convert Macro to Visual Basic**
1. Open macro in Design view.
2. Click Convert Macros to Visual Basic button.
3. Click Convert button.
4. Click OK.

**H I N T**

If you convert an embedded macro, Access also changes the property box in the form, report, or control Property Sheet to run the VBA procedure instead of the macro.

Macros enable you to add automation or functionality within Access without having to learn how to write programming code. In the Microsoft Office suite, Visual Basic for Applications (VBA) is the programming language used to build custom applications that operate within Word, Excel, PowerPoint, or Access. The macros used in this chapter have been simple and did not need VBA programming; however, when automation requires more complex tasks, a developer may prefer to write a program using VBA. A quick method to use to start a VBA program is to create a macro and then convert the macro to VBA code. To do this, open the macro in the Macro Builder window and then click the Convert Macros to Visual Basic button in the Tools group of the Macro Tools Design tab. Access opens a Microsoft Visual Basic window with the VBA code for the macro.

Convert Macros
to Visual Basic

---

**Project 1h**   **Converting a Macro to Visual Basic for Applications**   Part 8 of 8

1. With the **AL2-C7-RSRCompServ.accdb** database open, convert a macro to Visual Basic by completing the following steps:
   a. Right-click the HPhoneFind macro in the Macros group of the Navigation pane and then click *Design View* at the shortcut menu. The Macro Builder window opens with the macro actions and arguments for the HPhoneFind macro.
   b. Click the Convert Macros to Visual Basic button in the Tools group of the Macro Tools Design tab.
   c. At the Convert macro: HPhoneFind dialog box with the *Add error handling to generated functions* and *Include macro comments* check boxes selected, click the Convert button.
   d. At the *Convert macros to Visual Basic* message box with the message *Conversion Finished!*, click OK.

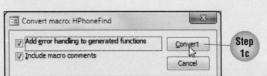

2. Access opens a Microsoft Visual Basic for Applications window when the macro is converted and displays the converted event procedure below an expanded Modules list in a Project window. If necessary, drag the right border of the Project window to expand the width in order to read the entire converted macro name and then double-click the macro name to open the event procedure in its class module window.
3. Read the VBA code in the Converted Macro-HPhoneFind (Code) window and then close the window.

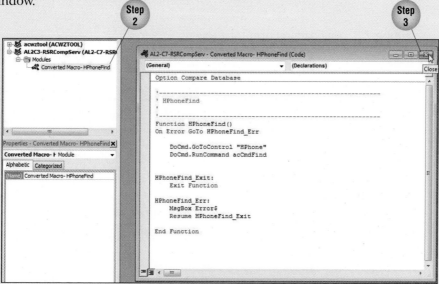

4. Click File on the Menu bar and then click *Close and Return to Microsoft Access* at the drop-down list.
5. Close the HPhoneFind Macro Builder window.

---

## Project 2    Create a Navigation Form

**2 Parts**

You will create a Navigation form to be used as a main menu for the RSR Computer Services database.

---

# Creating a Navigation Form ■■■■■■■■■■■■■■■■■■

Database files are often accessed by multiple users who need to enter the file for a specific purpose such as updating a customer record or entering details related to a completed work order. These individuals may not be well versed in database applications and simply want an easy method with which to accomplish the data entry or maintenance task. A Navigation form with tabs along the top, left, or right is used as a menu with which end users can open the forms and reports needed to update, view, or print data. The Navigation form can be set to display automatically when the database file is opened so that end users do not need to know which objects are needed from the Navigation pane.

To create a Navigation form, click the Create tab and then click the Navigation button in the Forms group. At the Navigation button drop-down list, choose the type of menu form you want to create by selecting the option in the drop-down list

**▼ Quick Steps**

**Create Navigation Form**
1. Click Create tab.
2. Click Navigation button.
3. Click desired form style.
4. Drag form or report name to *[Add New]* in Navigation Form.
5. Repeat Step 4 as needed.
6. Click Save.
7. Type form name.
8. Press Enter or click OK.

Navigation
Form

that positions the tabs where you want them to appear horizontally or vertically. A Navigation Form window opens with a title and tab bar created. Access displays *[Add New]* indicating the first tab in the form. Drag a form or report from the Navigation pane to *[Add New]* in the Navigation Form window to add a form or report to the form. Continue dragging form and/or report names from the Navigation pane to *[Add New]* in the Navigation Form window in the order you want them to appear. Figure 7.5 illustrates the navigation form you will create in Projects 2a and 2b.

**Figure 7.5** Navigation Form for Projects 2a and 2b

| RSR Computer Services | Exit RSR Computer Services database |

Navigation form with tabs along the top used to access forms and reports within the database.

| Customers | Technicians | Work Orders | Monthly Work Orders |

### Customer Data Maintenance Form

Customer ID 1000    First Name Jade    Last Name Fleming

Street Address 12109 Woodward Avenue

City Detroit    State MI    ZIP Code 48203-3579

Home Phone 313-555-0214    ☑ Service Contract?

Cell Phone 313-555-3485    Find Customer by Home Phone

Find Customer by Last Name

| Profiles | Service Contracts | Work Orders |

| Computer ID ▾ | Username ▾ | Password ▾ | Remote Access? ▾ |
| D1 | jade | Psck7 | ☐ |
| * | | | ☐ |

Record: ◄ ◄ 1 of 1 ► ►► ☒ No Filter Search

Revision number 1.0      Student Name

Record: ◄ ◄ 1 of 19 ► ►► ☒ No Filter Search

---

**Project 2a**    **Creating a Navigation Form**        Part 1 of 2

1. With the **AL2-C7-RSRCompServ.accdb** database open, create a Navigation form with tabs along the top for accessing forms and reports by completing the following steps:
   a. Click the Create tab.
   b. Click the Navigation button in the Forms group.
   c. Click *Horizontal Tabs* at the drop-down list. Access opens a Navigation Form window with a Field List pane open at the right side of the work area. The horizontal tab across the top of the form is selected with *[Add New]* displayed in the first tab.

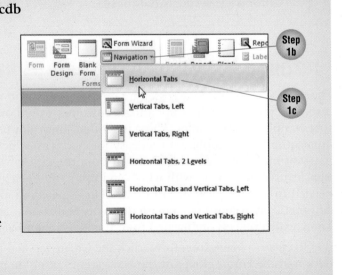

d. Position the mouse pointer on the CustMaintenance form name in the Navigation pane, hold down the left mouse button, drag the form name to *[Add New]* in the Navigation Form, and then release the mouse. Access adds the CustMaintenance form to the first tab in the form and displays a new tab with *[Add New]* to the right of the CustMaintenance tab.

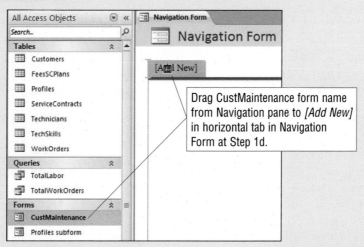

Drag CustMaintenance form name from Navigation pane to *[Add New]* in horizontal tab in Navigation Form at Step 1d.

e. Drag the TechMaintenance form name from the Navigation pane to the second tab with *[Add New]* displayed as the tab name.

f. Drag the WorkOrders report name from the Navigation pane to the third tab with *[Add New]* in the Navigation Form.

g. Drag the WorkOrdersbyMonth report name from the Navigation pane to the fourth tab with *[Add New]* in the Navigaton Form.

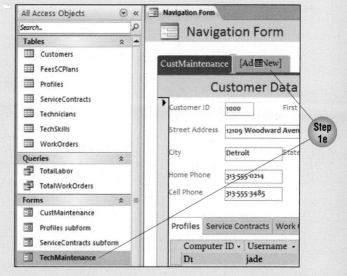

Step 1e

2. Close the Field List pane at the right side of the work area.

3. Click the Save button on the Quick Access toolbar. At the Save As dialog box, type **MainMenu** in the *Form Name* text box and then press Enter or click OK.

4. Switch to Form view.

5. Click each tab along the top of the Navigation form to view each form or report in the work area. When finished, leave the form open for the next project.

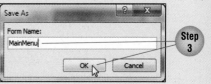

Step 3

A Navigation form can be edited in Layout view or Form view using all of the tools and techniques you learned in Chapter 4 for working with forms. Consider changing the title, adding a logo, and renaming tabs to customize the Navigation form.

1. With the **AL2-C7-RSRCompServ.accdb** database open and with the MainMenu form displayed in the work area, add a command button to the Navigation form by completing the following steps:
   a. Switch to Design view.
   b. Resize the title control object in the *Form Header* section to align the right edge of the object at approximately the 3-inch position in the horizontal ruler.
   c. Click the Button button in the Controls group and drag to create a button the approximate height and width shown in the *Form Header* section.

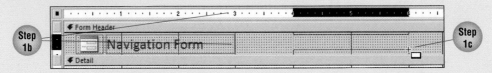

   d. Select *Miscellaneous* in the *Categories* list box and *Run Macro* in the *Actions* list box at the first Command Button Wizard dialog box and click Next.
   e. With *ExitRSRdb* already selected in the macros list box at the second Command Button Wizard dialog box, click Next.
   f. Click *Text*, select the current entry in the *Text* text box, type Exit RSR Computer Services database, and click Next at the third Command Button Wizard dialog box.
   g. Type Exitdb at the last Command Button Wizard dialog box and then click Finish.

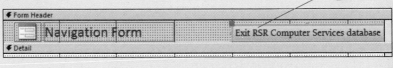

2. Click to select the logo container object at the left of the title in the *Form Header* section and then press Delete.
3. Edit the text in the Title control object in the *Form Header* section to *RSR Computer Services*.
4. Relabel the tabs along the top of the Navigation form by completing the following steps:
   a. Click to select the first tab with *CustMaintenance* as the tab name and then click the Property Sheet button in the Tools group of the Form Design Tools Design tab.
   b. With Format the active tab in the Property Sheet, select the current text in the *Caption* property box and then type Customers.
   c. Click the second tab with *TechMaintenance* as the tab name, select the current text in the *Caption* property box in the Property Sheet, and then type Technicians.
   d. Click the third tab with *WorkOrders* as the tab name, click in the *Caption* property box, and then insert a space between *Work* and *Orders* so that the tab name displays *Work Orders*.
   e. Click the fourth tab with *WorkOrdersbyMonth* as the tab name, select the current text in the *Caption* property box, and then type Monthly Work Orders.

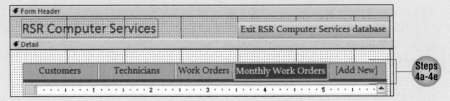

   f. Close the Property Sheet task pane.
5. Save the revised form and then switch to Form view.
6. Compare your form with the one shown in Figure 7.5 on page 253.

You will configure database options for the active database and error checking options for all databases, and customize the ribbon.

# Customizing the Access Environment ■■■■■■■■■■■■■■■

Click the File tab and then click the Options button located near the bottom of the left pane in the Info tab Backstage view to open the Access Options dialog box in which you can customize the Access environment. You can specify database options for all databases or for the current database. You can also define behavior for certain keys and set the default margins for printing. A form can be set to display automatically whenever the database file is opened. You can also choose to show or hide the Navigation pane in the current database. For example, if you have created a Navigation form that you want to use to provide limited access to only those objects that you want to make available, you may choose to hide the Navigation pane to prevent users from being able to open other objects within the database. Databases can be set to open by default in shared use or exclusive use. Exclusive use means the file is restricted to one individual user.

Figure 7.6 displays the Access Options dialog box with *Current Database* selected in the left pane. In the Current Database pane, you can define a startup form to open automatically when the database is opened. In Project 3a you will configure the current database to display the MainMenu form when the database is opened and in Project 3b you will customize the Navigation pane.

## ▼ Quick Steps

**Set Startup Form**
1. Click File tab.
2. Click Options.
3. Click *Current Database* in left pane.
4. Click down-pointing arrow next to *Display Form*.
5. Click desired form.
6. Click OK.

**Specify Application Title**
1. Click File tab.
2. Click Options.
3. Click *Current Database* in left pane.
4. Click in *Application Title* text box.
5. Type desired title.
6. Click OK.

Options

**Figure 7.6** Access Options Dialog Box with Current Database Pane Selected

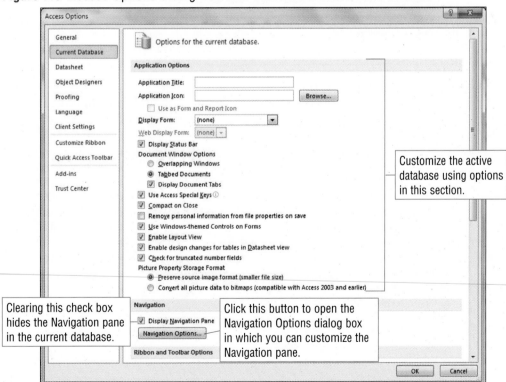

Clearing this check box hides the Navigation pane in the current database.

Click this button to open the Navigation Options dialog box in which you can customize the Navigation pane.

Customize the active database using options in this section.

1. With the **AL2-C7-RSRCompServ.accdb** database open, specify a form to be opened automatically when the database file is opened and a title to appear in the Title bar by completing the following steps:

   a. Click the File tab.

   b. Click the Options button located near the bottom of the left pane at the Info tab Backstage view.

   c. Click *Current Database* in the left pane.

   d. Click the down-pointing arrow next to the *Display Form* list box (currently displays *[none]* in the *Application Options* section) and then click *MainMenu* at the drop-down list.

2. Click in the *Application Title* text box and type RSR Computer Services Database.

3. Click OK.

4. Click OK at the Microsoft Access message box indicating you have to close and reopen the database for the options to take effect.

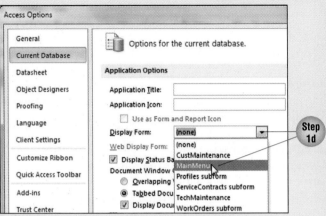

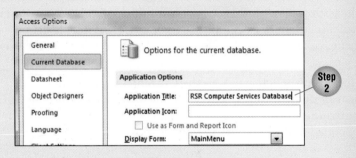

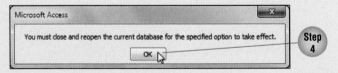

5. Close the **AL2-C7-RSRCompServ.accdb** database.

6. Reopen the **AL2-C7-RSRCompServ.accdb** database. The MainMenu form displays automatically in the work area and the Title bar displays the application title *RSR Computer Services Database*.

Application title and startup form option in effect when database is reopened at Step 6

# Limiting Ribbon Tabs and Menus in a Database

Often, when you are interested in securing the database by showing a startup form with limited access to objects, you also want to limit access to options in the ribbon and menus. Preventing an end user from seeing the full ribbon and shortcut menus allows you to avoid accidental changes made by someone switching views and editing or deleting objects without knowing the full impact of these changes. To do this, display the Access Options dialog box with the Current Database pane active. Scroll down the dialog box to the section titled *Ribbon and Toolbar Options*. Clear the check boxes for *Allow Full Menus* and *Allow Default Shortcut Menus* and then click OK. When the database is closed and reopened, only the Home tab will be available in the ribbon. The File tab Backstage view will only display Print options. You will not be able to switch views as the View buttons are removed and right-clicking will not show a shortcut menu.

If you need to work within the database and have access to the full ribbon and menus, you can bypass the startup options by holding the Shift key while double-clicking the file name to open the database.

# Customizing the Navigation Pane

Often, when a startup form is used in a database, the Navigation pane is hidden to prevent users from accidentally making changes to other objects by opening an object from the Navigation pane. To hide the Navigation pane, open the Access Options dialog box, click *Current Database* in the left pane, and then clear the *Display Navigation Pane* check box in the *Navigation* section.

Click the Navigation Options button in the *Navigation* section to open the Navigation Options dialog box shown in Figure 7.7. At this dialog box you can elect to hide individual objects or groups of objects, set display options for the pane, and define whether objects are opened using a single mouse click or a double mouse click. For example, to prevent changes from being made to table design, you can hide the Tables group.

▼ **Quick Steps**

**Customize Navigation Pane**
1. Click File tab.
2. Click Options.
3. Click *Current Database* in left pane.
4. Click Navigation Options button.
5. Select desired options.
6. Click OK.
7. Click OK.

**Hide Navigation Pane**
1. Click File tab.
2. Click Options.
3. Click *Current Database* in left pane.
4. Clear *Display Navigation Pane* check box.
5. Click OK.
6. Click OK.

**HINT**

Press F11 to display a hidden Navigation pane.

**Figure 7.7** Navigation Options Dialog Box

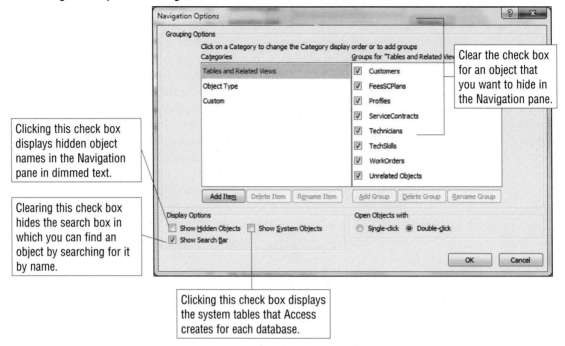

Clicking this check box displays hidden object names in the Navigation pane in dimmed text.

Clearing this check box hides the search box in which you can find an object by searching for it by name.

Clear the check box for an object that you want to hide in the Navigation pane.

Clicking this check box displays the system tables that Access creates for each database.

**Project 3b**  **Customizing the Navigation Pane**  Part 2 of 5

1. With the **AL2-C7-RSRCompServ.accdb** database open, customize the Navigation pane to hide all of the table and macro objects by completing the following steps:
   a. Click the File tab and then click the Options button.
   b. If necessary, click *Current Database* in the left pane. Click the Navigation Options button in the *Navigation* section.
   c. Click *Object Type* in the *Categories* list box.
   d. Click the *Tables* check box in the *Groups for "Object Type"* list box to clear the check mark.
   e. Clear the check mark in the *Macros* check box.
   f. Click OK to close the Navigation Options dialog box.

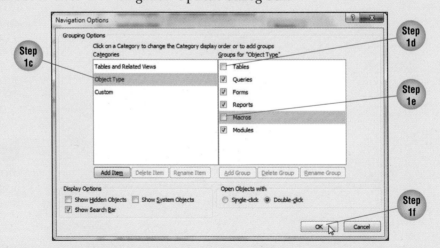

   g. Click OK to close the Access Options dialog box.

h. Click OK at the message box that says you must close and reopen the current database for the specified option to take effect.

2. Notice the Tables and Macros groups are hidden in the Navigation pane.

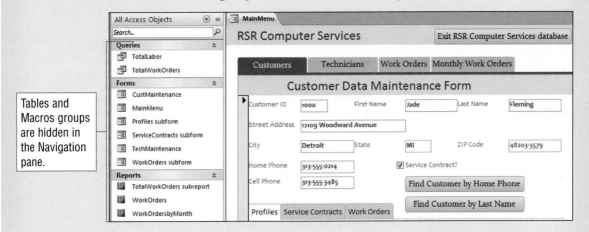

Tables and Macros groups are hidden in the Navigation pane.

3. After reviewing the customized Navigation pane, you decide the database would be more secure if the pane were hidden when the database is opened. To do this, complete the following steps:

a. Click the File tab and then click the Options button.

b. With *Current Database* already selected in the left pane, click the *Display Navigation Pane* check box in the *Navigation* section to clear the check mark.

Step 3b

c. Click OK.

d. Click OK at the message box indicating you have to close and reopen the database for the option to take effect.

4. Close the **AL2-C7-RSRCompServ.accdb** database.

5. Reopen the **AL2-C7-RSRCompServ.accdb** database. The Navigation pane is hidden with the MainMenu form open in the work area.

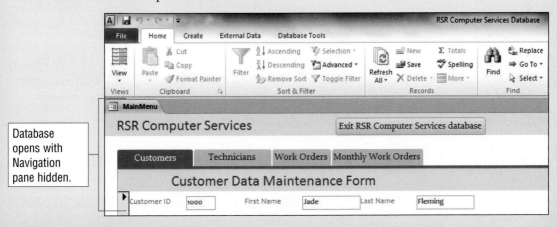

Database opens with Navigation pane hidden.

# Configuring Error Checking Options

**▼ Quick Steps**

**Customize Error Checking Options**
1. Click File tab.
2. Click Options.
3. Click *Object Designers* in left pane.
4. Scroll down to *Error checking in form and report design view* section.
5. Clear check boxes as required.
6. Click OK.

Recall from Chapter 5 that a green triangle displayed in the Report Selector button when the report width was wider than the page would allow. Clicking the error checking options button allowed you to access tools to automatically fix the report. A green triangle also appeared in a new label you added to a report to describe another control. Access flagged the label as an error because the label control object was not associated with another object.

By default, Access has error checking turned on with all error checking options active. Figure 7.8 displays the error checking option parameters that you can configure in Access. Open the Access Options dialog box and select *Object Designers* in the left pane. Scroll down the right pane to locate the *Error checking in form and report design view* section. Clear check boxes for those options for which you want to disable error checking and click OK. Table 7.1 provides a description of each option.

**Figure 7.8** Error Checking Options in Access

**Error checking in form and report design view**
- ☑ Enable error checking
- ☑ Check for unassociated label and control
- ☑ Check for new unassociated labels
- ☑ Check for keyboard shortcut errors
- ☑ Check for invalid control properties
- ☑ Check for common report errors

Error indicator color

**Table 7.1** Error Checking Options

| Error Checking Option | Description |
|---|---|
| Enable error checking | Turn on or off error checking in forms and reports. An error is indicated by a green triangle in the upper left corner of a control. |
| Check for unassociated label and control | Access checks a selected label and text box control object to make sure the two objects are associated with each other. A Trace Error button appears if Access detects an error. |
| Check for new unassociated labels | New label control objects are checked for association with a text box control object. |
| Check for keyboard shortcut errors | Duplicate keyboard shortcuts or invalid shortcuts are flagged. |
| Check for invalid control properties | Invalid properties, formula expressions, or field names are flagged. |
| Check for common report errors | Reports are checked for errors such as invalid sort orders or reports that are wider than the selected paper size. |
| Error indicator color | A green triangle indicates an error in a control. Click the Color Picker button to change to a different color. |

1. With the **AL2-C7-RSRCompServ.accdb** database open, assume you frequently add label control objects to forms and reports to add explanatory text to users. You decide to customize the error checking options to prevent Access from flagging these independent label controls as errors. To do this, complete the following steps:
   a. Click the File tab and then click the Options button.
   b. Click *Object Designers* in the left pane.
   c. Scroll down the right pane to the *Error checking in form and report design view* section.
   d. Click the *Check for new unassociated labels* check box to clear the check mark.
   e. Click OK.
   f. Click OK.

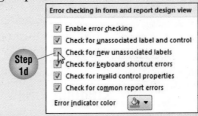

# Customizing the Ribbon ■■■■■■■■■■■■■■■■■■■■■

You can customize the ribbon by creating a new tab. Within the new tab you can add groups and then add buttons within the groups. To customize the ribbon, click the File tab and then click the Options button. At the Access Options dialog box, click *Customize Ribbon* in the left pane to open the dialog box shown in Figure 7.9.

**H I N T**

Consider creating a custom tab with the buttons you use on a regular basis to save mouse clicks from frequently switching tabs.

**Figure 7.9** Access Options Dialog Box with *Customize Ribbon* Selected

▼ **Quick Steps**

**Create a New Tab and Group**
1. Click File tab.
2. Click Options.
3. Click *Customize Ribbon* in left pane.
4. Click tab name to precede new tab.
5. Click New Tab button.

**Add New Group to Existing Tab**
1. Click File tab.
2. Click Options.
3. Click *Customize Ribbon* in left pane.
4. Click tab name for which the new group is associated.
5. Click New Group button.

The commands shown in the left list box are dependent on the current option for *Choose commands from*. Click the down-pointing arrow at the right of the current option (displays *Popular Commands*) to select from a variety of command lists such as *Commands Not in the Ribbon* or *All Commands*. The tabs shown in the right list box are dependent on the current option for *Customize the Ribbon*. Click the down-pointing arrow at the right of the current option (displays *Main Tabs*) to select *All Tabs*, *Main Tabs*, or *Tool Tabs*.

You can create a new group in an existing tab and add buttons within the new group, or you can create a new tab, create a new group within the tab, and then add buttons to the new group.

## Creating a New Tab

To create a new tab, click the tab name in the *Main Tabs* list box that you want the new tab positioned after and then click the New Tab button located below the *Main Tabs* list box. This inserts a new tab in the list box along with a new group below the new tab as shown in Figure 7.10. If you had selected the wrong tab name before clicking the New Tab button, you can move the new tab up or down the list box by clicking *New Tab (Custom)* and then clicking the Move Up or the Move Down buttons that display at the right side of the dialog box.

**Figure 7.10** New Tab and Group Created in the Customize Ribbon Pane at the Access Options Dialog Box

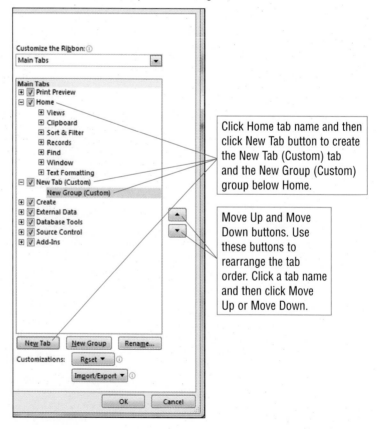

# Renaming a Tab or Group

Rename a tab by clicking the tab name in the *Main Tabs* list box and then clicking the Rename button located below the *Main Tabs* list box. At the Rename dialog box, type the desired name for the tab and then press Enter or click OK. You can also display the Rename dialog box by right-clicking the tab name and then clicking *Rename* at the shortcut menu.

Complete similar steps to rename a group. The Rename dialog box for a group name or a command name contains a *Symbol* list as well as the *Display name* text box. Type the new name for the group in the *Display name* text box and press Enter or click OK. The symbols are useful to identify new buttons rather than the group name.

# Adding Buttons to a Tab Group

Add commands to a tab by clicking the group name within the tab, clicking the desired command in the list box at the left, and then clicking the Add button that displays between the two list boxes. Remove commands in a similar manner. Click the command you want to remove from the tab group and then click the Remove button that displays between the two list boxes.

▼ **Quick Steps**

**Rename a Tab or Group**
1. Click File tab.
2. Click Options.
3. Click *Customize Ribbon* in left pane.
4. Click tab or group to be renamed.
5. Click Rename button.
6. Type new name.
7. Press Enter or click OK.

**Add Buttons to Group**
1. Click File tab.
2. Click Options.
3. Click *Customize Ribbon* in left pane.
4. Click group name in which to insert new button.
5. Change *Choose commands from* to desired command list.
6. Scroll down and click desired command.
7. Click Add button.

---

**Project 3d**  **Customizing the Ribbon**                                                   Part 4 of 5

1. With the **AL2-C7-RSRCompServ.accdb** database open, customize the ribbon by adding a new tab and two new groups within the tab by completing the following steps:
    a. Click the File tab and then click the Options button.
    b. Click *Customize Ribbon* in the left pane of the Access Options dialog box.
    c. Click the Home tab name in the *Main Tabs* list box located at the right of the dialog box.
    d. Click the New Tab button located below the list box. (This inserts a new tab below the Home tab and a new group below the new tab.)
    e. With *New Group (Custom)* selected below *New Tab (Custom)*, click the New Group button that displays below the list box. (This inserts another new group below the new tab.)

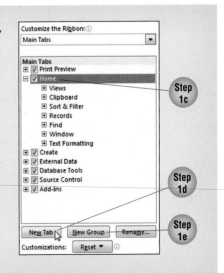

2. Rename the tab and the groups by completing the following steps:
   a. Click to select *New Tab (Custom)* in the *Main Tabs* list box.
   b. Click the Rename button that displays below the list box.
   c. At the Rename dialog box, type your first and last names and then press Enter or click OK.
   d. Click to select the first *New Group (Custom)* group name that displays below the new tab.
   e. Click the Rename button.
   f. At the Rename dialog box, type Views in the *Display name* text box and then press Enter or click OK. The Rename dialog box for a group or button displays symbols in addition to the *Display name* text box. You will apply a symbol to a button in a later step.
   g. Right-click the *New Group (Custom)* group name below *Views (Custom)* and then click *Rename* at the shortcut menu.
   h. Type Records in the *Display name* text box at the Rename dialog box and then press Enter or click OK.
3. Add buttons to the Views (Custom) group by completing the following steps:
   a. Click to select *Views (Custom)* in the *Main Tabs* list box.
   b. With *Popular Commands* the current option for *Choose commands from*, click *Form View* in the list box and then click the Add button located between the two list boxes. This inserts the command below the Views (Custom) group name.

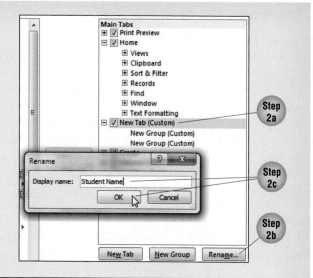

Step 2a

Step 2c

Step 2b

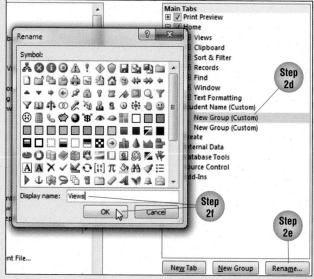

Step 2d

Step 2f

Step 2e

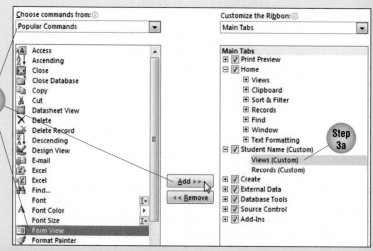

Step 3b

Step 3a

c. Scroll down the *Popular Commands* list box, click Print Preview, and then click the Add button.

d. Click *Report View* in the *Popular Commands* list box and then click the Add button.

e. If necessary, scroll to the bottom of the *Popular Commands* list box, click *View*, and then click the Add button.

4. Add buttons to the Records (Custom) group by completing the following steps:

a. Click to select *Records (Custom)* in the *Main Tabs* list box.

b. Click the down-pointing arrow at the right of the *Choose commands from* list box (currently displays *Popular Commands*) and then click *All Commands* at the drop-down list.

c. Scroll down the *All Commands* list box (the list displays alphabetically), click *Delete Record*, and then click the Add button.

d. Scroll down the *All Commands* list box, click *Find*, and then click the Add button.

e. Scroll down the *All Commands* list box, click *New* (choose the *New* option that displays with the ScreenTip *Home Tab | Records | New (GoToNewRecord)*), and then click the Add button.

f. Scroll down the *All Commands* list box, click *Sort Ascending*, and then click the Add button.

g. If necessary, scroll down the *All Commands* list box, click *Spelling*, and then click the Add button.

5. Change the symbol for the Spelling button by completing the following steps:

a. Right-click *Spelling* below *Records (Custom)* in the *Main Tabs* list box.

b. Click *Rename* at the shortcut menu.

c. At the Rename dialog box, click the blue book icon in the *Symbol* list box (fourth icon in eighth row) and then click OK.

6. Click OK to close the Access Options dialog box.

7. Click OK at the message that displays saying that you have to close and reopen the database for the option to take effect.

8. Use buttons in the custom tab to change views and start a spelling check in a form by completing the following steps:

a. Click the Technicians tab along the top of the MainMenu form.

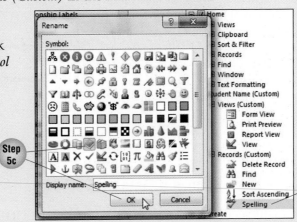

   b. Click the custom tab with your name and then click the Print Preview button in the Views group.

   c. Click the Form View button in the Views group to switch back to the form.

   d. Click in the *Last Name* field and then click the Spelling button.

   e. Click the Cancel button at the Spelling dialog box.

9. Insert a screen image of the database window showing the custom tab in a new Microsoft Word document using either Print Screen with Paste or the Windows Snipping tool (Start button, *All Programs*, *Accessories*). Type your name a few lines below the screen image and add any other identifying information as instructed (for example, the chapter number and project number).

10. Save the Microsoft Word document and name it **AL2-C7-P3-CustomRibbon.docx**.

11. Print **AL2-C7-P3-CustomRibbon.docx** and then exit Word.

## Resetting the Ribbon

Restore the original ribbon by clicking the Reset button that displays below the *Main Tabs* list box in the Access Options dialog box with the Customize Ribbon pane selected. Clicking the Reset button displays two options—*Reset only selected Ribbon tab* and *Reset all customizations*. Click *Reset all customizations* to restore the ribbon to its original settings and then click Yes at the Microsoft Office message box that displays the message *Delete all Ribbon and Quick Access Toolbar customizations for this program?*

---

### Project 3e    Restoring the Ribbon

Part 5 of 5

1. Open the Access Options dialog box.
2. If necessary, click *Customize Ribbon* in the left pane.
3. Click the Reset button located below the Main Tabs list box.
4. Click *Reset all customizations* at the drop-down list.
5. Click Yes at the Microsoft Office message box that appears.
6. Click OK to close the Access Options dialog box.
7. Click OK at the message that displays saying that you have to close and reopen the database for the option to take effect.

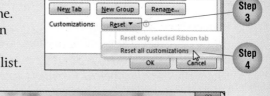

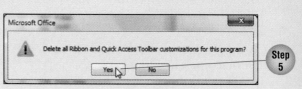

---

## Project 4   Secure a Database

2 Parts

You will secure a database by making an ACCDE file. You will also explore the default settings in the Trust Center.

# Creating an ACCDE Database File ▪▪▪▪▪▪▪▪▪▪▪▪▪▪▪▪▪

In Chapter 6 you learned how to split a database into two files to create a front-end and a back-end database. This method allowed you to improve performance and protect the table objects from changes by separating the tables from the queries, forms, and reports. Another method with which you can protect an Access database is to create an ACCDE file. In an ACCDE file, end users are prevented from making changes to the design of objects. An Access database stored as an ACCDE file is a locked-down version of the database that does not provide access to Design view or Layout view. In addition, if the database contains any Visual Basic for Application (VBA) code, the code cannot be modified or changed.

To save an Access database as an ACCDE file, click the File tab and then click the Save & Publish tab. Click *Make ACCDE* in the *Advanced* section of the Save Database As pane located at the right side of the Save & Publish tab Backstage view. Next, click the Save As button located at the bottom of the Save Database As pane to open the Save As dialog box. Navigate to the drive and/or folder in which to save the database, type the desired file name in the *File Name* text box, and click the Save button. Once the file is created, move the original database in .accdb format to a secure location and provide end users with the path to the .accde file for daily use.

▼ **Quick Steps**

**Make ACCDE File**
1. Open database.
2. Click File tab.
3. Click Save & Publish tab.
4. Click *Make ACCDE.*
5. Click Save As button.
6. Navigate to required drive and/or folder.
7. Type name in *File name* text box.
8. Click Save button.

---

| Project 4a | Making an ACCDE Database File | Part 1 of 2 |
|---|---|---|

1. With the **AL2-C7-RSRCompServ.accdb** database open, create an ACCDE file by completing the following steps:
   a. Click the File tab and then click the Save & Publish tab.
   b. Click *Make ACCDE* in the *Advanced* section of the Save Database As pane located at the right of the Save & Publish tab Backstage view.
   c. Click the Save As button located at the bottom of the Save Database As pane.

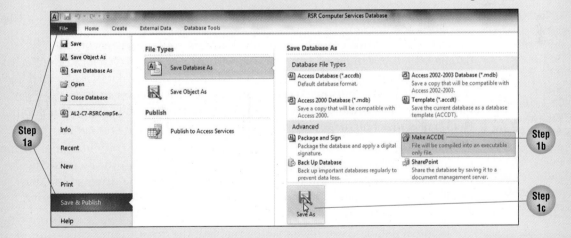

   d. At the Save As dialog box with the default location the Access2010L2C7 folder on your storage medium and **AL2-C7-RSRCompServ.accde** the default name in the *File name* text box, click the Save button.

2. Close the **AL2-C7-RSRCompServ.accdb** database.
3. Open the **AL2-C7-RSRCompServ.accde** database.
4. At the Microsoft Access Security Notice dialog box informing you the file might contain unsafe content, click the Open button.
5. With Customers the active tab in the MainMenu form and the Customer Data Maintenance Form open in Form view, click the Home tab if necessary. Notice the View button in the Views group is dimmed.
6. Click the Monthly Work Orders tab in the MainMenu form to view the Work Orders by Month report. Notice the View button in the Home tab is still dimmed. Also notice only one view button is available in the View group located at the right end of the Status bar.
7. Insert a screen image of the database window in a new Microsoft Word document using either Print Screen with Paste or the Windows Snipping tool (Start button, *All Programs*, *Accessories*). Type your name a few lines below the screen image and add any other identifying information as instructed.
8. Save the Microsoft Word document and name it **AL2-C7-P4-ACCDEWindow.docx**.
9. Print **AL2-C7-P4-ACCDEWindow.docx** and then exit Word.
10. Close the **AL2-C7-RSRCompServ.accde** database.

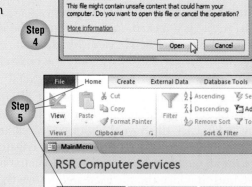

Step 4

Step 5

▼ **Quick Steps**

**View Trust Center Options**
1. Click File tab.
2. Click Options.
3. Click *Trust Center* in left pane.
4. Click Trust Center Settings button.
5. Click desired trust center category in left pane.
6. View and/or modify required options.
7. Click OK twice.

Changing the macro security setting in Access does not affect the macro security setting in other Microsoft programs such as Word or Excel.

# Viewing Trust Center Settings for Access ■■■■■■■■■■

In Access, the Trust Center is set to block unsafe content when you open a database file. As you have been working with Access, you have closed the Security Warning that appears in the message bar when you open a database by clicking the Enable Content button. Access provides the Trust Center in which you can view and/or modify the security options that are in place to protect your computer from malicious content.

The Trust Center maintains a *Trusted Locations* list with content stored within the location considered a trusted source. You can add a path to the trusted locations list and Access will treat any files opened from the drive and folder as safe. Databases opened from trusted locations do not display the Security Warning in the message bar and do not have content blocked.

Before a database can have macros enabled, the Trust Center checks for a valid and current digital signature signed by an entity that is stored in the *Trusted Publishers* list. The *Trusted Publishers* list is maintained by you on the computer you are using. A trusted publisher is added to the list when you enable content from an authenticated source and click the option to *Trust all content from this publisher*. Depending on the active macro security setting, if the Trust Center cannot match the digital signature information with an entity in the Trusted Publishers list or the macro does not contain a digital signature, the security warning displays in the message bar.

The default Macro Security option is *Disable all macros with notification*. Table 7.2 describes the four options for macro security. In some cases, you may decide to change the default macro security setting by opening the Trust Center dialog box. You will explore the Trust Center in Project 4b.

**Table 7.2** Macro Security Settings for Databases Not Opened from a Trusted Location

| *Macro Setting* | *Description* |
| --- | --- |
| Disable all macros without notification | All macros are disabled; security alerts will not appear. |
| Disable all macros with notification | All macros are disabled; security alert appears with the option to enable content if you trust the source of the file. This is the default setting. |
| Disable all macros except digitally signed macros | A macro that does not contain a digital signature is disabled; security alerts do not appear. If the macro is digitally signed by a publisher in your Trusted Publishers list, the macro is allowed to run. If the macro is digitally signed by a publisher not in your Trusted Publishers list, you receive a security alert. |
| Enable all macros (not recommended, potentially dangerous code can run) | All macros are allowed; security alerts do not appear. |

**Project 4b** **Exploring Trust Center Settings** Part 2 of 2

1. At the New tab Backstage view, explore the current settings in the Trust Center by completing the following steps:
   a. Click the Options button.
   b. Click *Trust Center* in the left pane of the Access Options dialog box.

   c. Click the Trust Center Settings button in the *Microsoft Access Trust Center* section.
   d. At the Trust Center dialog box, click *Macro Settings* in the left pane.
   e. Review the options in the *Macro Settings* section. Note which option is active on the computer you are using. The default option is *Disable all macros with notification*.

   *Note: The security setting on the computer you are using may be different than the default option. Do not change the security setting without the permission of your instructor.*

f. Click *Trusted Publishers* in the left pane. If any publishers have been added to the list on the computer you are using, the names of the entities will be shown in the list box. If the list box is empty, no trusted publishers have been added.

g. Click *Trusted Locations* in the left pane. Review the path and description of any folders added to the trusted locations list. By default, Access adds the folder created upon installation of Microsoft Access that contains the wizard database templates provided by Microsoft. Additional folders may also appear that have been added by a system administrator or network administrator.

h. Click OK to close the Trust Center dialog box.

2. Click OK to close the Access Options dialog box.

In this chapter you have learned some techniques to automate, customize, and secure an Access database. As you gain more experience with Access, explore further Access options to customize the environment that allow you to change behavior of actions and keys while editing. Also consider experimenting with other macro actions such as the OpenQuery action to automate queries.

# Chapter Summary

- A macro is used to automate actions within a database such as opening a form or report.
- Click the Create tab and click the Macro button in the Macros & Code group to open a Macro Builder window in which you create the actions you want to store.
- Add a macro action using the *Add New Action* list box or the Action Catalog pane.
- Action arguments are parameters for the action such as the object name, the mode in which the object opens, and other restrictions placed on the action.
- The available arguments displayed in the *Action Arguments* section are dependent on the active action.
- Run a macro by clicking the Run button in the Macro Builder window or by double-clicking the macro name in the Navigation pane.
- A macro can also be created by dragging and dropping an object name from the Navigation pane to the *Add New Action* list box in the Macro Builder window.
- Edit a macro by right-clicking the macro name and clicking *Design View* at the shortcut menu.
- A macro can be assigned to a button in a form to provide single-click access to run the macro.
- Use the Button tool to create a command button in a form.
- The Command Button Wizard creates an embedded macro for you that instructs Access on which macro to run when the button is clicked. You can view the macro by opening the command button's Property Sheet, clicking the Event tab, and then clicking the Build button in the *On Click* property box.

- A macro can be converted to Visual Basic for Applications code by opening the macro in the Macro Builder window and then clicking the Convert Macros to Visual Basic button in the Tools group of the Macro Tools Design tab.

- A Navigation form with tabs along the top, left, or right is used as a menu. Users can open the forms and reports in the database by clicking a tab rather than using the Navigation pane.

- Click the Create tab and then click the Navigation button to create a Navigation form. Choose the desired form style at the drop-down list and then drag and drop form and/or report names from the Navigation pane to *[Add New]* in the tab bar.

- A form can be set to display automatically whenever the database is opened at the *Display Form* list box in the Access Options dialog box with *Current Database* selected in the left pane.

- Change the title that appears in the Title bar for the active database by typing an entry in the *Application Title* text box at the Access Options dialog box with *Current Database* selected in the left pane.

- You can set options for the Navigation pane such as hiding individual objects or groups of objects at the Navigation Options dialog box.

- Hide the Navigation pane by clearing the *Display Navigation Pane* check box at the Access Options dialog box with *Current Database* selected in the left pane.

- Change default error checking options in the Access Options dialog box with *Object Designers* selected in the left pane.

- You can customize the ribbon by creating a new tab, creating a new group within the new tab, and then adding buttons within the new group.

- To customize the ribbon, open the Access Options dialog box and click *Customize Ribbon* in the left pane.

- Create a new ribbon tab by clicking the tab name that will precede the new tab and then clicking the New Tab button. A new group is automatically added with the new tab.

- Rename a custom tab by clicking to select the tab name, clicking the Rename button, typing a new name, and then pressing Enter or clicking OK. Rename a group using a similar process.

- Add buttons within a group by clicking the group name, selecting the desired command in the commands list box and then clicking the Add button located between the two list boxes.

- Restore the ribbon to the default by clicking the Reset button located near the bottom right of the Access Options dialog box with *Customize Ribbon* selected and then clicking *Reset all customizations* at the drop-down list.

- Create an ACCDE database file at the Save & Publish tab Backstage view to create a locked-down version of the database in which objects are prevented from being opened in Design view or Layout view.

- Open the Access Options dialog box, click *Trust Center* in the left pane, and then click the Trust Center Settings button to view and/or modify trust center options.

# Commands Review

| FEATURE | RIBBON TAB, GROUP | BUTTON |
|---|---|---|
| Convert Macros to Visual Basic | Macro Tools Design, Tools | |
| Create ACCDE file | File, Save & Publish | |
| Create command button | Form Design Tools Design, Controls | |
| Create macro | Create, Macros & Code | |
| Customize Access options | File, Options | |
| Customize Navigation pane | File, Options | |
| Navigation Form | Create, Forms | |
| Run macro | Macro Tools Design, Tools | |

# Concepts Check Test Your Knowledge

**Completion:** In the space provided at the right, indicate the correct term, command, or number.

1. This is the name of the window in which you create actions with associated action arguments for a macro.

2. Add a macro action at the *Add New Action* list box or in this pane.

3. To cause Access to display the Find dialog box in a macro, choose this action in the *Add New Action* list box.

4. Drag a form name from the Navigation pane to the *Add New Action* list box to insert this macro action.

5. Edit a macro by right-clicking the macro name in the Navigation pane and selecting this option at the shortcut menu.

6. At the first Command Button Wizard dialog box, click this option in the *Categories* list box to locate the *Run Macro* action.

7. This type of macro is not shown as a macro object within the Navigation pane.

8. When a macro has been converted to Visual Basic, Access opens this window. _____

9. This type of form is used to create a menu to allow end users to select forms and reports by clicking tabs. _____

10. Open this dialog box to specify a display form to open whenever the database is opened. _____

11. Hide the Tables group in the Navigation pane by opening this dialog box. _____

12. Click this option in the left pane at the Access Options dialog box to change an error checking option. _____

13. Click this option in the left pane at the Access Options dialog box to create a custom ribbon tab. _____

14. Save a database as this type of file to disallow Design view and Layout view for the database objects. _____

15. View and/or change the macro security setting at this dialog box. _____

# Skills Check  Assess Your Performance

## Assessment

### 1  CREATE AND RUN MACROS

1. Open the database named **AL2-C7-VantageVideos.accdb** and enable content.
2. Create the following macros. Run each macro to make sure the macro works properly and then close the macro.
   a. A macro named RPTWebOrders that opens the report named WebOrdersByProd. Use the macro action *OpenReport*. In the *Action Arguments* section, change the *View* argument to *Print Preview*.
   b. A macro named RPTWebSales to open the WebSalesByDate report in Report view.
   c. A macro named FORMCustOrd that opens the WebCustOrders form in Form view, activates the control named *LastName*, and then opens the Find dialog box. Test the macro using the customer last name *Gallagher*.
3. Open the RPTWebOrders macro in Design view. Click the File tab, click the Print tab, and then click Print at the Backstage view. At the Print Macro Definition dialog box, clear check marks as necessary until only the *Actions and Arguments* check box is checked and then click OK. Close the Macro Builder window.
4. Print the FORMCustOrd macro and the RPTWebSales macro by completing a step similar to Step 3.

## Assessment

### 2 EDIT A MACRO AND ASSIGN MACROS TO COMMAND BUTTONS

1. With the **AL2-C7-VantageVideos.accdb** database open, edit the FORMCustOrd macro to remove the *OpenForm* action. Save and close the revised macro. Rename the FORMCustOrd macro in the Navigation pane to FINDLastName.
2. Create command buttons to run macros as follows:
   a. Open the WebCustOrders form in Design view and create a command button at the right side of the *Form Header* section that runs the FINDLastName macro. You determine appropriate text to display on the face of the button, and a name for the command button. Save and close the form.
   b. Open the WebProducts form in Design view and create two command buttons as follows. Place each button at the bottom of the *Detail* section. You determine appropriate text to display on the face of the button and a name for the command button. Save and close the form.
      • A button at the left side of the form that runs the RPTWebOrders macro.
      • A button at the right side of the form that runs the RPTWebSales macro.
3. Open each form, test the button(s) to make sure the correct form or report displays, and then close each form or report.
4. Open the WebCustOrders form in Form view. Insert a screen image of the database window in a new Microsoft Word document using either Print Screen with Paste or the Windows Snipping tool. Next, switch back to Access and open the WebProducts form. Insert a screen image of the database window below the first image in the Microsoft Word document. Type your name a few lines below the screen images and add any other identifying information as instructed. Save the Microsoft Word document and name it **AL2-C7-A2-FormWindows.docx**. Print **AL2-C7-A2-FormWindows.docx** and then exit Word.
5. Close both forms.

## Assessment

### 3 CREATE A NAVIGATION FORM AND CONFIGURE DATABASE OPTIONS

1. With the **AL2-C7-VantageVideos.accdb** database open, create a Navigation form using the following information.
   a. Use the *Vertical Tabs, Left style*.
   b. Add the WebCustOrders form as the first tab.
   c. Add the WebProducts form as the second tab.
   d. Add the WebOrdersByProd report as the third tab.
   e. Add the WebSalesByDate report as the fourth tab.
   f. Save the form, naming it *MainMenu*.
2. In Layout view or Design view, edit the MainMenu Navigation form as follows:
   a. Delete the logo container object.
   b. Edit the text in the Title control object to *Vantage Classic Videos* and resize the object so that the right edge of the control ends just after the title text. In other words, the width of the control object is only as wide as it needs to be in order to display the title text.
   c. Change the Caption property for the first tab to *Customer Orders*.
   d. Change the Caption property for the second tab to *Classic Products*.
   e. Change the Caption property for the third tab to *Orders by Product*.
   f. Change the Caption property for the fourth tab to *Sales by Month*.

3. Create a new macro named *ExitDB* that will exit Access saving all objects. Assign the macro to a command button positioned in the *Form Header* section of the MainMenu form. You determine appropriate text to display on the face of the button and a name for the command button. Save and close the MainMenu form.

4. Set the MainMenu form as the startup display form.

5. Create an application title for the database with the text **Vantage Classic Videos Web Orders Database**.

6. Hide the Navigation pane.

7. Turn on the *Check for new unassociated labels* error checking option. ***Note: Skip this step if you did not complete Project 3c where this option was turned off***.

8. Close and reopen the database to test your startup options. Click each tab in the MainMenu form to make sure the correct form or report displays.

9. With the database open at the MainMenu form, insert a screen image of the database window in a new Microsoft Word document using either Print Screen with Paste or the Windows Snipping tool. Type your name a few lines below the screen image and add any other identifying information as instructed. Save the Microsoft Word document and name it **AL2-C7-A3-MainMenu.docx**. Print **AL2-C7-A3-MainMenu.docx** and then exit Word.

## Assessment

## 4 SECURE THE DATABASE

1. With the **AL2-C7-VantageVideos.accdb** database open, save a copy of the database in the same folder and using the same name as an ACCDE file.

2. Close the **AL2-C7-VantageVideos.accdb** database.

3. Open the **AL2-C7-VantageVideos7.accde** database.

4. Insert a screen image of the database window in a new Microsoft Word document using either Print Screen with Paste or the Windows Snipping tool. Type your name a few lines below the screen image and add any other identifying information as instructed. Save the Microsoft Word document and name it **AL2-C7-A4-VantageACCDE.docx**. Print **AL2-C7-A4-VantageACCDE.docx** and then exit Word.

5. Use the exit button in the MainMenu form to exit the database.

# Visual Benchmark  Demonstrate Your Proficiency

## AUTOMATE AND CUSTOMIZE RESERVATION DATABASE

1. Open **AL2-C7-PawsParadise.accdb** and enable content.
2. Review the database window shown in Figure 7.11. Create the Navigation form as shown including the command buttons and required macros assigned to the command buttons. Set the required startup and Navigation pane options.
3. Save a copy of the database as an ACCDE file.
4. Close the **AL2-C7-PawsParadise.accdb** database
5. Open the **AL2-C7-PawsParadise.accde** database. Check with your instructor for instructions on whether you need to print the macros and a screen image of the database window.

**Figure 7.11** Visual Benchmark

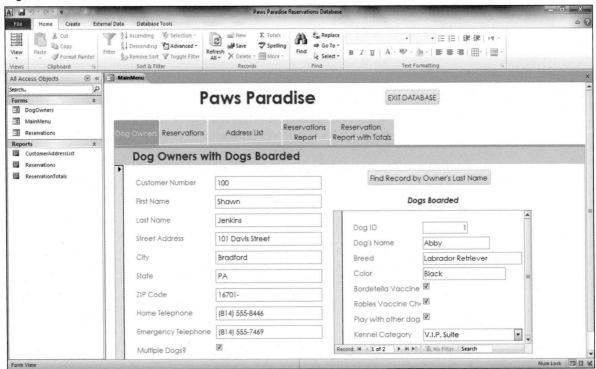

# Case Study  Apply Your Skills

**Part 1**

As you near completion of your work as an intern at Hillsdale Realty, you decide to automate the database to make the application easier for the next intern to use. Open **AL2-C7-HillsdaleRealty.accdb** and enable content. Create three macros to accomplish the tasks in the bulleted list. You determine appropriate macro names.

- Move to the *AgentLName* control and open the Find dialog box.
- Move to the *ListingNo* control and open the Find dialog box.
- Exit the database saving all objects.

Assign the first macro as a command button in the Agents form. Assign the second macro as a command button in the ListingsAndSales form. In both forms, you determine where to position the button, the text to display on the button, and the button name. Check with your instructor for instructions on whether you need to print the macros and a screen image of the Agents form and the ListingsAndSales form showing each command button.

**Part 2**

Create a navigation form to be used as a main menu to display the Agents form, the ListingsAndSales form, and the two reports. Set the form to display automatically when the database is opened. Add an appropriate application title for the database and hide the tables, queries, and macros in the Navigation pane. Assign the macro to exit the database as a button in the main menu form. Edit the main menu form as necessary to show descriptive labels in the tabs and apply other formatting enhancements as necessary. Close and reopen the database to test your startup options. Test each menu tab to make sure each option works. Check with your instructor for instructions on whether you need to print a screen image of the database window with the main menu form displayed.

**Part 3**

Open a Help window and search for help content using the phrase **access 2010 security** in the Search text box. Click the link to the article titled Introduction to Access 2010 security and then click the link to Package, sign, and distribute an Access 2010 database at the Introduction to Access 2010 security page. Read the information in Help and then compose a memo in your own words addressed to your instructor using Microsoft Word that provides the following answers.

- What is the file extension for an Access Deployment file?
- Why would you package and sign a database file?
- What is applied to the packaged file to indicate that the content has not been altered since the database was packaged?
- Where is the Package and Sign feature located in Microsoft Office Access 2010?
- How many databases can be added to a package?

Save the memo in Word and name it **AL2-C7-CS-P3-PackageMemo.docx**. Print the memo and then exit Word.

Microsoft®
# Access

**CHAPTER**

# 8

# Integrating Access Data

## PERFORMANCE OBJECTIVES

**Upon successful completion of Chapter 8, you will be able to:**

- Import data from another Access database
- Link to a table in another Access database
- Determine when to import versus link from external sources
- Reset or refresh links using Linked Table Manager
- Import data from a text file
- Save import specifications
- Export data in an Access table or query as a text file
- Save and run export specifications
- Save an object as an XPS document
- Summarize data by using a PivotTable
- Summarize data by using a PivotChart

### Tutorials

**8.1** Importing Data from Another Access Database

**8.2** Linking to a Table in Another Access Database

**8.3** Importing Data to Access from a Text File

**8.4** Saving and Repeating a Saved Import Process

**8.5** Exporting Access Data to a Text File

**8.6** Saving and Repeating Saved Export Specifications

**8.7** Publishing Database Objects as PDF or XPS Files

**8.8** Summarizing Data in a PivotTable

**8.9** Creating a PivotTable Form

**8.10** Summarizing Data Using PivotChart View

Integrating data between the applications within the Microsoft Office suite is easily accommodated with buttons in the External Data tab to import from Word and Excel and export to Word and Excel. Data is able to be exchanged between the Microsoft programs with formatting and data structure maintained. In some cases, however, you may need to exchange data between Access and a non-Microsoft program. In this chapter you will learn how to integrate data between individual Access database files and how to import and export in a text file format recognized by nearly all applications. You will also learn how to publish an Access object as an XPS file, which is an XML document format, and summarize data using a PivotTable and PivotChart. Model answers for this chapter's projects appear on the following pages.

Access
Access2010L2C8

*Note: Before beginning the projects, copy to your storage medium the Access2010L2C8 subfolder from the Access2010L2 folder on the CD that accompanies this textbook and then make Access2010L2C8 the active folder.*

## Technician Maintenance

|  |  |
|---|---|
| Technician ID | 01 |
| SSN | 000-45-5368 |
| First Name | Pat |
| Last Name | Hynes |
| Street Address | 206-31 Woodland Street |
| City | Detroit |
| State | MI |
| ZIP Code | 48202-1138 |
| Home Phone | 313-555-6874 |
| Cell Phone | 313-555-6412 |
| Certifications | Cisco CCNP, CompTIA A+, Microsoft MCTS |
| Operating Systems | Linux, Unix, Windows 7, Windows XP |
| Network Specialist? | ✔ |
| Design Websites? | ☐ |
| Programming? | ✔ |

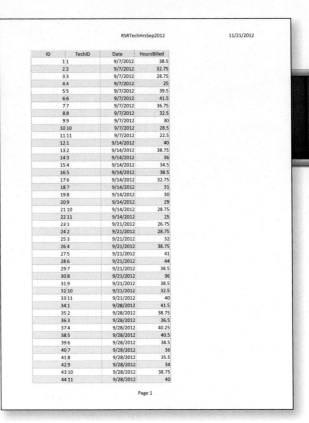

RSRTechHrsSep2012                11/21/2012

| ID | TechID | Date | HoursBilled |
|---|---|---|---|
| 1 | 1 | 9/7/2012 | 38.5 |
| 2 | 2 | 9/7/2012 | 32.75 |
| 3 | 3 | 9/7/2012 | 28.75 |
| 4 | 4 | 9/7/2012 | 25 |
| 5 | 5 | 9/7/2012 | 39.5 |
| 6 | 6 | 9/7/2012 | 41.5 |
| 7 | 7 | 9/7/2012 | 36.75 |
| 8 | 8 | 9/7/2012 | 32.5 |
| 9 | 9 | 9/7/2012 | 30 |
| 10 | 10 | 9/7/2012 | 28.5 |
| 11 | 11 | 9/7/2012 | 22.5 |
| 12 | 1 | 9/14/2012 | 40 |
| 13 | 2 | 9/14/2012 | 38.75 |
| 14 | 3 | 9/14/2012 | 36 |
| 15 | 4 | 9/14/2012 | 34.5 |
| 16 | 5 | 9/14/2012 | 38.5 |
| 17 | 6 | 9/14/2012 | 32.75 |
| 18 | 7 | 9/14/2012 | 31 |
| 19 | 8 | 9/14/2012 | 30 |
| 20 | 9 | 9/14/2012 | 29 |
| 21 | 10 | 9/14/2012 | 28.75 |
| 22 | 11 | 9/14/2012 | 25 |
| 23 | 1 | 9/21/2012 | 26.75 |
| 24 | 2 | 9/21/2012 | 28.75 |
| 25 | 3 | 9/21/2012 | 32 |
| 26 | 4 | 9/21/2012 | 38.75 |
| 27 | 5 | 9/21/2012 | 41 |
| 28 | 6 | 9/21/2012 | 44 |
| 29 | 7 | 9/21/2012 | 38.5 |
| 30 | 8 | 9/21/2012 | 36 |
| 31 | 9 | 9/21/2012 | 38.5 |
| 32 | 10 | 9/21/2012 | 32.5 |
| 33 | 11 | 9/21/2012 | 40 |
| 34 | 1 | 9/28/2012 | 41.5 |
| 35 | 2 | 9/28/2012 | 38.75 |
| 36 | 3 | 9/28/2012 | 36.5 |
| 37 | 4 | 9/28/2012 | 40.25 |
| 38 | 5 | 9/28/2012 | 40.5 |
| 39 | 6 | 9/28/2012 | 38.5 |
| 40 | 7 | 9/28/2012 | 36 |
| 41 | 8 | 9/28/2012 | 35.5 |
| 42 | 9 | 9/28/2012 | 34 |
| 43 | 10 | 9/28/2012 | 38.75 |
| 44 | 11 | 9/28/2012 | 40 |

Page 1

**Project 1 Import Data from External Sources**

Project 1b, Imported TechMaintenance Form

Project 1d, Imported RSRTechHoursSep2012 Table

```
                        TotalWorkOrders.txt
WO,CustID,Descr,ServDate,Total Labor,Parts,Total Work Order
65012,1000,Bi-annual computer maintenance,9/7/2012 0:00:00,37.50,$10.15,$47.65
65013,1000,Replace keyboard,9/10/2012 0:00:00,14.25,$42.75,$57.00
65014,1005,Replace power supply,9/10/2012 0:00:00,52.50,$62.77,$115.27
65015,1008,Restore operating system,9/11/2012 0:00:00,67.50,$0.00,$67.50
65016,1010,Install upgraded video card,9/11/2012 0:00:00,30.00,$48.75,$78.75
65017,1015,Replace DVD drive,9/15/2012 0:00:00,16.87,$55.87,$72.75
65018,1020,Upgrade Office suite,9/15/2012 0:00:00,22.50,$0.00,$22.50
65019,1025,Upgrade to Windows 7,9/17/2012 0:00:00,75.00,$0.00,$75.00
65020,1030,Troubleshoot noisy fan,9/17/2012 0:00:00,33.75,$62.77,$96.52
65021,1035,Customer has blue screen upon boot,9/18/2012 0:00:00,97.50,$0.00,$97.50
65022,1040,Customer reports screen is fuzzy,9/22/2012 0:00:00,45.00,$55.47,$100.47
65023,1045,Upgrade RAM,9/23/2012 0:00:00,37.50,$62.50,$100.00
65024,1005,Install malware protection,9/24/2012 0:00:00,15.50,$75.50,$91.00
65025,1010,Troubleshoot hard drive noise,9/28/2012 0:00:00,45.00,$0.00,$45.00
65026,1025,Upgrade memory,9/29/2012 0:00:00,22.50,$75.75,$98.25
65027,1010,Replace hard drive,10/2/2012 0:00:00,45.00,$375.50,$420.50
65028,1030,Reinstall operating system,10/2/2012 0:00:00,67.50,$0.00,$67.50
65029,1035,Set up automatic backup,10/3/2012 0:00:00,11.25,$0.00,$11.25
65030,1000,Clean malware from system,10/6/2012 0:00:00,15.50,$0.00,$15.50
65031,1045,Customer reports noisy hard drive,10/6/2012 0:00:00,52.50,$0.00,$52.50
65032,1008,Install second hard drive,10/13/2012 0:00:00,60.00,$425.75,$485.75
65033,1000,Install Windows 7,10/13/2012 0:00:00,97.50,$335.75,$433.25
65034,1035,File management training,10/14/2012 0:00:00,45.00,$0.00,$45.00
65035,1020,Office 2010 training,10/15/2012 0:00:00,75.00,$0.00,$75.00
65036,1008,Set up home network,10/16/2012 0:00:00,67.50,$85.22,$152.72
65037,1015,Bi-annual computer maintenance,10/19/2012 0:00:00,37.50,$8.75,$46.25
65038,1010,Install Windows 7,10/19/2012 0:00:00,75.00,$0.00,$75.00
65039,1030,Set up automatic backup,10/19/2012 0:00:00,16.87,$0.00,$16.88
65040,1025,Configure dual monitors,10/20/2012 0:00:00,30.00,$0.00,$30.00
65041,1020,Bi-annual computer maintenance,10/22/2012 0:00:00,37.50,$10.15,$47.65
65042,1030,File management training,10/22/2012 0:00:00,33.75,$0.00,$33.75
65043,1020,Troubleshoot video fuzziness,10/23/2012 0:00:00,15.00,$0.00,$15.00
65044,1008,DVD drive is not working,10/23/2012 0:00:00,30.00,$55.40,$85.40
65045,1025,Set up automatic backup,10/26/2012 0:00:00,11.62,$0.00,$11.63
65046,1010,Windows 7 training,10/26/2012 0:00:00,60.00,$0.00,$60.00
65047,1030,Set up automatic backup,10/29/2012 0:00:00,11.25,$0.00,$11.25
65048,1020,Replace LCD monitor,10/29/2012 0:00:00,15.00,$169.95,$184.95
65049,1040,Set up dual monitor system,10/31/2012 0:00:00,22.50,$0.00,$22.50
65050,1045,Reinstall Windows 7,10/31/2012 0:00:00,45.00,$0.00,$45.00
```

Page 1

```
                        TotalLabor.txt
WO      ServDate       Hours   Rate    Total Labor
65012  9/7/2012 0:00:00        1.25    $30.00  37.50
65013  9/10/2012 0:00:00       0.50    $28.50  14.25
65014  9/10/2012 0:00:00       1.75    $30.00  52.50
65015  9/11/2012 0:00:00       2.25    $30.00  67.50
65016  9/11/2012 0:00:00       1.00    $30.00  30.00
65017  9/15/2012 0:00:00       0.75    $22.50  16.87
65018  9/15/2012 0:00:00       1.00    $22.50  22.50
65019  9/17/2012 0:00:00       2.50    $30.00  75.00
65020  9/17/2012 0:00:00       1.50    $22.50  33.75
65021  9/18/2012 0:00:00       3.25    $30.00  97.50
65022  9/22/2012 0:00:00       1.50    $30.00  45.00
65023  9/23/2012 0:00:00       1.25    $30.00  37.50
65024  9/24/2012 0:00:00       1.00    $15.50  15.50
65025  9/28/2012 0:00:00       1.50    $30.00  45.00
65026  9/29/2012 0:00:00       0.75    $30.00  22.50
65027  10/2/2012 0:00:00       1.50    $30.00  45.00
65028  10/2/2012 0:00:00       2.25    $30.00  67.50
65029  10/6/2012 0:00:00       0.50    $22.50  11.25
65030  10/6/2012 0:00:00       1.00    $15.50  15.50
65031  10/6/2012 0:00:00       1.75    $30.00  52.50
65032  10/13/2012 0:00:00      2.00    $30.00  60.00
65033  10/13/2012 0:00:00      3.25    $30.00  97.50
65034  10/14/2012 0:00:00      1.50    $30.00  45.00
65035  10/15/2012 0:00:00      2.50    $30.00  75.00
65036  10/16/2012 0:00:00      3.00    $22.50  67.50
65037  10/19/2012 0:00:00      1.25    $30.00  37.50
65038  10/19/2012 0:00:00      2.50    $30.00  75.00
65039  10/19/2012 0:00:00      0.75    $22.50  16.87
65040  10/20/2012 0:00:00      1.00    $30.00  30.00
65041  10/22/2012 0:00:00      1.25    $30.00  37.50
65042  10/22/2012 0:00:00      1.50    $22.50  33.75
65043  10/23/2012 0:00:00      0.50    $30.00  15.00
65044  10/23/2012 0:00:00      1.00    $30.00  30.00
65045  10/26/2012 0:00:00      0.75    $15.50  11.62
65046  10/26/2012 0:00:00      2.00    $30.00  60.00
65047  10/29/2012 0:00:00      0.50    $22.50  11.25
65048  10/29/2012 0:00:00      0.50    $30.00  15.00
65049  10/31/2012 0:00:00      0.75    $30.00  22.50
65050  10/31/2012 0:00:00      1.50    $30.00  45.00
```

**Project 2 Export Access Data to a Text File**

Project 2a, Exported TotalWorkOrders Query

Project 2b, Exported TotalLabor Query

| | Months ▾ | | |
|---|---|---|---|
| | ⊞ Sep | ⊞ Oct | Grand Total |
| | ± − | ± − | ± − |
| LName ▾ | Sum of Total Work Order | Sum of Total Work Order | Sum of Total Work Order |
| Bodzek | $173.25 | $41.63 | $214.88 |
| Carmichael | $67.50 | $723.87 | $791.37 |
| Cobb | $22.50 | $322.60 | $345.10 |
| Fahri | $206.27 | | $206.27 |
| Fennema | $100.00 | $97.50 | $197.50 |
| Fleming | $104.65 | $448.75 | $553.40 |
| Friesen | $72.75 | $46.25 | $119.00 |
| Lemaire | $123.75 | $555.50 | $679.25 |
| Machado | $100.47 | $22.50 | $122.97 |
| Pierson | $96.52 | $129.38 | $225.90 |
| Woodside | $97.50 | $56.25 | $153.75 |
| Grand Total | $1,165.16 | $2,444.22 | $3,609.38 |

Drop Filter Fields Here

**Project 4 Summarize Data in a PivotTable and PivotChart**
Project 4b, PivotTable for CustomerWorkOrders Query

---

## Project 1  Import Data from External Sources                4 Parts

You will link and import data from a table in another Access database and from a comma delimited text file. You will also save import specifications for an import routine you expect to repeat often.

# Importing Data from Another Access Database ▪▪▪▪▪▪

Data stored in another Access database can be integrated into the active database by importing a copy of the source object(s). You can choose to copy multiple objects including duplicating the relationships between tables. When importing, you can specify to import the definition only or the definition and the data. To begin an import operation, click the External Data tab and then click the Import Access database button in the Import group to open the Get External Data - Access Database dialog box shown in Figure 8.1.

Specify the source database containing the object(s) that you want to import by clicking the Browse button to open the File Open dialog box. Navigate to the drive and/or folder containing the source database and double-click the desired Access database file name to insert the database file name in the *File name* text box below *Specify the source of the data*. With *Import tables, queries, forms, reports, macros, and modules into the current database* selected by default, click OK. This opens the Import Objects dialog box shown in Figure 8.2. Select the objects to be imported, change options if necessary, and click OK.

### ▼ Quick Steps

**Import Objects from Access Database**
1. Open destination database.
2. Click External Data tab.
3. Click Import Access database button.
4. Click Browse button.
5. If necessary, navigate to drive and/or folder.
6. Double-click source file name.
7. Click OK.
8. Select desired import object(s).
9. Click OK.
10. Click Close.

If an object with the same name as an imported table already exists in the destination database, Access does not overwrite the existing object. The imported object is named with the number 1 appended.

Access

**Figure 8.1** Get External Data - Access Database Dialog Box with Import Option Selected

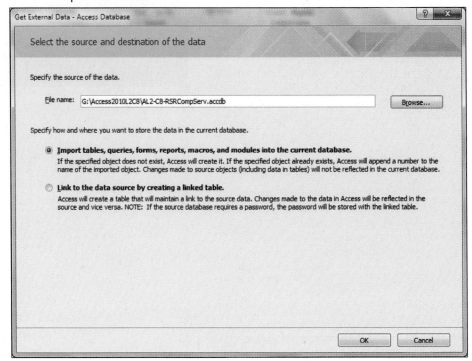

**Figure 8.2** Import Objects Dialog Box

Click tab for object type to be imported, click object name, and then click OK. Use standard Windows selection keys Shift (adjacent objects) or Ctrl (nonadjacent objects) to select multiple objects.

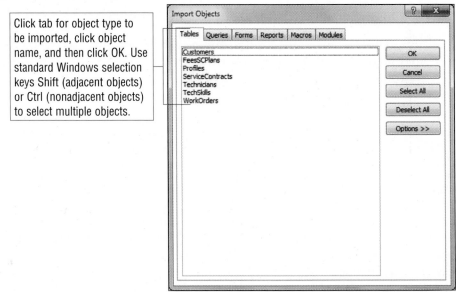

If you import a query, form, or report, make sure you also import the underlying tables associated with the object.

Click the Options button to display the *Import*, *Import Tables*, and *Import Queries* options shown in Figure 8.3. By default, Access imports relationships between tables, imports table structure definition and data, and imports a query as a query as opposed to importing the query as a table. Select or clear the options as required before clicking OK to begin the import operation.

**Figure 8.3** Import Objects Dialog Box with Options Displayed

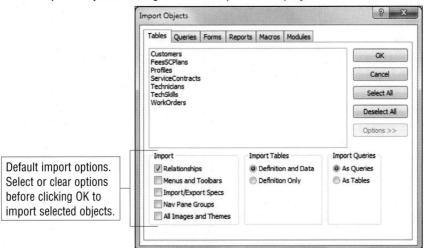

Default import options. Select or clear options before clicking OK to import selected objects.

---

**Project 1a**    **Importing a Form from Another Access Database**    Part 1 of 4

1. Open the **AL2-C8-RSRTechPay.accdb** database and enable content.
2. Import the Technicians form from the **AL2-C8-RSRCompServ.accdb** database by completing the following steps:
   a. Click the External Data tab.
   b. Click the Import Access database button in the Import & Link group.
   c. At the Get External Data - Access Database dialog box, click the Browse button.
   d. At the File Open dialog box, double-click the file named *AL2-C8-RSRCompServ.accdb*. *Note: Navigate to the Access2010L2C8 folder on your storage medium if necessary*.
   e. With *Import tables, queries, forms, reports, macros, and modules into the current database* already selected, click OK.

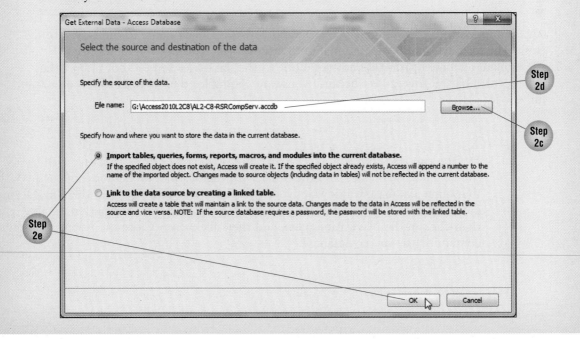

f. At the Import Objects dialog box, click the Forms tab.

g. Click *TechMaintenance* in the Forms list box and click OK.

h. At the Get External Data - Access Database dialog box with the *Save import steps* check box cleared, click Close.

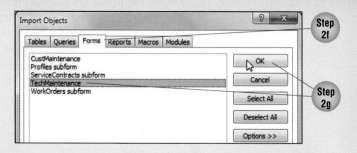

Step 2f

Step 2g

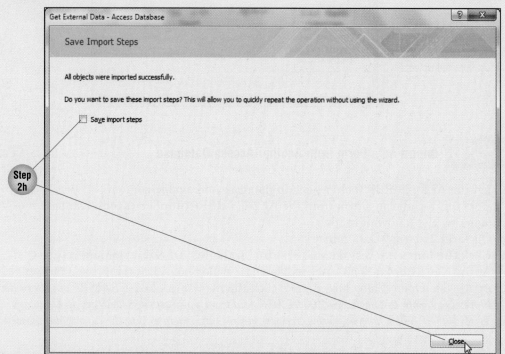

Step 2h

3. Access imports the TechMaintenance form and adds the object name to the Navigation pane. The form will not be operational until after Project 1b since the tables needed to populate data in the form do not yet reside in the database. You did not import the dependent tables in this project because you want the tables that contain the records to be linked.

You can also copy an object by opening two copies of Access, one with the source database opened and the other with the destination database opened. With the source database window active, right-click the source object in the Navigation pane and click *Copy*. Switch to the window containing the destination database, right-click in the Navigation pane, and then click *Paste*. Close the Access window containing the source database.

# Linking to a Table in Another Access Database ■■■■■■■

In Project 1a you imported a form that duplicates the source object from one database to another. If the source object is modified, the imported copy of the object is not altered. Link the data when importing if you want to ensure that the table in the destination database inherits any changes made to the source table. To create a linked table in the destination database, click the External Data tab and then click the Import Access database button. Click the Browse button, navigate to the drive and/or folder in which the source database is stored, and then double-click the source database file name. Click *Link to the data source by creating a linked table* at the Get External Data - Access Database dialog box and then click OK as shown in Figure 8.4.

The Link Tables dialog box shown in Figure 8.5 opens with the *Tables* list box in which you select the tables to be linked. You can use the Shift key or the Ctrl key to select multiple tables to link all in one step. Linked tables are indicated in the Navigation pane with a right-pointing blue arrow.

▼ **Quick Steps**

**Link to Table in Another Database**
1. Open destination database.
2. Click External Data tab.
3. Click Import Access database button.
4. Click Browse button.
5. If necessary, navigate to drive and/or folder.
6. Double-click source file name.
7. Click *Link to the data source by creating a linked table.*
8. Click OK.
9. Select desired table(s).
10. Click OK.

**Figure 8.4** Get External Data - Access Database Dialog Box with Link Option Selected

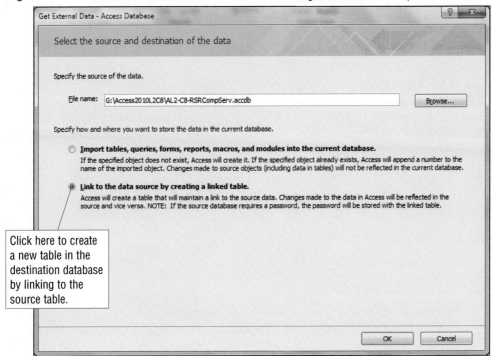

Click here to create a new table in the destination database by linking to the source table.

**Figure 8.5** Link Tables Dialog Box

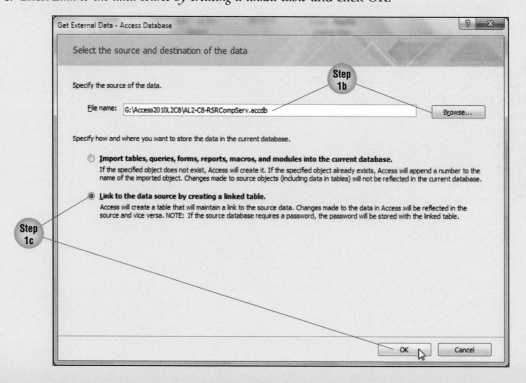

1. With the **AL2-C8-RSRTechPay.accdb** database open, link to two tables in the **AL2-C8-RSRCompServ.accdb** database by completing the following steps:
   a. With the External Data tab still active, click the Import Access database button.
   b. Click the Browse button and double-click the file named *AL2-C8-RSRCompServ.accdb*.
   c. Click *Link to the data source by creating a linked table* and click OK.

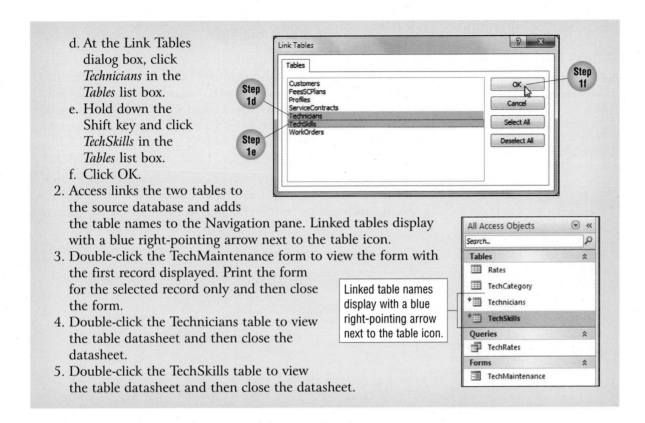

d. At the Link Tables dialog box, click *Technicians* in the *Tables* list box.

e. Hold down the Shift key and click *TechSkills* in the *Tables* list box.

f. Click OK.

2. Access links the two tables to the source database and adds the table names to the Navigation pane. Linked tables display with a blue right-pointing arrow next to the table icon.

3. Double-click the TechMaintenance form to view the form with the first record displayed. Print the form for the selected record only and then close the form.

4. Double-click the Technicians table to view the table datasheet and then close the datasheet.

5. Double-click the TechSkills table to view the table datasheet and then close the datasheet.

Linked table names display with a blue right-pointing arrow next to the table icon.

When a table is linked, the source data does not reside in the destination database. Opening a linked table causes Access to dynamically update the datasheet with the information in the source table in the other database. You can edit the source data in either the source database table or the linked table in the destination database.

## Deciding between Importing versus Linking to Source Data

In most cases you would import data into Access from another Access database or some other external source if the source data is not likely to be updated. Since importing creates a copy of the data in two locations, changes or updates to the data must be duplicated in both copies. Duplicating the change or update increases the risk of data entry error or missed updates in one or the other location.

If the data is updated frequently, link to the external data source so that all changes are only required to be entered once. Since the data exists only in the source location, the potential for error or missed updates is reduced.

In another situation you may choose to link to the data source when several different databases require a common table such as Inventory. To duplicate the table in each database is inefficient and wastes disk space. The potential for error if individual databases are not refreshed with updated data is also a risk that favors linking over importing. In this scenario a master Inventory table in a separate shared database would be linked to all of the other databases that need to use the data.

## Resetting a Link Using Linked Table Manager

**▼ Quick Steps**

**Refresh Link(s)**
1. Click External Data tab.
2. Click Linked Table Manager button.
3. Click Select All button or click individual linked table.
4. Click OK.
5. Navigate to drive and/or folder.
6. Double-click source database file name.
7. Click OK.
8. Click Close button.

Linked Table
Manager

When a table has been linked to another database, Access stores the full path to the source database file name along with the linked table name. Changing the database file name or folder location for the source database means the linked table will no longer function. Access provides the Linked Table Manager dialog box shown in Figure 8.6 to allow you to reset or refresh a table's link to reconnect to the data source. Click the Linked Table Manager button in the Import & Link group of the External Data tab to open the Linked Table Manager dialog box.

Click the check box next to the link you want to refresh and then click OK. Access displays a message box stating that the link was successfully refreshed or displays a dialog box in which you navigate to the new location for the data source.

**Figure 8.6** Linked Table Manager Dialog Box

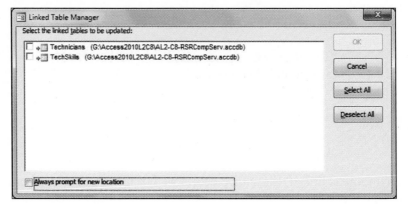

---

**Project 1c**  **Refreshing a Link**  Part 3 of 4

1. With the **AL2-C8-RSRTechPay.accdb** database open, move the location of the **AL2-C8-RSRCompServ.accdb** database by completing the following steps:
   a. Click the File tab and then click Open.
   b. Right-click *AL2-C8-RSRCompServ.accdb* in the file list box and then click *Cut* at the shortcut menu.
   c. At the Open dialog box, click the drive representing your storage medium in the *Computer* section of the Navigation pane, for example, *KINGSTON (G:)*, or click the drive letter in the Address bar.
   d. Right-click in a blank area of the file list box and click *Paste*.
   e. Close the Open dialog box. With the location of the source database now moved, the linked tables are no longer connected to the correct location.
2. Refresh the links to the two tables by completing the following steps:
   a. If necessary, click the External Data tab.
   b. Click the Linked Table Manager button in the Import & Link group.

c. At the Linked Table Manager dialog box, click the Select All button to select all linked objects.

d. Click OK. Access attempts to refresh the links. Since the source database has been moved, Access displays a dialog box in which you select the new location.

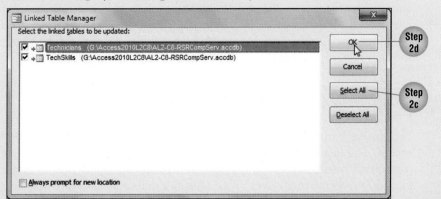

e. At the Select New Location of Technicians dialog box, locate and then double-click ***AL2-C8-RSRCompServ.accdb***.

f. Click OK at the Linked Table Manager message box that indicates all selected links were successfully refreshed.

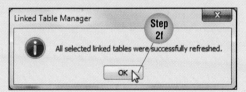

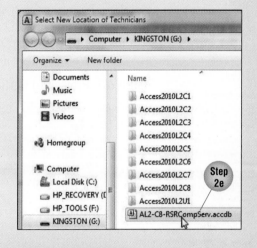

3. Click the Close button at the Linked Table Manager dialog box.

# Importing Data to Access from a Text File

A text file is often used to exchange data between dissimilar programs since the file format is recognized by nearly all applications. Text files contain no formatting and consist of letters, numbers, punctuation symbols, and a few control characters only. Two commonly used text file formats separate fields with either a tab character (delimited file format) or a comma (comma separated file format). A partial view of the text file you will use in Project 1d is shown in a Notepad window in Figure 8.7. If necessary, you can view and edit a text file in Notepad prior to importing if the source application inserts characters that you wish to delete.

**HINT**

Most programs can export data in a text file. If you need to use data from a program that is not compatible with Access, check the source program's export options for a text file format.

## Quick Steps

**Import Data from Comma Separated Text File**
1. Click External Data tab.
2. Click Import text file button.
3. Click Browse button.
4. If necessary, navigate to drive and/or folder.
5. Double-click .csv file name.
6. Click OK.
7. Click Next.
8. If applicable, click *First Row Contains Field Names* check box.
9. Click Next.
10. Choose primary key field.
11. Click Next.
12. Click Finish.

**Save Import Specifications**
1. At last Get External Data dialog box, click *Save import steps*.
2. If necessary, edit name in *Save as* text box.
3. Type description in *Description* text box.
4. Click Save Import button.

Text File

To import a text file into Access, click the Import text file button in the Import & Link group of the External Data tab. Access opens the Get External Data - Text File dialog box which is similar to the dialog box used to import data from another Access database. When importing a text file, Access adds an append option in addition to the import and link options in the *Specify how and where you want to store the data in the current database* section. Click the Browse button to navigate to the location of the source file and double-click the source file name to launch the Import Text Wizard, which guides you through the import process through four dialog boxes.

# Saving and Repeating Import Specifications ▪■▪■▪■■▪■

You can save import specifications for an import routine that you are likely to repeat. The last step in the Get External Data dialog box displays a *Save import steps* check box. Click the check box to expand the dialog box to display the *Save as* and *Description* text boxes. Type a unique name to assign to the import routine and a brief description that describes the steps. Click the Save Import button to complete the import and store the specifications. Click the *Create Outlook Task* check box if you want to create an Outlook task that you can set up as a recurring item for an import or export operation that is repeated at fixed intervals.

**Figure 8.7** Project 1d Partial View of Text File Contents in Notepad

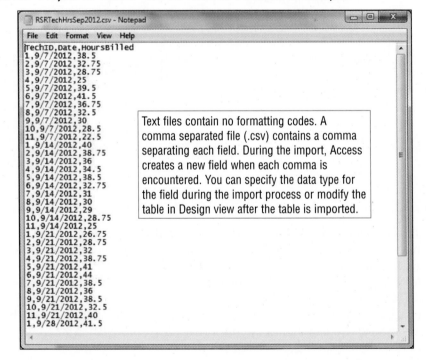

Text files contain no formatting codes. A comma separated file (.csv) contains a comma separating each field. During the import, Access creates a new field when each comma is encountered. You can specify the data type for the field during the import process or modify the table in Design view after the table is imported.

1. With the **AL2-C8-RSRTechPay.accdb** database open, select a text file to import that contains the weekly hours billed for each technician for the month of September 2012 by completing the following steps:

   a. If necessary, click the External Data tab.

   b. Click the Import text file button in the Import & Link group.

   c. At the Get External Data - Text File dialog box, click the Browse button.

   d. At the File Open dialog box, navigate to the Access2010L2C8 folder on your storage medium if necessary.

   e. Double-click the file named *RSRTechHrsSep2012.csv*.

   f. With *Import the source data into a new table in the current database* already selected, click OK. This launches the Import Text Wizard.

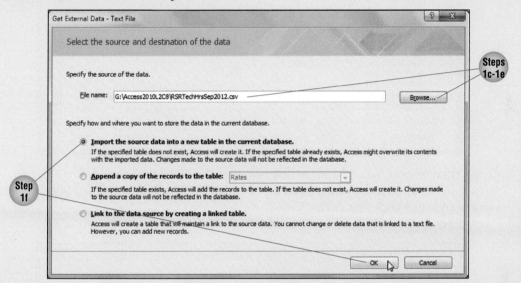

2. Import the comma separated data using the Import Text Wizard by completing the following steps:

   a. At the first Import Text Wizard dialog box, with *Delimited* selected as the format, click Next. Notice the preview window in the lower half of the dialog box displays a sample of the data in the source text file. Delimited files use commas or tabs as separators while fixed width files use spaces.

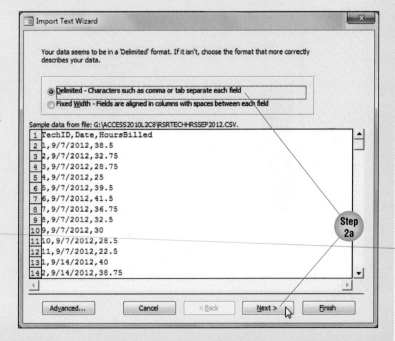

b. At the second Import Text Wizard dialog box with *Comma* already selected as the delimiter, click the *First Row Contains Field Names* check box and then click Next. Notice the preview section already shows the data set in columns similar to a table datasheet.

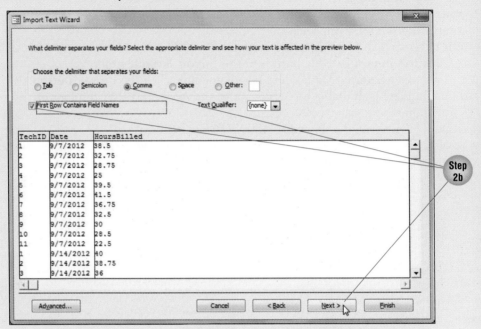

c. At the third Import Text Wizard dialog box with the *TechID* column in the preview section selected, click the down-pointing arrow next to *Data Type* in the *Field Options* section and then click *Text* at the drop-down list.

d. Click Next.

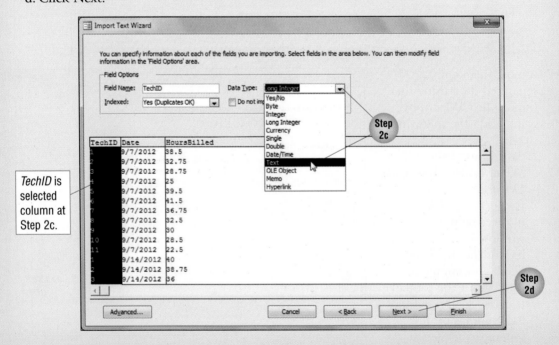

e. At the fourth Import Text Wizard dialog box, with *Let Access add primary key* already selected, click Next. Notice Access has added a column in the preview section with the field title *ID*. The column added by Access is defined as an AutoNumber field where each row in the text file is numbered sequentially to make the row unique.

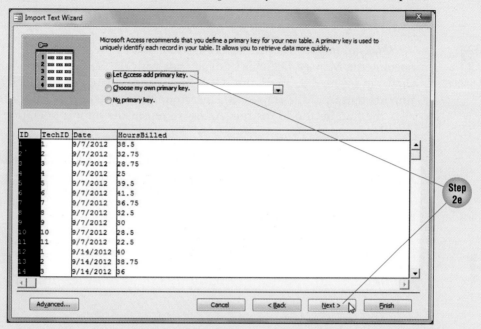

f. At the last Import Text Wizard dialog box, with *RSRTechHrsSep2012* entered in the *Import to Table* text box, click Finish.

3. Save the import specifications in case you want to run this import again at a future date by completing the following steps:

a. At the Get External Data - Text File dialog box, click the *Save import steps* check box. This causes the *Save as* and *Description* text boxes to appear as well as the *Create an Outlook Task* section. By default Access creates a name in the *Save as* text box with *Import-* preceding the file name containing the imported data.

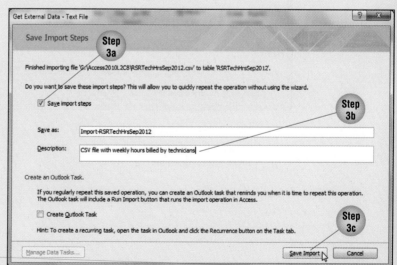

b. Click in the *Description* text box and type **CSV file with weekly hours billed by technicians**.

c. Click the Save Import button.

4. Double-click the RSRTechHoursSep2012 table in the Navigation pane to open the table datasheet.
5. Print the datasheet with a bottom margin set to 0.5 inch and then close the datasheet.
6. Close the **AL2-C8-RSRTechPay.accdb** database.

Saved Imports

Once an import routine has been saved, you can repeat the import process by opening the Manage Data Tasks dialog box with the Saved Imports tab selected shown in Figure 8.8. To do this, click the External Data tab and click the Saved Imports button in the Import & Link group. Click the desired import name and click the Run button to instruct Access to repeat the import operation.

**Figure 8.8** Manage Data Tasks Dialog Box with Saved Imports Tab Selected

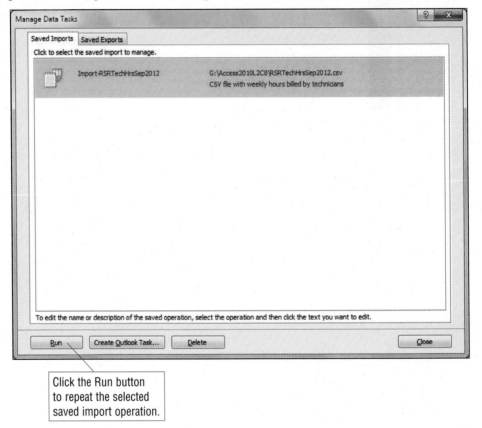

Click the Run button to repeat the selected saved import operation.

# Project 2   Export Access Data to a Text File   2 Parts

You will export a query as a comma delimited text file and another query as a tab delimited text file including saving the second export steps so that you can repeat the export operation.

## Exporting Access Data to a Text File ■■■■■■■■■■■■■■■■

The Export group in the External Data tab contains buttons with which you can export Access data from a table, query, form, or report to other applications such as Excel or Word. If you need to work with data from Access in a program that is not part of the Microsoft Office suite, you can click the More button in the Export group to see if a file format converter exists for the application that you will be using. For example, the More button contains options to export in Word, SharePoint List, ODBC Database, HTML Document, and dBase file formats.

If a file format converter does not exist for the program that you will be using, export the data as a text file since most applications recognize and can import a text data file. Access includes the Export Text Wizard, which is launched after you select an object in the Navigation pane, click the Export to text file button, and then specify the name and location to store the exported text file. The Export Text Wizard uses similar steps to those that you used when you imported a text file in Project 1d.

### ▼ Quick Steps

**Export Data as Text File**
1. Select object in Navigation pane.
2. Click External Data tab.
3. Click Export to text file button.
4. Click Browse button.
5. If necessary, navigate to desired drive and/or folder.
6. If necessary, change file name.
7. Click Save button.
8. Click OK.
9. Click Next.
10. Choose delimiter character.
11. If appropriate, click *Include Field Names on First Row* check box.
12. If appropriate, choose *Text Qualifier* character.
13. Click Next.
14. If necessary, change *Export to File* path and/or name.
15. Click Finish.
16. Click Close button.

Text File

---

### Project 2a   Exporting a Query as a Text File   Part 1 of 2

1. Display the Open dialog box and move the **AL2-C8-RSRCompServ.accdb** database back to the Access2010L2C8 folder on your storage medium.
2. Open the **AL2-C8-RSRCompServ.accdb** database and enable content.
3. Export the TotalWorkOrders query as a text file by completing the following steps:
   a. Select the query named TotalWorkOrders in the Navigation pane.
   b. Click the External Data tab.
   c. Click the Export to text file button in the Export group.

d. At the Export - Text File dialog box, click the Browse button.

e. At the File Save dialog box, if necessary, navigate to the Access2010L2C8 folder on your storage medium.

f. With the default file name of *TotalWorkOrders.txt* in the *File name* text box, click the Save button.

g. Click OK.

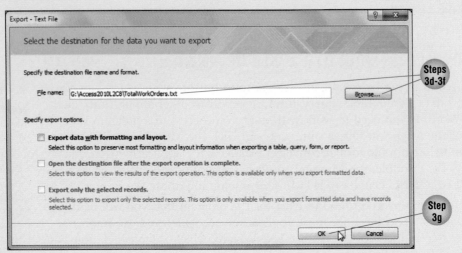

h. At the first Export Text Wizard dialog box with *Delimited* selected as the format, click Next. Notice in the preview section of the dialog box that a comma separates each field and that data in a field defined with the Text data type is encased in quotation symbols.

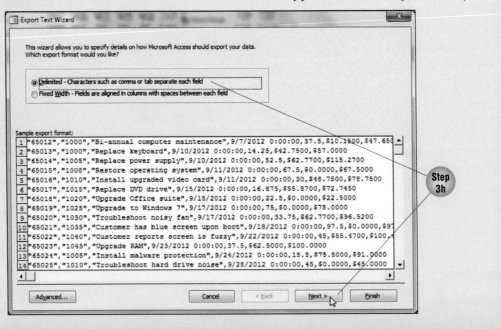

i. At the second Export Text Wizard dialog box, with *Comma* selected as the delimiter character that separates the fields, click the *Include Field Names on First Row* check box. Access adds a row to the top of the data in the preview section with the field names. Each field name is encased in quotation symbols.

j. Click the down-pointing arrow next to the *Text Qualifier* list box and click *{none}* at the drop-down list. Access removes all of the quotation symbols from the text data in the preview section.

k. Click Next.

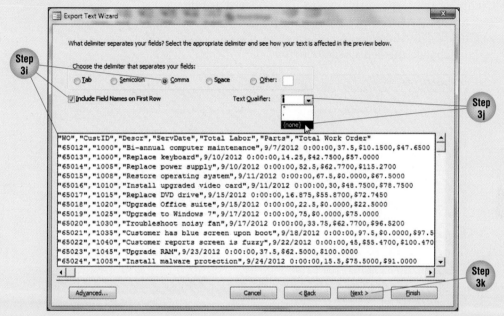

l. At the last Export Text Wizard dialog box, with *[d]:\Access2010L2C8\TotalWorkOrders.txt* (where *[d]* is the drive for your storage medium) entered in the *Export to File* text box, click Finish.

m. Click the Close button at the Export - Text File dialog box to close the dialog box without saving the export steps.

4. Click the Start button, point to *All Programs*, click *Accessories*, and then click *Notepad*.

5. At a blank Notepad window, click File and then click Open. Navigate to the Access2010L2C8 folder on your storage medium and then double-click the exported file named **TotalWorkOrders.txt**.

6. Click File and then click Print to print the exported text file.

7. Exit Notepad.

# Saving and Repeating Export Specifications ■■■■■■■

Access allows you to save export steps similar to how you learned to save import specifications for an import routine that you are likely to repeat. The last step in the Export - Text File dialog box displays a *Save export steps* check box. Click the check box to expand the dialog box options to display the *Save as* and *Description* text boxes. Type a unique name to assign to the export routine and a brief description that describes the steps. Click the Save Export button to complete the export operation and store the specifications for later use.

▼ **Quick Steps**

**Save Export Specifications**
1. At last Export - Text File dialog box, click *Save export steps.*
2. If necessary, edit name in *Save as* text box.
3. Type description in *Description* text box.
4. Click Save Export button.

1. With the **AL2-C8-RSRCompServ.accdb** database open, export the TotalLabor query as a text file using Tab as the delimiter character by completing the following steps:
   a. Select the query named TotalLabor in the Navigation pane.
   b. Click the Export to text file button in the Export group of the External Data tab.
   c. With *[d]:\Access2010L2C8\TotalLabor.txt* (where *[d]* is the drive for your storage medium) entered in the *File name* text box, click OK.
   d. Complete the steps in the Export Text Wizard as follows:
      1) Click Next at the first dialog box with *Delimited* selected.
      2) Click *Tab* as the delimiter character, click the *Include Field Names on First Row* check box, change the *Text Qualifier* to *{none}*, and then click Next.

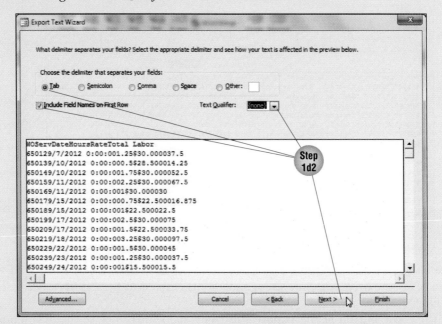

   3) Click Finish.
   e. Click the *Save export steps* check box at the Export - Text File dialog box.
   f. Click in the *Description* text box and type TotalLabor query for RSR Computer Service work orders as a text file.
   g. Click the Save Export button.

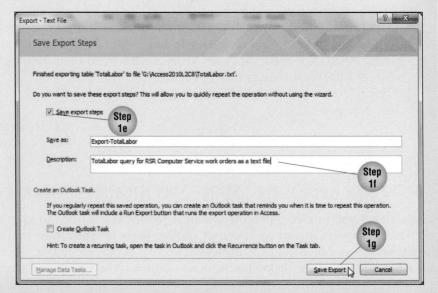

2. Start Notepad.
3. At a blank Notepad window, open the exported file named **TotalLabor.txt**.
4. Print the exported text file and then exit Notepad.

Once an export routine has been saved, you can repeat the export process by opening the Manage Data Tasks dialog box with the Saved Exports tab selected shown in Figure 8.9 by clicking the Saved Exports button in the Export group in the External Data tab. Click the desired export name and click the Run button to instruct Access to repeat the export operation.

Saved Exports

**Figure 8.9** Manage Data Tasks Dialog Box with Saved Exports Tab Selected

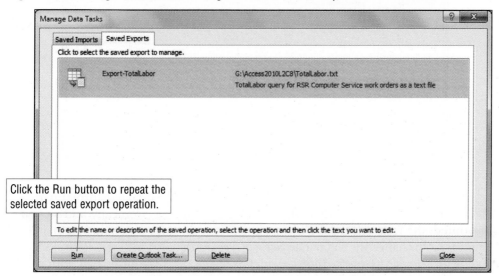

Click the Run button to repeat the selected saved export operation.

Project ⑧ **Publish a Database Object as an XPS Document**   **1 Part**

You will publish a report as an XPS file.

# Publishing and Viewing Database Objects as XPS Documents ■■■■■■■■■■■■■■■■■■■■■■■■■■■■■■

In Level 1, Chapter 7 and Chapter 8, you learned to publish database objects as a PDF document using the Save & Publish tab Backstage view and the PDF or XPS button in the Export group of the External Data tab. Recall that clicking the PDF or XPS button in the Export group of the External Data tab with an object selected in the Navigation pane causes the Publish as PDF or XPS dialog box shown in Figure 8.10 to open.

PDF or XPS

**Figure 8.10** Publish as PDF or XPS Dialog Box

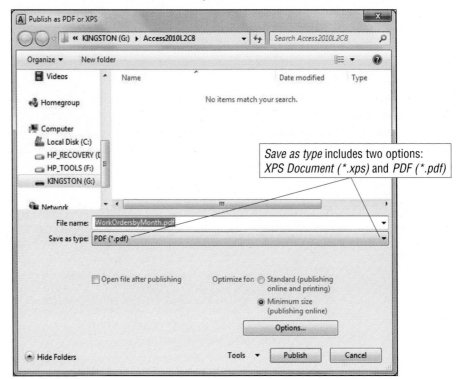

*Save as type* includes two options: *XPS Document (\*.xps)* and *PDF (\*.pdf)*

**Quick Steps**

**Publish Object as XPS**
1. Select object in Navigation pane.
2. Click External Data tab.
3. Click PDF or XPS button.
4. If necessary, navigate to desired drive and/ or folder.
5. If necessary, change file name.
6. Change *Save as type* to *XPS*.
7. Click Publish button.
8. Click Close button.

XPS stands for *XML Paper Specification,* which is a fixed-layout format with all formatting preserved so that when the file is shared electronically and viewed or printed, the recipients of the file see the format as it appeared in Access and cannot easily change the data. The *Save as type* option also includes *PDF*. PDF stands for *Portable Document Format,* which is also a fixed-layout format with all formatting preserved for file sharing purposes.

Once you have selected the required file format, navigate to the desired drive and/or folder in which the file should be stored and change the file name if necessary. Click the Publish button when finished to create the file.

---

**Project 3**  **Publishing a Report as an XPS Document**                 Part 1 of 1

1. With the **AL2-C8-RSRCompServ.accdb** database open, export the WorkOrdersbyMonth report as an XPS document by completing the following steps:
   a. Click to select the WorkOrdersbyMonth report in the Navigation pane.
   b. Click the PDF or XPS button in the Export group of the External Data tab.
   c. If necessary, navigate to the Access2010L2C8 folder at the Publish as PDF or XPS dialog box.

d. With *WorkOrdersbyMonth* entered in the *File name* text box, publish the report as an XPS document by completing the following steps:

    1) Click the *Save as type* option and then click *XPS Document (*.xps)*.

    2) If necessary, click the *Open file after publishing* check box to clear the check mark.

    3) Click the Publish button.

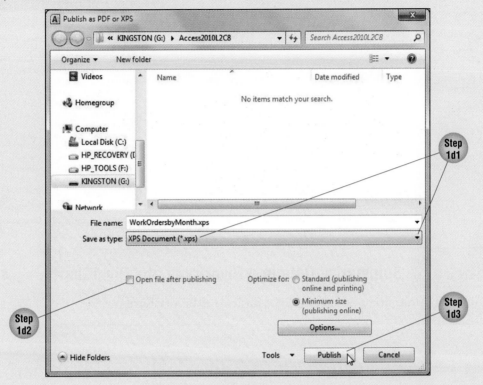

e. Click the Close button at the Export - XPS dialog box to close the dialog box without saving the export steps.

    Similar to PDF files that require the Adobe Reader program in which to view documents, you need a viewer in order to read an XPS document. The viewer is provided by Microsoft and is included with Windows Vista and Windows 7.

    The WorkOrdersbyMonth.xps document created in Project 3 is shown in an XPS Viewer window in Figure 8.11.

**Figure 8.11** WorkOrdersbyMonth.xps Opened in XPS Viewer Window

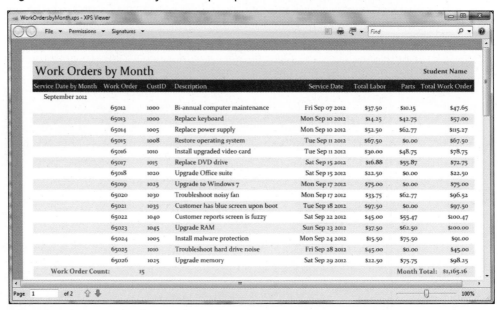

<br>

**P**roject **4** **Summarize Data in a PivotTable and PivotChart** **4 Parts**

You will summarize data in a PivotTable and PivotChart.

## Summarizing Data in a PivotTable and PivotChart ▪▪▪

Pivot Table

Access provides additional views in a table and query that you can use to summarize data. Change to the PivotTable view to create a PivotTable, which is an interactive table that organizes and summarizes data. Use the PivotChart view to create a PivotChart that summarizes data in a graph.

### Summarizing Data in a PivotTable

**Quick Steps**

**Create PivotTable**
1. Open table or query.
2. Click PivotTable View button.
   OR
   Click View button arrow and click *PivotTable View.*
3. Drag fields from *PivotTable Field List* box to desired dimmed text locations.

A PivotTable is an interactive table that organizes and summarizes data based on fields you designate as row headings and column headings. A numeric column you select is then grouped by the row and column field and the data summarized using a function such as Sum, Average, or Count. PivotTables are useful management tools since you can analyze data in a variety of scenarios by filtering a row, a column, or another filter field and instantly see the change in results. The interactivity of a PivotTable allows one to examine a variety of scenarios with just a few mouse clicks.

To create a PivotTable, open a table or query in Datasheet view and then click the PivotTable View button in the view area at the right side of the Status bar, or click the View button arrow in the Views group in the Home tab and then click *PivotTable View* at the drop-down list. This displays the datasheet in PivotTable layout with four sections along with a *PivotTable Field List* box as shown in Figure 8.12. Dimmed text in each section describes the types of fields you should drag and drop.

**Figure 8.12** PivotTable View

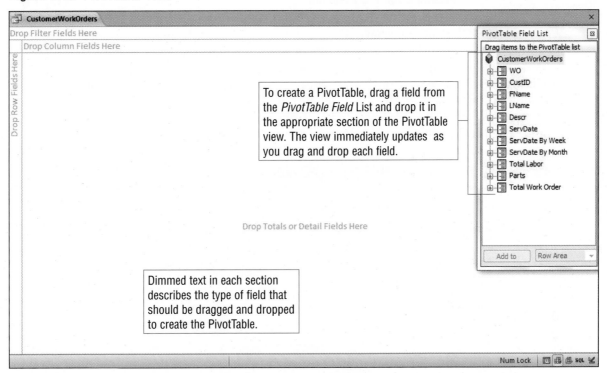

To create a PivotTable, drag a field from the *PivotTable Field* List and drop it in the appropriate section of the PivotTable view. The view immediately updates as you drag and drop each field.

Dimmed text in each section describes the type of field that should be dragged and dropped to create the PivotTable.

Drag the fields from the *PivotTable Field List* box to the desired locations in the PivotTable layout. The dimmed text in the PivotTable layout identifies the field you should drop in the location. In Project 4a, you will drag the *LName* field to the Row field section, the *ServDate by Month* field to the Column field section, and the *Total Work Order* field to the Totals or Details field section. After adding summary totals and hiding details, the PivotTable will display as shown in Figure 8.13.

**Figure 8.13** PivotTable for Project 4a

| LName | ⊞ Sep Sum of Total Work Order | ⊞ Oct Sum of Total Work Order | Grand Total Sum of Total Work Order |
|---|---|---|---|
| Bodzek | $173.25 | $41.63 | $214.88 |
| Carmichael | $67.50 | $723.87 | $791.37 |
| Cobb | $22.50 | $322.60 | $345.10 |
| Fahri | $206.27 | | $206.27 |
| Fennema | $100.00 | $97.50 | $197.50 |
| Fleming | $104.65 | $448.75 | $553.40 |
| Friesen | $72.75 | $46.25 | $119.00 |
| Lemaire | $123.75 | $555.50 | $679.25 |
| Machado | $100.47 | $22.50 | $122.97 |
| Pierson | $96.52 | $129.38 | $225.90 |
| Woodside | $97.50 | $56.25 | $153.75 |
| Grand Total | $1,165.16 | $2,444.22 | $3,609.38 |

1. With the **AL2-C8-RSRCompServ.accdb** database open, modify an existing query to add fields needed for summarizing data in a PivotTable by completing the following steps:
   a. Open the TotalWorkOrders query in Design view.
   b. Click the Show Table button in the Query Setup group. At the Show Table dialog box, double-click *Customers* in the Tables list box and then click the Close button.
   c. Drag *FName* from the Customers field list box to the *Descr* field in the query design grid. The *FName* column is added to the query and the existing *Descr* column and the remaining columns shift right.

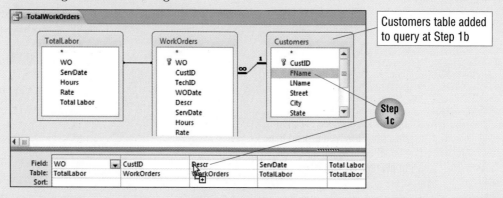

Customers table added to query at Step 1b

Step 1c

   d. Drag *LName* from the Customers field list box to the *Descr* field in the query design grid.
   e. Run the query.

Customer first and last names added to TotalWorkOrders query

2. Click the File tab, click Save Object As, type **CustomerWorkOrders** at the Save As dialog box, and press Enter or click OK.
3. Click the Home tab, click the View button arrow in the Views group, and then click *PivotTable View* at the drop-down list.
4. At the PivotTable view, drag and drop the *LName* field to the Row field section by completing the following steps:
   a. Position the mouse pointer on the *LName* field in the *PivotTable Field List* box.

Step 3

b. Hold down the left mouse button, drag to the dimmed text *Drop Row Fields Here* located at the left side of the PivotTable view, and then release the mouse button. Access updates the view to show one row for each unique customer name in the query results datasheet.

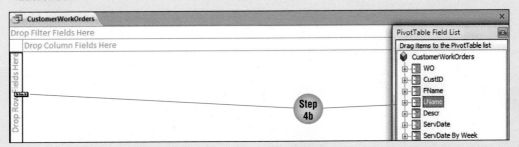

5. Add the column field to summarize the work orders by month by completing the following steps:
   a. Click the expand button (displays as a plus symbol) next to *ServDate by Month* in the *PivotTable Field List* box. This expands the list to show the *ServDate* field in various time intervals such as *Years*, *Quarters*, *Months*, and so on.
   b. Drag the *Months* field in the expanded *ServDate by Month* list from the *PivotTable Field List* box and drop it on the dimmed text *Drop Column Fields Here*. Access updates the view to show one column for each month in the query results datasheet.

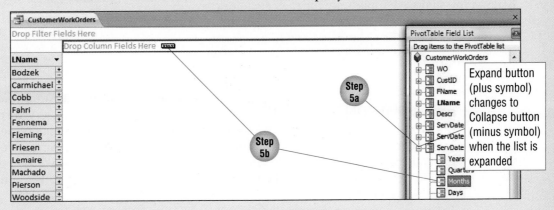

6. Scroll down the *PivotTable Field List* box if necessary and then drag the *Total Work Order* field from the *PivotTable Field List* box and drop it on the dimmed text *Drop Totals or Detail Fields Here*. Access organizes the data and shows the total work order value for each work order by customer by month in the PivotTable.
7. Remove the *PivotTable Field List* box from the screen by clicking the Field List button in the Show/Hide group in the PivotTable Tools Design tab.
8. Add summary totals and hide details by completing the following steps:
   a. Click either one of the *Total Work Order* column headings below *Sep* or *Oct* in the PivotTable. This selects all of the values in the PivotTable.

b. Click the AutoCalc button in the Tools group of the PivotTable Tools Design tab and then click *Sum* at the drop-down list. Access adds a subtotal of the work order values for each customer below each month and a total of all work orders for each customer in the *Grand Total* column at the right.

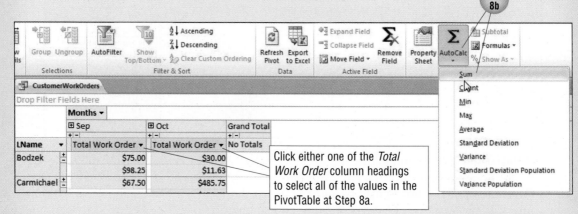

Click either one of the *Total Work Order* column headings to select all of the values in the PivotTable at Step 8a.

c. Click the Hide Details button in the Show/Hide group of the PivotTable Tools Design tab. Access removes the individual work order values and shows the summary totals only for each customer.

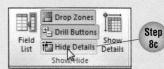

9. Compare your results with Figure 8.13 on page 303.
10. Save and then close the CustomerWorkOrders query.

When you create a PivotTable in a query or table, it becomes a part of and is saved with the table or query. The next time you open the table or query, display the PivotTable by clicking the PivotTable View button in the view area on the Status bar or by clicking the View button arrow in the Views group in the Home tab and then clicking *PivotTable View* at the drop-down list. If you make changes to data in fields that are part of the table or query, the data is automatically updated in the PivotTable.

The power of a PivotTable is the ability to analyze data for numerous scenarios. For example, in the PivotTable you created in Project 4a, you can display work orders for a specific date or a specific customer or group of customers. Use the plus and minus symbols that display in a row or column heading to show (plus symbol) or hide (minus symbol) data. Use the down-pointing arrow (called the *filter arrow*) that displays next to a field name to filter the PivotTable by one or more values in the field.

### Project 4b    Analyzing Data in PivotTable View                    Part 2 of 4

1. With the **AL2-C8-RSRCompServ.accdb** database open, open the CustomerWorkOrders query.
2. Click the View button arrow in the Views group in the Home tab and then click *PivotTable View* at the drop-down list.

3. Display only those work orders from September by completing the following steps:
   a. Click the filter arrow (down-pointing black arrow) at the right of *Months* (located above the *Sep* and *Oct* columns in the PivotTable).
   b. At the drop-down list that displays, click the *(All)* check box to remove the check mark.
   c. Click the expand button (displays as a plus symbol) next to *2012*.
   d. Click the expand button next to *Qtr3*.
   e. Click the *Sep* check box to insert a check mark.
   f. Click OK. Notice the arrow on the *Months* button changes color to blue to indicate the PivotTable is filtered by the field.
4. Redisplay all months by clicking the *Months* filter arrow, clicking the *(All)* check box, and then clicking OK.
5. Display only those work orders for Fahri, Fennema, and Fleming by completing the following steps:
   a. Click the filter arrow next to the *LName* field.
   b. At the drop-down list, click the *(All)* check box to remove the check mark before each customer name.
   c. Click the check box next to *Fahri*.
   d. Click the check box next to *Fennema*.
   e. Click the check box next to *Fleming*.
   f. Click OK.
6. Redisplay all customers by clicking the *LName* filter arrow, clicking the *(All)* check box, and then clicking OK.
7. Save, print, and then close the PivotTable.

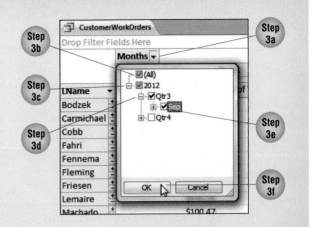

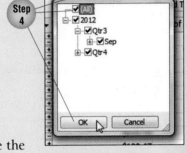

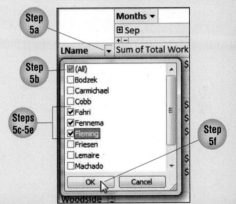

## Summarizing Data in a PivotTable Form

When you create a PivotTable in a query or table, the PivotTable settings are saved and become part of the table or query. When you open a table or query in which you have created a PivotTable and then switch to PivotTable view, the table or query displays with the PivotTable settings you created. If you want to view different fields or perform other functions in PivotTable view, you have to edit the last settings. For example, if you created a PivotTable in a Work Orders query that summed the total work order field by customer and by month, and then wanted to sum by quarter, you would have to edit the previous PivotTable. If you want to routinely view data in PivotTable view by different criteria (such as by month and by quarter), consider creating a PivotTable form. A PivotTable form is a separate object from the query or table, so you could create one showing the sum by month and another showing the sum by quarter. This way, you do not have to constantly edit the PivotTable's settings each time you want to change the way the data is summarized.

To create a PivotTable form, click the desired object in the Navigation pane and then click the Create tab. Click the More Forms button in the Forms group and then click *PivotTable* at the drop-down list. This displays the object in PivotTable layout. Click the Field List button in the Show/Hide group to display the *PivotTable Field List* box. (You may need to click the button twice to display the list box.)

---

**Project 4c**  **Creating a PivotTable Form**  Part 3 of 4

1. With the **AL2-C8-RSRCompServ.accdb** database open, save the CustomerWorkOrders query as a form by completing the following steps:
   a. Click to select the CustomerWorkOrders query in the Navigation pane.
   b. Click the File tab and then click *Save Object As* at the Info tab Backstage view.
   c. At the Save As dialog box, type **CustWorkOrders** in the *Save 'CustomerWorkOrders' to* text box.
   d. Click the down-pointing arrow at the right of the *As* list box (currently reads *Query*) and then click *Form* at the drop-down list.
   e. Click OK.
   f. Click the Home tab and then close the CustWorkOrders form.

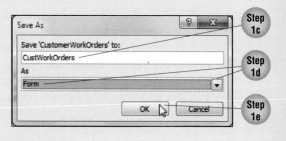

2. Create a PivotTable form by completing the following steps:
   a. Click the CustWorkOrders form in the Navigation pane.
   b. Click the Create tab.
   c. Click the More Forms button in the Forms group and then click *PivotTable* at the drop-down list.
   d. At the PivotTable form, click twice on the Field List button in the Show/Hide group in the PivotTable Tools Design tab.
   e. Drag the *LName* field in the *PivotTable Field List* box and drop it on the dimmed text *Drop Row Fields Here*.
   f. Expand the *ServDate By Month* field in the *PivotTable Field List* box, and then drag the *Months* field to the dimmed text *Drop Column Fields Here*.

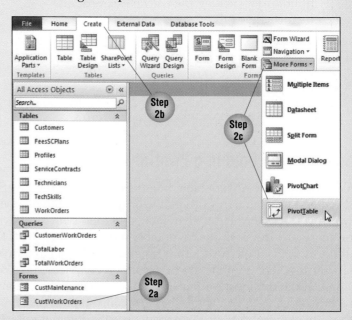

g. Drag the *Total Work Order* field from the *PivotTable Field List* box and drop it on the dimmed text *Drop Totals or Detail Fields Here*.

h. Close the *PivotTable Field List* box.

3. Click to select either one of the *Total Work Order* column headings, click the AutoCalc button in the Tools group of the PivotTable Tools Design tab, and then click *Sum* at the drop-down list.

4. Display only the work orders for Fleming and save the filtered PivotTable in a new form by completing the following steps:

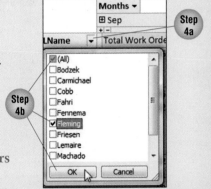

a. Click the filter arrow at the right of the *LName* field.

b. Click the *(All)* check box to remove all of the check marks, click the *Fleming* check box to insert a check mark, and then click OK.

c. Click the Save button on the Quick Access toolbar.

d. At the Save As dialog box, type **FlemingWorkOrders** and then press Enter or click OK.

5. Close the FlemingWorkOrders PivotTable form.

## Summarizing Data Using PivotChart View

A PivotChart performs the same function as a PivotTable with the exception that Access displays the source data in a graph instead of a table or query. You create a chart by dragging fields from the *Chart Field List* box to the *Filter, Data, Category,* and *Series* sections of the chart. As with a PivotTable, you can easily alter the PivotChart using the filter arrows.

    To create a PivotChart, open a table or query in Datasheet view, click the PivotChart View button in the view area at the right side of the Status bar, or click the View button arrow in the Views group in the Home tab, and then click *PivotChart View* at the drop-down list. This changes the datasheet to PivotChart layout, which contains four sections, and displays the *Chart Field List* box. Dimmed text in each section describes the types of fields that you should drag and drop. If a table or query datasheet has previously had a PivotTable that has been saved with the table or query, PivotChart view automatically graphs the existing PivotTable. For example, Figure 8.14 displays the PivotChart that appears if you open the CustomerWorkOrders query and change the view to PivotChart view. The PivotChart is dynamically linked to the PivotTable you created in Project 4a.

### Quick Steps

**Create PivotChart**
1. Open table or query.
2. Click PivotChart View button.
   OR
   Click View button arrow and click *PivotChart View*.
3. Drag fields from *Chart Field List* box to desired dimmed text locations.

Pivot Chart

**Figure 8.14** PivotChart Connected to PivotTable Created in Project 4a

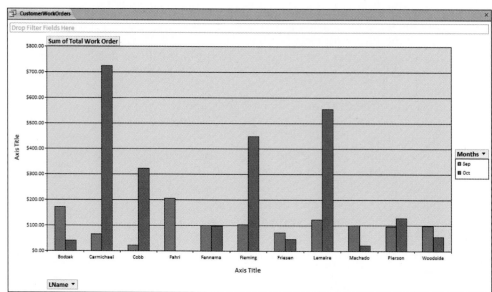

Figure 8.15 illustrates the PivotChart layout for a query or table for which no previous PivotTable exists. Drag the fields from the *Chart Field List* box to the desired locations in the PivotChart layout. The dimmed text in the PivotChart layout identifies the field you should drop in the location. In Project 4d, you will create a new query to summarize the work order values by the technicians who performed the service work. You will begin by creating a new query with the fields from two tables and then change the view to build the PivotChart from scratch.

**Figure 8.15** PivotChart View for Table or Query with No Pre-Existing PivotTable

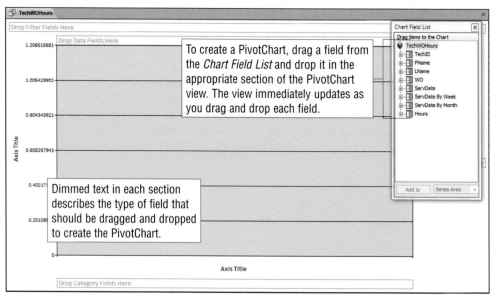

1. With the **AL2-C8-RSRCompServ.accdb** database open, create a new query in Design view with the following specifications:
   a. Add the Technicians and WorkOrders tables to the design grid.
   b. Add the following fields from the specified tables:

   | | | |
   |---|---|---|
   | *TechID* | = | Technicians table |
   | *FName* | = | Technicians table |
   | *LName* | = | Technicians table |
   | *WO* | = | WorkOrders table |
   | *ServDate* | = | WorkOrders table |
   | *Hours* | = | WorkOrders table |

   c. Run the query.
   d. Save the query and name it *TechWOHours*.

   **TechWOHours**

   | Technician ID ▾ | First Name ▾ | Last Name ▾ | Work Order ▾ | Service Date ▾ | Hours ▾ |
   |---|---|---|---|---|---|
   | 01 | Pat | Hynes | 65020 | Mon Sep 17 2012 | 1.50 |
   | 01 | Pat | Hynes | 65033 | Sat Oct 13 2012 | 3.25 |
   | 01 | Pat | Hynes | 65038 | Fri Oct 19 2012 | 2.50 |
   | 02 | Hui | Chen | 65014 | Mon Sep 10 2012 | 1.75 |
   | 02 | Hui | Chen | 65019 | Mon Sep 17 2012 | 2.50 |
   | 02 | Hui | Chen | 65026 | Sat Sep 29 2012 | 0.75 |

   Steps 1a-1d

2. Click the View button arrow in the Views group in the Home tab and then click *PivotChart View* at the drop-down list.
3. At the PivotChart layout, drag and drop the following fields:
   a. Drag the *LName* field from the *Chart Field List* box and drop it on the dimmed text *Drop Category Fields Here*.
   b. Expand the *ServDate By Month* field in the *Chart Field List* box and then drag the *Months* field to the dimmed text *Drop Series Fields* here. **Hint: You may need to drag the Chart Field List *box out of the way to see the dimmed text* Drop Series Fields *here*.**
   c. Drag the *Hours* field (make sure you drag the *Hours* field name that appears last in the list) from the *Chart Field List* box and drop it on the dimmed text *Drop Data Fields Here*.
4. Remove the *Chart Field List* box from the screen by clicking the Field List button in the Show/Hide group.
5. Click the Legend button in the Show/Hide group of the PivotTable Tools Design tab. A legend appears below the Months field button at the right side of the PivotChart.

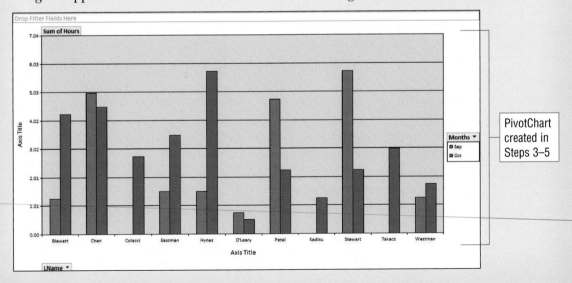

PivotChart created in Steps 3–5

6. Save the PivotChart.
7. Click the View button arrow in the Views group and then click *PivotTable View* at the drop-down list. Notice that Access automatically created a PivotTable behind the scenes as you built the PivotChart.
8. Close the TechWOHours query.

| | | Months ▾ | | |
|---|---|---|---|---|
| | | ⊞ Sep | ⊞ Oct | Grand Total |
| | | +|- | +|- | +|- |
| LName | ▾ | Sum of Hours | Sum of Hours | Sum of Hours |
| Blewett | ± | 1.25 | 4.25 | 5.50 |
| Chen | ± | 5.00 | 4.50 | 9.50 |
| Colacci | ± | | 2.75 | 2.75 |
| Eastman | ± | 1.50 | 3.50 | 5.00 |
| Hynes | ± | 1.50 | 5.75 | 7.25 |
| O'Leary | ± | 0.75 | 0.50 | 1.25 |
| Patel | ± | 4.75 | 2.25 | 7.00 |
| Sadiku | ± | | 1.25 | 1.25 |
| Stewart | ± | 5.75 | 2.25 | 8.00 |
| Takacs | ± | | 3.00 | 3.00 |
| Westman | ± | 1.25 | 1.75 | 3.00 |
| Grand Total | ± | 21.75 | 31.75 | 53.50 |

TechWOHours

Drop Filter Fields Here

Step 7

In this chapter you have learned to import data from another Access database and to import and export using a text file format to exchange data between Access and other non-Microsoft programs. To distribute Access data with formatting preserved in a non-editable format, publish an object as a PDF or XPS document. Finally, numeric data can be summarized and analyzed by creating a PivotTable and/or a PivotChart.

# Chapter Summary

- An object in another Access database can be imported into the active database using the Import Access database button in the Import & Link group of the External Data tab.

- If the source object is a table, you can choose to import or link the source table.

- In a linked table, the data is not copied into the active database but resides only in the source database.

- You can edit source data in a linked table in either the source or destination database.

- Use an import routine if the source data is not likely to require changes or updates.

- Link to source data that requires frequent changes to reduce the potential for data entry or missed update errors.

- You may also decide to link to a source table that is shared among several different databases within an organization.

- Access stores the full path to the source database when a table is linked. If you move the location of the source database the links will need to be refreshed.

- A text file is often used to exchange data between dissimilar programs because a text file is recognized by nearly all applications.

- Import a text file into an Access database by clicking the Import text file button in the Import & Link group of the External Data tab.

- When a text file is selected for import, Access launches the Text Import Wizard, which guides you through the steps to import the text into a table.

- If an import operation is often repeated, consider saving the import steps so that you can run the import routine without having to walk through each step every time you import.

- Open the Manage Data Tasks dialog box to run a saved import by clicking the Saved Imports button in the Import & Link group of the External Data tab.

- Export Access data in a text file format using the Export Text Wizard by clicking the Export to text file button in the Export group of the External Data tab.

- Within the Export Text Wizard you are prompted to choose the text format, delimiter character, field names, text qualifier symbols, and export path and file name.

- You can save export steps at the last Export - Text File dialog box in order to repeat an export operation.

- Click the Saved Exports button in the Export group of the External Data tab to run a saved export routine.

- Access includes a feature that allows you to save an object in XPS or PDF format in order to distribute Access data with formatting preserved in a non-editable format.

- Publish an object by selecting the object name in the Navigation pane and then clicking the PDF or XPS button in the Export group in the External Data tab.

- A PivotTable is an interactive table that organizes and summarizes data which can easily be filtered to display the effects of different scenarios.

- Open a table or query datasheet and change to PivotTable view to build a PivotTable by dragging field names from the *PivotTable Field List* box to the appropriate dimmed text locations in the view.

- Create a PivotTable form by clicking the More Forms button in the Forms group of the Create tab and then clicking *PivotTable* at the drop-down list.

- Create separate PivotTable forms for those situations where you need to routinely view the same data by different filter criteria. Each PivotTable form is a separate object that allows you to maintain individual PivotTable settings.

- A PivotChart allows you to analyze data in a graph format rather than a table format. Change to PivotChart view to view the chart for an existing PivotTable, or create a new chart from scratch.

# Commands Review

| FEATURE | RIBBON TAB, GROUP | BUTTON |
|---------|-------------------|--------|
| Export data as text file | External Data, Export | |
| Import or link data from Access database | External Data, Import & Link | |
| Import data from text file | External Data, Import & Link | |
| Linked Table Manager | External Data, Import & Link | |
| PivotTable form | Create, Forms | |
| PivotTable view | Home, Views | |
| PivotChart view | Home, Views | |
| Save object as XPS document | External Data, Export | |
| Saved exports | External Data, Export | |
| Saved imports | External Data, Import & Link | |

# Concepts Check Test Your Knowledge

**Completion:** In the space provided at the right, indicate the correct term, command, or number.

1. Click this button at the Import Objects dialog box to choose whether or not relationships between tables will be imported.

2. Click this option at the Get External Data - Access Database dialog box to create a table in which changes to data are automatically updated in either the source or destination databases.

3. Data that is not likely to be changed should be brought into the active database from another database using this method.

4. Data that is updated frequently should be brought into the active database from another database using this method.

5. If the location of a source database has moved, open this dialog box to refresh the link to the source table.

6. This type of file format is used to exchange data between programs for which an application-specific file format converter is not available. _____

7. A file in which each field is separated by a comma has this file extension. _____

8. Click this check box at the last Get External Data dialog box to store the steps used in the import process in order to repeat the import routine at a future date. _____

9. The Export Text Wizard is launched from this button in the Export group in the External Data tab. _____

10. XPS is a document format that stands for this type of document specification. _____

11. Change to this view to create an interactive table that organizes data by fields you specify for row and column headings and calculates a Sum function for each group. _____

12. This type of form allows you to store an interactive table and is created using the More Forms button in the Forms group of the Create tab. _____

13. Change to this view to create an interactive chart that graphs data by fields you specify. _____

# Skills Check  Assess Your Performance

## Assessment

### 1  IMPORT AND LINK OBJECTS FROM ANOTHER ACCESS DATABASE

1. Open the database named **AL2-C8-VantageStock.accdb** and enable content.
2. Using **AL2-C8-VantageVideos.accdb** as the data source, integrate the following objects into the active database.
   a. Import the form named WebProducts.
   b. Link to the tables named WebProducts, WebOrders, and WebOrderDetails.
3. Display the Relationships window and create a relationship between the WebProducts and WebProductsCost tables using the field named *WebProdID*. Save and close the Relationships window.
4. Modify the WebProducts form as follows:
   a. Open the form in Layout view.
   b. Delete the *Retail Value* label and text box control objects at the bottom of the form. This will leave the form with four fields: *Product ID, Product, In Stock,* and *Selling Price.*
   c. Display the Field List pane and show all tables in the pane. Expand the field list for the WebProductsCost table.
   d. Add the field named *CostPrice* below the *Selling Price* field in the form.

e. Move, resize, and format the field as necessary so that the cost price displays similarly to the selling price.

f. Modify the form title to *Inventory Stock and Pricing*.

5. Save the revised form, print the form for the first record only, and then close the form.

6. Open the WebProdCostsWithSupp query in Design view and modify the query as follows:

a. Add the WebProducts table to the query.

b. Add the *SellPrice* field to the query design grid, placing the field between the *Product* and *CostPrice* columns.

c. Add a calculated column at the right of the *CostPrice* column that subtracts the cost price from the selling price. Display the column heading *Gross Profit*.

7. Save the revised query and then run the query.

8. Print the query in landscape orientation and then close the query.

## Assessment

### 2 IMPORT A TEXT FILE

1. With the **AL2-C8-VantageStock.accdb** database open, append records from a text file using the following information:

- The data source file is named **WebProducts.csv**.

- Append a copy of the records to the end of the existing WebProductsCost table.

- Save the import steps. You determine an appropriate description for the import routine.

2. Open the WebProductsCost table and print the table datasheet.

3. Close the datasheet.

4. Close the **AL2-C8-VantageStock.accdb** database.

## Assessment

### 3 EXPORT AND PUBLISH ACCESS DATA

1. Open the **AL2-C8-VantageVideos.accdb** database and enable content.

2. Export the query named CustWebOrders to a comma delimited text file using the following information:

- Include the field names and remove the quotation marks.

- Save the export steps. You determine an appropriate description for the export routine.

3. Open Notepad, open the **CustWebOrders.txt** file, and then print the document.

4. Exit Notepad.

5. Publish the WebSalesByDate report as an XPS document named **WebSalesByDate.xps**.

6. Open the **WebSalesByDate.xps** document in an XPS Viewer window (Windows 7 users) or in an Internet Explorer window (Windows Vista users) and print the document.

7. Exit XPS Viewer or Internet Explorer.

## Assessment

### 4 ANALYZE WEB SALES USING A PIVOTTABLE AND A PIVOTCHART

1. With the **AL2-C8-VantageVideos.accdb** database open, open the WebSalesWithTotal query and then create a PivotTable using the following information:

   - Display the customer last names in rows.
   - Sum the total sale by months in columns.
   - Hide details so that only the total for each month displays next to each customer's last name.
   - Add titles and make any other formatting changes you think improve the appearance of the table.
   - Save and print the PivotTable and then close the query.

2. Open the WebOrdersByProd query and then create a PivotChart using the following information:

   - Display the Months (*DateOrd by Month*) as the category axis labels.
   - Graph the average of the selling price field.
   - Add titles or make any other formatting changes you think improve the appearance of the chart. ***Hint: You can add a title to an axis by right-clicking the axis title, selecting* Properties, *and then typing the desired title in the Caption property of the Format tab.***
   - Save and print the PivotChart and then close the query.

3. Close the **AL2-C8-VantageVideos.accdb** database.

# Visual Benchmark  Demonstrate Your Proficiency

## ANALYZE RESERVATION DATABASE

1. Open **AL2-C8-PawsParadise.accdb** and enable content.
2. Create a PivotTable similar to the one shown in Figure 8.16 using the ReservationTotals query. Note that the table is filtered to show only the V.I.P. Suite data.
3. Save, print, and then close the PivotTable.
4. Open the DaysBoarded query.
5. Create a PivotChart similar to the one shown in Figure 8.17. Note that the chart is filtered to show only the number of days boarded for each dog in week 47. ***Hint: To adjust the scale in the value axis, right-click any value to select the axis, click* Properties *at the shortcut menu and change the major unit to a whole number in the Scale tab***.
6. Save, print, and then close the PivotChart.
7. Close the **AL2-C8-PawsParadise.accdb** database.

**Figure 8.16** Visual Benchmark Assessment PivotTable

| Type ▾ | | |
|---|---|---|
| V.I.P. Suite | | |
| | Drop Column Fields Here | |
| LName ▾ | Sum of Amount Due | Sum of Days Boarded |
| Doherty | $192.50 | 5 |
| Gallagher | $115.50 | 3 |
| Jenkins | $231.00 | 6 |
| Murphy | $154.00 | 4 |
| Rivera | $192.50 | 5 |
| Torres | $154.00 | 4 |
| Grand Total | $1,039.50 | 27 |

**Figure 8.17** Visual Benchmark Assessment PivotChart

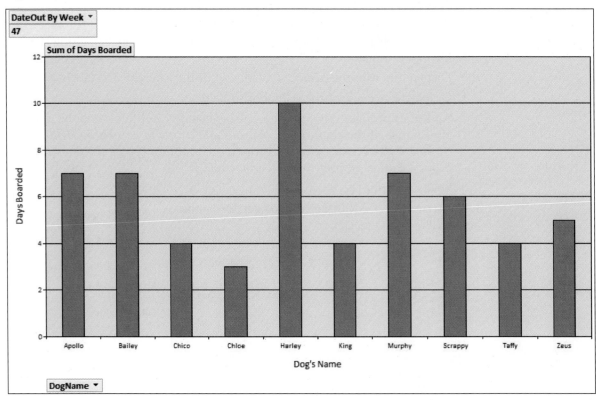

# Case Study   Apply Your Skills

**Part 1**

The office manager at Hillsdale Realty has asked you to assist her with summarizing data for the monthly sales meeting. Open the **AL2-C8-HillsdaleRealty.accdb** database and enable content. Using the SalesByAgentWithComm query, create a PivotTable that illustrates for each sales agent, the total sale price and the total commissions earned. Organize the PivotTable so that the sales and commissions are in columns by city. This will enable the office manager to filter the report to view the data by city. Show totals only for each salesperson. Save, print, and then close the PivotTable.

**Part 2**

The office manager would like the Listings table data exported from the database to use in a custom software package that accepts comma separated data files. Create the text file for the manager including field names and quotations symbols as text qualifiers. Save the export steps since the manager has advised this data exchange file will be required often. Print the text file for your records.

The CEO has requested an electronic copy of the SalesAndCommissions report. The CEO is not familiar with Access and has asked that you send the report with the formatting as displayed in Access but in a file that can be opened on her laptop that does not have Microsoft Office software. Publish the report as an XPS document using the default name and email the report to your professor as an email attachment using an appropriate subject line and message. ***Note: Check with your instructor for alternate instructions before emailing the file in case he or she would prefer you submit the XPS file in a different manner***.

**Part 3**

You want to find out if Access and Outlook can integrate to collect data using email messages and automatically update tables when replies are received. You decide to research this topic using Access Help. Use the search phrase *collect data using email* to locate a related Help topic. Locate and read an article that describes when to use data collection and the steps that should be completed before starting to ensure a successful data collection process. Compose a memo in your own words addressed to your instructor using Microsoft Word that provides the following information.

- Describe two scenarios in which data collection using Access and Outlook would be appropriate.
- What do you need to create if the data collection will be used to update more than one table in the Access database?
- What software is needed by the recipients of the email message in order to view the form?

Save the memo in Word and name it **AL2-C8-CS-P3-DataCollectionMemo**. Print the memo and then exit Word.

# Access
Microsoft®

# Performance Assessment

Access2010L2U2

*Note: Before beginning unit assessments, copy to your storage medium the Access2010L2U2 subfolder from the Access2010L2 folder on the CD that accompanies this textbook and then make Access2010L2U2 the active folder.*

# Assessing Proficiency ▪▪▪▪▪▪▪▪▪▪▪▪

In this unit you have learned to design and create reports with grouping, sorting, totals, and subreports; to use Access tools to analyze tables and improve database efficiency; to automate a database using macros and a Navigation form; to configure startup options and customize the database and Navigation pane; to integrate Access data with other programs; and to summarize data using PivotTables and PivotCharts.

## Assessment 1 Import Data from Text Files and Create Reports for a Property Management Database

1. Open **AL2-U2-BenchmarkPropMgt.accdb** from the Access2010L2U2 folder on your storage medium and enable content. In this unit you will continue working with the residential property management database started in Unit 1. The database design and objects have been modified since Unit 1 based on feedback from the property manager and the office staff.
2. Import data into tables from two text files as follows. Save each set of import specifications for future use. You determine an appropriate description for each set of import steps.
   a. Append the data in the text file named *TenantsU2.csv* to the Tenants table.
   b. Append the data in the text file named *LeasesU2.csv* to the Leases table.
3. Design and create reports as follows:
   a. A report based on the LeasesByBldg query with all fields included except the building code field. Group the records by the building name and sort by Unit No within each group. Name the report *BuildingsAndLeases*. Include the current date and page numbering in the page footer. Add your name as the report designer in the report footer. Insert an appropriate clip art image in the report header. You determine the remaining layout and formatting elements including a descriptive report title.

b. A report based on the RentalIncome query with all fields included except the building code field. Group the records by the building name and sort by Unit No within each group. Name the report *IncomeByBuilding*. Sum the rent and annual rent columns and count the unit numbers. Show the statistics in the group footer and as grand totals at the end of the report. Include appropriate labels to describe the statistics and format the values to a suitable numeric format if necessary. Add your name as the report designer in the report footer. Insert an appropriate clip art image in the report header. You determine the remaining layout and formatting elements including a descriptive report title.

4. Print the BuildingAndLeases and IncomeByBuilding reports.

### Assessment 2 Use Access Tools to Improve the Property Management Database Design

1. With the **AL2-U2-BenchmarkPropMgt.accdb** database open, use the Performance Analyzer feature to analyze all objects in the database. In the *Analysis Results* list, use the Optimize button to fix each *Suggestion* item (displays with a green question mark).

2. Use the Database Splitter to split the database into two files in order to create a back-end database. Accept the default file name at the Create Back-end Database dialog box.

3. Close the **AL2-U2-BenchmarkPropMgt.accdb** database.

4. Open the **AL2-U2-BenchmarkPropMgt_be.accdb** database and enable content.

5. Use the Database Documenter feature to generate a table definition report for the Leases table with the following options: *Include for Table* set to *Properties* and *Relationships*, *Include for Fields* set to *Names, Data Types, and Sizes* and *Include for Indexes* set to *Nothing*. Print and then close the report.

6. Close the **AL2-U2-BenchmarkPropMgt_be.accdb** database.

### Assessment 3 Automate the Property Management Database with Macros and Command Buttons

1. Open the **AL2-U2-BenchmarkPropMgt.accdb** database and enable content.

2. Create the following macros. Run each macro to make sure the macro works properly, print each macro's definition, and then close the macro.

a. A macro named *QLeasesByTenant* that opens the LeasesByTenant query in Datasheet view and Edit mode. Use the macro action *OpenQuery*.

b. A macro named *QLeaseTerms* that opens the LeaseTermsAndDeposits query in Datasheet view and Edit mode. Use the macro action *OpenQuery*.

c. A macro named *RBldgLeases* that opens the BuildingsAndLeases report in report view.

d. A macro named *RIncome* that opens the IncomeByBuilding report in report view.

3. Open the BldgsAndMgrs form in Design view.

4. Create two command buttons in the Form Header section as follows. You determine the placement of the button within the section, text to display on the face of each button, and a name to assign each button.
   a. A button that runs the RBldgLeases macro.
   b. A button that runs the RIncome macro.
5. Test each button to make sure the macros display the correct report and use Print Screen or the Windows Snipping tool to make a screen capture of the BldgsAndMgrs form with the buttons displayed. Print the screen capture by pasting the image into a blank Word document. Exit Word without saving.
6. Make sure all objects are closed.

## Assessment 4   Create a Navigation Form and Configure Startup Options for the Property Management Database

1. With the **AL2-U2-BenchmarkPropMgt.accdb** database open, create a Navigation form named MainMenu using the Horizontal Tabs style with forms and reports in the following tab order.
   - BldgsAndMgrs form
   - TenantsAndLeases form
   - BuildingsAndLeases report
   - IncomeByBuilding report
2. Edit the form title and delete the logo container object. You determine appropriate text to replace *Navigation Form*.
3. Edit the tab captions. You determine appropriate text for each tab.
4. Create a macro named *ExitDB* that quits Access saving all objects and then create a command button placed at the right end of the MainMenu form header section that runs the macro. You determine the text to display on the face of the button and a name for the button.
5. Display the form in Form view and click each tab to make sure the correct form or report displays.
6. Set the MainMenu form to display as the startup form, add an appropriate title as the application title for the database, and hide the Navigation pane.
7. Close and then reopen the **AL2-U2-BenchmarkPropMgt.accdb** database.
8. Use Print Screen or the Windows Snipping tool to capture an image of the database window. Paste the image into a Word document. Print the Word document and then exit Word without saving.

## Assessment 5   Configure Security for the Property Management Database

1. With the **AL2-U2-BenchmarkPropMgt.accdb** database open, make an ACCDE file from the database saving the copy in the same folder and using the same file name.
2. Close the **AL2-U2-BenchmarkPropMgt.accdb** database.
3. Open the **AL2-U2-BenchmarkPropMgt.accde** database.
4. Change the database startup option to display the Navigation pane with the Tables and Macros hidden.
5. Close and then reopen **AL2-U2-BenchmarkPropMgt.accde**.
6. Use Print Screen or the Windows Snipping tool to capture an image of the database window. Paste the image into a Word document. Print the Word document and then exit Word without saving.

## Assessment 6 Export and Publish Data from the Property Management Database

1. With the **AL2-U2-BenchmarkPropMgt.accde** database open, export the LeaseTermsAndDeposits query as a text file using the default name and making sure the file is saved in the Access2010L2U2 folder on your storage medium. Include the field names in the first row and remove the quotation symbols. Do not save the export steps.
2. Open Notepad, open the **LeaseTermsAndDeposits.txt** file, and then print the document.
3. Exit Notepad.
4. Publish the IncomeByBuilding report as an XPS document named **AL2-U2-BenchmarkRentInc.xps** making sure the file is saved in the Access2010L2U2 folder on your storage medium. Do not save the export steps.
5. Open the **AL2-U2-BenchmarkRentInc.xps** document in an XPS window (Windows 7) or Internet Explorer window (Windows Vista) and print the report.
6. Exit the XPS or Internet Explorer window

## Assessment 7 Summarize Rental Income in a PivotTable and PivotChart

1. With the **AL2-U2-BenchmarkPropMgt.accde** database open, open the LeaseTermsAndDeposits query in Design view.
2. Add the *Rent* field from the Tenants table to the design grid placing it between the *EndDate* field and the *SecDep* field.
3. Save the revised query.
4. Create a PivotTable using the following information:
   - Show the names of the buildings in rows.
   - Show the end dates of the leases in months in columns.
   - Add the rent field as the detail field.
   - Add subtotals and grand totals and then hide details.
5. Filter the table to show only those months with end dates in 2013.
6. Save and then print the PivotTable in landscape orientation.
7. Switch to PivotChart view.
8. Filter the chart to display only the data for Mornington Place.
9. Print the PivotChart.
10. Redisplay all of the buildings and then save and close the query.
11. Close the **AL2-U2-BenchmarkPropMgt.accde** database.

# Writing Activities

The following activities give you the opportunity to practice your writing skills along with demonstrating an understanding of some of the important Access features you have mastered in this unit. Use correct grammar, appropriate word choices, and clear sentence constructions when required.

## Activity 1 Create a New Database for Renovation Contracts by Importing Data

You work for a sole proprietor home renovation contractor. The contractor has an old computer in his basement that he has been using to keep invoice records for renovation contracts. The computer is from the Windows XP operating system era and the software program the contractor used is no longer being sold or updated. The contractor was able to copy data from the old system in a tab-delimited text file named **DavisRenos.txt**. Create a new Access database named **AL2-U2-DavisRenos.accdb** and import the data from the old system into a new table. Modify the table design after importing to change the *Amount* field to Currency. Design and create a form based on the table to be used for entering new records. Design and create a report to print the records including a total of the invoice amount column. The proprietor is not familiar with Access and would like you to create a user-friendly menu that can be used to add new records using the form you designed and view the report. Create the menu using a Navigation form and configure startup options so that the menu is the only object displayed in the work area when the database is opened. Test your menu to make sure each tab functions correctly. Using Microsoft Word, compose a quick reference instruction page for the proprietor that instructs him on how to open the database, add a new record, view and print the report, and exit the database. Save the Word document and name it **AL2-U2-Act1-DavisRenos**. Print the document.

## Activity 2 Design and Publish a Report for a Painting Franchise

You are helping a friend who has started a student painting franchise for a summer job. Your friend has asked for your help designing a database to store job information and revenue earned from the jobs over the summer. Create a new database named **AL2-U2-StudentPainters.accdb**. Design and create tables to store the records for painting contract jobs that include the date the job is completed, the invoice number, the homeowner name, address, and telephone number, and the contract price. Enter at least 10 records into the tables. Design a report to print the records in ascending order by date completed. Include statistics at the bottom of the report that provide your friend with the maximum, minimum, average, and total of the contract price field. Include appropriate titles and other report elements. Add your name in the footer as the report designer. Publish and print the report as an XPS document named **AL2-U2-PaintingContracts.xps**.

# Internet Research

## Buying a Home

Within the next few years you plan on buying a home. While you save money for this investment, you decide to maintain a database of the homes offered for sale within the area where you are interested in buying. Design and create tables and relationships in a new database named **AL2-U2-Homes4Sale.accdb**. Include fields to store data that would be of interest to you such as: the address, asking price, style of home (condominium, ranch, two stories, semi-detached, etc.), number of bedrooms, number of bathrooms, type of heating/cooling system, property taxes, basement, and garage. Design and create a form to be used to enter the information into the tables. Research on the Internet at least five listings within the area that you wish to live and use the form to enter records for each listing. Design and create a report that groups the records by style of home. Calculate the average list price at the end of each group and at the end of the report. Include five hyperlink control objects that will link to the web page from which you retrieved the information for each listing. Include appropriate titles and other report elements. Add your name in the footer as the report designer. Publish and print the report as an XPS document named **AL2-U2-AvgHousePrices.xps**.

# Job Study

## Meals on Wheels Database

You are a volunteer working in the office of your local Meals on Wheels community organization. Meals on Wheels delivers nutritious, affordable meals to citizens in need of the service such as seniors, convalescents, or people with disabilities. The organization requires volunteers using their own vehicle to drive to the meal depot, pick up meals, and deliver them to clients' homes. The volunteer coordinator has expressed an interest in using an Access database to better organize and plan volunteer delivery routes. Create a new database named **AL2-U2-MealsOnWheels.accdb**. Design and create tables and relationships to store the following information. Remember to apply best practices in database design to minimize data redundancy and validate data whenever possible to ensure accuracy.

- Client name, address, telephone, gender, age, reason for requiring meals (senior, convalescent, or disability), meals required (breakfast, lunch, dinner), date service started, and estimated length of service required.

- Volunteer name, address, telephone, gender, age, date started, availability by day and by meal (breakfast, lunch, dinner), and receipt of police check clearance.

- Incorporate in your design an assignment for both the client and the volunteer to the quadrant of the city or town in which he or she is located. The volunteer coordinator divides the city or town by north, south, east, and west and tries to match drivers with clients in the same quadrant.

- Any other information you think would be important to the volunteer coordinator for this service.

Create a user-defined form template so that each of your forms has a consistent look. Design and create forms to be used to enter the information into the tables and then use the forms to enter at least eight client records and five volunteer records. Make sure you enter records for both clients and volunteers in all four quadrants and for all three meals (breakfast, lunch, dinner).

Design and create queries to extract records of clients and volunteers within the same quadrant. Include in the query results datasheet the information you think would be useful to the volunteer coordinator to set up route schedules. Design and create reports based on the queries. Print the reports.

Create a main menu for the database to provide access to the forms and reports. Configure startup options to display an application title, the main menu form, and hide the tables in the Navigation pane when the database is opened. Close the database and then reopen it. Use Print Screen or the Windows Snipping tool to capture an image of the Access window. Print the image from Word and then exit Word without saving.

## A

ACCDE database file, creating, 289–290
Access
  customizing environment, 277–283
  viewing Trust Center settings for, 290–292
Access Options dialog box, 277, 283, 288
Action Arguments, 259, 260
Action Catalog pane, 259
  creating macros using, 263–264
action queries, performing operations using, 88–94
action queries, types of
  append, 88, 91–93
  delete, 88, 90, 91
  make table, 88, 89
  update, 88, 93–94
actions, 258
adding
  automation with macros, 272
  buttons to a tab group, 285
  calculated control objects, 124–126
  calculations to a form in Design view, 124–126
  captions, 10
  combo boxes to custom forms, 137
  combo boxes to custom reports, 204–205
  command buttons to Navigation forms, 276
  fields to custom forms, 108–110
  fields to custom reports, 174–175
  functions to custom reports, 188–195
  graphics to custom forms, 128–132
  graphics to custom reports, 186–188
  hyperlinks to custom reports, 205–209
  list boxes to custom forms, 137–141
  list boxes to custom reports, 204–205
  page numbering, 182–186
  records to table using append queries, 91–93
  tab control to custom forms, 116–117
  tab control to custom reports, 204
  tables to queries, 78–80
Add mode, 259
alias, 81
  creating for a table, 81
aligning multiple controls at same position, 126
Append dialog box, 92
Append Only property for a Memo field, 22

append queries, 88
  adding records to a table using, 91–93
Application Parts template, creating objects using, 226–232
arguments, 259
asterisk (*) as wildcard character, 142
attached files
  editing, 26
  removing, 27
  saving to another location, 27
Attachment data type, 8
Attachment dialog box, 24, 26
Attachment field, creating, and attaching files to records, 24–27
automation, adding with macros, 272
AutoNumber data type, 6, 8
AutoNumber field, 15

## B

back-end database, 243–246
blank form templates, 219
blank form tools, creating forms using, 137–141
  adding combo boxes, 137
  adding list boxes, 137–141
blank report tools, creating reports using, 204–209
  adding combo boxes, 204–205
  adding hyperlinks, 205–209
  adding list boxes, 204–205
  adding tab control, 204
  changing shape of control objects, 205
  changing tab order of fields, 205
Boolean logic, 6
bound objects, 105
buttons, adding to a tab group, 285

## C

Calculated data type, 8
calculated objects, 105
calculations, adding to a form in Design view, 124–126
Caption property, 7, 10, 21
captions, adding, 10
Cartesian product, 82
charts. See also PivotCharts
  inserting, editing, and formatting in custom reports, 198–204
combo boxes, adding
  to custom forms, 137

to custom reports, 204–205

command button, creating to run a macro, 266–273

Command Button Wizard, 270

  viewing macro actions created by, 271

comma separated file, importing data from, 313–316

composite key, 45

compressed files (.zip), 24

conditional expression, 6

configuring error checking options, 282–283

control objects, 105

  adding and formatting calculated, 124–126

  changing shape of in creating custom reports, 205

  moving and resizing, 111, 112–113

  moving to another section in custom reports, 176–177

controls

  adjusting sizing and spacing between, 127–129

  aligning multiple at the same position, 126

  anchoring to forms, 133–134

  formatting, 112

  formatting multiple, 114–115

Create Relationship Wizard, 226

Create Relationship Wizard dialog box, 226, 227, 228

creating

  ACCDE database file, 289–290

  alias for a table, 81

  Attachment fields, 24–27

  command buttons to run macros, 266–273

  custom formats for Date/Time field, 17–18

  custom formats for numeric field, 15–17

  custom formats for Text field, 13–14

  custom input masks, 20–21

  custom reports using blank report tools, 204–209

  database using template, 221–225

  datasheet form, 134–136

  fields that allow multiple values, 50–53

  fields to look up values in another table, 46–50

  forms using blank form tools, 137–141

  indexes, 53–55

  label objects, 106

  macros, 258–264

  macros to open form and find records, 260–262

  macros using Action Catalog pane, 263–264

Navigation forms, 273–277

new database using templates, 221–225

new tables using queries, 89–90

new tables with multiple-field primary key, 46

new tabs, 284

objects, using Application Parts template, 226–232

PivotCharts, 331

PivotTables, 324

queries to prompt for starting and ending date, 74

restricted-use forms, 134–136

self-join queries, 80, 81–82

subforms, 118–123

subqueries, 83–85

tables in Design view, 9–10

tables with lookup fields including a multiple-value field, 51–52

titles, 106

user-defined forms, 232–234

cross products, 82

crosstab queries, 88

Currency data type, 8

Currency field, 15

custom formats, creating

  for Date/Time field, 17–18

  for numeric field, 15–17

  for Text field, 13–14

custom forms

  adding bound, unbound, and calculated control objects, 106

  adding calculations to in Design view, 124–126

  adding combo boxes to, 137

  adding fields to, 108–110

  adding graphics to in Design view, 129–132

  adding list boxes to, 137–141

  adding tab control to, 116–117

  anchoring controls to, 133–134

  changing tab order of fields, 115–116

  creating subforms, 118–123

  creating titles and label objects, 106

  creating using Design view, 105–123

  formatting controls, 112

  moving and resizing control objects, 111, 112–113

  restricting form actions, 134–136

  sorting and finding records in, 141–144

  using the blank form tool, 137–141

customizing

  Access environment, 277–283

Navigation pane, 279–281
ribbon, 283–288
custom reports
adding combo boxes, 204–205
adding graphics to, 186–188
adding hyperlinks, 205–209
adding list boxes, 204–205
adding page numbering and date and time
controls to, 182–186
adding tab control, 204
changing shape of control objects, 205
changing tab order of fields, 205
creating using blank report tools, 204–209
detail in, 173
grouping records and adding functions to,
188–195
inserting, editing, and formatting chart in,
198–204
keeping group together on same page,
196–198
modifying section properties in, 195–196
page footer in, 173
page header in, 173
report footer in, 173
report header in, 173

**D**

data
deciding between importing versus linking
to, 309
exporting to text file, 317–319
importing from another Access database,
303–306
importing to Access from a text file,
311–312
requiring in field, 10
segmenting, 6
summarizing in a PivotTable, 324–329
summarizing in a PivotTable form,
329–331
summarizing using PivotChart view,
331–334
Date and Time dialog box, 183
database(s)
creating new using template, 221–225
designing tables and fields for new, 5–10
diagramming, 7
documenting, 246–247
importing data from another Access,
303–306
limiting ribbon tabs and menus in, 279
linking to table in another Access,
307–311

macro security settings for, not opened
from a trusted location, 291
relational, 6
renaming and deleting objects in, 248–249
source, 303
splitting, 219, 243–246
database designers, 5, 35, 103
Database Documenter, 219
database index, 53
database normalization, 35, 56
first normal form, 56
second normal form, 56
third normal form, 56
database objects, publishing and viewing as
XPS documents, 321–324
data dictionary, 5
data display, restricting using field
properties, 10–12
data entry, restricting
using field properties, 10–12
using input mask, 18–21
Data Mode argument, 259
data redundancy, 6
datasheet form, creating, 134–136
data types, 8
assigning, 7
Attachment, 8
AutoNumber, 6, 8, 15
Calculated, 8
Currency, 15
Date/Time, 8
Hyperlink, 8
Number, 7, 8, 10, 15
OLE, 8
Text, 8, 10
Yes/No, 8, 10
date and time controls, adding, 182–186
Date/Time data type, 8
creating custom format for, 17–18
dBase file format, 317
Default Value, 21
delete queries, 88, 90
deleting a group of records using, 91
deleting
embedded macros, 270
macros, 264–266
Design view
adding calculations to form, 124–126
adding fields to form, 108–110
adding graphics to form, 129–132
adding tab control to form, 116–117
applying theme to report, 177–178

bound, unbound, and calculated control
  objects in form, 106
Caption property in, 21
changing tab order of fields in form,
  115–116
connecting table or query to report and
  adding fields, 174–175
creating custom form, 105–123
creating custom report, 172–182
creating subforms, 118–123
creating tables, 9–10
creating titles and label objects in form,
  106
Default Value property, 21
formatting controls in form, 112
inserting subreport, 178–182
moving and resizing control objects in
  form, 111, 112–113
moving control objects to another section
  of report, 176–177
Validation Rule property, 21
Validation Text property, 21
detail in custom report, 173
Dialog mode, 259
dictionary, data, 5
Documenter dialog box, 246
documenting databases, 246–247

**E**

editing
  attached file, 26
  charts in custom reports, 198–204
  macros, 264–266
  relationships, 40–42
Edit mode, 259
Edit Relationships dialog box, 40, 41
embedded macros, 270
Enter Parameter Value dialog box, 72
entity, 6
error checking options, configuring, 282–283
exporting Access data to a text file, 317–319
export specifications, saving and repeating,
  319–321
Export Text Wizard, 317

**F**

field(s)
  adding to custom forms, 108–110
  adding to custom reports, 174–175
  changing tab order of, 115–116
  creating that allow multiple values, 50–53
  creating to look up values in another table,
    46–50

designing for new database, 5–10
disallowing zero-length strings in, 10–11
requiring data in, 10
selecting records using multiple-value,
  86–87
field length, using the field size property to
  restrict, 8–9
field names
  abbreviated, 7
  hyphen (-) in, 7
  spaces in, 7
  underscore character (_) in, 7
field properties, restricting data entry and
  display using, 10–12
field size property, using to restrict field
  length, 8–9
file(s), attaching to records using Attachment
  field, 24–27
File New Database dialog box, 221
File Open dialog box, 303
filter, saving as a query, 70–71
filter arrows, 328, 331
first Command Button Wizard dialog box,
  266
First Database Splitter Wizard dialog box,
  244
first normal form, 56
First Table Analyzer Wizard dialog box, 237
foreign key, 37
form(s). *See also* custom forms; PivotTable
  forms
  creating macros to open, 260–262
  importing from another Access database,
    305–306
  summarizing data in a PivotTable,
    329–331
format. *See also* custom format
format codes for Date/Time fields, 17
format codes for Text or Memo fields, 13
form control defaults, setting, and creating a
  user-defined form template, 232–234
Form Footer section, 106
Form Header section, 106
Form tool, 105
Form Wizard, 105
front-end database, 243–246
functions, adding to custom reports,
  188–195

**G**

Get External Data Access Database dialog
  box, 303, 304, 307, 312
GoToControl action, 260

graphics, adding
   to custom forms in Design view, 129–132
   to custom reports, 186–188

## H

Hidden mode, 259
HTML Document format, 317
Hyperlink data type, 8
hyperlinks, adding to custom reports, 205–209
hyphen (-), in field names, 7

## I

Icon mode, 259
image files (.bmp, .jpg, .gif, .png), 24
importing
   data from another Access database, 303–306
   data to Access from a text file, 311–312
Import Objects dialog box, 303, 304, 305
import specifications, saving and repeating, 312–316
indexes, 53
   creating, 53–55
inner join, 75
   selecting records in a query using an, 77
input masks, 18
input masks, commonly used codes, 19
input masks, creating custom, 20–21
input masks, restricting data entry using, 18–21
Input Mask Wizard, 18

## J

join properties
   defined, 75
   modifying, in a query, 75–82
join properties dialog box, 75
join type, specifying, 75–77
junction table, 44

## K

Keep Together property, 196–198

## L

label control object, 111
label objects, creating, 106
left outer join, 75
   selecting records in a query using, 78
link, resetting using Linked Table Manager, 310–311

Linked Table Manager, resetting link using, 310–311
Linked Table Manager dialog box, 310
linking to table in another Access database, 307–311
Link Tables dialog box, 308
list boxes, adding
   to custom forms, 137–141
   to custom reports, 204–205
log files (.log), 24
lookup list, assigning multiple values in a, 52–53
Lookup Wizard, 46, 50

## M

Macro Builder Window, 259, 260
macros, 257
   adding automation with, 272
   assignment of to command button, 258
   converting to Visual Basic for Applications, 272–273
   creating, 258–264
   creating a command button to run, 266–273
   creating by dragging and dropping an object, 263
   creating to open form and find record, 260–262
   creating using an Action Catalog pane, 263–264
   defined, 258
   editing and deleting, 264–266
   embedded, 270
macro security settings for databases not opened from a trusted location, 291
Make Table dialog box, 89
make-table queries, 88, 89
Manage Data Tasks dialog box, 316, 321
many-to-many relationships, establishing, 44–45
Memo data type, 8
Memo fields
   Append Only property for, 22
   enabling rich text formatting and maintaining a history of changes in, 22–24
   format codes for, 13
   working with, 22–24
menus, limiting in a database, 279
multiple controls
   aligning at the same position, 126
   sizing, aligning, and spacing, 127–129
multiple-field indexes, creating, 54

multiple-field primary key
   creating new table with, 46
   defining, 45–46
multiple-value field, selecting records using, 86–87
multiple values, assigning in a lookup list, 52–53

## N

Name & Caption dialog box, 10
Navigation form, 257
   adding command button to and editing, 276
   creating, 273–277
Navigation pane, customizing, 279–281
new tab, creating, 284
New tab Backstage view, 9, 221
Normal mode, 259
Number data type, 7, 8
Number field, 15
   properties of, 10
numeric fields, creating custom format for, 15–17

## O

objects
   adjusting for consistency in appearance, 126–129
   bound, 105
   calculated, 105
   control, 105
   creating macros by dragging and dropping, 263
   creating using Application Parts template, 226–232
   moving and resizing control objects, 111
   renaming and deleting in database, 248–249
   unbound, 105
ODBC Database format, 317
OLE Object data type, 8
one-to-many relationship, establishing, 37–40
one-to-one relationship, establishing, 42–44
OpenForm action, 259
operations, performing action queries using, 88–94
orphan records, 41
outer join, 75
   left, 75
   right, 76

## P

page footer, 173
page header, 173
page numbering, adding, 182–186
Page Numbers dialog box, 182
parameter query, 72
   prompting for criteria using, 72–73
Paste Table As dialog box, 235
PDF (Portable Document Format), 322
PDF documents, publishing database objects as, 321
performance, optimizing using Performance Analyzer, 240–243
Performance Analyzer, optimizing performance using, 240–243
Performance Analyzer dialog box, 241
PivotCharts. *See also* charts
   creating, 331
   summarizing data using, 331–334
PivotTable forms, summarizing data in, 329–331
PivotTables. *See also* table(s)
   summarizing data in, 324–329
primary key, 37
   defining multiple-field, 45–46
   deleting, 45
primary key field, 7
Property Sheet, 195–196
Publish as PDF or XPS dialog box, 321, 322
publishing
   database objects as XPS documents, 321–324
   reports as XPS documents, 322–323

## Q

queries
   action, 88–94
   adding tables to and removing tables from, 78–80
   connecting to report and adding fields, 174–175
   creating to prompt for a starting and ending date, 74
   creating a self-join, 80, 81–82
   creating new table using, 89–90
   crosstab, 88
   exporting as a text file, 317–319, 320–321
   extracting records using select, 70–74
   modifying join properties in, 75–82
   nesting within query, 84–85
   prompting for criteria using a parameter, 72–73

running with no established relationships, 82

saving filter as, 70–71

selecting records in using inner join, 77

selecting records in using left outer join, 78

selecting records in using right outer join, 79–80

using multiple-value field in, 86–87

Query Design view, criteria in selecting records in, 70

question mark (?) as wildcard character, 142

## R

Read only mode, 259

records

  adding to a table using a query, 91–93

  creating an Attachment field and attaching files to, 24–27

  creating macros to find, 260–262

  deleting group of using a query, 91

  extracting using select queries, 70–74

  grouping, and adding functions in a custom report, 188–195

  modifying using an update query, 93–94

  orphans, 41

  selecting in a query using inner join, 77

  selecting in a query using left outer join, 78

  selecting in a query using right outer join, 79–80

  selecting using multiple-value field, 86–87

  sorting and finding in forms, 141–144

referential integrity, turning on in a one-to-many relationship, 41

relational databases, 6

relationships

  editing options, 40–42

  many-to-many, 44–45

  one-to-many, 37–40

  one-to-one, 42–44

  running query with no established, 82

removing attached files, 27

Rename dialog box, 285

report footers, 173

report headers, 173

reports. *See* custom reports; subreports

restricted-use forms, creating, 134–136

ribbon

  customizing, 283–288

  resetting, 288

  restoring, 288

ribbon tabs, limiting in a database, 279

rich text formatting, enabling, 22

right outer join, 76

  selecting records in a query using, 79–80

RunMenuCommand action, 260

## S

Save & Publish tab Backstage view, 321

Save As Query dialog box, 70

Save Attachments dialog box, 26, 27

saving attached file to another location, 27

saving export specifications, 319–321

saving import specifications, 312–316

second Command Button Wizzard dialog box, 267

second normal form, 56

section properties, modifying in custom reports, 195–196

Security Warning, 290

select queries, 70

  extracting records using, 70–74

self-join queries, 80

  creating, 80, 81–82

SharePoint List format, 317

sizing, adjusting between controls, 127–129

Snap to Grid feature, 111

source data, deciding between importing versus linking to, 309

source database, 303

spacing, adjusting between controls, 127–129

Split Form tool, 105

subforms, creating, 118–123

subqueries, 83

  creating and using, 83–85

subreports, 178

  inserting, 178–182

summarizing data

  in a PivotTable, 324–329

  in a PivotTable form, 329–331

  using PivotChart view, 331–334

## T

tab control, adding

  to custom forms, 116–117

  to custom reports, 204

tab group, adding buttons to, 285

table(s). *See also* PivotTables

  adding and removing from a query, 78–80

  adding records to using a query, 91–93

  connecting to report and adding fields, 174–175

  copying table structure to create new, 234–236

creating alias for, 81
creating field to look up values in another, 46–50
creating in Design view, 9–10
creating new using a query, 89–90
creating new with multiple-field primary key, 46
creating with lookup fields including a multiple-value field, 51–52
designing for new database, 5–10
linking to in another Access database, 307–311
modifying using the Table Analyzer Wizard, 236–240
Table Analyzer Wizard, modifying tables using, 236–240
Table Definition Documentation Report, generating, 247
Table Design view, field properties in, 259
tab order of fields, changing, 115–116
in custom reports, 205
tabs
creating new, 284
renaming, 285
templates, 219
blank form, 219
creating new database using, 221–225
setting form control defaults and creating a user-defined form, 232–234
text box control object, 111
Text data type, 8
properties of, 10
Text field
creating a custom format for, 13–14
format codes for, 13
text files (.txt), 24
exporting Access data to, 317–319
exporting queries as, 317–319
importing data to Access from, 311–312
theme, applying to custom reports, 177–178
third Command Button Wizard dialog box, 267
third normal form, 56
titles, creating, 106

Trust Center
exploring settings, 291–292
viewing settings, 290–292
trusted locations, macro security settings for databases not opened from, 291
Trusted Publishers list, 290

## U

unbound objects, 105
underscore character (_) in field names, 7
update queries, 88
modifying records using, 93–94
user-defined form template, setting form control defaults and creating, 232–234

## V

Validation Rule property, 21
Validation Text property, 21
value(s)
creating field that allows multiple, 50–53
creating field to look up in another table, 46–50
Visual Basic for Applications, 272
ACCDE database files and, 289
converting macros to, 272–273

## W

wildcard characters, 142
Window mode argument, 259
wizards, 219. *See also specific*

## X

XPS (XML Paper Specification), 322
XPS documents, publishing and viewing database objects as, 321–324

## Y

Yes/No data type, 8
properties of, 10

## Z

zero-length strings, disallowing in field, 10–11

**Access 2010 Feature Reference**

| Access 2010 Feature | Ribbon Tab, Group | Button, Option | Shortcut |
|---|---|---|---|
| Advanced Filter Options | Home, Sort & Filter | | |
| Append query | Query Tools Design, Query Type | | |
| Application Parts | Create, Templates | | |
| Copy | Home, Clipboard | | Ctrl + C |
| Create ACCDE file | File, Save & Publish | | |
| Create table | Create, Tables | | |
| Customize Access options or Navigation Pane | File | Options | |
| Cut | Home, Clipboard | | Ctrl + X |
| Delete query | Query Tools Design, Query Type | | |
| Delete record | Home, Records | | Delete key |
| Design view | Home, Views | | |
| Export as PDF or XPS document | External Data, Export | | |
| Export to Excel worksheet | External Data, Export | | |
| Export to Word document | External Data, Export | , Word | |
| Filter | Home, Sort & Filter | | |
| Find | Home, Find | | |
| Form | Create, Forms | | |
| Form wizard | Create, Forms | | |
| Import Excel worksheet | External Data, Import & Link | | |
| Import from Access Database | External Data, Import & Link | | |
| Labels | Create, Reports | | |

| Access 2010 Feature | Ribbon Tab, Group | Button, Option | Shortcut |
|---|---|---|---|
| Macro | Create, Macros & Code | | |
| Make Table query | Query Tools Design, Query Type | | |
| Navigation Forms | Create, Forms | | |
| New record | Home, Records | | Ctrl + + |
| Paste | Home, Clipboard | | Ctrl + V |
| Performance Analyzer | Database Tools, Analyze | | |
| Primary Key | Table Tools Design, Tools | | |
| Property Sheet | Form Design Tools Design, Tools or Report Design Tools Design, Tools | | F4 |
| Query design | Create, Queries | | |
| Query wizard | Create, Queries | | |
| Relationships | Database Tools, Relationships | | |
| Report | Create, Reports | | |
| Report Design | Create, Reports | | |
| Report wizard | Create, Reports | | |
| Sort ascending | Home, Sort & Filter | | |
| Sort descending | Home, Sort & Filter | | |
| Spelling | Home, Records | | F7 |
| Split database | Database Tools, Move Data | | |
| Table Analyzer Wizard | Database Tools, Analyze | | |
| Total row | Home, Records | | |
| Update query | Query Tools Design, Query Type | | |